STOCKWELL-MUDD LIBRARIES

3 5044 00358 4791

James Mark Baldwin

THOUGHT AND THINGS

A Study of the Development and

Meaning of Thought

or

GENETIC LOGIC

Volume 2

EXPERIMENTAL LOGIC, OR GENETIC
THEORY OF THOUGHT

Elibron Classics

www.elibron.com

D1378020

BC
121
.B2
V.2

Elibron Classics series.

© 2005 Adamant Media Corporation.

ISBN 1-4021-9761-6 (paperback)
ISBN 1-4021-2225-X (hardcover)

This Elibron Classics Replica Edition is an unabridged facsimile
of the edition published in 1908 by Swan Sonnenschein & Co.,
London.

Elibron and Elibron Classics are trademarks of
Adamant Media Corporation. All rights reserved.

This book is an accurate reproduction of the original. Any marks, names, colophons, imprints, logos or other symbols or identifiers that appear on or in this book, except for those of Adamant Media Corporation and BookSurge, LLC, are used only for historical reference and accuracy and are not meant to designate origin or imply any sponsorship by or license from any third party.

Press Notices of Volume I

" *I record my fullest appreciation of a notable book, one that can not fail to add to the author's already splendid reputation, and one which will enlarge not a little our knowledge in a great field of science. . . . The time has come for the reconstruction of the entire discipline of logic—a reconstruction of logic on the basis of a genetic explanation of our actual knowledge seems to be manifest destiny in the light of Professor Baldwin's present work.*"—Prof. J. E. Russell in JOURN. OF PHILOSOPHY.

" *This is a most earnest, profound, laborious, systematic analysis of cognition, such as cannot fail to be of continual utility to students of psychology. It appears to be a signal setting forth of science— what the Germans would call an ' epoch-making ' book. When one has to build a house, a definite plan is drawn, in which all the conditions are duly considered—and this plan becomes the focus of study. Such a preliminary project it is with which Professor Baldwin has now enriched the psychology of cognition. The vocabulary of well-considered new terms is in itself a precious gift to psychological investigation. For with each of these new terms there goes a valuable new conception. The publication must serve as a precious landmark in future investigation, in that it lays down for the first time a definite project of structure of the theory of cognition in great detail.*"—THE NATION.

" *The genetic method has been wielding an influence shaking up the old distinctions ; but there has not been such a traversing of the whole psychological field solely by its intellectual right and its scientific authority, as that made by Baldwin's* Thought and Things. *It promises a complete reconstruction of psychology and also of the cognate philosophical disciplines of logic and epistemology, leaving the time-honoured distinctions far behind. The achievement can be interpreted as an age-movement, and be closely related to the current intellectual need which has been finding wide-spread satisfaction in pragmatism. The item of historical interest is that the initiative has come from within psychology, and the results stand closer to the assured gains of the science than do the quasi-metaphysics of the time.*"— Prof. Buchner in a résumé of Psychological Progress in 1906.

" *This is the most comprehensive attempt in logic yet made in America. The fact that such a program is offered, and the general standpoint and method of treatment are further evidence that philosophy in America is rapidly passing from the absorbing, translating, albeit necessary period of German apprenticeship, into a free creative adulthood.*"—Pro. A. W. Moore in THE PSYCHOLOGICAL BULLETIN.

" *The first instalment of what promises to be an important inquiry into the actual movement of the function of knowledge. Prof. Baldwin's account of the process by which cognition is built up is so coherent that it is impossible to give more than a fraction of its substance. But one finds that the writer has always something true and important to say.*"—NATURE.

" *One must heartily acknowledge the importance of Professor Baldwin's contribution in a comparatively new field.* [It is] *worked out with great thoroughness of detail and with a comprehensive grasp of the guiding principles. One cannot fail to recognize both the importance of the problem, and the real value of his results.*"—Prof. J. E. Creighton in the PHILOSOPH. REVIEW.

THOUGHT AND THINGS

BY THE SAME AUTHOR. ·

HANDBOOK OF PSYCHOLOGY: Vol. I. SENSES AND INTELLECT. Second Edition. 1891. New York, Holt & Co.; London, Macmillans.

HANDBOOK OF PSYCHOLOGY: Vol. II. FEELING AND WILL. 1892. Same publishers.

ELEMENTS OF PSYCHOLOGY. 1893. Same publishers. Second Edition, tenth thousand.

MENTAL DEVELOPMENT IN THE CHILD AND THE RACE. New York and London, Macmillans. 1895. Third Edition, seventh printing, 1907. German Translation, Berlin, Reuther u. Reichard, 1897. French Translation, Paris, F. Alcan, 1897.

DEVELOPMENT AND EVOLUTION. Same publishers, 1902.

SOCIAL AND ETHICAL INTERPRETATIONS IN MENTAL DEVELOPMENT. Same publishers. Fourth Edition, 1907. In French, German, Spanish, etc. Awarded Gold Medal Royal Acad. of Denmark.

DICTIONARY OF PHILOSOPHY AND PSYCHOLOGY. 3 Vols. in 4 Parts. Edited (with an international corps of contributors) by J. MARK BALDWIN. 1901–5. New York and London, Macmillans.

STORY OF THE MIND. London, Newnes. New York, Appletons. For popular reading. In several languages.

FRAGMENTS IN PHILOSOPHY AND SCIENCE. COLLECTED ESSAYS. · London, Nimmo; New York, Scribners, 1902.

THOUGHT AND THINGS; OR, GENETIC LOGIC. Vol. I. FUNCTIONAL LOGIC OR GENETIC THEORY OF KNOWLEDGE. London, Swan, Sonnenschein & Co.; New York, Macmillans, 1906. French trans., Paris, Doin, 1908. German trans., Leipzig, Barth, 1908.

THOUGHT AND THINGS

A Study of the Development and
Meaning of Thought

OR

GENETIC LOGIC

BY

JAMES MARK BALDWIN

*Ph.D., Hon. D.Sc. (Oxon.), LL.D. (Glasgow); Author of Mental Development
Social and Ethical Interpretations, etc.; Editor of Dictionary of Philosophy
and Psychology, and The Psychological Review; Professor in the
Johns Hopkins University*

VOL. II

EXPERIMENTAL LOGIC, OR GENETIC
THEORY OF THOUGHT

LONDON
SWAN SONNENSCHEIN & CO., LIM.
NEW YORK: THE MACMILLAN CO.
1908

TO THOSE PHILOSOPHERS MAINLY
BRITISH
WHO BY INVESTIGATING
THOUGHT
HAVE ADVANCED OUR KNOWLEDGE OF
THINGS

Τὸ καλόν πᾶν

PREFACE

THE Preface to the first volume of this work was of course intended to answer for the whole. It was there explained that the different volumes were written in form suitable for separate and independent reading and use in the Universities. The place and scope of this volume in reference to its fellows is also indicated there, and is further commented upon in the "Introduction to Vol. II."

A word is necessary, however, on a point or two which, if left unexplained, might excite criticism. I am in this volume in nowise attempting to make an exhaustive or adequate presentation of the principles of the ordinary Formal Logic. It is not even proposed to cite the literature widely. The treatment here given to the topics ordinarily discussed in Formal Logic is from a definite point of view, and only so much citation of theories and authorities is made as is found sufficient to suggest the relation that this point of view bears to others. With a view to this I have selected certain works for citation, as both representative and recent: Keynes' *Studies and Exercises in Formal Logic*, 4 ed., and Bradley's *Studies in Logic*, the one strictly formal, in its point of view, and the other more psychological. While using these two able and influential works as background, and often as objects of seeming criticism, I do it with the explicit expression of genuine admiration and indebtedness. In Bradley's book especially I find certain anticipations of the positions that I arrive at from the genetic point of view, as well as certain distinctions that I believe to be fundamental; among the latter the distinction between what he calls " mere suggestion " and judgment. With these I also cite the articles of C. S. Peirce, C. Ladd Franklin and Robert Adamson, especially those of Peirce, in my *Dictionary of Philosophy and Psychology*.

This limitation in number of references and citations in the book accounts for the lack of more historical matter and for the failure to point out important agreements, no less than differences, between my results and those of others. For example, the very able work of M. Ribot on *The Evolution of General Ideas* might well be cited in certain connections.[1] It also excuses the absence of a show of erudition (to which indeed I make no pretensions). There is nowadays, especially in English books, so much straining to justify one's views by recondite citations from Aristotle, Kant, Mill, and the prophets generally, so much disputation over what these worthies really meant, so much of what seems to be not a hiding of one's candle in a bushel, indeed, but a losing of it in the searchlights of earlier time—that it may be a relief to readers to find a book in which conclusions and their reasons are simply stated for what they may be worth. Wherever I am aware of having taken a thought from another, I have acknowledged it ; but that does not mean of course that most of what is in this work may not have been said, and said better, by some one else.

The problem of this volume is simply that of interpreting the movements and results of the functions generally called logical or discursive as part of the larger movement of development of knowledge or cognition as a whole. As has been said by Professor J. E. Russell, in a review of the first volume of *Thought and Things*, " The time has come for a reconstruction of the entire discipline of logic. . . A reconstruction of logic on the basis of a genetic explanation of our *actual* knowledge seems to be manifest destiny." Whether it be a reconstruction of the old logic or a new construction which will supplement and fortify the old logic, remains to be seen ; but this volume may be taken to be an attempt to do what Prof. Russell thinks ought to be done—an attempt to interpret the processes usually handed over to formal logic in terms of the movements of actual know-

---

[1] I hope later on to make use of M. Ribot's fruitful researches on " Affective Logic."

ledge. Most of the larger problems of logic are accordingly treated in this broad way.

I am aware that my use of certain new terms has proved a stumbling stone to many ; it was bound to be so. I deliberately adhere to my view, however, that for new distinctions, and for old ones too that have no proper names, unambiguous terms are absolutely requisite. In this matter I enrol myself under the banner of the American apostle of clear terminology in this field, C. S. Peirce. If any of the views expressed in my work survive, the terms will " win out " too ; if the views do not survive, the terms may perish with them ! A word on this point and also on other criticisms will be found in the Appendix to this volume (II.), and certain of the points made there, especially the remarks on " meaning " and on " assumption," may be referred to as supplementary to topics of Vol. I. The intimations in the matter of the " aesthetic," also in the Appendix, anticipate conclusions reached in Volume III.

An error was made in the Preface to Vol. I., in the statement that the third volume was to appear in a year. It was this volume, the second, that was intended. The third volume is writing, but not written.

I have again to thank Prof. Muirhead, the editor of the Library of Philosophy, for valuable suggestions and comments ; also the French and German translators, Professor P. Cahour and Herrn W. F. G. Geisse for their careful and painstaking work.

JOHNS HOPKINS UNIVERSITY,
November, 1907.

TABLE OF CONTENTS

VOLUME II.[1]

EXPERIMENTAL LOGIC.

PART I.[2] INTRODUCTION TO EXPERIMENTAL LOGIC.

PART II.[3] GENETIC THEORY OF THOUGHT: HOW THINKING GOES ON.

[1] Being Book ii. of the entire treatise on *Genetic Logic*.
[2] Being Part iv. of the entire treatise.
[3] Being Part v. of the entire treatise.

[1] Being Part vi. of the entire treatise on *Genetic Logic.*

Contents

PART IV.[1] THE DUALISMS AND LIMITATIONS OF THOUGHT.

[1] Being Part vii. of the entire treatise on *Genetic Logic.*

GENETIC LOGIC

BOOK II

EXPERIMENTAL LOGIC

Experimental Logic[1]

PART I[2]

INTRODUCTION TO EXPERIMENTAL LOGIC

Chapter I

WHAT EXPERIMENTAL LOGIC IS[3]

§ 1. DEFINITION

In opening the discussion of the more refined operations of the logical mode, together with its meanings for consciousness, **Experimental Logic.** we should first of all justify the term Experimental Logic which we are applying to this branch of the larger subject of Genetic Theory of Knowledge. This we may do by distinguishing first the sense in which the matter constitutes Logic, and second, the sense in which it is Experimental.

1. The treatment of the operations of thinking, that is, of the discursive or reasoning faculty generally, under the term **1. As Logic.** Logic, is so conventional and established, that further defence of it is not necessary.[4] It is only the nature of the method adopted—the method called " genetic "—involving as it does, a peculiar point of view, that distinguishes the present treatment. That method consists in tracing out the movement of the function of cognition—in this case, the logical mode of it as such—in its great typical movements or " progressions,"

---

[1] Being Book II of the entire treatise on Genetic Logic.

[2] Being Part IV of the entire treatise.

[3] The §§ 1 to 3 of this chapter have been already printed as an article in the *Psychological Review*, November, 1906.

[4] See the account of " Formal Logic " in vol. i. chap. i. § 2.

with the attempt to determine the " how," " why," and " where-unto " of each stage in the advance.   Thinking is thus considered in the light of an *effective function*, working upon the objects of cognition, having adequate motives for its passage from one stage to another, and pursuing its characteristic method in achieving each successive stage.   It is this general conception of a logic that is genetic[1] that justifies the isolation of the function of thinking for special treatment.

2. In adopting the term *Experimental* Logic, a certain general result of the treatment itself is anticipated.   That result **2. As Experi-** is, in brief, as follows.   The logical operations as **mental.** such, considered as the essential method of advance or progress in the mode of thought, *proceed by experimentation*, or to use the more special term employed in the first volume of this work (chap. viii. §§ 6 ff.), by a process of Schematism.   This con-sists essentially in the *experimental* erection of an object already made-up in consciousness,[2] and its treatment as having a meaning or value which *it has not yet been found to have*, with the expecta-tion and intent that in the result it may be found to have it.   It is, in the logical mode, an intentional and conscious use of a method established and found fruitful in the pre-logical stages of psychic assimilation and handling of objective contents, as has been shown in another place.[3]   The results of what may be called the

---

[1] See the detailed exposition of the field and scope of Genetic Logic, vol. i. chap. i.

[2] What Bradley (*Principles of Logic*) calls a " suggestion " as con-trasted with a judgment whose differentia is an act of assertion (*loc. cit.* p. 14).   It is this distinction, in fact, that I work out, making it radical and thoroughgoing.

[3] Vol. i. chap. v. § 6 ; chap. vi. § 4 ; chap. viii. §§ 6–8.   It will be seen from the division given in the table in chap, i. § 6 of that volume, that the larger topic of " Functional Logic " includes what is here called Experi-mental Logic ; for it is the *function* of knowledge in the mode called " logical " that is now to be taken up.   Both on account of its special characters, however, and also on account of its traditional monopolizing of the term " Logic," it is worthy of detailed treatment and also of a special name.   To those, we may add, who do not admit that experimentation or schematism is always the mode of procedure of thinking, we have only to say—let the scope, then, of " Experimental Logic " be restricted to those operations which are and are shown to be experimental.   There will then be left over for another discipline—formal, deductive, rational or whatever it be called—the problems which such non-experimental pro-cesses present.   To such thinkers the problems of this volume will be found to be among those of the discussions sometimes known as " Em-pirical Logic."

"progression of experimentation" as a method may be summarized for our present purposes under a separate heading.

§ 2. THE PROGRESSION OF THE EXPERIMENTAL MODE.

3. The development of cognition, in its essential progress, is always one of increasing determinateness in the two great
Control   moments that enter into its objects or meanings. These two moments are the *content* and the *control*. The content is what it is because *it is determined and controlled to be that* and no other object. Besides its determination as having this or that make-up, consistency, subsistence, it is controlled as capable of being referred to one or other of those spheres or classes which become, *for consciousness*,[1] existences, substances, and realities. The process of contextuation of content might go on *ad libitum* by the mere presence together of items, images, fancies, etc. ; and it might have no further meaning. If, however, meanings are to arise whereby such contexts have reference to the spheres in which in some sense *they hold good*, then different controls must also be derived and developed.

Now it is on the side of such reference, such control, such assignment of possible and present combinations of contents to
As Experimentally Established.   their spheres of fulfilment, that a method of finding, testing, exerting or acknowledging control is necessary ; and this we find, as the result of our detailed examination of cognitive process, to be one of experimentation. The main stages of its development—its progressive modes, so to speak, as worked out in vol. i.—are as follows.

(1) The semblant or make-believe use of an object having merely inner character as image of fancy, whereby it is treated
1. Semblant Stage.   for playful or other personal purposes as having further meaning or reference. The object thus becomes a "scheme," a *Schema*, charged with the further meaning which it has not as yet been found to have in its own right.

(2) The erection of such schemata in an *experimental* way,

---

[1] This is italicised because of certain misconceptions of the theory of control worked out in vol. i. The dualism of control is all the while "for consciousness," not for our final theory of reality. When a control that "is or seems foreign to the process itself " is spoken of, this means "seems to the process itself to be foreign," not "seems to the observer to be foreign to the process " (a meaning given to it by certain reviewers of vol. i.), which suggests a question that is to come up later on in the treatment of "Real Logic."

under the urgency of a desired or intended fulfilment. There

2. Stage of direct Experiment. results either fulfilment or non-fulfilment, and either is a marked accretion to the original meaning so erected. Thus by the experimentation both the determination and the control are essentially advanced. In the prelogical modes, consciousness has no other way—barring possibly certain brute intrusions upon it [1]—of advancing or effectively selecting its meanings.

(3) The most important instance of this before the rise of reflection is that which issues in " generalization." By the

3. Stage of Generalization. use of a schema as a meaning adequate to embrace many instances, and hence *experimentally taken to mean them*, it is discovered what cases in the particular instance may properly be meant. The individuation of objects as general, particular, singular and universal—as is shown in the earlier discussion—is secured by this process of schematism.

(4) The transition to the logical mode as one of reflection, is accomplished again by an act of essential experimentation.

4. Stage of Judgment. The contexts which are still ambiguous in their meanings as general and particular, under whatever control, are all alike erected as schemata within the larger control they have in common—that of the inner life or experience. From the point of view of experience under a control functioning as Judgment, the contents receive severally *whatever further assignments the experimentation of this mode may secure*. The entire context of experience—idea, hypothesis, imagination—becomes available for experimental treatment in the problematic forms of judgment which embody variations in *belief*. The schematism of the logical mode becomes the method of determining belief ; and the entire development of logical meanings may be treated from the point of view of ascertaining the forms in which the

---

[1] To these, however, it must still accommodate itself by " trial-and-error " processes which are in type experimental. Yet from the point of view of *the process itself*, the meaning is one of intrusion and foreignness. The passage stating this in vol. i. (chap. iii. § 15) has been wrongly construed as denying the processes of accommodation. It is such misunderstandings arising from confusion of points of view that justify—and indeed demand—the adoption of an explicit and full terminology. In this connexion I have deliberately adopted the term "schematism" (with " schema " and " schematic ") to mean experimentation as a process of *psychic meaning* (*i.e.* meaning *for the process itself*) as opposed to psychological meaning (*i.e.* meaning for an observer of the process).

relative determinateness or indeterminateness of belief takes form in presupposition, postulation, implication, or other mode of acknowledgment or assurance.

In other words, as in cognition generally, so here, there is the established and there is the not-yet-established, the content and the intent, the anticipatory schema and the richer fulfilment. The method whereby consciousness, by using a meaning experimentally, establishes and advances it, holds for thinking also.

4. If this be the exclusive method, or even the principal method, whereby thinking does its work, then it is quite proper to call this department of Genetic Logic " experimental." The further questions—as to the limits of experimentation and the possible advancement of meanings by some other process or by no process at all—these may in turn be solved by the inquiry itself, or, if left over, made subject of separate disciplines.

It will, therefore, serve the interest of clearness, if we define Experimental Logic as that inquiry which, pursuing genetic **Definition.** and functional methods, *investigates thinking with a view to tracing the derivation, development, and embodiments* [1] *of Belief.*

§ 3. THE TWO TYPES OF SCHEMATISM.

5. Speaking still on the general topic of experimentation, we may say that there are two contrasted ways in which a content **Two sorts of Meaning used.** may be made schematic and so be used experimentally. These illustrate respectively the methods of advance of the two great sorts of meaning, recognitive and selective—meaning established by recognition and held up as true, and meaning selected by and for appreciation and held up as, in some immediate sense, good or " fit."

6. It is evident that these two types of meaning result from

---

[1] These three words indicate the problems " why," " how," and " what " of the logical mode, although in the treatment which follows the topics are taken up rather with reference to divisions current in the literature. " How " belief embodies itself in Judgments is taken up in chap. ii., and in " Common " Judgments in chap. iii. ; " why " it is thus embodied is the question of " schematism " of chaps. iv. and v. The question " what ? " suggests the topic of the organization of logical meanings in a system of Implications and Truths, treated in chapters vi. to xiii. ; and the limitations of thinking, together with the new problems set by the logical function itself, are treated in the final chapters, xiv. and xv.

and appeal to different motives. The items of established

1. Recog- fact are taken as just what they are, and used for the
nitive, giving. discovery of further items of fact.   Only so far as the
content is stripped of selective and personal meaning, of all
interpretation beyond its bare outline as a context of knowledge, only so far is it available for the schematism whose motive
is theoretical.   The schema of this sort is instrumental to the
development of knowledge as such, of a representative and convertible system of cognitions ; in short, to the development of
Scientific what is to be acknowledged as true.   This may be
Schematism. called " scientific " or " theoretical " schematism.   On
the other hand, the furtherance of special personal purposes and
interests requires a schematism of its own sort.   This consists in
the selective use of a context as " fit " to fulfil a purpose or end
2. Selective, and thus " good " for that purpose or end.   The items
giving
Appreciative chosen are *appreciated* as " good " or " fit," and
Schematism. the further advance is in the confirmation and development of this sort of appreciable fitness.   The development
of selective meanings in the prelogical modes is by this sort
of schematic or experimental use of contents.[1]   In the logical
mode it may be called " selective " or " appreciative " schematism.

7. The further treatment of these two sorts of experimental
use of contents is to follow ; they are mentioned in this Intro-
Latter re- duction in order to point out that with the rise of
duced to
former in judgment as characteristic control in reflection, all
Judgment, appreciations as such become truths, all selective
meanings become theoretical meanings—*so far as they are
made subject-matter of reflection.*   Experimental Logic, therefore, after it has found it to be the fate of appreciations to be
thus taken up in judgments of experience or fact, has no longer
anything to do with them as appreciations ; for it then deals
with such meanings from the point of view of judgments of truth
motived by theoretical interest.[2]   Appreciation will have its

---

[1] See vol. i. chap. viii. § 9.

[2] To be sure this realization may not be pure, but mixed with personal
preferences, as in what is called " will to believe."   But, as I show in the
discussion later on (chap. viii. § 9), in that case the statement reached
remains in some degree schematic, and is not fully a judgment.   The
wish may be "father to the thought," but it cannot be its mother
also !   It may direct the selection of materials, but it cannot guarantee
the " truth " of the construction made out of the materials.

place as among the motives that give rise to the schemata or "proposals" set for further determination in judgment.

The further development of these appreciative meanings goes on, it is true, in its own right; but experimental logic, as theory of reflective or logical procedure, loses its claim upon them. There is indeed the special need of inquiring in detail as to the function whereby the items of selective schematism arise and are found eligible or "fit"; this is to be discussed in the treatment of the hyper-logical modes. The operations of the constructive Imagination, in its selection of materials with reference to what *which is* may be called purposive or normative ideals, is to be *subject of* distinguished from that other sort of schematic use *Experimental* *Logic.* of a context whose aim is to extend its application in the domain of fact or truth. It is the latter with which the developments of our text heretofore have had mainly to do, and to which this volume is to be exclusively devoted.

8. The preservation of this distinction is subject, however, to a complication which we may as well point out now, especially as it enables us to introduce a scheme of definite terminology, that will later on stand us in good stead. It is the complication that, while disclaiming any motive of a personal or purposive sort in its theoretical schematism and experimentation, yet reflective process is itself motived by a special interest. The interest and purpose resolutely to know and to know only what is true to fact, requires a certain restriction of the scope and *Theoretical* function of the mental life to that more direct field of *Interest has* psychic vision we call the "theoretical." This results *fulfilment in* *an Apprecia-* in a fulfilment, a renewed appreciation, of its own type. *tion.* We shall find, therefore, that the separation of the two modes of rendering the meanings of knowledge is not final; nor are they exclusive *inter se* as to content. Not only do appreciated experiences become when judged theoretical; but judged contents are appreciated as fulfilling the ideal set up by theoretical interest. A logical solution of a problem meets the demand for logical validity and so fulfils the interest of its theoretical pursuit.

9. There is, therefore, when we reach the logical mode, need of careful distinction of the various sorts of "interest" that *Four sorts of* motive these great progressions of meaning. Accept- *interest.* ing the distinction already advanced between the psychic and psychological points of view, we may recognize "practical," "pragmatic," "pragmatelic," and "theoretical"

interests. " Practical " interest is that which motives the mass of contents of cognition and action[1] fused together in their early flow and development. The interest of the child in his tea-spoon is practical. It is an interest in which the factors of knowledge and action have not yet been isolated. " Pragmatic " interest is the practical interest considered from the objective and psychological point of view. For example, with my knowledge of the child's processes, I may describe his interest as having consequences, bearings, and motives which he himself does not apprehend. My account of his interest makes it a pragmatic interest.[2] The dualism of the factors of knowledge arises, however, in later modes in consciousness, and the relative opposition between recognitive and selective meanings appears. This is consummated in the segregation of the interests that motive and achieve knowledge, over against those that evaluate and use it. So there arise " theoretical " interest, on the one side—interest in maintaining and furthering the system of knowledge [3]—and over against it, "pragmatelic " interest, which terminates upon that system as satisfying, fulfilling, consequential, etc. These fulfilments may not be isolated, set up as separable meanings, or made *ends* of pursuit ; but they are part of the full intent of that which is so set up.

10. The two points made just above—both still to be taken up, in later discussions—may be stated in terms of interest.

Fulfilments become Theoretical. The objects of pragmatelic interest, *appreciated as fulfilling*, are, when judged to be objective experiences, placed in a context of recognitive and common meanings, and are thus made objects of theoretical interest. And, on the other hand, the items of knowledge in a measure reduced to a context of theoretical interest, are thereby made pragma-

---

[1] Action in the large sense, as including fulfilments, consequences, etc., in what is called " practical life."

[2] This is, as I conceive, about what is common in the various uses of the term " pragmatic " in current discussions of knowledge. They contemplate the larger reference of knowledge, its bearings, utilities, consequences which are wider than the forms of such " practical " reference in consciousness itself.

[3] From the objective point of view this is the " logical " interest. It might be named with reference to its psychic end, " noötelic." Interests of the type that motive objects of the " semblant " sort are—drawing still upon the Greek—" autotelic " in the Play-mode (see vol. i. chap. vi. § 5) and " syntelic " in the Aesthetic mode (vol. iii.). These terms, it may be added, are used very sparingly in the discussions that follow, and always with sufficient explanation.

Truths are Appreciated. telic, since the fulfilment of the theoretical interest is a real fulfilment and satisfaction, although its ideal involves the denial of the interest in fulfilments as such.[1]

§ 4. ACCEPTANCE AND QUESTION.

11. It may serve the interests of clearness if we now set these movements together in a way that gives a view of the progressions of meaning as a whole with reference to what we **Presumption and Assump-** have called "control" in a sphere of some sort of existence or reality. The different stages of experi- **tion.** mental meaning called, from the psychic point of view, schematic, are those in which an established recognitive context, accepted for what it is, is *also read for what it may become.* This gives in the prelogical mode, two possible attitudes toward the control of a given content. That attitude whereby the meaning is recognized *as determined for what it is*, gives what we may call a "presumption" of existence, control, or reality. The meaning *is depended upon* or expected to have its own appropriate co-efficients, its own "real" value; but the aspect that constitutes it thus "real" is not isolated or asserted, as a separate element of meaning. Over against this, also in the prelogical modes, there is, however, the contrasted attitude toward what is not presumed but "assumed"—*made schematic for further determination*. The "assumption" is the use of a meaning in a control or with a reference that is not yet established, not yet a presumption.[2] When a child, for example, cries for an

[1] So much, without raising the question here whether all appreciations or "goods" can be exhausted in cognitions or "truths," and the reverse. This is to be a matter of detailed enquiry later on.

For a relevant point of view, see the chapters "Origin v. Nature," in *Devel. and Evolution* (chap. xiii.), and "The Cosmic and the Moral," in *Fragments in Philos. and Science* (v.). In this latter chapter, published originally in the *International Journal of Ethics* (Oct. 1895), it is contended that the "ends" of ethical pursuit—the content of the "ought"— are, as they are attained, added to the context of theoretical truth—the content of the "is." See also Bawden, in *The Philosophical Review*, March, 1906.

[2] In this scheme the term "Assumption" is a translation of *Ahnahme*, as used by Meinong. The term "Presumption" in this sense was suggested by Professor Urban (*Psychological Review*, January, 1907, p. 23), and I follow his recommendation. In my first volume, this is called

object in the next room, he " presumes " its existence and availability in the world of his practical interests ; but when he goes
through the process of " feeding " his toy-dog, he " assumes " a
sphere that he does not regularly " presume."

In the logical mode, the existence marks harden into a dualism
of spheres, and the intent of existence or control becomes itself
a separable and predicable meaning. And this exist-
Presupposition ence or " reality " meaning may be again entertained
and higher
Assumption. in the same two ways. It may be specifically asserted
in a judgment of existence or taken for granted as something
capable of such assertion ; or it may be set up hypothetically
and schematically. These two attitudes are for the logical mode
what the " presumption " and the " assumption " are for the
prelogical. Apart from the case of specific judgment of existence, we may call them respectively the " presupposition " and
the " higher assumption " We have, therefore, two modes of
taking for granted, " presumption " and " presupposition,"
*the former genetically preceding, and the latter following upon,
the judgment of existence*; and also the two modes of assumption,
" lower " and " higher," also with the judgment of existence
midway between. If we further call the judgment of existence
—the existential, considered as an attitude—a mode of " acknowledgment," we have the following genetic scheme.[1]

simply " schematic meaning " in the lower modes. The term " acknowledgment " is in somewhat general use for judgmental attitude towards
content. " Presupposition " (of belief) is a restriction of the term
Voraussetzung of Meinong to the logical level, in order to mark the genetic
distinction between it and the lower *Voraussetzung* called above " Presumption." The distinction between " presumption " and " presupposition " goes with that between " simple apprehension " and " reflection ";
the " real " is " simply apprehended," given or presumed, in the one case,
and made a reflective presupposition in the other. In the French translation, " presumption " is rendered by " appréhension."

[1] I think no one can read the work of Meinong without seeing the
need and the value of the close distinctions covered in this terminology.
I may also refer to the recent thorough papers of Prof. Urban on worth
theory as also bearing this out. After the appearance of my first volume
I became acquainted with Prof. Urban's articles in mss., together with
other papers which are to constitute chapters in his book ; and I intentionally modify my usage somewhat—as he also has kindly done—to
bring our respective discussions into more harmony in their terms. This
is fully justified by the harmony of methods and results. His forthcoming
book, *Valuation : its Processes and Laws*, is, in my opinion, a very important contribution to the theory of value.

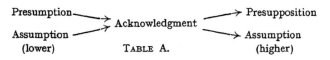

TABLE A.

The assignment of these meanings, with reference to their place in the life of cognition, may be seen in the arrangement of the tables given in the Appendix.

PART II [1]

GENETIC THEORY OF THOUGHT : HOW THINKING GOES ON

Chapter II

THE CHARACTER OF LOGICAL MEANING : ACKNOWLEDGMENT AND BELIEF

§ 1. JUDGMENT AS BELIEF MODE

If we single out the aspect of reflection generally considered the criterion of logical function, namely the Judgment, we may introduce our discussions with its consideration.

1. The treatment of judgment, both in logic and philosophy, has tended to lose sight of the function and deal exclusively with

Propositional View of Judgment. the content.[2] This is seen in the application of the term judgment to the meaning expressed in a verbal proposition or statement ; and the position has been explicitly advocated that a judgment is a relation of two terms or objects. The criterion of logical content, or of experience as such, is carried over to judgment, and judgment is denied in any case in which there is not a two-fold determination of content

Predication Theory. in a larger whole of relation. It is this tendency, I think, that issues in—and in a measure justifies— what is known as the " predication " theory of judgment. This theory maintains that in every judgment one term is asserted or " predicated " of another, the latter being the logical " subject " and the former the logical " predicate." [3]

---

[1] Being Part V. of the entire treatise on Genetic Logic.

[2] That is the " thought-content," the " whole " thought about, which to avoid ambiguity I shall call the *subject-matter* or the " judgmental content." It includes, as a related whole, both the " logical subject " and the " logical predicate," as distinguished in the text below.

[3] The full treatment of predication is to be found in chaps. vi. ff.

2. The force of such a view is further brought out when we recall to mind the genetic place of judgment, considered as control attitude toward a content. We have found judgment to be well described as " acknowledging function " terminating upon an object or meaning. Now, it is evident that in a mode in **Judgment as** which an earlier meaning is taken up and acknow- **Specification.** ledged, it must be by so much classification, limitation, or "specification " of some sort as may establish the meaning in some context. A judgment must in some way *specify* a meaning, by asserting its how, why, where, when, what, etc. The individuation by judgment serves to render explicit and relational certain lines of complication, classification, etc., upon which the direct acceptances of the pre-logical consciousness have already proceeded. This we may call the "specification " or logical determination of the subject-matter, which is thus isolated from the auxiliary or supplementary meanings not included in the particular specification ; and the relation that is included stands out in an assertion or predication.

3. There are, moreover, two positive considerations, drawn from our earlier discussions, which reinforce this position. One **Two Reasons** of them is our view of the genetic motive which urges **for Predica-** on to the function of reflection, and the other is the **tion Theory.** meaning of negation in this mode.

(1) It appears that it is a certain embarrassment that urges on to the erection of objective meanings in the sphere of inner **(1) Judgment** presence called experience, or world of ideas. Two or **motived** more meanings attach to mind and also to body[1]; the **by rival** **Meanings.** interpretation is more or less forced and ambiguous, and it is also often mistaken. The solution takes the form of judgment, as acknowledgment of one *rather than the other*, or of a meaning partly fulfilling both, the positive assertion being that the relational meaning is this and not that or not those. **It issues in** This, it is evident, requires the holding up of the rival **Predication.** determinations of meaning as available to thought, and the linking of the logical subject of the judgment in a relational context. The whole subject-matter is now judged or asserted in the form of a predication.

(2) The other consideration is drawn from the theory of opposition, which in this mode becomes actual negation as

---

[1] Each seems on occasion to be both "inwardly " and "outwardly " controlled. See vol. i. chap. xi. § 2.

relational meaning.   The dual character of opposition by ex-
(2) Negation as Exclusion is dual and Predicative. clusion has already been remarked upon, and it has been called relational opposition for the reason that in such negation a determinate content is removed by exclusion from a determinate sphere or class.   It is only, there-fore, to bring this out to say that the correlative affirmative meaning is also a relational meaning, involving two positive terms.   This point receives further emphasis when we find that negation is the rejection of an attempted or suggested affirma-tion.[1]

4. While these considerations are quite just, and go far to establish a predicative theory of the proposition, yet **Belief Meaning or Intent.** they do not lead us to reject the theory that the subject-matter of judgment as function is a single whole.   The content is relational, but the whole meaning that is suggested by this relation is what the acceptance or rejection of judgment, considered as mode of belief, terminates upon.

The content does not embody the entire meaning of an act of judgment, and in this fact we see the necessity of preserving the distinction between the two criteria respectively of content and function.   The function as such, the act of judgment, has its *intent* as well as its content; its presuppositions, as well as its subject-matter ; *its envelope of control no less than its kernel of determinate meaning.*   The " pre-**The Presup-position, not a Part of the Subject Matter.** suppositions " of the mode itself, as we may now call them, following Meinong,[2] are present to con-sciousness as part of its full meaning.   Judgment has the *intent* to acknowledge these presuppositions—the sphere of real existence, the mode of psychic process, the class of general meanings, the avenue of expression, or any other of the psychic pre-conditions of the meaning.[3]

---

[1] This is taken up again in the treatment of logical negation below, chap. viii. §§ 3 ff.

[2] Meinong, *Gegenstandstheorie* and *Die Annahmen,* uses *Voraussetzung* over against *Annahme* (" Assumption "). *Annahme* suggests hypothetical or problematical meaning, while *Voraussetzung* embodies or includes the full acceptance of a sphere of reality or existence as a *presupposition.* My own usage limits " presupposition " to the level of logical process, " presumption " applying to the earlier stages.   See Table A., chap. i., sect. 11, and the Appendix.   No doubt it is true, however (see Marty, *Über Annahmen* in *Zeitsch. f. Psychol.,* Bd. 40, pp. 1 ff), that Meinong is not entirely consistent in the use of these terms.

[3] This gives " acknowledgment " the force of acceptance or rejection

Now these presuppositions, thus described as intent of the judgment, are just what we have found, in a preceding chapter, to be the " existence meanings " within which respectively the various objects are built up. When I speak of " dog " I mean something determined in the dog-class of externally existing objects ; when I say " person " I mean, on the contrary, that sort of object that can only have the peculiar kind of existence that persons are determined as having. So long as there is no occasion to recognize or make a point of discussing or asserting this existence-meaning, it remains what I have called an " envelope " of presupposition, wrapped about the subject-matter. It remains a sort of suppressed predicate, a part of the whole meaning, but not a " term " thrown into the form of explicit relation in the content.

But of course this meaning or intent may itself become, on occasion, object of thought and assertion ; it may become content of thought, part of the " subject-matter." Instead of simply presupposing or intending the existence-meaning of dog, for instance, I may assert it—" the dog exists." The suppressed predicate or envelope of presupposition then becomes one term of a relational predication. But before it was not so.

In what sense is existence itself then a predicate ?

5. The existence meaning which the judgment always presupposes in the sense given, may, *when explicitly asserted, be* **Existence a** *called a predicate* ; but it is not an *attributal predicate*, **Predicative** not a separate element of presented context or **but not an** **Attributal** recognitive meaning, an attribute of the subject- **Meaning.** matter. It is only the explicit assertion of the presupposition of belief in the sphere in which the subject-matter is constituted as object of thought. It is only to go back to the traditional use of " attribute " to denote a separable

---

of the whole related content. See below, chap. viii. §§ 2, 11. " Judgment proper is the act which refers an ideal content (recognized as such) to a reality beyond the act " (Bradley, *Principles of Logic*, p. 10). This view of judgment, which I hold to be essentially sound, leads Bradley to a position from which he organizes logical meanings in many respects from the point of view worked out below. He makes the " reality " thus referred to—or in our terminology " presupposed "— the " real " or ultimate " subject " of judgment, and makes the judgmental forms modes of qualifying this " subject." While this only embarrasses the theory of " subject "—for " reality " is predicate, not subject, as I point out below—yet it amounts to treating logical meanings as embodying presuppositions of reality with belief attitudes toward it.

part of a presented content, without which it is not, as a content, complete, to deny that existence is such an attribute, and so to deny that assertion of existence is an attributal predication.[1]

6. We may, in illustration, consider any of the sorts of assertion made in ordinary discourse. The subject-matter in each is the relational whole of the verbal meaning ; the presupposition is the intent to convey a meaning that is true or fictional or playful. Thus in humour, semblance of reality is the presupposition.

Illustrations. My child strokes my face and says, " Papa, you are a lamb." Here a certain intent of affection gives meaning to the relational context ; that is its presupposition. Or again, I say, " Adam Bede was a noble fellow," presupposing the meaning that fiction is the sphere of reference. What is called in logic a " universe of discourse " arises from the recognition of one of these tacit intentions or presuppositions, enveloping our judgmental content—a sort of neuroglia in which the network or context of stained tissue, made up of the cell and fibre of relational subject-matter, lies embedded.

7. The possibility of these presuppositions arises from the nature of the mode of reflection itself, as may be seen to advantage from a point of view developed above. We saw

Presuppositions are the Reference Points of a mediating Context. that control in this mode is mediate, it is *via* a mediating context, through which the further reference to a sphere of fulfilment is accomplished. The self is mediated through the context treated as an inner system of experience held in the form of judgment. The external reality is mediated by the same context treated as a convertible and representing system of ideas, referable outward. These points of reference lie in the background ; they are not given in the thought system, but taken-for-granted as presuppositions of it. Taken together they underlie the whole of experience

---

[1] It is an interesting question, raised, I think, by Hillebrand, whether the existential judgment presupposes an earlier "idea of existence" which may or may not be predicated. Hillebrand seems to intimate, what I should explicitly claim, that genetically it is through the judgment of existence that such an idea is isolated and released. The mere reality feeling is sharpened into belief only by the situation which demands judgment, and the existential judgment is at once both the recognition of the control which existence means and the relating of such a control-meaning to the object-content. Only thus does existence or reality become a separable "idea" or subject-matter of thought. See also below, sect. 15 of this chapter.

in its distributive meanings. The judged content is what it is, an object of thought, because it is the issue of a process which has behind it the control characteristic of the individuation of an earlier meaning, which is now used by thought for its own purposes.

8. We should expect to find, and we do find, the cases of meaning showing differences that may be explained by the **Contrast of** distinction of criteria now made. (1) Judgment has **two Cases.** a content which is dual or relational in meaning ; but this dual or relational meaning, while it is the criterion of thought-content, does not always exhaust the meaning of judgment. **(1) Relational** For example, when I say " Parsifal is a fool," the **Content** **under Pre-** meanings Parsifal and folly constitute a dual or **suppositions.** relational whole. But the sphere of meaning with reference to which I make the assertion is a presupposition not exhausted by the verbal content. This is one case ; with it a second is to be contrasted.

(2) The presupposition of judgment, the intent part of the entire meaning, may itself be made a term of a further judgmental **(2) Assertion** content. That is, the control may be no longer left **of the Pre-** **position** in the limbo of presupposition, but brought forward **itself.** as itself an object of thought, a term of the whole subject-matter. This leads to a judgment which acknowledges, asserts, or confirms a specific control as relative to the logical subject of the judgment ; as when I say, " the fool Parsifal is mythological." The presupposition of the meaning has now become a term of the relational content of thought.

This progression of meaning is involved in all existential or other judgments which make explicit the sphere of discourse intended. Other categorical judgments remain in the status of assertions based upon presuppositions. When looked at from this point of view there is no lack of clearness in existential or other judgments by reason of their " real " implications. It is to be our task (this and later chapters) to classify and interpret judgments within their respective presuppositions, and afterwards in the theory of Implication (chaps. x. ff) to deal with them in relative independence of such a reference.[1]

9. The topic has been made unnecessarily difficult, however,

---

[1] The real reference itself is considered in vol. iii., *Real Logic.* The movement by which the existence meaning is rendered as predicate is illustrated by Figs. 1, 2 in sect. 31 below.

by reason of the intrusion of philosophical views. The meaning
Theory that of judgment has been found to be assertion of, or of
Reality is something about, the reality—or in terms of our
Subject of
Judgment present distinctions—the control presupposed by
judgment. We are told that the subject of all judgment is
reality,[1] and the content as a whole is predicated of that ; the
universe becomes the logical subject, and the judged content
the predicate.

10. (1) This puts the emphasis quite in the wrong place,
besides being without adequate reason. The cognitive meaning
Not true, of the mode is the relational content, the object of
because thought stripped of its control ; the characteristic
mark of the function is the joint or mediate control, which now
becomes possible just because the reference to reality has become
remote.[2]   The dualism of the mode is that of subject-self and
thought-content, in which the pre-logical dualisms are
(1) Reflection transcended and made mediate. This is confirmed,
makes
Reality a besides, by the existential judgment itself, by which
Presupposi-
tion, not Sub- just the remoteness and unexpressed-ness of the "real"
ject-matter.
presuppositions are recognized and overcome.   When I
say, "Parsifal did not exist," I assert something about reality
(as not including Parsifal in one of its modes) ; but it certainly
cannot be claimed that I have already made such an assertion
about reality when I simply say, "Parsifal was mad." The
existential statement "Parsifal is fanciful" is in the same way a
meaning added to the relational meaning, "Parsifal is mad,"
although the presupposition of a sphere of the "fanciful" may
be made in this latter statement when taken alone.

(2) A further enforcement of this point comes from the fact
that the existential judgment often *for the first time* [3] determines

---

[1] Or the entire universe, or the Absolute.

[2] How this "remoteness"—a term used in lieu of a better—should
be interpreted in the theory of reality is to be a matter of further inquiry.
Here we may say that a "presupposed" reality is remote only in the
sense of not being cognitive subject-matter, not in the sense of being
inferential or less "real" because "intended" and not "presented."
I use the term reality here simply as a general term for the spheres of
"existence" of the varied presuppositions of judgment. The distinction between "presupposition" and "postulation" (explained in chap.
v.) must precede the theory of Reality.

[3] See note to sect. 5 in this paragraph, above. Instead of saying with
Bradley (*Principles of Logic*, p. 11) that in judging "The sea-serpent
exists," "we have qualified the real world by the adjective of the sea-

the real reference or control of a context which has already had
(2) **Reality may be still Undetermined.** formulation in a predicative or relational context.
The relational meaning may be determined in the
logical mode, while the real reference is still schematic,
alternative, or quite undetermined.[1] For example, I may say,
" Sea-serpents hiss," meaning to express a quite definite meaning
of a relational sort ; at the same time that I am not prepared to
say that sea-serpents do or do not or may or may not exist in
this, that, or the other realm. The " real " reference is problematical, while the judgment of relation is categorical. It is,
accordingly, an additional meaning, when I go on to acknowledge
such or such real existence in a judgment.

After these explanations we are prepared to put the matter
Belief. in terms of Belief, for we are now able to give that
word its definite connotation.

11. In the more recent discussions of belief a distinction has
been made which embodies, from a different point of view from
that here taken, that of the two cases of judgment mentioned
just above. It is the distinction between what is variously
known as " spontaneous belief," " mere acceptance," " realizing
sense," " reality feeling," etc., on the one hand, and " reflective
Reality-feeling and Belief Proper. belief," " conviction," " belief proper," etc., on the
other hand. Retaining the terminology which I have
used in more extended discussions of the topic of belief in an earlier publication,[2] to which reference may here be
allowed, we may distinguish " reality-feeling " from "belief."

Reality-feeling is an intent-consciousness, an element of
an entire cognitive meaning, which attaches to an object con-
Reality-feeling structed simply under its appropriate control. It
is the case in which that control is not disturbed, or
embarrassed, by other and alternative or rival dispositions or
interests. The *cachet* of mere presence, or present sameness,

---

serpent," I should say that we have qualified the sea-serpent by the
adjective of real-ness of a restricted sort. The " real-ness " is constituted
just by the act of recognition of the sea-serpent as a " controlled " content. Of course, after reality as a logical universal has arisen, we may
use it substantively to the various contents as adjectives, as is seen
especially in negative judgments of existence (see below, chap. viii. § 10).

[1] The case dealt with in detail under the heading " Postulation," in
chap. v. below.

[2] " Interest, Reality and Belief," chap. vii. of *Handbook of Psychology*,
ii. *Feeling and Will*.

set upon an object before it is thrown upon the defensive or put to question in consciousness, is the reality sign,—*the sign of what is to be or mean reality in later modes of process*.[1] This is found, of course, in the case just spoken of—the case of absence of all rival tendencies through which the smoothness of the flow of cognitions would be in any way disturbed.

The feeling of reality is then only the sense of presence, when there is no question, doubt, or hesitation to accept. Let

or Sense of mere Presence. this be disturbed, however, by experiences of disappointment, lack, and absence, and then unreality feeling takes its place. Doubt, hesitation, perplexity, arise, and the resolution of doubt brings in the sort of assured confidence we call belief.

I think it is clear that whenever judgment is absent from consciousness, that is when the cognitive process is in a pre-

It is present in the Prelogical Modes. logical mode, there is reality-feeling as thus described ; the meaning is an intent, a sign of mere presence, an aspect of the object which belongs to its control as *being just what it is*. For example, a dog or a very young child sees my mahogany chair, and the polish, colour, etc., are to him simply there for his acceptance as part of the entire object of perception and memory, whose existence the entire experience " presumes."

12. It is, on the contrary, the springing up of rival dispositions and interests that motives the dualisms by which judgment is made possible. Judgment is a determination issuing from preceding rivalries, embarrassments, hesitations and adjustments

Belief Proper. of alternative meanings ; these are the occasion of judgment, and with it reality-feeling passes into belief.[2] Belief is the affective-dispositional side of judgment ; *belief is the disposition to judge or acknowledge a thing as in some sense existing or real*. Belief embodies, therefore, intent no less than content—

---

[1] In contrast with any meaning of reality later to arise and attach to an object, we may say that it is here simply " presumed," taken for granted that the object is real. There is a " presumption " of the dependableness of the thing. But even this may imply too much. It is only as some question arises that the " presumption " comes to consciousness, or that an " assumption " of the dependableness of the thing arises. The attitude of acceptance of the object is one of " presumption " (cf. Table A, given in chap. i. sect. 11).

[2] Between them are the various modes of hesitation, caution, doubt, etc., that make the object " schematic " as already described, and are classed as attitudes of " assumption."

a factor of meaning additional to the relational content, and **Embraces Intent.** together with it making up the entire meaning of the judgment. By my belief, I intend something beyond merely entertaining a fugitive thought. I intend the particular control which assigns that thought to a sphere of existence, inner, external, semblant or other. For example, when I say, " Mahogany takes a high polish," I express a belief ; I mean that besides a mere object set up to inspect or not to inspect—a fugitive scheme or context which is a relation of terms that might hold in **Illustration.** fiction, in verbal play, in art, anywhere—there is here *acknowledged a content controlled in the real world of woods and processes of polishing.*

13. This is the case of meaning of the sort called judgment with presuppositions. The belief-intent is the presupposition. It is now a positive element of meaning, not a mere reality-**Belief intent** feeling or presence sign. I make the assertion not only **is Presuppo-** to join the terms in a relation, but to do this explicitly **sition.** in the sphere of existence in which mahogany *is*. I am surprised when my auditor says, " I come from Greenland ; pray, is there a wood called mahogany ? " He has not fully taken in my presupposition.

14. Most of our everyday judgments are of this sort. The belief meaning is in the background, for its reasons are suffi-**It becomes** ciently established to form a common presupposi-**Conventional.** tion of profitable intercourse. The more conventional presuppositions of our thought have become so established in certain great spheres of control, such as those of physical existence, fancy, humorous semblance, etc., that the intent of belief is scarcely stirred up. The habitual coefficients are so automatic in their action, and the flow of cognitive constructions so smooth-running, that mere reality-feeling comes again to suffice. The play of ideas glows with that gentle feeling of familiarity with which we accept the accustomed.

Our belief then becomes simply a *disposition to judge* or to pursue a series of judgments ; the underlying presumptions and assumptions of all sorts have passed into " beliefs." A mass of such beliefs is recognized and their sphere of reference is presupposed.

15. Another case is seen in the judgments already referred to as existential—the case in which the dualism of coefficients of control, of subject and object, testifies to the presence of the mode of reflection as such. It is the case that comes genetically

midway, that which in the formative process exhibits the **Judgment of** birth and self-assertion of judgment. When the **Existence is** child says, " fire ! "; when the adult says, "rain!"; **Assertion** **of Belief.** when I say, " Mermaids do not exist," or " Parsifal is not a historical character "—we not merely acknowledge each a relational content or meaning, but to this we add the assertion of our own belief. We shell off the envelope of control, already the intent meaning, from the content controlled, and pass it also over to the subject-matter, making it a " term " of thought and assertion.[1]

In this formation the predicate is just the crystalizing of the control in a separable meaning. The child's " fire ! " is not the assertion of an existence meaning separable from the meaning " fire "; the control aspect of the entire meaning, the presupposition is emphatic. If it is not emphatic, there is not judgment but mere cognition of the simple presence sort; and the exclamation " Fire ! " is motived by reality-feeling. Between these two **Seen in** lie, besides, the various schematic and semblant **Exclamatory** constructions which spoken language expresses vocally **and** **Impersonal** by devices of intonation supplemented by gesture. **Judgments.** The interrogatory " Fire ? " for example, is schematic, an "assumption,"[2] preparing to issue in the judgment of existence, " Fire ! " The impersonal " it rains " is only another verbal form of stating belief in a judged content, and has the same variations, as we may see from illustrations in a less conventional control-sphere. The *on dit* of common report, a matter of reality-feeling, passes into the "*y a-t-il ?*" of inquiry, and then into the *voila* ! of confirmation and judgment of existence.

16. The judgment does not, therefore, make assertions about the universe—except when the universe is what assertion is made **Universe and** about. The universe may be judged; so may reality **Reality may** of any sort, like anything else. Even in the existential **be Judged** and impersonal forms of judgment, however, it is some restricted " universe," the external, the inner, etc., that becomes part of the asserted meaning; and even then it is the need of bringing out a hidden presupposition for confirmation and acknowledgment, that motives the meaning. Of course,

---

[1] This general position was first worked out in an article entitled " Feeling, Belief and Judgment " in *Mind*, July, 1892, pp. 403 ff. (reprinted in *Fragments in Philos. and Science*, xii. p. 239), in which bibliographical citations are also to be found.

[2] See chap. iv. § 4 on " Interrogative Judgments."

when this sphere is the metaphysical universe, as in the judgment "God is the Absolute," then the presupposition is the universe as an all-embracing category. Yet one may then make this meaning explicit by asserting "God the absolute is real." In short, the presupposition of a sphere of existence or reality is always the sleeping-partner in the entire firm-meaning expressed as "Content, Ltd.," [1] until this partner claims the right, in the existential judgment, to have his name written out in the firm-title, "Content, Reality & Co."

The need is again evident, in this connexion, of recognizing both function and content. The judgment does in its reference always acknowledge its subject-matter as in some sense real ; but it also acknowledges it as set up "in idea" or for thought. The reference to reality is dependent upon the mode of setting-up and judging-about found in the relational content.

17. Another quasi-philosophical theory of judgment makes it essentially a movement of self-assertion, the self-expression of the subject of experience. This, too, has its more or less adequate grounds. From the point of view of the mode of reflection, of which judgment is the expression, the criterion of logical meaning is the dualism of subject and object. The self is expressed in each of its judgments.

Judgment as Self-assertion.

Moreover, experience, of which each judged content is part, is a whole of inner meaning, a life of ideas, and this meaning is controlled by the subject-self functioning for the realization of its interests and purposes. It would seem then to be altogether true that judgment is self-assertion.

18. Yet it is easy to see that the subject-self is a meaning of the sort called a presupposition. The dualism of subject and object is a remoulding of the earlier dualisms of control. The intent-meanings called reality-feelings and beliefs attach to the subject term no less than to the object term, and they pass through the same progressions. Self-hood is a reality feeling in all cognitive process ; it becomes a presupposition in reflection ; it is an object of thought, the empirical ego, in judgments of self-assertion. There is a progression from "rain !" to "I think it rains" and "I think of rain, there-fore I am" ; or if the self is the content throughout, from "me," to "my thinking," and "I exist, having the experience of thought." So far, therefore, the self and the world of the not-self are in the same sense present at each correspond-

Self a Progressive Mode.

It may become Object.

---

[1] "Ltd." or "controlled ! "

ing stage of meaning.   Either *may be judged* with the presupposition of its own sort of existence, or either *may be simply the presupposition* of a judgment of an objective subject-matter. Inner existence, like outer existence, is the presupposition of its own appropriate subject-matter, except when taken up and made predicate of a judgment of existence.

The truth of this appears more clearly when we ask how we proceed to test the presuppositions made in the two cases respectively. It would appear that in each case the test consists in going back to the direct form of control by which the objective content is finally established.[1]   When I say " Pigmies exist," my proof of the existence predicate is reached by an appeal to sense and memory tests suitable to establish physical existence. So of inner existence or self-hood. I can prove my existence as a personal thinking self only by "secondary" and "tertiary" conversion, that is by having another match my inner events with his own, or by whatever process of establishing the class of self-objects as originally set-off and confirmed.   The conclusion is that all judgments presuppose the spheres of existence in which their objects are respectively determined.

19. There is, however, a more subtle distinction to be made out between the two sets of presuppositions.

It is evident that it is the objective self, the me, that is analogous to the external things which are subject-matter of judgment. The " me " is object of experience as things are, being a relational meaning. It has the intent of control, not only as being in the sphere of inner experience, but also as being inner in its essen-
Objective Self is Subject-matter of Judgment. tial objective marks.   Accordingly, the intent of the act of judging a relational objective self is to declare or acknowledge the self judged to be existent in the sphere of discourse or belief called mind.   When I say, " I think, therefore I am a self," I declare the existence of myself as an object in the realm of beings of inner or psychic constitution. So far the belief meaning is correlative with that of the outer or of any other sphere of accepted existence.

But the further meaning now arises that this self—the
The Subject is a second Intent of the Control sort. " myself " asserted—is also in some way identical with the subject of the experience who makes the assertion.   The entire thought situation is within the " inner " life.   There is a second intent, a further control,

[1] That is, in terms of later discussions (chap. iv.), I " assume " or " postulate " the control and test it experimentally.

not objectified in the existential meaning of the first control. This second intent, this acceptance meaning, extends also to all personal judgment of content as existing. The intent *to be experiencing, to be a competent thinker, to maintain reflection, even to think the self properly, goes along with all the acts of judging.* It is the subject intent as such, which is never exhausted by any subject-matter. That old subtlety, that serpent of disturbance in the garden of peace of any purely presentative interpretation of consciousness, here raises its head in the person of the subject, the I. The "I" intent is a second and more remote presupposition of reflection as such—that is, in those judgments in which it is not so lost in the direct objective relational meanings that it ceases to rank as a presupposition or belief at all, and appears at the level of mere reality-feeling or "presumption." But in either case, it is there.

That it may so rank, even to the extent of assertion, is seen in the famous Cartesian motto, where self-existence is made object of thought, in "I am," declared explicitly to be part of the meaning of the experience, "I think." That is, Descartes did not mean merely, "I believe I exist as a self or object of the sort called mind"; he meant, "I am an inner

The Motto of Descartes— an illustra- tion. life or subject having experience." The Cartesian motto is an existential judgment, attempting to render as objective subject-matter the essential control meaning of all thought as such, the subjective principle.

20. Usually, however, since men are commonly not interested in demonstrating or even in asserting their own existence as

When and how the Subject is a Presupposi- tion. subject of reflection, the meaning remains simply one of immediate control, an acceptance of presence, a "presumption," which becomes a conscious presupposition when a subjective intent attaches to the motive for assertion.[1] We live and act, feel and desire, argue and

---

[1] It is well to say this lest we fail to maintain an even balance in our later interpretations. It is a commonplace of the idealists that a rational self, a subject, is a "presupposition of reflection or of experience"—the very phrase smacks of their round of connotations. But it is only to the acutely reflective consciousness—at its best in the philosopher—that this can be said to be a meaning for consciousness itself; that is that consciousness itself holds this meaning. It is a presupposition of experience to a thinker who *reflects upon his experience.* In the prelogical modes of cognition, it is not a presupposition at all to the function itself: it is only our presupposition who think and talk *about* the function. On the other hand we will have also to protest against the procedure of the

dispute, within the circle of reflection without even raising the question of the control we are exercising as subjects of our own thought processes ; it does not rise to the level of a presupposition.[1] Let any one, however, call us a fool, or a child, and we say, " I'm doing this thinking—I am competent to control my thought to a valid outcome—that we must *presuppose*, if you consent to argue with me at all."

This is about the actual state of things with reference to the theory of judgment.   The self is the *subject-agent* of judgment, but not commonly the *subject-matter* ; the *psychic* subject, not

Self as
Subject-
agent is not
Subject-
matter.

the *logical* subject.   Nothing is predicated about this self except when the process turns in upon it, objectifies it as content, and makes it subject-matter.   As meaning it is reality-feeling, presumption of control, and at best a presupposition of belief.   To make it subject-matter is to pass it over to the content side, and again to exercise that very control, *in judging it*, which is presupposed or asserted in judging anything else.

21. There is, therefore, to conclude, in all judgment, a second-intent, a universal control, a meaning attaching to the subject over and above that belief-presupposition which assigns and specifies the subject-matter judged.   This it is that constitutes experience what it is to itself, and makes it what it means to an observer.   To the former it is the *subject as acknowledging function of judgment* ;   to the latter it is *the presupposition of reflective thought*.[2]

22. The relation between the characters respectively of judgment as function, found to be acknowledgment or belief, and of the logical content, found to be relation, is brought out in

Propositions
have two
Terms.

discussions of judgment and proposition.   A proposition is a verbal expression of the content of a judgment ; it is a relational whole in which two terms appear.   It is maintained on the strength of this, that judgment

" levelling " philosopher who reads the situation in terms of the lower mode, or the lowest mode—" pure experience "—and makes no use of the presupposition at all or of the simpler " presumption " of inner reality.

[1] As found in the Cartesian's thought, however, it is a typical and precise case of what we are calling presuppositions.   Having demonstrated the existence of the active subjective principle, it is to him thereafter once for all to be presupposed.

[2] Or its " postulate " in the sense explained below (chap. iv. § 1, and chap. v.).   See also, on the subject-self, chap. xv. § 4.

itself is also always relational and synthetic—the bringing of two separate subjects-matter into the relation expressed in the proposition.

This disregards the aspect of judgment in which it is an act of belief, of acceptance of the one whole of content taken up **They do not** by the act of acknowledgment, as in the exclam- **always ex-** atory "Mad-dog!" or in the impersonal "it rains." **press entire** **Import of** In these the single term of content is acknowledged and **Judgment.** asserted as existing, e.g., a "mad-dog"; there is not the ascription of madness to any particular dog. In the first place we may at once dispose of the "proposition" as such, the verbal declarative statement, by saying that it is always two-membered or relational.[1] Then there remain the questions whether judgment requires for its essential meaning the two-foldness or duality which the corresponding propositions exhibit, and whether the relationships in the content are all that it is the intent of the judgment to express. The question as a whole is that as to the passage of a meaning from its single-term stage to its dual or relational stage, through the act of judgment, the question usually put as that of the relation of the "concept" to the judgment. Some light will be cast on this topic by the further elucidation of the "acknowledging" function of judgment in which the unity of the judged content *as a whole* is emphasized. Later on we find that the relationships *within the whole*, that give duality to the meaning, are emphasized by the social rôle that the meaning fulfils through its linguistic embodiment (chap. vi.).

§ 2. JUDGMENT AS ACKNOWLEDGMENT

23. If we apply the general term acknowledgment to that mode of function which involves belief proper, the *Beurtheilung* **Judgment an** of Brentano,[2] or "assertion with presuppositions" **Acknow-** in the sense given above, we may further define the **ledgment.** relation of such acknowledgment to the group of meanings individuated as logical. We have already said that logical individuation by judgment makes a meaning relational. What

---

[1] As such a form of predication, involving two "terms," it is fully treated below, chaps. viii.–ix.

[2] *Beurtheilung* is a word suggested by Windelband for Judgment in Brentano's sense: i.e., subjective acceptance or rejection over and above the presentation of an objective context for such acceptance or rejection. Brentano's psychological view is developed in its logical bearings by Hillebrand, *Die neuern Theorien der katagor. Schlüsse.*

Albion
College
Library

place has this in the individuation process which gives general
or what we may now describe as "conceptual" meaning?

The problem thus indicated may be sharpened by noting
two current views which seem to require different interpretations of the relation of judgment to conception. If
we mean by conception the individuation of meanings
as general and particular (these two terms involving
also the further meanings, universal, ideal, etc.), and call all
such meanings "concepts," then we have to ask what judgment *does to* such meanings, if, indeed, it does anything.

**Judgment
and
Conception.**

24. Two contrasted views may be cited called respectively
the "predicative" and the "existential." They are
restatements of the two points of view already cited
above in the discussion of the nature of judgment.

**Two Extreme
Views**

One of them, characterized above as the "extreme predicative" theory, holds that judgment assumes two earlier existing terms or meanings, *S* and *P*, and consists of the bringing
together of these two meanings in a predicated relation. Thus
considered it makes conception a process which precedes judgment and supplies separate meanings ready to be joined up or
connected together in a proposition by the act of judgment.

The other view may be called the "extreme existential."
It holds that a predicative or relational content either may or
may not *exist*, and that such a concept or meaning is then individuated by judgment *as in* a sphere of existence or control.
This act of individuation, characterized by belief, is a subjective
function independent of the make-up of the content, and its
force is not to predicate anything, but to give a reference to
a sphere of existence.[1]

---

[1] In another place, *Dict. of Philos.*, art. "Proposition," i., the writer
has suggested a reason for the difference in standing between judgment
and proposition, which may be quoted here as introductory to the
"conceptual" theory of judgment now to be developed.

The passage is as follows (slightly altered) :—" The difference of view
on this subject is probably in large part due to the distinction between
judgment and proposition, especially when this distinction is ac-
counted for genetically by the 'communicative' or 'declarative' function of language. The normal psychological process seems to be the
formation of judgment by the acceptance of a whole of mental content,
and then the rise of propositions, in words, by analysis and for communication ; this in the mind of the *speaker*. But in the mind of the *hearer*, to
whom the relation expressed in the proposition is new, this procedure is
apparently reversed : two more or less familiar terms are given to him in

25. These positions are both here stated in their " extreme " form rather to show tendencies with view to their reconciliation than to characterize the theories of particular writers.[1] We may proceed at once, therefore, to the statement of the view which gives the genetic basis for the divergence between them, and suggests a middle ground.

If judgmental meaning is a revision and restatement of earlier prelogical meanings, we seem to side at once with the declarative or " predicative " theory ; but if, on the contrary, judgment is an act of control, of subjective attitude to a content, it becomes an essential reference of the meaning to a sphere of existence apart from its character as having relational content. This recognizes what is essential to the " existential " view.

The solution is to be found in the fact that the very function by which prelogical meanings are brought into the relational context of thought is *also* that by which the reference to the original control or existence spheres is brought out. Both the criteria—that of relational content, and that of acceptance or belief—must be recognized.

As to content, judgment is predicative in the sense of being declarative. It declares, in the form of the pre-

language, joined in a certain relation ; and he, by accepting this relation, forms a new judgment. The logician, if he restrict himself to the point of view of the hearer, should deal strictly with propositions and their communication from one mind to another, holding that they are always synthetic (relational) ; the psychologist, approaching the proposition from the point of view of mental process and meaning, finds that the proposition is always the analytic statement of the content of an earlier judgment. Even when the hearer *hears* the proposition ' *a* is *b*,' it is not *his* proposition until he has gained the concept *ab* and by acknowledging the relation of the parts *a* and *b* to each other achieved the meaning as one of his own judgment." See also what is said below in the note to Sect. 31 of this chapter. The distinction between the attitudes of " speaker " and " hearer " is made fundamental in the treatment given below to the topic (chap. vi., especially §§ 4, 5). The *elucidation* of a single whole meaning by the *speaker*, comes to the *hearer* as a *proposal* of relation between separate meanings—in the terms of the later discussion. This brings a social or common strain into all predication in a way still to be fully pointed out.

[1] It would be safe to say that Brentano himself represents the " existential " tendency, and the older formal logicians generally the " predicative " or propositional. Bradley, who falls in the former class through his doctrine of the " real " reference of judgment, puts very forcibly the truth that the content of the judgment is a single whole of meaning or " idea " (*Principles of Logic*, chaps. i.–iv.).

dication of *P* about *S*, the relational meaning already
Judgment reached in the movement that establishes the general
asserts stage
of Conceptual concept.   Not, indeed, "already" reached in a
Meaning. chronological sense, but presupposed in the meaning
which the individuation as general achieves.   For example, the
judgment, "This dog is fierce," is a declarative or predicative
acknowledgment within the general concept, fierce-dog.   The
terms "fierce" (*b*) and "this dog" (*a*) are individuated in a
single content, "this fierce-dog" (*ab*).   Judgment is, then, the
form which this meaning takes on when its movement from *a* to
ab is acknowledged and asserted.   "Judgment . . . sets forth,"
as the writer has said in another place,[1] "in a conscious contem-
plative way the actual stage of the thought movement."   It
brings the earlier meaning, "this dog" (*a*), up to the latest
reading justified by experience, "a-fierce-dog" (*ab*), and by a
declaration exhibits the genetic or progressive change by which
knowledge has grown.   If we call a general meaning which is
relatively fixed for communication and other purposes, a concept,
then the-before-and-after movement of such a meaning, the
movement in which the concept is a stage—the movement by
which increments of meaning are achieved and acknowledged
in successive individuations—*this is judgment*.   It brings out
the newly found relationships in the content—the dog is now
thought of as fierce ; and also recognizes the sphere of control or
existence that this relation presupposes—the physical existence
of this fierce dog.

Put in this way—and this is the writer's view—judgment
may be said to be always "predicative" ; it is, however, different
Judgment is from that narrower form of the predication view noted
Predicative. above, which holds that judgment is always a statement of relation between two separate and given contents of
idea or presentation.   For the interpretation now suggested

[1] *Handbook of Psychol.* i., *Senses and Intellect,* 1st ed. p. 285.   The
context of this quotation is also by no means irrelevant to our present
discussion ; the passage goes on : [the judgment] "brings out and emphasizes the belief immanent in the concept in its progressive stages.   In the
generalizing of the concept, this belief was present . . . and in the judgment each such esoteric belief becomes explicit.   Belief is necessary to
judgment and constitutes its distinguishing mark.   It is here, in its
belief force, rather than in its content, that judgment is a distinct mental
act.   This belief is an immediate reference to reality in all cases"—
giving what I now call the "presupposition" of existence.

allows the form of judgment of existence or of mere presupposition on which the "existential" theory in turn
rests its case. Acknowledgment, on the writer's interpretation of predication, *may be simply the passage
to a determination* of acceptance or the reverse. The assertion
of the existence of a sea-serpent involves a movement of
conceptual meaning based upon experience, evidence, etc.—
as does the progress from dog to fierce-dog. But there are not
two contents of presentation involved. There is only the one
object, sea-serpent, now determined under a definite control, as
a content of acknowledgment, and it is this control that is
made predicate in the existential statement.

But it allows Existential Predication.

On this view of acknowledgment and predication, the existential is a judgment, and existence is a predicate; but the *relational
whole as existing* is the subject-matter, and *it is a single whole
of conceptual meaning*.

26. The "existential" view emphasizes the need of interpreting the existence meaning of judgment; but to do so
it goes to the extreme of denying or tending to deny
the declarative and relational character of the content
judged. Existence, we are told, is not an attribute, it
is not something additional attributed to or added to
the concept—let us say, the sea-serpent. So the meaning of
existence, which is the essential intent of judgment, cannot
be stated in terms of predication.

Existential Theory: Existence not a Predicate.

This is so far true that if we define predication as attribution
of one given presentative content to another such content, then
only relational meanings of the type of the proposition, *S* is *P*,
would be judgments. But existence meaning may not be so
expressed; and that alone would be fatal to such an
extreme theory. But as we have seen above, it is
possible to conceive the existence predicate, not as
presentative content, but as control meaning; not as object-
matter, but as mode of subsistence; and this intent-meaning
can be made object of thought and assertion for the purposes of
predication.

True only on Attributal Theory.

27. Thus middle ground is discovered.[1] From a genetic
point of view, this position is plainly valid. The entire objective
meaning of a concept is not exhausted in its context; its control

[1] Erdmann reaches a somewhat similar position, making judgment
"declarative" of the synthesis reached in conception (*Logik*, i. pp. 205,
216).

D

(as being mind, body, fiction, history, etc.,) is an element of
Concept has Control as well as Context, meaning. This control is just what judgment as a function of reflection enables consciousness to isolate and think about separately. In my reflection I say to myself, " Sea-serpent ?—Is it a fish ? a fiction ? an illusion ? a joke ? " The meaning is not determined. Then when I make up my mind, and make, let us say, a humorous assertion : " Oh, yes, 'tis a fish-story ! " I have then made a determination of **and that is Asserted.** control in the semblant mode. I then judge with the acknowledgment and declaration of *this sort of existence meaning.* Semblance of a fish, for purposes of consistent " humorization," prevails, and this I may now predicate of the former bare context of the sea-serpent's reported shape and size.

28. Moreover, nothing hinders, on this view, the regular development of the relational meaning inside the established **Context Develops within the Sphere of Control.** and predicated control. Granted the status of sea-serpent stories, as circulated in the newspaper press, to be that of serio-comic " humorization," we all consent to the new items that accrue to the relational whole that the word denotes. We hear with composure that sea-serpents breathe fire and are given to hypnotizing row-boats ! The bubble of presupposition remaining unpricked, the declarative process of forming propositions goes on apace.

29. What may be called the " conceptual " view of the judg-ment and of the more complex processes of reasoning in syllo-**Conceptual View.** gisms is, therefore, the true one. The meaning given in a concept is relational and by analysis predicative ; but this meaning is not exhausted by the attribual predications into which the context is analysed. The vital process of growth and the transformations of control are also phases of the entire meaning. These may remain in the background as presupposi-tions ; but they may also, for the purposes of reflection, be taken up as meanings to be separately acknowledged and predicated in judgments of existence in all their varied forms.[1]

---

[1] I think it is a germ of some such synthesis that lead to what has been called (see Bosanquet, loc. cit. i. p. 30 f, and Dewey, loc. cit., p. 59) the inconsistency of Lotze on this point. Lotze remarked upon the " static " character of a concept, as contrasted with the changing character of actual experience. There is so much truth in this, that we may say the concept is a generalization of *what is* ; it is a *retrospective meaning* inclusive of actually given and, *so far as now utilized in the generalization,* unchanging

30. It should be insisted, in conclusion, that a judged meaning is not in any sense a different subject-matter from the concept nor a later one ; it is the same content, viewed *in* its transformations, rather than *after* them. In function, conception and judgment are one ; they are just *the mode of operation of reflection in its peculiar individuation of its meanings.* Every conception *is* at once a judgment and a belief, and every conceptual meaning is, by virtue of its own force, judged and believed ; but it is also true that every subject-matter of judgment predicates only the relations present in the general meaning which it embodies and declares.

31. The entire matter may be presented to the eye in diagrams which show the essential points of the " Conceptual " theory as now presented.

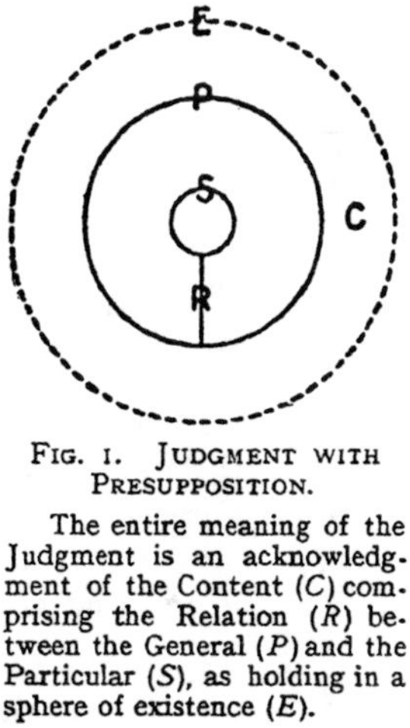

If we represent the relation of the general term (*P*, predicate) " woman " to the particular " Romola " (*S*, subject), as expressed in the sentence " Romola is a woman," by a larger circle (*P*) outside a smaller one (*S*) as in Fig. 1, then the relation of general to particular which characterizes the meaning as a concept may be represented by the line *R inside the larger circle* and connecting the two. This entire meaning is the " subject-matter " or content (*C*) of the judgment.

Diagrams.

FIG. 1. JUDGMENT WITH PRESUPPOSITION.

The entire meaning of the Judgment is an acknowledgment of the Content (*C*) comprising the Relation (*R*) between the General (*P*) and the Particular (*S*), as holding in a sphere of existence (*E*).

But judgment involves not only the content of the given general-particular meaning, but also the intent or presupposition of the sphere of existence in which the meaning is acknowledged. Let this be represented by the dotted circle (*E*) around the

data. Of course, concepts change ; no meanings are or can remain, in their real reference, static ; but it is the ideal of the concept as such not to change. If it change, it is then just the function of judgment to pass upon, assert, or embody that change as the *growth of meaning from one concept to another.* It is in a form of *judgment* that I say, " My opinion was *that* (concept), but it has now become *this* (concept)." As meanings, the two several concepts are different affairs and each is static. Of course, so far as Lotze found in the static aspect of conceptual meaning a reason for making judgment a new function of uniting or combining such meanings after any process to which mechanical analogies would apply, he lays himself fairly open to criticism.

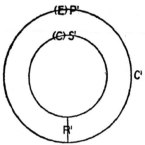

FIG. 2. EXISTENTIAL
JUDGMENT.

In the Existential Judgment
the sphere of Existence (*E*)
has become predicate (*P'*), and
the former Subject-matter (*C*)
has become subject (*S'*) of the
new relation *R'*, now made Subject-matter or Content (*C'*).
The factors are just the same as
in Fig. 1, except that the existence presupposition (*E*) has now
become predicate.

whole. The act of judgment isolates
and declares the relation *R* as holding between *P* and *S* ; a relation,
however, which is simply the maturing *within the envelope of belief* of
the one meaning in which both *P*
as general and *S* as particular are
individuated under the interest by
which the judgment is itself motived.

If now we pass on to the assertion " The woman Romola really
existed," the function simply repeats
itself. The circle of existence (*E*)
hardens into a general meaning (*P'*)
with reference to the particular, " the
woman Romola " (*S'*), and we only
have to extend the line of relation
(*R'*) so that it connects the new
predicate (*P'*) with its subject (*S'*).
" The woman Romola " is a par-
ticular in the class of " really-existing " things. Together they
constitute the new subject-matter (*C'*). That is, the existential is a judgment in exactly the same sense that the earlier
meaning was. Both are acknowledgments of relations established in the essential growth of a conceptual meaning.[1]

---

[1] It may be said that while this gives an account of " analytic " judgments, it does not properly interpret " synthetic " judgments ; those in
which two familiar terms are brought together and a relation is now for
the first time asserted between them. In reply to this I should say that
a relation between terms can not be *asserted* until it is *discovered* : it can
not be *meant* until it is *understood* : it can not be *acknowledged* until it is
thought ; and these are all ways of saying that it is not a judgment at all
until it· is a relational whole involving the two terms. Before that it is
hypothetical meaning, information, or some other form of construction
which is not subject-matter of personal belief. Most of our adult
thinking is of this synthetic type. We are told " Othello was a Moor,"
" Mexico is an elevated plateau," etc. ; but only as in each case the
meaning Othello or Mexico becomes particular to a new general—the
subject-matter being this larger whole—can I acknowledge the meaning
as holding in the sphere appropriate to it. Otherwise we are shut up to
the quite unpsychological view that in judgment certain separate and
static terms, each maintaining its independence, are " put in relation "
by an activity working *ab extra*. As is shown later on, this same
" conceptual " interpretation holds throughout the development of mean-

§ 3. MODES OF BELIEF

32. The position taken above, that the judgment of a subject-matter embodies a variable attitude of acknowledgment or belief, suggests further consideration of these variations as they appear in typical assertions and propositions. We may ask not only, " *Do* I acknowledge this subject-matter ? " and " What do I acknowledge it *as being ?* "—but also, " *How* do I acknowledge it—simply, conditionally, alternatively, schematically ?—how ? " That is to say, there are modes in the outgo of belief, as well as in the existence or reality of the object on which belief terminates. For example, I may say, " His morals are corrupt " ; " If this story is true, his morals are corrupt " ; " Either he is a fool, or his morals are corrupt " ; " He is pretending to be corrupt"; " It is only a rumour that his morals are corrupt " ; " His morals are not corrupt," etc. The variations here are not, it is clear, in the meaning of the relation as to which my belief is or may be questioned ; such variations are given in the relational content, " his corrupt morals." But there are variations in the outgo of my belief upon the meaning propounded once for all in the question, " What do you think ?—are his morals corrupt ? " The answer, " This is what I think," gives this, that, or the other modal expression of belief in the meaning thus set for my acknowledgment.

Variations in Belief.

Modes of Acknowledging a Content.

This is not to say, of course, that the *actual content* in mind does not change in its setting and also in its extent, but that the conceptual meaning singled out for acknowledgment in the pursuit of a selective purpose, is held in different modes of acceptance and assumption through the growth of the whole content into the form finally acknowledged. I begin, let us say, with denial that Mr. A. is corrupt, but with the accumulation of evidence my attitude passes through the disjunctive, conditional and other modes until, when my thought of Mr. A. has changed enough to justify it, I say "His morals are corrupt ! " There is now an acknowledgment and declaration of the same subject-matter I had before rejected.

It is not difficult to see that the variations reflect the different belief-attitudes which may be taken toward any of the controls possible to objects. The subject may in reflection take up an attitude toward any one of the sorts of objects given in reality-feeling in the modes preceding the logical—a memory

ings in all the operations of reasoning. On analytic and synthetic propositions, see chap. ix. § 1.

attitude, a play-attitude, a sceptical attitude, etc. This follows from our theory that judgment is a reflective process, mediating in thought any of the original existence spheres.

33. We find the following modes of control, all dealing with meanings of un-reflective knowledge :—(1) *Direct* external [1] and **The Typical** inner control, taken up by reflection and issuing in the **Modes.** *Assertorial* forms of judgment (with the negatives) : "His morals are corrupt "; (2) *Semblant* and other *selective* controls issuing in *Appreciative* judgments : "Let him be corrupt"; "Let us pretend he is corrupt "; "Away with so corrupt a man ! " ; (3) *Alternative* control, issuing in *Disjunctive* judgments : "He is corrupt or my informant is mistaken "; (4) *Experimental* or schematic control, giving the *Hypothesis* [2] : "Suppose he should be corrupt ! " and the Interrogative, " Is he corrupt ? " (5) the attitude toward accidental or *Anomic* constructions expressed in statements such as, " I dreamed he was corrupt ! " " What a conceit, fancy him corrupt ! "

These attitudes toward earlier meanings shade all the way from "*acceptance with presupposition*" *to neutrality*, the latter being the absence of all reference of the meaning to a control. We may file them for discussion in three classes, representing, first and second, the two extremes, and third, the range of modes of acknowledgment between the extremes. So treated we have *the believed as controlled*, the *believed as not controlled* or the *neutral*, and the *partially believed*. Considering these attitudes of belief as referring their objects to spheres or domains of some sort of subsistence or existence, we may distinguish the spheres of *Reality*, *Unreality*, and *Possibility*.[3] We will take up these three spheres for further discussion, beginning with

---

[1] Of course, external in the large sense of what is taken to be foreign, not merely the physical.

[2] A little later on we shall come upon another great form, the *Contingent*, which arises only in the logical mode itself (see sect. 25), and is not placed here where meanings of prelogical origin are taken up. Cf. the distinction brought out in chap. v. § i. between the schematism or " assumption of the general " and that of the " postulation of reality." Indeed the tenor of our discussions later on is to show that there is generally what may be called a " mixed mode " of belief—an acceptance of an object in and for a restricted sphere or use, and a question or assumption of the object's further place in a larger or different sphere. Most judgments have presuppositions of belief, and also make assumptions of a further context and meaning.

[3] In logic, these variations constitute the " Modality " of the corresponding propositions (see chap. ix. sect. 36).

Unreality, confining ourselves, however, strictly to the movements of belief. The meaning of Reality itself is a topic of detailed discussion later on (Vol. iii).

§ 4. ASSERTORIAL JUDGMENTS

34. (1) The question, in any preliminary consideration of what reality and unreality mean, is first of all that as to the presence of a secondary sphere of reference in which the item in question could find its reality. As we saw above the only sort of contents or objects that have no such reference are the fugitive images read off as being only psychically existent. These may be taken in certain conditions to have no reality, to be unreal, although recognized as existing actually in the inner life. As meanings their peculiarity is that they lack the belief with presuppositions, and have only the *presupposition of non-belief*. Of my fugitive dreams I judge and declare them non-believed as to any further sphere of reality in which they might "make-good." I judge them to lack any form of control which I might acknowledge by my belief ; but just by my judgment I imply the presupposition of this belief of my own.[1]

Unreality judgments, then, as attitudes of reflection, are not neutral in the sense of not implying belief ; on the contrary, they Judgments of do imply belief ; and as meanings of thought they go Unreality further in presupposing a mode of existence characterized as "unreal." They imply belief in no further reference beyond mere psychic subsistence or existence in idea. In the dualism of reflection realities are remote spheres of reference, each claiming marks which entitle it to be called a mode of reality. A meaning carry Belief set up may be referred to one or the other, or it may in absence be judged to remain merely set up, merely present, of positive Control, merely fancied, having no claim to further reference in a context of controlled meanings. But there remains the presupposition of reflection itself ; for all judged meanings are in experience, and in and are psychic objects as such. The judgment of un-Psychic reality, therefore, is not entirely negative, nor neutral ; Existence. it is a judgment of psychic existence,[2] of that bare inwardness wherewith a fugitive fancy floats before the eye of

[1] See what is said below, chap. xi. sect. 5, on the "Presupposition of Reflection."

[2] The exposition and further justification of the distinction between existence and reality is to follow in the explicit treatment of reality as

reflection. It is not neutral in the sense of being undetermined, but in the sense of being determined not to go either here or there in the alternative classes of the real. The presupposition of this sort of judgment is merely that of the sphere of reflection itself.

Speaking in terms of existence we may say that such a subject-matter has psychic existence—a sphere described above. Its relation to those other spheres of existence to which some sort of reality attaches is seen in its character as being "fugitive" or anomic. Other sorts of experience all have some control which is *mediated* by the context presented for judgment. Their meanings are convertible in some sense in a direct control-mode. Even the psychically existent is, *when judged real*, referred to the system whose control **Mere** is the subject-self. But when the psychic, the fugi-**Psychic** **Existence** tive, has no moorings in any sphere beyond just **is judged** its bare psychic happening, it mediates no further **Unreal** meaning ; in this sense it is neutral. This curious [1] presupposition of the absence of control, or of unreality, may itself as a meaning be made object of thought and assertion. It then becomes predicate of a judgment of unreality. "My castle-in-Spain is unreal" is such a judgment. The positive content or subject-matter is the fugitive and uncontrolled

meaning. Mere *subsistence* or texture becomes *existence* when it is in a sphere of *special* meaning, such as inner or psychic, and outer or external ; it becomes *reality* when, being given in experience, it has a further reference by judgment to a definite sphere of control. Cf. the passages on "existence" in vol. i. chap. x. §§ 9–11.

One of the limitations of formal logic is seen here. While attempting to give the import of propositions and the sorts of dependence of one on another, it cannot take account of implications of meaning from one sphere or universe to another. From "This is unreal" formal logic allows no inference to "This is fanciful." Many of the general treatises on logic do, however, become less "formal" by attempting to recognize the implications of different modes of reality and existence.

[1] Curious, because, as will be seen later on, it leads to a discrimination against this particular sort of existence—the "merely psychic"—in the make-up of the meaning of reality. All the other spheres of existence seem to have some sort of "reality" assigned to them, and so to be set over against this, which is unreal because, as we say to one another, it is "in your mind." As will be seen later on, these judgments of un-reality are not at all the same as those of *disbelief*, ordinarily described as "negative judgments," such as "his morals are not corrupt" (discussed in chap. viii. § 8 ; especially sect. 24, note).

" castle-in-Spain "; but its presupposition of unreality is taken up for acknowledgment in the judgment which declares it.[1]

Beginning with this case, we will proceed to the more specific cases of belief. As judgments the unreal meanings are " assertorial "; they express a positive belief or assertion. They differ from other assertorial judgments in the fact that the presupposition is a sphere of lack of control instead of one of a definite sort of control. We will call this the " unreal presupposition," and the belief which accompanies this judgment " belief in the unreal," as opposed to the presupposition and belief of a positive or " real " control.

35. (2) The cases of partial belief being reserved, we may now cite the other extreme of the assertorial judgment, in which **Assertorial as controlled Meaning.** a meaning is assigned to a definite control over and above its mere presence as subject-matter of reflection. The presupposition itself may now take form in an existential assertion, predicative in its character; or it may remain in the background as the belief-envelope of a relational content. If, for example, my former judgment of unreality terminated upon the notion of the sea-serpent, I might either give the subject-matter reality by saying, " sea-serpents exist," or " presuppose " a common sort of existence for our discourse about sea-serpents, as in " sea-serpents are said to sleep in winter."

Most of our judgments are of this latter sort; assertorial judgments involving the presupposition of some sort of reality. They take the verbal form of the conventional " categorical " proposition " S is P " of the formal logic. Under this one form, the differences of real reference, like so many essential differences of psychic meaning, are effectually concealed.

We may find it useful, as we proceed, to employ a symbolism to distinguish these modes; and we may start with the symbol $\underline{A}$ to denote the unreal inner object, and $\widehat{AB}$ [2] to denote the judgment with " real " presuppositions (the sub-arc beneath the letters indicating the positive determination of the relation of the terms, and the upper curve or over-arc the positive determination of the sphere of existence). These, then, are the two extremes in the modal determination of belief—the meanings

---

[1] The judgment of unreality is then a good instance of a negation by " pure exclusion," as described below, chap. viii. § 7. By its positive marks, the fugitive image is excluded from the several classes that go to make up reality.

[2] B may be either the related predicate term or existence rendered predicatively.

unreality and *specific reality*—" reality," we may again re-iterate, being a generic term for that which is a sphere of control—inner, outer, etc.—*for the judging process itself*, over and above mere presence in the mind.

§ 5. JUDGMENTS OF APPRECIATION AS ASSERTORIAL

36. A moment's reflection, however, cannot fail to convince us that there are certain differences in this function of "taking-up" or "passing-upon" earlier meanings in an assertorial form of statement according as these are *recognitive* or *selective* in their type. Selective meanings are meanings of fulfilment, satisfaction, worth-while-ness. They embody meanings added to the mere skeletons of schematic or presented contexts. And the question is a very important one as to whether, in reflection, these meanings when taken up in belief, confirmed, and declared by judgment, are reduced to relational content, in just the same way that the meanings of recognition are.

How are Selective Meanings Judged?

On an earlier page a distinction of terms has been made between judgments of *Acknowledgment* and judgments of *Appreciation*, in anticipation of the detailed treatment of this very topic. That treatment is still to follow in its proper place below.[1] In judgments of appreciation, we have acknowledgment in the sphere of that control which is not foreign to itself but more or less selective and fulfilling of personal interests and purposes. The question arises as to how judgments of appreciation, granted they exist—whether or not they be exhaustive of the original worthful experience—differ from other judgments.

Judgments of Appreciation.

37. Such meanings, *as subject-matter*, do not claim a distinctive character ; a selective meaning like any other may be taken up and asserted in judgment. They give a relational content, expressing any sort of relation in which appreciation can be embodied. Moreover, another of our criteria of the reflective mode, that of the *dualism of subject and object*, is also realized in our reflection upon our experiences of appreciation. We can think about satisfactions, just as we can about anything else, as objective items of experience. There remains, therefore, only the one criterion left, that of *belief*,

both Relational and Dualistic.

---

[1] See what is said in the Introduction on the two types of schematism that underlie these judgments respectively (chap. i. § 3). The question of the limits of the logical rendering of appreciations is taken up in chap. xiv.

whereby to distinguish these judgments from other forms of acknowledgment. Do they differ in this?

38. They differ, we may reply, not in the essential act of acknowledgment, but in the different sort of control attaching to the meaning acknowledged. The meaning acknowledged as a judgment of appreciation is one of *immediacy*—a sweet taste, an artistic effect, etc.—and as originally constituted it does not allow variations of attitude.

The difference then is this. We do not find attaching to our appreciative experiences a foreign control toward which we can take up varying attitudes of acknowledgment. We do **Appreciation** not say: "This milk may taste good," "This milk **not under** tastes either good or bad," "If this milk is white it **various** **Controls,** tastes good," "Let us assume that the milk tastes good"—none of these variations appear. The given milk tastes good or bad! It is the milk as recognitive meaning that passes through the phases of belief; the taste in each case remains fixed. The "whiteness" of the milk is a meaning fixed by the context and controlled externally to me; the "goodness" of it is a meaning that requires a certain fulfilment of the requirements of taste. This latter is set up for objective and "common" recognition only with certain reservations (pointed out below, chap. xiv.).

In other words, there is a certain immediateness about an experience of appreciation which at once justifies judgment without further reference or confirmation. Beforehand, there is all manner of doubt; the new supply of milk may be good, bad or indifferent. But the experience once had, the judgment of it is positive. Even the judgment, "I am uncertain whether I like it or not," is an assertorial statement of a certain neutral experience of appreciation. It is the experience that is neutral; the judgment of it is assertorial.

The control of simple appreciation is then apparently independent of the modes of reality assigned to the thing which is **but added** appreciated.[1] "Adam Bede's character pleases me"— **to each of** this is my appreciation; and it may be independent **them.** of the mode of reality or existence (fact, fiction, humour,

---

[1] I say "simple" appreciation, for in cases of developed worth, artistic, economic, etc., their sphere of fulfilment or reality becomes part of the meaning appreciated, thus greatly complicating the question. I think it may be said, however, that in every case of assertion of subjective worth, there is the intent to *assert* merely and *not to prove*, to say so by personal right, not to *propose for discussion and testing.*·

or other) that I go on to assign to Adam Bede. This, of course, leaves many considerations open, and so they may be left for the present. Suffice it to say that there is a relative detachment of the appreciation from the thing appreciated. Though assigned *to the object*, the good taste is *somehow in me* : I say *I* like it, *I* find it so, etc. And the judgment of appreciation confirms the finding, isolating for acknowledgment the appreciative aspect of the entire meaning. The judgment " I like milk " is true of *me*, not of the milk ; but it is equivalent to saying, " I find the *milk good*."

39. This may now suffice to justify us in saying that *appreciative judgments are always assertorial*. They *acknowledge the* **Judgments of** *thing* to which the appreciation attaches *as possible,* **Appreciation** *probable, or certain*, in this or that sphere or realm, **are always** **Assertorial.** but they *appreciate the thing as, once for all, what it is found to be, fit or unfit.*

In other words, belief as judgment of appreciation has its reference to the sphere of inner control or satisfaction ; and since such control is immediate in its mode,[1] there can be no

---

[1] There is indeed the subtle question, and some reader may be disposed to raise it, as to whether the thought of satisfaction does not make it part of the cognitive context which is then mediate in its reference to the original control ; whether—to cite an instance—my assertion that " yesterday's breakfast was enjoyable " does not make the whole experience one now of remote reference into which my present thought is to be in some way converted. There can be, indeed, no doubt that the appreciative part, no less than the recognitive part of the past experience, yesterday's breakfast, may be treated in this way ; I may prove both by having the same breakfast again. But it is still true that *I need not* treat my enjoyment in this way. The central sphere of the enjoyment part of the meaning being that also of my present selective and appreciative meaning, this latter suffices and needs no further mediation. I may say, " I am uncertain whether that was a real, or a fancied, or a dream breakfast, but *in any case I enjoyed it just the same*, and do in thought again." Whatever uncertainty there may be about the proper assignment of the recognitive context to a sphere of reality, such uncertainty does not attach to the appreciation of it.

Speaking of subtilties there is here the additional one, to which we must return again, that the sphere of the " real" which appreciative judgments presuppose —that of an unambiguous immediate inner existence—is just the sphere which, as we have seen above, judgments of mediate belief find " unreal "—at least as to that part of its context described as uncontrolled or " fugitive." The distinction is that already contained in the illustration given above : the breakfast may be a mere fancy and thus " unreal," although the satisfaction of it is said to be " real." This suggests the query, at least, whether the " real-ness "

doubts or hesitations. Judgment of appreciation is then always simply assertion or denial of the presence of a selective meaning or worth. It is a case of "real" presupposition and belief, giving its own sort of reference to reality, but in a sense different, as will appear later on, from the "real" belief attaching to recognitive meanings. It is a "real" that is in some sense more "singular" and "private" than are the judgments that are used to render it ; a matter brought out in chap. xiv. below.

We may gather up our results so far in the accompanying Table B, noting only that it anticipates the conclusion of a later page that justifies the use of the term "problematical" to cover all the forms which embody partial belief or judgments of "possibility" (together with the description of these judgments).

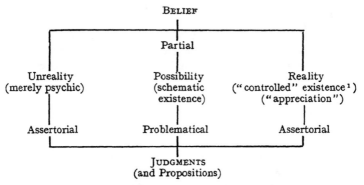

TABLE B. MODES OF BELIEF IN JUDGMENT.

§ 6. JUDGMENTS OF PARTIAL BELIEF

40. (3) Our third group of meanings is very varied. They fall into three great forms, all recognized in the current discussions of logic. As meanings in the prelogical modes we have come across some of them, and given them names. We may distinguish, for further discussion, *Problematical* or schematic from

of appreciations is the same meaning as the "real-ness" of things. In seeking a solution, we should remember that it is the images, the recognitive parts of "inner" experience, that require confirmation (by "tertiary" conversion, see vol. i. chap. iv. § 25), not the fulfilments, the selective parts. These latter are in type what we found (vol. i. chap. x. § 2) to constitute the immediate and continuous fund of the inwardly "persisting" and real.

[1] That is both the "external" and the "inner," when the latter is of the "funded" or organized type (as contrasted with "fugitive").

Assertorial meanings ; and further, within the problematical, *Hypothetical* from *Alternative*. To these must be added a further

Three great Modes as Judgments, meaning called the *Contingent*. Recalling our earlier remarks upon these meanings, all of which are now taken up in analogous judgments or propositions, we may distinguish them as :—

a. Experimental statements, rendering Semblant and Hypothetical meanings in propositional form.

b. Disjunctive Judgments and Propositions, rendering Alternative meaning.[1]

c. Conditional Judgments and Propositions, rendering Contingent meaning.

For these the respective forms, when the belief predicate is explicit, are the existential propositions—

a. Suppose sea-serpents exist.

b. Either sea-serpents exist or the newspapers lie.

c. If the newspapers are veracious, sea-serpents exist.

When the content is relational and the belief reference is a pre-supposition only, we have—

a. Suppose sea-serpents have lungs.

b. Sea-serpents have either lungs or gills.

c. If sea-serpents are fish, they have gills.

41. It is clear that in the second and third we are only recognizing distinctions of meaning which have been taken up,

Arranged according to Determinate- ness of Control and Content. ratified, and declared by reflection. The relationships of content, resting before under the *cachet* of mere acceptance or reality-feeling, now receive assertion as objects of belief. In the forms in which the reality is presupposed, but not asserted, the degree of determinateness of the relation judged is the motive for the distinctions of form ; and in the existential forms the motive is the degree of determinateness of the assignment of the subject-matter to a sphere of belief. So we may arrange these forms *with reference to the determination both of the control of the whole meaning,* as reflected in the acknowledgment or belief of the subject-matter, *and of the relationships which are made subject-matter of judgment,* as being fully or partially established. It is evident from the illustration given that there are degrees of relative fixity—or determinateness—in the relation of subject and predicate, and also degrees of relative confidence or assurance

---

[1] Considered as embodying " grounded " implication, or logical dependence, these are later on called " inferential " (chap. ix. § 5).

as to the sphere of belief within which the predication is made. The question of the relative independence, however, of these two sorts of variation is still ;to be discussed (see chap. viii. § 11, on " Acceptance, Denial and Rejection ").

§ 7. PROBLEMATICAL PROPOSITIONS AS HYPOTHESES

Experimental Mode. 42. (a) First in order, excluding the meanings of the assertorial type, $\widehat{A}$ and $\widehat{AB}$ (see sect. 35 above), we have the *experimental* or schematic mode of meaning, which although not strictly speaking a judgment, is in its verbal form propositional.[1]

In this the meaning is not yet subject-matter of judgment ; it is merely erected as a proposal for discussion, inquiry, and later determination. This we may denote by a **It is doubly Indetermi- nate.** symbol for tentative meaning, *ab*, the small *b* being the experimental predicate, which is not yet accepted. It does not have the sign of determinateness of content, the *sub-arc* beneath it, nor the sign of acceptance of the whole meaning in an act of judgment, the *over-arc*. It is the reflective use of a schematic content, with the careful preservation of its essential meaning as still problematical, still open to proof or disproof.

The indeterminateness holds both of the experimental content and also of the existential force of such meanings. In saying, **Illustration.** " Suppose sea-serpents are green," I may suggest not only a mere relationship whereby sea-serpents may or may not be pictured as green ; but also, a supposition of belief in green sea-serpents, as existing in some sphere or other.

---

[1] The use of the term " proposition " for something proposed or supposed is common. There is, however, something more to be said about the "hypothesis " or "proposition " of science, when it arises in the logical mode and becomes a device for the development of Implication—what is called below " proposal." For that reason I have just above called the meaning reached here " semblant hypothesis," a meaning that is wholly schematic. Later on, a distinction is recognized between schematism of content or relation, " proposal," and that of remote control or reality, " postulation." While it would be confusing to use " proposition " in both the current senses, that of schematic meaning or " assumption " in experimental science, and that of categorical statement in logic—still the passage of the meaning from the former to the latter rôle is so normal and usual that the very ambiguity of the term is suggestive. I shall confine the term to its logical meaning—a verbal expression of predication (see chap. viii.).

The meaning is one of "assumption" with suspense of judgment pending investigation or other means of obtaining proof. When this passes into one of the forms of positive judgment, not only is the relation—green sea-serpent—established, but a presupposition of belief also falls upon the whole meaning. But before this the entire meaning is really prelogical still (and for this reason put in small letters in our symbolism). So long as it is schematic, it means *absence of belief*[1] as to any sphere of existence.

Accordingly, we are not able to describe such meanings as judgments ; they do not fulfil the belief criterion. They are expressed in the form of the proposition, the form in which judgments also usually are ; but only with the accompanying reservation, embodied in verbal intonation, written interrogation, etc. that the meaning is problematical and, it may be, *set up as a semblant hypothesis with "assumption"* of some sort of reality.

They are not Judgments, but "Proposals."

43. The placing of this meaning in the semblant mode, in our earlier treatment of its genetic beginnings, is here fully justified. The procedure of our reflection, in treating contents experimentally, is distinctly of the nature of semblance or make-believe. The scientific hypothesis is not only proposed as a content, it is also *assumed to be, and erected as if it were, in some sense true*, in order that its relations and control may be established. It is here, as in the lower mode, *made-up* of known items, but *treated* as embodying meaning not yet finally determined.

Still a Semblant meaning.

§ 8.   Alternative or Disjunctive Judgments

44. (*b*) The movement toward determinateness shows itself in what we have above called *Alternative* meaning. Its genetic[2] motives and control have already been worked out. It is a meaning which suggests dual or rival determinations, each claiming to embody and express the internal relationships of a whole meaning, which, however, remain indeterminate. The meaning is determinate as to the larger whole, within

Alternative Meaning

---

[1] In the classification of meanings according to belief given in sect. 55 of this chapter, this meaning is at one extreme end of the scale, and both the assertorial meanings already spoken of (unreality and unconditional reality) are at the other end.

[2] See vol. i. chap. x. § 4.

which the rival claims are still to be adjusted ; but indeterminate
Determinate as to the issue in one of them or the other. So far as
only as a belief in the whole is concerned, the judgment is
Whole. assertorial ; so far as the relationships of the content
are concerned the meaning remains problematical.

This is the meaning embodied in the "disjunctive" judgment
and proposition of formal logic. It is a judgment only with
It gives respect to the presupposition of reality which belief
Disjunctive in the entire meaning justifies.[1] " Sea-serpents have
Judgment. scales or skins," presupposes belief in a sphere of
existence *in which either supposition may have confirmation,*
whether it be physical existence, newspaper report, humour, etc.
But it is not a final judgment in respect to determinateness of
relational content ; there is suspense as to which of the possible
assertions is to be accepted.

45. Expressing this meaning in the same symbolism as be-
fore, we have $\overparen{a \text{ or } b}$. The over-arc of determinateness attaches to
Symbolic the whole meaning as (1) having a presupposition of
Expression
of the belief, but not having the sub-arc of final relationship
Disjunctive. of content. The certainty of the issue—as indeed to
be *a or b*—is expressed by " is." The two alternatives are
still put in small letters as in the schematic meanings, since
it is (2) by the further experimental use of *a* and *b*, or one of
them, that the disjunction or alternation is to be removed, and
the terms placed in a logical relationship.[2]

46. This latter mental movement is interesting as illustrating

---

[1] It is this presupposition, called by him the " real subject," by which
Bradley justifies his view that the disjunctive is a categorical statement
(*Principles of Logic*, p. 123).

[2] Both these points (1) and (2) were definitely stated in the writer's
first sketch of this theory of judgment (*Handbook of Psychol.* i., *Senses and
Intellect*, 1st ed., p. 299), in these words : " The disjunctive judgment has
also a hypothetical reference, . . . The assertion extends only to the entire
disjunction, and rests suspended in reference to the single alternatives.
. . . There is, however, a direct mental tendency to further assertion
by the erection of one of the alternatives into a hypothesis, when the
judgment takes on a distinctly hypothetical form."

As far as the belief attitude is concerned, the view of Venn, *Emp.
Logic*, pp. 246 f, is about the same as that given here, but the genetic
order is not expressed in his view that the disjunctive " widens the reference " of the categorical. It has indeed a wider reference, since its
subject-matter includes all the alternatives ; but, genetically, the order
is from the wider disjunctive to the narrower categorical.

E

the processes of flux and transition in meaning between the
typical recognized modes. The disjunctive judgment
has varying shadings from mere tentative suggestion
of possibility to quasi-assertion of strong probability.
We customarily say, " It is this or that," meaning " It
may be this, but is probably that " ; and often also, " It may be
either of these, I have no means of deciding " ; and sometimes,
again, " It may be that, but let us try this."   While, that is,
the circle of determinateness closes around the entire group of
alternatives, it does not in just the same sense hold aloof from
each of them.   On the contrary, it has its points of emphasis,
its selections, its preferences, due to the attitude—the selective
interest, the dispositional character, etc.—of the thinker.   Some
disjunctions should read, " It may be that, but I hope it is this."

Disjunction as illustrating Transitions of Meaning.

47. In the further development of an alternative meaning
three cases should be distinguished.   One (1) is that already
spoken of in which the disjunction is motived by
rivalry or positive duality in the issue of a single
developing meaning.   This is the case, in actual experience, in
which the judgment most fairly exhibits the change taking place
in the content, by which new meaning is determined.
If it be a case of *a*, the dog, becoming *ab*, the fierce-
dog, or *ax*, the tame dog, the alternative is one of *exclusive
or definite alternation* : both cannot be true.[1]   The form " A is
B, or C "—the comma emphasizing the exclusion—may express
this meaning.

Cases of Disjunction.

1. Exclusive Alternation.

This is usually the case also in the actual use of the disjunctive proposition to express the alternative meaning.   The communication to another is intended to tell him something
he does not know, and if one use this form, the supposition is that one is telling the other all one knows
—that one is still uncertain whether the dog is fierce or tame.[2]

Usual form in Conversation.

(2) Yet this is not always the meaning of the disjunctive
judgment ; it is not always exclusive, but may be indefinite as
to inclusion.   For example, when I say, " The apple
or the orange fell off the table," I do not mean to
assert that they did not both fall off.
In this case, to be called *indefinite disjunction*, the
range of indeterminateness is wider.   The whole meaning is

2. Indefinite Disjunction: both Alternatives may be true.

---

[1] See the treatment of the corresponding logical meaning under the
term " exhaustive disjunction," below, chap. iv. § 2.

[2] This point has been noted in vol. i. chap. x. sect. 22, note.

not so shut in by a circle of belief, nor narrowed down to so contracted a content. I may not have the subject-matter so fixed that it is a question of one of the alternatives only, in my growing experience. On the contrary, it may be a meaning of a more indefinite character to which the alternation gives a tentative filling. By the sentence given above I may mean, "something fell off the table—apple, orange, or what ? " The result may show that both things fell, and possibly more.

If we use the form " A is B, or C " (one of them only), for exclusive disjunction, then the form " A is B or C " (either or both may do) will serve for indefinite disjunction. This latter is recognized below (chap. iv. § 2) as " schematism of the general " ; it is interesting as showing a state of mind resting in mere analogy or indefinite sameness of content which may be interpreted by any one of certain alternatives, *all of them being for the moment equally eligible*.[1]

(3) The third case is that called *inclusive disjunction*, in which Inclusive the members of a class are assigned to one or other Disjunction. of certain sub-classes or terms, these sub-classes being either exhaustively determined or in part still indefinite.

A form of inclusive disjunction in which the terms are exhaustive of the meaning is that which we may call " disjunction in extension " or " disjunction in division " ; for example, " coins are either gold, or silver, or copper." Here the determinateness of the belief appears in the exhaustion of the range or extension of the general class " coins " by the alternatives into which it is divided, " gold coins," " silver coins," etc. But the indeterminateness of the content appears in the relation of general class

---

[1] Mr. Bradley's argument (*Principles of Logic*, pp. 124 ff) to the effect that all disjunction is exclusive, the alternatives being " incompatible," seems a laboured bit of special pleading. He admits that the meaning expressed is not always exclusive, but calls such a meaning " loose," " careless," " inaccurate." But " looseness "—that is indefiniteness and uncertainty—may be part of the belief attitude the meaning is to express. It may be " loose " and inaccurate to say " some " or " few," rather than exactly how many, but it serves a purpose when we do not know how many, or when the exact how many is indifferent. All particular quantity, as we shall see later on, is " inaccurate " in the sense of indefinite. " Some A is B " means also " B is A or something else " (being both). Mr. Bradley seems to assume that all alternative meanings are incompatible, and says therefore they are exclusive ; certainly not an illuminating argument ! With this position falls Mr. Bradley's special corollary to it, that the content of the disjunction is two hypothetical judgments (If A then not B, and If B then not A). This holds, of course, only of incompatible terms.

to particular case. Any one coin is one of the three, gold, silver, or copper ; but *which* it is to be is not expressed.

This case is evidently a restating of the case of exclusive disjunction, from the point of view of the general. The inclusiveness of the general comprises the entire sphere within which the exclusiveness of the particular alternatives holds. It embodies what is called below " schematism of the particular " in contrast with that of the " general," which appears in indefinite disjunction.[1]

The written form for this meaning may be this : " A is B or C, either " (indifferently).

48. It is the exclusive form of disjunctive judgment, however, that lies in the line of progression of meaning. This we **Exclusive** have seen above, both in discussing the transition **Disjunction** from experimental to general individuation, and also **leads to** **further** in discussing opposition. The fruitful situations are **Modes.** those of the rivalry, embarrassment, or conflict, which forces the issue to new adjustments and meanings. We accordingly find in this sort of disjunctive judgment the motive that urges on to the next mode of judgment, the conditional. So construed the disjunctive judgment means, " This *or* that, let us see *which* "—as in the scientific disjunctions " volcanoes are due either to explosive or to continuous forces," " these markings are those either of erosion or of stratification." In the result, the " either to " may give place to " to either."

§ 9. Contingent Meaning and Conditional Judgments

49. (*c*) The contingent meaning is one which we have not heretofore had occasion to discuss separately, both because it is **Contingent** partly covered under the terms problematical and **Meaning is** **first Prob-** hypothetical in the preceding discussions, and also **lematical.** because, as a matter of fact, it arises late in the movement of consciousness itself. There is no prelogical motive

---

[1] This is the much discussed case in which " either-or " seems equivalent to " both-and," as in " human nature is either male or female." It *is* so equivalent, from the point of view of the general (*pace* Mr. Bradley's argument !), for it is determined as inclusive of both the particular cases. But from the point of view of the particular, it is an exclusive disjunction : one person is not both.

The different cases, with their varieties, are distinguished with reference to the general and particular forms of schematism in the treatment of logical disjunction below, chap. iv. § 2, where diagrams are also given illustrative of their respective " quantities."

for cutting the problematical or experimental meaning as a whole into those aspects of it which are disjunctive and those which are contingent. This will appear as the motives for the rise of contingent meaning are pointed out, along with the definition of such meaning itself.

We have accordingly to read off a mass of meanings which are usually known by the terms " conditional," " hypothetical," etc., as falling in the class already treated as " schematic "; they are " proposals " and " assumptions," having the symbol, *ab*. The burnt child that dreads the fire has such a meaning and acts as if it judged, " if this is fire, it will burn." But it may not so judge. Its meaning may be only the experimental hypothetical of the semblant or simple problematical sort. It may mean, that is, " in the presence of this thing I propose ' fire-that-burns ' to myself, assuming such a situation." This is not contingent meaning.

50. A contingent meaning expressed in judgment is one in which the relative determinateness and indeterminateness of the factors of acknowledgment and inner relationship are the reverse of those belonging to the disjunctive judgment. Instead of *belief in a whole of uncertain details, there is belief in the details of an uncertain whole.* I believe the statement, " If mermaids sing, they play," but I have my doubts about " playing and **Contingent** singing mermaids." It is mere acceptance of a re-**Meaning is** **Determinate** lational meaning—a connection of terms as such. It **in Content,** is accordingly determinate as to A and B (written in capitals as logical). But as to the assertion of the AB content as **but In-** a concept claiming acknowledgment in a sphere of **determinate** existence —that is not part of its intention. The A **in Control.** and B are thus joined by the inner determination sign, the sub-arc, ͡B if A, but they are not set in the over-arc of acknowledgment and belief. In this it is in contrast with the

͡a or *b* of the disjunctive.

51. As soon as we see the full force of this it becomes clear that it is not in the prelogical stages of the progression of **Prelogical** meaning that the contingent is shaken free from **Meaning** **always the** the larger mass of what is problematical. For in the **Reverse.** prelogical the relations are the reverse—a determinate whole going on to acquire determinateness of detail—a whole of habit, of vagueness of application, of schematic outline, gaining progressively more detailed individuations. The mode in which a determinate content looks not forward for its issue, but back-

ward for its ground, as the contingent does, is not one that
arises short of the stage in which experience itself takes form as
a system of ideas—that is, as logical.

Of course, this is not to say that consciousness does not
earlier cope with situations of the contingent type, say those of

Conscious-
ness treats
Contingency
under lower
Meanings,

cause and effect. It does ; but it interprets them by
meanings which do not involve the contingency of one
event upon another. The entire *fire-burn* meaning,
for example, is one taken in as a whole and progressively developed *forwards*, by accretions due to its schematic
and experimental use. Furthermore, there is, no doubt, the

until the
Rise of
Reflection.

meaning of togetherness or relationship of parts in the
whole. But it must go farther to be contingent. The
fire is sometimes found without the burn, while the
burn never occurs without the fire. This is just the sort of

Selective
Treatment of
Particulars.

situation which motives logical individuation : the determination of a general meaning through *discri-
minative and selective treatment of particulars*. The
meaning arises which hits off the cases " (some) fires with
burns " and " all burns with fires " in a single judgment : " If
burns then fires." This is contingent. It may be characterized
as a judgment of a one-sided relation of dependence.[1] It clearly
involves two general concepts which overlap, but are not coincident—a meaning of reflection.

The force of the contingent appears more emphatically when
we bring out the intent given to the subject term " fire " in
the disjunctive meaning, " fire with or without burns." The
determinate whole meaning here is of uncertain detail, a true
disjunctive ; while in the judgment " if burns, then fire," the
meaning is of determinate details in a whole whose existence in
any actual sphere may not be asserted.

52. It may be said that contingent meaning may be reciprocal—two-sided or mutual—each term being contingent upon the

Mutual
Contingency
mere Toge-
therness

other. Of course, in reflection such a reciprocal relation may be meant.[2] But in the prelogical modes it
would not be contingency at all, but mere together-

---

[1] Just what such a relation means we find later on to be simply that of
established unity or identity individuated in judgment. The meaning
" if fire, then (fire-) burn " is the judgment in which the identity of " fire "
is acknowledged in the new setting or situation " fire-that-burns." See
chap. xi. §§ 2, 3.

[2] A judgment of reciprocal contingency does not add anything to the

ness of parts in a total meaning—as is the case with every cognition as such taken as one object, e.g., "apple-red," "red-apple "— with no motive to the isolation of a contingent meaning as **until rise of** such. Contingency seems to arise in situations which **Reflection.** give a preponderant rôle—that of adequate condition—to the antecedent term, and a relative invariability of occurrence to the subsequent term, a relation which may fail when the terms are reversed.[1]

Contingent meaning is, therefore, logical. It takes the form of the *conditional*[2] judgment, " If sea-serpents are scaly, they are **Contingent** fish." What is asserted is the relation between scaly-**Meaning is** ness and fish ; the content is determinate. What is **Logical.** left unasserted, indeterminate, is a sphere of existence in which the " scaly-fish sea-serpent " combination is realized.

53. The important thing to note about this mode of judgment is, that in it the *logical criterion is carried over to the content, to* **Criterion** *the assertion of a relation* within the whole meaning, **carried over** which is independent of the thinker's attitude of **to the** **Relation in** belief or disbelief towards the whole. It is pecu-**the Content,** liarly a meaning of reflection because it.marks and proceeds upon this distinction. There is the recognition of a sort of independence, on the part of the thought context—of the

meaning of contingency ; it only gives a meaning in which two contingent relations are together asserted, one reversing the subject-predicate relation of the other. It is equivalent to the compound meaning, " A if B, and B if A." As a fuller meaning, however, this in turn is fruitful, especially as underlying judgments of identity and cause. In arguing that " a hypothetical judgment, when ideally complete, must be a reciprocal judgment," Bosanquet (*Logic*, I, pp. 261 ff) seems to mean, if I understand him, a judgment of identity reached either by inclusion in a " system," with reference to which the terms are abstracted, or by some other motive which excludes irrelevant elements from both terms of the relation of " conditioning." No doubt the principle of " identity," which serves as law of " ground," is in this sense one of reciprocal contingency.

[1] This is taken account of in the rules of " logical conversion," or reversal of subject and predicate. If all contingent judgments were reciprocal, all universal propositions could be " simply " converted.

[2] The term " conditional " is used to denote only those judgments in which contingent meaning is expressed. The term " hypothetical proposition," commonly used in the logical text-books, may be retained for statements of the form, " If S then P," considered as propositions, and expressing hypothetical meaning as defined in vol. i. chap. x. sect. 21 f. Both the hypothetical and the contingent judgments may be called problematical, inasmuch as one or other of the sorts of determination remains in question in each.

experience-system—as holding together merely by its immanent
apart from relationships, whatever one's attitude to it may be.
Control. It is the beginning of a *new form of presupposition*,
that called "ground" or "reason." In ground or reason,
the justification of a thought-content is placed not in the
attitude of the thinker, nor in the secondary reference to a remote
Presupposi- context by what the thinker's belief is secured ; but
tion of
Ground or in the *relationships of subject-matter itself, by which the*
Reason. *meaning is self-consistent and self-maintaining.*[1] In
the terms of the formal logic of propositions this is a transition
from "modality" to "relation," from the mode of acceptance
to that of the relation of terms.

This is the force of the conditional judgment. When I
say, "If S, then P," I assert not only the contingency of P upon
S, but also the lack of dependence of the proposition upon my
belief in the existence of either. I remove the presupposition
of existence in any specific mode, and invoke the presupposition of what may be called an "enabling" type of relation.
This contingent meaning lies at the root of implication, therefore, since it deals with what is set up in idea or under the presupposition of reflection only. All "inference" rests upon this
fact that what is "contingent" as to belief—the acceptance of
one term being contingent upon the acceptance of another is
necessary as to relation—the presence of one term implying the
presence of the other. As a proposition, it is "inferential."

It may be said that it is impossible for reflection thus to dispense with a real-reference of its content ; and this is in a sense
true. But the force of the contingent judgment is that of its
being so cut off. We find it best in cases of the pure abstraction of relation as such (see chap. xi. § 5, and the discussion of
"pure exclusion" in chap. viii. § 7). But the reference to "reality,"
so far as it is there, may be of the nature of "postulation" itself
hypothetical. When saying, "if A then B," we intend also
"if there be a world in which there is A."

54. This exhausts, in my opinion, the modes of belief embodied in typical judgments. Other propositions called judg-
These ments are reducible as meanings to these, or to those
exhaust the earlier forms of meaning which are prelogical. The
Modes, opening for other typical modes would be found, of
course, did they exist, under the heading called "Judgments of

---

[1] What is discussed below (chap. x. § 1) as the "reasonableness" of
a system of implication ; see also chap. xi., especially § 5.

Partial Belief," in which three modes have now been distinguished. It is difficult, however, to see where such a meaning **barring** could fall when it is remembered that the variations **the Special** **Treatment** in determinateness and indeterminateness can only **of Cases.** occur in the two factors of content and control—relation and belief. But within the types pointed out there are all the sub-varieties of relation and acceptance which our special purposes of treatment may distinguish, our practical intercourse allow, and our language be made to embody.

55. Summing up the conclusions of these paragraphs, we may bring together symbolically the modes of acknowledgment, **Résumé** ranging them in their true genetic order, from proble- **Symbolism.** matical meanings in prelogical form, which are not yet judgments, through partial-belief judgments to assertorial judgments, as follows, the small letters denoting prelogical and the capitals logical meaning :—

1. *Problematical—*

   1. *ab.* Experimental meaning, lack of determination in judgment.

   2. $\overgroup{a \text{ or } b}$. Alternative meaning, disjunctive judgment.

   3. B if A. Contingent meaning, conditional judgment.
     $\undergroup{}$

2. *Assertorial—*

   4. $\underset{\smile}{A}\underset{\smile}{B}$. Determination as real, categorical judgment.

   5. A. Determination as unreal, categorical judgment.

   6. $\underset{\smile}{A}\underset{\smile}{B}$. Selective meaning, appreciative judgment.

It may be added that in the case of the existential judgment proper, the determinate control acknowledged in belief, **Existence** symbolized in the figures by the *over-arc*, is **and Worth** **made** *itself made predicate*, taking the place of the content **Predicates.** B. As predicate, B may be *any object of thought*, and the belief or fact of determinate control may itself be and is on occasion such an object. Similarly the presence of selective meaning in judgments of appreciation may be what B denotes, since it is the predicate attached to the subject-matter that expresses the appreciation. In the judgment " oranges taste good " the predicate is the appreciative meaning " good taste."

Topic of Having in this chapter treated of the *Acknowledg-* **Relation as** **Criterion of** *ment* of Belief, the criterion of logical function, we **Content.** have yet to take up *Relation*, as mark of content. If we should describe the marks of the meaning of a judgment as those of a relational whole, we could then say that belief is its differentia.[1] The marks as such will demand consideration later on (chaps. vi.–ix.) after the subjects of "common acknowledgment," "acknowledgment of the problematical" and "contingent acknowledgment" have had discussion.

---

[1] This is the way it is put in some treatises ; see the writer's *Handbook of Psychol.* i., 1st ed., p. 288.   In that work (2nd ed., p. 293) it is also pointed out that Venn, in his *Empirical Logic*, pp. 243–250, opens the way to a classification and treatment of judgments according to the sort and amount of belief they embody.   This is the method of treatment of my present text, where I think it is for the first time carried through. Its relation to the underlying thought of Bradley's treatment has been spoken of in an earlier note.   On this point Bradley is explicit, saying (*loc. cit.* p. 14), " The *differentia* of judgment will be found in what differences the content as asserted from the content as merely suggested."

Chapter III

COMMON ACCEPTANCE AND ACKNOWLEDGMENT

§ 1. Stages of Common Meaning

1. In an earlier discussion the different types of common meaning were distinguished[1], and the promise was made that we should attempt to trace these types respectively in the modes in which they arise. To that task we may now address ourselves, the material being organized with reference to that progress in " acceptance " which culminates in the " acknowledgment " of judgment.

Our task has been made somewhat less difficult, by reason of the progress made in the foregoing chapters, which have brought us well into the logical mode as such ; and we may now **We will Consider Logical, then Prelogical Forms.** abbreviate the consideration of the prelogical modes with reference to this discussion, by working backwards from the logical to the prelogical. Our question will be, first, what form of common meaning attaches to logical consciousness—consciousness in which judging takes place —and second, what sorts of common meaning are present when the logical function is absent. This method of discussion will henceforth be profitable, seeing that we are now fairly familiar with the typical modes of cognitive process, and are prepared in a general way for their characteristic variations of meaning.

2. At the outset, however, certain general distinctions in common meaning appear, which we may now describe.

(1) In the first place, it is very evident that all judgments which explicitly invoke the corresponding judgments of other

---

[1] Vol. i. chap. vii. §§ 4–9, where " aggregate," " syndoxic." and other forms are distinguished and named.

individuals are common meanings in the sense named above
"syndoxic".[1] We shall have, therefore, to ask as to
the limits and differentia of such judgments. Let
us call them "syndoxic judgments." This problem

Range of Syndoxic Judgments.

will involve that as to the possible presence of common meaning
in one's judgments when they do not explicitly carry reference
to others. That is, we must ask how far judgments which are
not psychically common—not explicitly common in the meaning given them by the judging person—are nevertheless in their
meaning what they are *only because they are fit to be common, or in some way presuppose or implicate common acceptance*. For example, the extreme case is that of a judgment of
existence of a physical object. How far is such a judgment
indebted to or moulded upon the common recognition of the
object by other persons in such a way that this fact is
engrained in the intent or belief-presupposition of the judgment ?

(2) We must ask in what sense cognitive process, which is not
reflective, not issuing in judgments at all but belonging
to earlier modes, has common meanings. Such meanings we may investigate under the heading of "pre-

Prelogical Common Meaning.

logical common meaning"—the term "prelogical" including
the quasi-logical modes, as well as those which are still earlier.

(3) It will also be interesting to ask as to what forms common
meanings take on in cases involving the refinements of
what we have called "social" and "public" meaning :
cases embodying further development, in the hyper-

Social and Public Mean-ings.

logical modes, of the type of meaning called "syndoxic."[2]

§ 2. All Judgments Syndoxic

3. When we recall, at the outset, the definition of syndoxic
meaning, and put beside it the full understanding of what is
called judgment, an important truth comes within our
ken. This truth may be formulated simply in these

All Judgment is Syndoxic.

terms : *all judgment as such is syndoxic.*

This I call important, in the sense that it is far-reaching and
illuminating if it be true. It means that the psychic
function whereby objective meanings and contents
are taken up in the mode of reflection and held as

All Reflective Meaning is Common

[1] I.e., meanings not only held "in common" or "aggregately," but
also held "as common" (see the table given in vol. i. chap. vii., sect. 27).

[2] This last topic must await the treatment of the hyper-logical modes
in volume iii.

a context of ideas or experiences, always establishes an experience *which is common in the sense that its meaning is meant as common.*[1] This is to say that a single mind always takes its experience as such—its world of established ideas organized in a system of judgments—to be, at the same time, the experience or world of ideas of other minds as well, so far as they have the same data to go upon. This follows from certain positions which have been made out in the preceding pages. To these we may first attend, and afterwards consider the apparent exceptions to the statement.

4. Experience, in the sense now adopted, is a system of meanings, taken over from the preceding modes of individuation,
Judgments
are Meanings
individuated
as General
and Universal. and constituted as a reflective content. The preceding individuations upon which the process proceeds, are those of the development of both the sorts of interest, the recognitive and the selective or appreciative.[2] Let us speak first of the former of these.

I. The recognitive meaning or context we found to pass through a stage of individuation, in which the meaning derived from recognition takes on general and universal significance.[3] It is indeed in judgments of recognitive meaning that "generals" and "universals" are established and acknowledged as contents of thought. The function whereby this is done is, moreover, as we have seen in chapter ii. § 2, of the essence of judgment, which is just the acknowledgment of the stage reached in the progress of general and particular meanings.

In the aspect in which such a meaning is individuated as universal, we find the point of departure for its further inter-
The Univer-
sal is Self-re-
peating. pretation as syndoxic. It is universal in that it is a meaning established by a process applicable to repeated particular cases. In so far as the meaning departed from that of the recognitive type, or was individuated not as universal but as singular, it would represent a variation toward the fulfilment of a special personal interest, or the

---

[1] To say, "meant as common," it may be remarked at this early stage of the discussion, is not to say actually accepted by others, but accepted by me as "appropriate" terminus of common psychic process, as fully explained below.

[2] It has been pointed out that both the recognitions and the selective appreciations of the unreflective mental life are built into a common reflective context of theoretical interest.

[3] See vol. i. chap. x. § 5.

satisfaction of a caprice.[1] Such a meaning we recur to below.
But the relation of recurrence or " identity in difference " in the
application of the general meaning to its particulars, is *ipso facto*
universal. And upon this the further aspect of meaning now
ensues, that this universal or self-repeating meaning is also
repeatable in other minds as well. This aspect it is which comes
when the meaning already established as thus *self-repeating for
cases* appears as presupposition of judgment ; it becomes *self-
repeating for minds.* This we may explain further.

5. Judgment is the function of personal acknowledgment and
ratification. The control of reflection isolates the meaning as
It is also   what it is in the experience of a thinker. This
"repeating" acknowledged context, just because it is isolated by a
in Minds
generally. subjective or psychic factor of control, constitutes a
meaning which is self-repeating, *a common " idea " for any such
control or subject.* The subject that now thinks the meaning
is the control function of the system of meaning which it
thinks ; and the outcome of the movement is that *the content
which becomes experience for thinking becomes also experience fit
for any and all thinkers.*

It cannot fail to be so, indeed, unless there be some reservation whereby the process, by a special movement, secures
its own privacy or denies itself common character. Such we have
seen to be the case in meanings of which some " singulars " are
examples. But they stand out *just in this* from the normal case of
judgments of experience ; to these no such privacy is attached ;
and it remains to be questioned whether meanings which have the
reservation of " privacy " can rise to the status of judgments at
all. This we are to discuss below.

6. The two factors involved, therefore, are so far these.
First, the individuation of a meaning as general makes it universal,
Self-Repeti- because through its application to the particulars
tion of Con- it is once for all established as self-repeating. And
trol Factor. second, the movement which makes it universal to
one typical thinker makes it a meaning fit for all thinkers, inasmuch as that movement implicates no further control by which
the individuation could result differently. The self-repetition
of the content involves the self-repetition of the control
function ; and it becomes this and no other content to every such

---

[1] This may be said here, pending the discussion below of the " essentially " or objectively singular, which is found to involve a special sort of
generalization (see chap. x. sect. 30 and chap. xiv. §§ 4, 8.)

process. The judgments of others are simply cases of the self-repetition of the control. In other words, the control of reflection as such is the common presupposition and intent of judgment.

To illustrate, I cannot judge the term " fixed star " as general, as in the judgment " the fixed stars are those that twinkle," without making a meaning which is universally true of fixed stars ; **"Fixed Star"** and I cannot judge this universal meaning to hold for **as Universal** all the particular fixed stars without making the fact **is a syndoxic** **Meaning.** that they are *such to thought* part of the meaning which is thus universal. That is, " twinkling fixed stars " becomes a syndoxic meaning. It is not only universal meaning for experience, but also meaning for universal experience. It is then true that *a judgment which constitutes a meaning as universal for a process of thought, also universalizes the process of thought by which that meaning is constituted.*

7. The same result appears, from a different point of view, when we analyse the meaning as a whole with reference to the **Experience is** interests involved. The recognized content of ex-**always "sem-** perience is meaning in the sense of context, while the **bled" mean-** **ing.** fact that it is experience to the knower gives it the additional element of meaning of the type called presupposition or intent ; for the judgment means that the context is not only objective, as in the earlier modes, but also experience—a system of ideas expressing fulfilment of the intent or belief of a subject. This suggests a meaning of the type described as " sembled " [1] —a meaning presupposing inner control and psychic life—in the respect that the context is necessarily held in an experience or inner control. *All experience as such is in this respect a sembled meaning ; it is not only context, it is also a developing inner life.* It follows that such a content is the same to each self to which its determination as experience is present; that is, to put it in the terms used above, the subject having the experience intends *any process of constituting this experience as well as this experience as constituted by his own process.*

8. Another quite valid argument is this : any judgment establishing the logical identity of the judging function would find **Argument** its particular illustrations in successive operations of **from Judg-** that function, apart from the special contents of **ment of** **Identity.** the several cases. But the determination in the concrete case of any one of my judgments is a matter of content.

---

[1] Vol. 1, chap. vi. § 6.

There would be no difference, therefore, between the cases of *different judgments of my own, and judgments of myself and others,* as regards the identical function ; the differences in both cases alike would arise only from differences of content. Lacking such differences, the judgments *would be identical both in function and in content.*[1] That is, the content once determined for one act of judgment would be the same for other acts of judgment, whether they were my own or another person's.

In other words, whatever assurance I may have, whatever reason for believing, that I will to-morrow accept my judgment of to-day, extends, by the same right, to my attitude toward *another's acceptance of my judgment of to-day.*

9. There is, yet again, another way of getting at the same result. The difference, in the earlier modes, between the self-content and other objects was, it will be remembered,

Mind Content is always Syndoxic because Ejective. that the external control of the latter separated off the object called external from the inner life of the perceiver. So that while the self is a content intrinsically subject to ejection, and to identical reading from one mind to another, external objects evidently cannot be so treated. In other words, minds, even in the prelogical modes, are always in large part identical and syndoxic, while things may be only "aggregate" meanings. But the progression into the mode of reflection, has been to reinstate a mediate control in which the direct extra-psychic control is no longer operative.

Experience as Content is Ejective also. The entire system of external objects, hanging together under its own organization in a context, is passed over to the inner realm and becomes the content of the thought processes of a self. The control now becomes the psychic act of judgment. The subject of control claims and owns the entire organization of ideas as its experience—as making up its

---

[1] In another connection (sect. 75, note) it is pointed out that there is no *logical* difference between the successive self-experiences, utilized in the conversion of images into perceptions—both being individuated as self-experiences—and the synchronous self-experiences of self and others utilized in the conversion of one's thoughts into those of another. That is, in the logical mode " primary " and " secondary " control lose their difference. The successive personal self-thoughts of one person illustrate the identity of self-function ; and so, in precisely the same sense, do the concurrent self-thoughts of separate persons. The characteristic differences are a matter of the further individuation of persons as singular. The principle is worked out under the heading " Difference of Discernibles " in chap. xiv. § 9. See also sect. 51 below.

very self, the "me" of the whole of experience. It thus becomes
at once available for ejection. All other selves are
subjects also, and all subjects are subjects of experience ; *the whole of experience is yours as well as mine*
unless there be characters of personal or private meaning which
I have right and reason to reserve from the body of my ejection.
A self is a function of ratification and endorsement of the one
system of organization in experience, and all ratified and
endorsed meanings are therefore common to all judging selves.

Judgment is the establish-ment of Inner Control.

10. It may be said in opposition to this that just by being
taken up into experience, under mediate control, a common
content of perception might lose that stable resistance,
or other mark, by which the common or syndoxic
character for different minds might be established.
"Surely," it will be said "my thought of a table is less truly
common to me and you than is our percept table which arises
when the object is touched and seen by us in common."

Objection that Percep-tion is most Common.

This is in a sense true ; it is not the same commonness, but
a new commonness that judgment establishes. It proceeds
upon the old and confirms it upon a new level. The judged table
is part of a context of experience ; and not only the perceptual but
all the other meanings of the table go to make it up. The result
is a system of related meanings in which this table stands for
one case. My judgment in asserting the one case asserts the
whole class of experiences for me, you, and other competent
observers. Another's judgment is not correctly read by me except
by that ejection of my own experience of the table that gives
him the same control processes that my experience now presupposes. So while we might not have the same perceptual
meanings, still the judgment must render them as a common
class-experience.

The various ways now suggested of looking at the topic
are simply paths converging to the same conclusion ; they do
not cite new facts, respectively, nor stand each independent
of the others. But when we put together these aspects of the
problem, the truth that commonness of meaning is a presupposition of judgment stands out, I think, as fully proved.

11. The bearing of this appears very evident when we consider the case which seem to present the chief exception to it : the case of judgment which is explicitly
private, in the sense of not only not presented as
held by other thinkers besides myself, but presented as *not being*

Private Meaning not self-repeating.

F

so held. This case yields readily to analysis in support of our present contention. Such a so-called judgment may not be self-repeating as a universal meaning ; it is then not a truly established nor Universal. general.   Lacking in this respect, it is *not a judgment at all* in the sense in which we use that term. Just in so far as I include in my meaning the possibility or the reality of others' not accepting it also, I impair its It is not Judgment but a Hypothetical Meaning. closed judgmental intent *to myself* as well.   For it then becomes so far lacking in determination that its control *may issue in variations upon my present experience.*   This destroys its character as object of judgment, for it reduces it to the hypothetical, alternative, of other instrumental mode of meaning which is not general nor universal.[1]

For example, when I say " I believe my grandfather's ghost to exist, but I don't expect you to believe it," it is the second clause that asserts the privacy of the meaning. This second clause may express either of two meanings : the one, " the evidence would not convince you," which removes the presupposition of a control sphere for my own belief ; or the other, " this is not a matter of evidence, but of personal acceptance," which in turn makes the meaning one of selective force.   Fully stated the two meanings are, (1) I accept this ghost, but not as a case of a class of which you might also find an illustration for my acceptance—not a case, that is, of a general class under an objective control which my judgment is now acknowledging as the only one possible ; and (2) I accept this ghost because I elect to—because it satisfies my interest and purpose so to do. The former is not a judgmental meaning ; the latter, a selective and appreciative meaning, is to be treated separately below (sect. 19, see also chap. viii. § 9).

12. The matter seems plain in the case in which a disjunctive proposition is made. This is a real judgment in respect to the The Disjunctive Judgment is Syndoxic. whole meaning. Its presupposition of belief is universal and syndoxic.   I expect the disjunction to be recognized and judged to be such by others as it is by myself. The indeterminate details, which are not yet stated for acceptance by others, are also those which are not yet matter of separate judgment by me.   " Sea-serpents are mammals or fish " asserts

---

[1] This is true so far as the admission of another's different judgment upon the same data is also an admission that one's own judgment might be different. The case of mere lack of prevalence or catholicity is of course not involved (see chap. vi. § 8).

a sphere of common acceptance, but does not judge as between the alternatives.

13. Further illustration and confirmation is afforded, also, by another extreme case : that in which something is really quite private in the sense of entering into only one person's psychic field, say a recognized illusion. In this case, the meaning may be in its type a matter of immediate psychic presence, not made over into the body of ideas, nor made part of a systematized context of experience. This indicates that it is not judged, not taken up as reflective or theoretical meaning. If, on the contrary, it be judged " unreal," it then becomes syndoxic as illustrating the " unreal " class, accepted and recognized *as unreal* by others also.

Private Images are Fanciful.

The case is different when consciousness refuses to give such an image or object any syndoxic or common meaning. In that case there is a real judgment of privacy or singularity ; and we have then a second great class of judgments to consider : those which do not terminate in universal but in singular meanings. To this we return below, as well as to the consideration of those selective meanings which we allow each other to entertain and judge in relative privacy.

Singular Judgments deferred.

14. The essence of the matter, so far as we have gone, is that experience, as judged content, is constituted by a progression of factors present in the earlier semblant mode, and struggling for a higher adjustment. The adjustment effected is just the passage into the mode characterized by a control-self over against the content of which it is the control. It is just as necessary that one of these factors, the control, should be what it turns out to be, as that the other, the content, should. The case in which the judgment issues in a universal or self-repeating content, is the case also in which the control-self *is one which justifies this content and this only*. To import the meaning that a different result might come out of the data in another's thought, would be to impair the universality of meaning which is the distinctive result of the individuation upon which the entire movement depends.

Meaning and Control must be what they are.

15. The objection arises that, as matter of fact, nothing is so variable as opinion ; that is, as the different judgments which different men form on the same subject-matter ; and that we expect more than half of our judgments to be rejected and finally disproved. The fact which this objection points out is, of course, to be fully admitted ; but there

Opinions vary as a Fact,

are two qualifications which destroy its force as an objection.

(1) In the first place, it is the psychic point of view, that of syndoxic meaning, from which the claim is made that all judg-
when treated ment is common. This does not necessarily mean
Objectively that we cannot, from the psychological point of view, compare judgments and opinions as held by different minds, and find them diverse. That would be to say that all judgment is! " con-aggregate "—held, that is, not only *as common* to me and others, but also in common by me with others—which need not be true. Of course, there is no limit to the passing of various possible quasi-experiences, opinions, knowledges through our minds, comparing them objectively, and discarding some of them ; and even the opinions of yesterday, now revised, let us say, by a new act of judgment, may be reflected upon and criticised. We may indeed treat our own present opinion objectively and anticipate its criticism ; but that is just to make it, from the psychic point of view, a hypothetical meaning of a type no longer a judgment. The essential fact upon which future revision would proceed would be the giving up of that psychic confidence in the present
and Hypo- opinion which is the presupposition of judgment.
thetically. This confidence requires the maintenance of the psychic point of view *with the presuppositions which it makes*. Once impair this, even by supposing oneself possibly mistaken, and *schematic assumption takes the place of judgment*.

(2) It should be remembered that it is not the unratified, instrumental schema, the hypothetical and experimental mean-
Hypothetical ing, that is held to be always syndoxic. It is just
Meanings the character of such meaning that it is still *sub*
may or may *judice*, still only *opinion*, still not endorsed as being re-
not be
Syndoxic. cognized in the context of experience as a whole. Such meanings as these are not judgments at all. They may or may not be held as common to self and others. What they lack is the ratification or acknowledgment which comes through the issue of the subjective control processes in an act of judgment. Judgment is not a process of stirring up doubt, but a process of declaring belief ; not a process instrumental to adjustment, but the adjustment itself, terminating in its own meaning. So soon as we reach a state of judgment, then the expectation of variation of opinion about the same data—what we call the evidence or proof—at once disappears. The coming of the judgment is the

fulfilment at once of the interest in the relational adjustment of the data, and also of that in the subjective function of control.

16. II. Taking up the case not covered under the heading of general meaning we find that they may be reduced in type to two : those judgments in which lack of participation by others is intended and those in which such participation is impossible. They may be illustrated by such propositions as these : (1) " I alone believe my grandfather's ghost to exist, because (2) I alone can feel his presence." Here there is a statement of singular objective individuation, the one ghost only; and further a statement of a private event, the feeling of his presence. We will take up the second clause first, seeing that as conveying a type of meaning it can be reduced to the first.

Two Additional Cases :

Statement of (1) Singular Individuation and (2) Private Events.

17. When we talk about a purely private event, a feeling, say, we make this event object of thought and communication. However purely affective a chill may be, for example, I take it up in idea and make it a term of experience when I say, " I feel cold." It has become now an event of that connected inner context called, as I look back upon it, my experience. It must, therefore, being an object, be individuated as a meaning in some mode of objective subsistence. This means it is made either a case of a general meaning—" my feeling is that of cold "—or that it is so bare of all schematization and general force that it is a singular. In the former case, it is at once, for the reasons given above, classed as syndoxic, since the general class to which it belongs is a meaning in which other persons join, and by which they now interpret this. So while we may contend that the cold feeling is private, we must allow that the judgment, " I feel cold," is common, so far as it employs the meaning cold as a general. Here, of course, we must bear in mind the caution given above. The judgment does not intend " you are also feeling cold " or " you before this were thinking that I was feeling cold," but my meaning is that *you and others, so far as you might have the data of experience for a judgment such as I am making, would reach a common judgment with me.* In other words, if you felt exactly as I now do, you also would be justified in saying " I feel cold," and not in saying " I do not feel cold "; you would identify and class the feeling as I do.

Private Events are

made Objects of Experience

either General or Singular.

As General they are Syndoxic ;

18. The other case—mentioned above as that in which there is

individuation of a singular—falls into the large class already distinguished which is to come up forthwith for discussion.

I have intentionally pursued the method of exclusion in this discussion, narrowing the problem down to singular objects as such, because it enables us to still further "pool" our issues. It will be remembered that we started with the distinction of meanings as recognitive and selective. So far we have disposed of all the recognitive meanings save the singular. It now remains to treat of the selective meanings, and show that they either do not become judgments at all, or that if they do they too take on the form of singular meanings. It is only, of course, cases in which they become judgments that concern us here.

Singulars.

They raise Questions of Selective Meanings.

19. In other chapters, full discussion is given to the question of the logical individuation of selective meanings of the extreme type commonly known as "appreciations" (chap. ii. § 5, and chap. xiv. §§ 4 ff). It is shown that judgments of appreciation are subject to the same criteria as are judgments of any other sort. The function is the same, the content or subject-matter alone is different. They are shown above, indeed (chap. ii. § 5),[1] to be assertorial judgments, presupposing either the "remote" control of an established context of past experience, or the immediate givenness of the psychic sphere itself.

The Extreme Case is Judgments of Appreciation.

As Function they are

When I say, "I am having fun," I judge the object "fun" or pleasure in the modes of general or singular meaning, precisely as when I say, "I am analysing a nerve." The result gives a meaning either general, as when I make a statement about fun, or singular as when I declare my present fun to be peculiar and indescribable. So it is only this latter case again that concerns us; for we have found that all general meanings are syndoxic. Our progress, therefore, now consists in this, that we find many appreciations or selective meanings also—when taken up in judgment—to be covered by the formula that all judgment is common. The remaining judgments of appreciation are singular. So the *singular judgment turns out to be the final pool in which our issues are cast.*

either General or Singular : Former is Syndoxic.

20. We have at hand, I think, means for the ready disposition of this final case of judgment. In discussing singular

---

[1] See also chap. i. § 3.

individuation we found it necessary to distinguish between " essential " singularity, as we may now call it, and that in which the singularity is " imported."[1]   One thing is singular because it resists generalization with other things : it is the one of its kind, recognized as such by its marks. Another thing is singular because of a selective interest or purpose that finds it so : the singularity here is not "essential," but " imported " by the appreciations which the object fulfils.   A man loves his wife only, although in appearance he cannot tell her from her twin-sister ; she is a singular only to his appreciation, not to his discrimination.

Singularity "Essential" and "Imported."

21. Now the latter case, that of " imported " singularity, is not judgment, because it is not taken up into a context of experience.   It finds its meaning in the immediate fulfilments for which the singular object is appreciated ; or—as it is pointed out below—it returns to direct or personal experience for the testing or proving of the " essential " singularity asserted by a judgment.   For example, I either appreciate apples as sweet, which is not judgment at all ; or I appreciate them as sweet in proof of your report or judgment that they are sweet.   So far, then, as singularity is of the " imported " sort, an appreciation, it is prelogical or hyper-logical (in either case its meaning is not a judgment) ; or it is incidental to a general meaning or presupposition of belief—a " common " judgment— for the testing of which the appreciation is resorted to.

"Imported" Singularity not a Judgment,

but an immediate or personal Fulfilment.

Otherwise it is "essential," and is a Judgment.

22. There is left over, then, only the *judgment of essential singularity*.   Is this syndoxic or in any sense common ? It is.   It is syndoxic.   This follows from what we know of the singular as an object of thought.   It will be recalled that the meaning correlative to general is "particular." The process of individuation proceeds by the establishment of such correlative meanings.   The general is established with reference to particular cases.   The " singular," on the contrary, is a meaning in *opposition* to the general.[2] It is the case that resists generalization ; it is constituted over against the general and particular.

Essential Singularity is Syndoxic.

The Singular is opposed to the General.

The determination of such a meaning as object of belief or judgment, however, involves a presupposition which is on a

---

[1] Vol. i. chap. x., § 6, especially sect. 32.

[2] See vol. i. chap. x. § 6.

level with all the other similar presuppositions. Singular mean-
Singularity is common Predicate of different Singulars. ing becomes a predicate as general meaning does, and as make-believe and the rest do. The very character that stands guard and differentiates the content as ungeneralizable, itself furnishes the motive to that larger generalization in which *common singularity* consists. Singularity becomes the mark of a general class.[1] When I judge an object to be singular, I place it in a general class of objects which *have the mark of singularity in common with it.*

23. The case stands out clearly from the point of view found so useful in many of our discussions, that of the distinction be-
The Common Control of Context of Experience. tween content and control. The singular, like other judgments, requires some control of the object *in a context of experience*; and it is this control which imports commonness of the sort attaching to the logical mode. Singular judgments, therefore, must have this commonness. The common force of the meaning lies in the control, not in the content; for this, by resisting generalization, stands unique. It is common to all perceivers. All alike will pronounce the object singular. It is *the singular object of general or common experience.*[2]

24. Our conclusion, so far, is that *all meanings established*
Conclusion. *by judgment are syndoxic in the sense explained.*[3]

---

[1] We have seen this to be peculiarly so of minds as such ; a case, indeed, that illustrates most forcibly the truth of this theory of the singular. Minds, though *common meanings*, are *as things* most essentially singular.

[2] That is, it is a general in " community " (see chap. xiv. § 8).

It is curious to note the variations in the interplay of the apprecia-tive and recognitive factors involved in singular judgments. For instance, in the judgment, " I am the only person present who likes this taste," I make a singular judgment which is common in meaning (involving the acceptance of my report by all), and confirm it by an appreciation (my own taste) which is not a judgment at all ; I express this confirmation by a judgment of singularity, invoking others' private appreciations, and their corresponding assertions of singularity (each his own taste). The whole situation is held together only by the *common* or *syndoxic* character of these judgments. I might say : " You all would agree with me could you know what I feel as my ground for saying that you may not agree with me in what you feel." The judgments are common in asserting the privacy of the appreciations as such.

[3] In the place already cited (*Soc. and Eth. Interps.*, chap. iii. §§ 3, 4), this conclusion is already advanced. I mention this because certain of the movements described in the following paragraphs of the present text are treated more fully in the detailed examination of the child's social de-velopment given in that work, and also because the text here fulfils the

With so much justification, therefore, we may now leave the matter, only pointing out that judgment stands as a sort of **Judgment a** watershed or "divide" in the development of common **midway stage in Common** meanings. On the side of later development, certain **Meaning.** types of material of experience, as personal or impersonal, yield meanings as to which the values called "social and public" come in question. They follow upon and issue from those of the syndoxic type. On the other hand, in the lower modes of development, the common meanings shade into the simpler forms described briefly on an earlier page. To these latter we turn attention later on. Before taking up the common meanings in the Prelogical Modes, however, certain further questions must be discussed.

25. An important distinction may be introduced by the following question : how does judgment as syndoxic meaning differ from other such meanings ? If there is prelogical syndoxic meaning, in what respect does the "commonness" of judgment differ from that. In answer to this question, we may anticipate here the general conclusion reached below, i.e. that prelogical commonness is "syndoxic" (held *as* common), *while and because it is also "aggregate"* (held *in* common) ; but judgmental meaning is syndoxic, *whether or not* it be aggregate (or logically, "catholic"). A meaning that is syndoxic without being also of necessity aggregate or catholic, we will call "synnomic." This general distinction we may now go on to justify and expand.

§ 3. Meanings as "Actually" or "Appropriately" Common

26. The further consideration of common meaning requires the more explicit treatment of a distinction suggested in the way **Judgment may** of caution in two places in the preceding paragraph. **be Syndoxic,** It will be recalled that we found judgment to be

promise there made to examine the topic in more detail. It is there held (*loc. cit.* p. 130), that "without assuming this view with reference to all judgments—although I think it is true—we may yet say : so far as a personal attitude is involved in a judgment, so far *the organization of the personal self* [here called the inner control] *is the ground of the selection of the particular thought as true.*" . . . " Of other truths, only those come to be real and valid to him which holds for others also." " This might be called in a sense a social deduction of the category of universality " (p. 133 ; cf. also the context before and after).

syndoxic, not in the sense that the person judging required others to be at the time *actually* judging as he himself was ; but in the sense that he required them, *if* they judged the same meaning

either "Actu- or situation that he did, to reach the same result.
ally" or Their judgment should *concur with his.* This is a
"Appropri-
ately." distinction that has had cursory recognition in recent discussions in social psychology,[1] but has never, to the writer's knowledge, been exhaustively explored and defined. To facilitate discussion I shall distinguish judgments which are taken to be actually present in others' minds as " actual," and those only taken to be *appropriate or fit to be concurred in by others* as not actual, but " appropriate " or " concurring."

The distinction between a process recognized by the subject as only his and one which he supposes to be shared by others
Function only is itself on the surface ambiguous, in so far as it does
may be shared, not define whether it is the function merely that is
or the Object
also. common or shared, or also the resulting meaning.

27. The commonness of function as such is completely guaranteed by the nature of the material of the self whose process it is. All objective self-material, notably on the side of its function, which is another name for its control, is ejectively
The Function read outward from the self that apprehends it. To
is made
Common by say that I even raise the question of your judging
Ejection. with me in this matter or that is to make the *pre-supposition that you judge* ; and the only meaning that can be entertained as to what the act of judging involves is drawn from direct experience of judging.

28. With reference to function, the question as between actual or merely concurring commonness is ordinarily of little im-
Common portance. We assume the other person's competence
Function
often and pass over to the results of his thought ; unless,
assumed. indeed, he prove very incompetent, when we ask, " are you asleep ? " or exclaim, " you blockhead ! "[2]

---

[1] In my own development of the competence of the person's judgment in social situations (*Social and Eth. Interps.*, chap. iii. §§ 3, 4), I have before reached this distinction, now made more general here and fixed by terms. It has been misconstrued by certain critics, who have charged that it required other persons' actual judgment at the time. Such is the need of exact terminology !

[2] As simple as this seems, it is yet open to all sorts of misreadings in comparative and social psychology, where the presupposition is made that a process of judgment is actually present in another person or in an animal, when there are only objective signs to go upon. In law the

29. This commonness of function seems to be a sort of protoplasm—a presupposition—within which the commonness of specific acts of control are differentiated. These modes of control have been dwelt upon above as giving syndoxic intent to judgments generally. The specific control—as well as the general function—is embodied in a given meaning or object; and that is in many cases directly identified with the common meaning of the object.[1] When I say, "we are both proud of our pedigree," it is the control of reflection upon the object of thought, "pride," made subject-matter of judgment, that gives syndoxic meaning to the judgment, in addition to and based upon the aggregate consciousness of our actual pride in common. "I am proud of my pedigree," is also syndoxic, through the specific control which claims commonness of concurrent or appropriate experience in you also, even though there is no actual present experience in your case to justify it.

(marginal notes: Specific Control gives Object as Common, / even when Singular.)

30. It is the commonness of objective content or meaning, resulting from judgmental control, that remains important for our further discussions. Assuming commonness of function, how far are *meanings* as such common?

(marginal note: When are Meanings Common, as distinct from Functions?)

To put this question in terms of control is, I think, to get a certain preliminary illumination. We may distinguish, as we have, between "actual" and "appropriate" objects or meanings, the "appropriate" being those which properly belong to certain control processes. This is the sense given the term syndoxic in the discussion of judgment above. But as soon as we inspect *actual meaning* with reference to control, we take an objective point of view and compare meanings in different minds. This gives what we have called above "aggregate" meanings.

(marginal note: How can "Actual" become merely "Appropriate" Meanings?)

theory of "intention" as mark of responsibility is open to this ambiguity. In interpreting children's and animals' minds we often argue from commonness of content or of action to commonness of function.

[1] We may suppose such a case as this: the dog baying the moon, as in our earlier illustration, first alone and later in full unison with another dog, who is also baying the moon. In the latter case, it would seem likely that the emphasis of meaning in the first dog's mind is shifted from the moon to the other dog's baying, since that stirs up a mass of organic and dispositional processes in which his gregarious instincts are embodied. The syndoxic character of his meaning is largely due to the functional commonness, and not so much to the common object, the moon.

Aggregate meanings are those which issue from specific control processes in different minds, as observed by an outsider. This is the sense in which meaning is syndoxic in the pre-judgmental modes. It recognizes *other minds as actually doing* what the one mind is also doing. Now in judgment the case is different. The need of actual judgment by others is lost ; and the individual still reads his result as " appropriate " or " fit " for a *concurring judgment*, whose ever it may be and whenever it may be exercised.

The vital question, then, concerning these two meanings—the appropriate and the actual or aggregate—becomes, *how can the force of a personal control process, in another's mind, come to be reflected as a synnomic or appropriate shading of meaning in the thinker's own mind*—how can a meaning be common as appropriate, though not at all common as actual or aggregate ? For example, how can the child's confidence in something *when I* " actually " confirm it, pass over into confidence in the same truth when *he alone* judges it as worthy of or appropriate to my concurring judgment ?

This, I think it is easy to show, is one of the most important and interesting problems of genetic theory of knowledge. It introduces us to what I shall designate as indicated above—extending the scheme of terminology wherein the affix " nomic" connotes control—*synnomic meanings* and *synnomic judgments*.[1] If we say of a judgment that it expresses syndoxic meaning, we have in mind meaning either (1) meant as actually common (aggregate), or (2) meant as both actually and appropriately common (aggregate and synnomic), or (3) meant as appropriately common, whether or not also actually. The last two are *synnomic*, and the judgments embodying such meanings are *synnomic judgments*. The question then as to the " commonness " of judgments finally takes the form of an enquiry into their synnomic force—their appropriateness and self-sufficiency as intending " concurrent " assent, whether they actually secure it or not.

Rise of Synnomic Meanings

and judgments.

---

[1] The term synnomic is applied to a control which *is motived by an earlier dualism* of control modes of any sort, but *which is itself a mode that supersedes and reconciles the terms of the dualism.* What we have, in the case now under discussion, is not the union of the great modes of inner and outer control, but that of the modes of two or more persons' aggregate inner control processes, *the result being reflected in the judgment of one of these persons.*

§ 4. SYNNOMIC MEANINGS

31. The investigation of synnomic meanings begins appropriately with those of the logical mode in which these meanings

Synnomic meaning in Judgment are thrown in the form of judgments. This appears all the more appropriate when we recall that in our discussion of judgment above we found the common ingredients of meaning to rest both upon the self-repeating

rests on Universality character of universal meaning and also upon the correlative self-repeating character of the control process or function. It will be remembered that these two lines of derivation of syndoxic meaning in judgment were there worked out.

of both Content and Control, A universal judgment asserts a general meaning the force of which is both that it *applies to all cases*, and also that it *is true for all minds*. In the phrasing of the British

being both without Exception and also Appropriate. philosophy it is not only *without exception*, it is also *catholic*. This we have now found to be really the case of universal judgments : they are universal as meanings and they are " appropriate " as judgments.

The word " catholic," however, is again ambiguous. It suggests both appropriateness to all judgment process and actual presence or acceptance by all minds. This latter is the historical meaning — actual *prevalence*, in many or all minds — and I follow this usage in the discussion of " catholicity " both here and below.[1] The other meaning I shall continue to call " appropriateness."

32. The question at once arises, however, as to whether there is concomitance of universality and catholicity proper; that

But some Meanings are not both. is, whether in the logical or other modes one may be found without the other. To put this question is at once to have a troop of cases come into one's mind illustrating the divorce of these two meanings. Evidently it is true that the universal must be " appropriate " also, while nothing compels the catholic to be appropriate.

There are catholic meanings in the prelogical stages of cognition. This is what our preceding discussion has prepared us to find. Commonness as catholicity of *function* may extend to pre-judgmental contents which make no claim to appropriateness.

---

[1] Chap. vi. § 8. Historically, indeed, catholicity carried both connotations, the " prevalence " being attributed to the *a priori* or " native " character of the meaning. This has imported great confusion into the discussion of " universality."

33. The essential advance into the mode of judgment, it will be recalled, takes the form of the passage of an experimental or schematic meaning into a general or logical meaning. Before this takes place, the cases are, or may be, re-petitions, of course, but not self-repetitions in the sense of our theory. That is, they are " this," and again " this," and yet again " this," with no assignment of all the " this-es " to a general class of which each is a particular instance. The universal meaning is therefore not then present.

No Universal in the Pre-logical Modes.

34. But the catholic meaning as such may be a much simpler matter than that. It does not necessarily require repetition at all ; that is, repetition of objective contents or mean-ings. It does not even require two or more acts of cognition whereby objects are found to be self-repeat-ing, the same, or related. All that it requires is that nascent dualism of inner and outer whereby other persons as minds are dis-tinguished from me. So much, *however crude the self may be, guarantees the other persons of the environ-ment as knowers, perceivers, with myself*, in the same state of relative crudeness and incomplete development. The catholicity of the dog's barking-meaning, for example, does not require that he should bark at the same object twice, or that other dogs should bark at the same object that he barks at ; it does require a sufficient dog-self-hood to be aware of other dogs whose inner control-process, directed upon objects, *issues, like his own, in barking*. The commonness of catholicity is commonness of an aggregate sort brought over into the psychic meaning of the one perceiver ; it is a case of the first of the three forms of syndoxic meaning distinguished above.[1]

Catholic Meaning is simpler and earlier.

It requires only Dualism of Inner and Outer.

35. Common meaning goes through certain stages of de-velopment, readily made out by the study of children. The stages, including the logical, may be distinguished summarily in their genetic order, for the purposes of our discussion, as follows:—

TABLE C.[2] SYNDOXIC MEANINGS

A. Catholic. Meanings held as actually common or preva-lent. Pre-judgmental.

I. The commonness of mere *sameness of function* : psycho-nomic commonness.

---

[1] Usually, however, the universal phase of meaning given in the logical consciousness is mixed up with it.

[2] Cf. vol. i. chap. vii. sect. 27, table, for the place of syndoxic with reference to other sorts of common meaning.

II. The commonness of *observed aggregateness.*

III. The modes of specific commonness differentiated by experiment : *inter-psychic commonness* due to " secondary conversion."

B. Appropriate. Meanings held as fit for concurring function.

IV. Commonness of *competent personal judgment* : synnomic commonness.

V. Commonness of *judgmental content* as synnomic and universal.

§ 5. COMMONNESS OF COMMON FUNCTION AND CONTROL.

36. I. The first stage in the development of common meaning is that which is spoken of above as sameness of function. **Sameness of Function** In the logical mode it is a presupposition of belief. In its earliest form it is mere reality-feeling—a *cachet* of mere presence to which no mark of privacy has yet come to be attached. The puzzle, I imagine, in the sense mode, say to an animal entangled in the gregarious habits of his tribe, is not, " how do we get these things and do such things in common ? " but " how lonely certain situations are ! " and " how peculiar those actions feel in which I shiver alone ! " The commonness is so guaranteed by common situations which bring out common instincts, appetites, reactions, **is part of Reality-Feeling** and afford satisfactions enjoyed in common, that the full meaning of objects is normally one of co-operation and collective life. This has been dwelt upon in the recent literature of the origin of social co-operation as rooted in the gregarious company-life of animal communities. The social environment is simply a part of the whole larger environment of objective presences, and the response to the whole **Such Commonness the Normal Colouring of Consciousness** carries with it the response to the part, without specific differentiations of meanings and motives to action. The real problem, as has been said in effect by the writer in an earlier discussion,[1] is not how do persons act together and know together ?—but how is common personality and knowledge broken up into isolated selves and spheres ? So **without Specific Differentiation.** of these meanings, none are specifically common, because none are specifically private ; but the normal presence of objective meaning is one in which the

[1] *Social and Eth. Interpretations,* chap. ii. § 6.

elements of both common and private meanings are already given in a neutral mass of collective or "aggregate" experiences.[1]

As an early form of common meaning this may be called psychonomic from the point of view of control. It is condi-
As Common or Private. tioned upon and controlled by the biological facts of common endowment, instinct, predisposition, etc. Its full interpretation would take us far afield, since the topic has bearings in both biological and social evolution theory.

37. II. The second stage observable in children is that in which the hero himself observes and utilizes the fact that differ-
Observation of Common-ness of Objects. ent persons, including himself, do get the same objects. The social act of calling another's attention to a thing requires the germ of such observation. Animals have it to a very marked degree. A dog will go to great pains to have you see what he sees. In this way "aggregate" meaning is taken over into the consciousness of the knower himself.

38. This is a great advance in the progression of common meaning in two ways: first, it is the recognition *that the foreign control of things is found in common by persons or minds.*
Involves (1) Recognition of Common-ness of For-eign Control, It involves some advance in the inner-outer distinction, even if not—as would seem to be required by Avenarius' theory of introjection—itself the prime motive to the birth of that distinction. The dog that bays the moon by instinct in company with other dogs has the commonness of common function, no doubt; but to be able to mean by "moon" an object that is being bayed separately by one or more other dogs in common with him, requires greater development. The meaning is aggregate to a spectator; but when it is apprehended as "same-object-for-all-of-us-dogs," it is syndoxic.

Another way, second, in which this is a great advance is in this respect—it serves to distinguish that which is *not common but private.*
and (2) the distinction of the Private The commonness of function no longer pervades all presences alike. Cases having common objective control stand in contrast to those that lack such control, whether this be from failure of the object to sustain the tests of externality, or from failure of the

---

[1] Cf. Ibid. Appendix D, where it is found that social meaning would probably arise simply from the action of animals of similar habit when these actions are imitatively performed. Any such result of association or collective perception reflected into the consciousness of one is common meaning in this first sense.

function to secure a common object. The first of these two forms

of two sorts. of failure establishes the privacy of certain objects as not common because *not outer, but inner*; the second, the privacy of objects which are not common because, although *quasi-outer, they are still deceptive*. In the latter case, the meaning is more or less eccentric and inappropriate. Both cases are fruitful in the further development of common meaning.

39. From the point of view of the development of psychic process, there does not seem to be any great difficulty in making

All a matter of Behaviour of Contents, this advance. The dualism is strictly one of terms of experience in which mind-material is set off from body-material by certain marks. The connecting links of context thus established are complex in that the body content stands in connection with several actually different mind contents. The commonness of meaning is simply the presence of these plural connections, which go on to be developed

in forming Dualism of Knower and Known. into relationships of the type knower-and-known, illustrated in the knower's own dualism of self and object. This purely experiential differentiation has been sketched already above as the mind-body progression. The commonness meaning develops from *objects-present-to-minds-in-common*, to *such objects apprehended as common by those minds*.[1]

§ 6. COMMONNESS THROUGH SECONDARY CONVERSION AND IMITATION

40. III. In the semblant mode, common like all other cognitive meaning passes into experimental and schematic

Specific commonness Experimental, forms. Its progress is toward specific determination, within the general recognition of aggregate over against private meanings. It operates largely through the "secondary" or inter-psychic conversion explained above in the discussion of the memory of events.[2] This is its

and arises by Secondary Conversion. general method—*the establishing of specific common meanings by conversion into the actual context of meanings entertained by other minds*. By this

---

[1] As in earlier discussions, we may here maintain the purely intra-psychic (or individual) point of view, entertaining the "inter-psychic" as it is reflected in the mind of the individual. The *inter-psychic* as "trans-subjective," an objective or *psychological* meaning, is matter of later discussion, as is the final interpretation of experience itself.

[2] Vol. i. chap. iv. § 5.

·derivation such meaning issues in two forms, in opposition to
the two forms of germinating private meaning distinguished
above. The privacy of *unconfirmed cognition* develops in
opposition to the commonness of *actual inter-psychic control*;
and the privacy of *eccentric or inappropriate process*
in opposition to the commonness of *individual judgment as "appropriate" or synnomic*, in which
the values of explicit conversion processes are reflected in the progress of the individual's competence to stand
alone and judge for himself. Before discussing these two movements, which take their initial divergence in the
mode of secondary conversion, we may illustrate
them by instances, and also recall the main problem
of this chapter, upon which our discussions are now to be
directly focussed.

(1) Common-
ness of
actual
Social
Control, and

(2) of appro-
priate or
Synnomic
Judgment.

The privacy of "unconfirmed cognition" is simply that of failure
to find agreement with another's context; the commonness in contrast with it is confirmation by such agreement. My
child says, "I saw an angel," and learns that it was
a "private angel," when I tell him, "No, you didn't; you
dreamed it." But he says, "I wasn't asleep—it must have been
mama," and I reply, "Yes, it was your mama." Mama is now
the confirmed common meaning.

Illustrations
of (1)

Again the child says, "No, it was not mama, it was an angel,
for it had wings." This is the privacy of eccentric or inappropriate process, the case of the persistence of marks
which do not yield to the inter-psychic conversion test.
These cases are private in the sense of going behind all the
conversion returns, and insisting on the meaning to which
the individual's psychic life is committed. We say it is a
fancy, an illusion, something not only not common, but not
sharable [1]—something "in the mind," like the "possessions"
of Don Quixote or the imaginary nosegay of poor Ophelia.

and of (2).

41. With these illustrations before us of what we mean by
the commonness of secondary conversion, we may again state the
large question whose answer remains as our goal:
how can aggregate commonness—*the commonness of
actually aggregate knowledge processes*—pass into *the*

Return to
Question of
Synnomic
Function.

---

[1] It is not merely, of course, the eccentric in the sense of illusion or
positive mal-operation of any sort; in the logical mode it appears in what
is called "bad judgment" or lack of competence, due to untamed or
undisciplined function.

commonness of appropriateness, the meaning rendered by private judgment as worthy and appropriate to all other judging processes, though actually supported, it may be, by none. How can syndoxic meaning pass from the aggregate to the synnomic type ?

The Context
is enlarged
by We decided, it will be remembered, that meaning may become syndoxic in the sense of being aggregate or catholic, without becoming universal. It is this phase of the development, therefore, as it goes on before the rise of judgment, that now concerns us in explaining the results of the resort to secondary conversion. The chief (1) Imitative
Absorption
and (2) Dis-
ciplinary
Enforcement. result is that the context of recognitive meaning is enlarged and extended by two great agencies of accommodation or adjustment to the social environment—*imitative absorption* and *disciplinary enforcement*.

42. The attempt to determine experimentally the value of this or that memory object or other image must go forward Treatment is
by Trial and
Error essentially here as everywhere by acts of trial and error or schematic assumption. The image must be treated *as if* it held, in order to find out *whether* it holds. In the case of objects generally, this leads to a practical testing in the external environment ; and so it does for the substantive terms of the whole image context. This is the By Primary
and sphere of " primary " conversion, and it goes as far as the material permits. The need of secondary or social conversion arises in connection with those parts of imaged meanings for which the primary tests are ineffectual or essentially unavailable—notably for the transitive or relational parts. The also
Secondary
Conversion. child says, " Yes, this is a match, but did it light ? " This requirement is met by the same sort of treatment as in the primary tests, but with reference now not to the physical but to the *psychological environment*—an environment of socially available contexts. The child must simply " try-it-on " with his companions or associates, and see whether any one else's context is like his in the given case.

43. This issues, of course, in a certain advance. There is an elimination no less than a selection ; and the results are for the The Child's
Anticipation,
by
Imitation, time secure. But the demands of active life go beyond such a slow mode of acquisition. We find that, so far from testing only what he already fancies, the ·child has a much more direct and ready means and method of

anticipating and making available the inner contexts of others. This is, of course, the method of active imitation.

The working of this great impulse and also the results accruing from its exercise have been so fully explained in recent books **of the** that we need not here do more than claim the legiti- **Mental** mate fruits of these discussions. The child sets up **Contexts of** **Others.** the thoughts of others in his own mind, either by directly and actively imitating the activities of movement, speech, etc., of others, or by an imitative interpretation of them ; and by this means he acquires models so far already shaped upon the mental contexts into which his own are to be converted. We find him straining every energy to anticipate one's opinion and action. " It is that, *isn't it ?* " is his repeated question. " I told you so," is his constant boast. The value of **This** this is, in the first instance, to abbreviate enormously **Abbreviates** the process of his learning. As his imitations **the Process** grow in refinement and the method of them becomes automatic, he keeps ahead of the expressed views of his associates by a certain quick interpretation of their moods and dispositions. He thus finds himself building up broad platforms of fact and opinion on which these recurring **and magnifies** social anticipations are confirmed. But with this **the Sense of** another psychic movement is getting under weigh, **Competence.** one motived in the activity and sense of power and initiative fostered by successful imitation.

44. He passes on to magnify beforehand the element of agreement between his anticipation and the confirmed result which comes only *after the fact*. This satisfies the demand which motives the whole procedure—the need of a direct personal meaning which will stand as common. He announces the outcome *as his own result*. He says, " I say so " ; and only when pressed for a reason, adds, " father says so, too." [1]

This latter shading of meaning, the self-assertive, arises quite legitimately through the selective character of the imitative process. It distinguishes the case of active imitation from that of the disciplinary enforcement which is to be spoken of below, both being real factors in the progression. For this active

---

[1] Cases are common like the following sent me by Professor Muirhead : " Officials in Egypt tell me the way to get a thing done is casually to suggest it to an Egyptian official. He will say nothing about it, but in a month or two will bring it out as *his own* and carry it through."

anticipation, with its partial confirmation, lends a sense of
The Result personal achievement to the result. The child goes
becomes a on to say, with partial truth, " I knew it already,"
Personal
Achievement. " father needn't have told *me*," " *he* agrees with *me*."
The inner control process so far claims the result as to place the
outer and confirmatory factor in a secondary place.

45. This is important, since it shows the beginning of that
education of " judgment " in " sizing-up " situations with per-
This is sonal independence, in which the synnomic aspect
Schematic
before the of meaning largely consists. In this mode, the outgo
Fact of anticipation is essentially schematic. The child, even
when most confident in a new formulation which is not socially
confirmed, takes the accommodating and questioning attitude
toward the better-informed. He does not use a meaning
finally assertorial. But there are differences in the forward
The Meaning reach of his expectation, and variations in his attitude.
may be
Disjunctive or He may, indeed, go so far as to say, " I knew it was
Probable, this *or* that—green or blue," getting alternative
meaning, or " I knew it *wasn't* that—red," having exclusive
negative meaning, or " I knew it *usually* rained on Sunday "
expressing a highly probable meaning ; these actually occur.
or Semblant He may, indeed, give things a semblant, humorous,
or or serio-comic turn, simply to bring out his growing
Humorous. independence and personal competence, saying, " I
was only joking," or " I thought you meant mermaids, they *are*
green." In it all he is accommodating himself to an environment,[1] and doing so by submitting his schematic context to a
conversion process ; but his own self-assertion appears in
the assumptively imitative method of it. In saying, " I did it
myself," he is truthful to the extent of meaning, " but for
my consent and co-operation it would not have been so—*you
wouldn't have had a chance to agree with me* ! "

46. This is not an accidental matter, nor does it result from
superficial motives. On the contrary, it results from two of the
It is rooted great movements of mental development. It exhibits
in Motives the essential sort of self-assertion seen in ejection,
that deter-
mine the whereby others' contexts are interpreted in terms
Synnomic, of one's own ; and it shows the beginning of that line
of cleavage whereby the dualism of mind and body arises in
the substantive mode. Both these movements mature in the

---

[1] Even in this he imitates the very attitude of those about him ;
for we adults also caricature knowledge by our conceit of omniscience.

next stage of the progression of common meaning, treated below ;
here we may bring out in a sentence or two the way

and is
transitional
to it.

that this start toward a synnomic shading of meaning
affords a transition to the later and fuller state of mind.

47. The ejecting motive is that by which the gains of imitative or other accommodations, and the attendant selection

Ejection
conserves
and fixes the
Context
selected,

of contents by conversion, are conserved. The fixing
of the selected and established meaning as a stable
common possession, requires that this meaning become part of that recognized inner context upon which
the individual's control processes have a permanent hold. If the
process of conversion were necessary in each successive case of
a recurring context, then our mortal life would be forever in the
assumptive and pre-judgmental stage of development.   But it is
not so.   The gains are integrated into the context of recognition,

for all
Minds,

and carry their conversion coefficient up into the
later modes of individuation. This proceeds, as to
" you," *the " other," by ejection.* The items set in the child's
context of established meaning are read as henceforth *taken by
you to be so no less than by him* ; and the private-to-him,
meaning the unconfirmed, allows also a private-to-you, which
is that of which he in turn has no confirmation in his
context.   He must think of you as being an inner life,

either as
Common or
as Private.

having both common and private spheres of
meaning like his own. The limit of the common
in your thought must be the limit he has
already set up in his own ; and your conversion of contexts must take his as model for imitation just as his takes
yours.   In short, *in his meaning you depend upon him by the
very movement which establishes his dependence upon you.*

This is seen also in the transition in the child's attitude

A Re-conver-
sion into the
original
Context.

from one of imitation of an elder to one of self-assertion
toward a younger person—a matter brought out in
detail in the fuller treatment of the topic with reference
to the growth of self-consciousness in the work mentioned
above.[1] If—using the first and second persons—we call my
checking-off of my contexts by yours, " secondary conversion,"
then the reciprocal phase of meaning, your checking-off
of your contexts by mine, might perhaps be called "secondary
re-conversion."

[1] *Social and Eth. Interps.*, chap. i., the " Dialectic of Personal Growth,"
which is summarily stated above in this work, vol. i, chap. viii. § 9.

When, for example, the child's associate says, " the light is green," he may reply : " Oh, no ! that is the red light you showed to me yesterday ; you shouldn't see it green. Your green is a private meaning, for I can, on the basis of yesterday's confirmation of my image by yours, now to-day demand that yours be re-converted into mine."

Example.

It is through the sense of *competence* thus springing up that the first claim of common meaning to be synnomic is registered. It is the stage at which a mode of personal competence arises which begins to *lose sight of its social origin and support.*

48. In the other movement suggested, that of the growing dualism of mind and body, there is another important motive to a concurrence between the individual's meaning and that which he finds " actual " to several, a concurrence that his own synnomic judgment later fully maintains. This dualism is between minds and personal bodies, not one between different minds.   The substantive form of it is the complete diremption of personality into these two parts.   The mind-parts become in common " mind," and the body-parts, in common with things, become " body."   Minds in common can readily become a substance " mind," by the processes of common control and ejected content already described ; but how can the body-parts become, in common with things, the substance " body " ?

Another motive is

the Dualism of Minds in common as Mind,

and Bodies in common as Body.

49. When we say that " body " is here a common meaning, there must be some ground of conversion or matched contents to produce and fulfil that meaning.   I think it is found in the actual commonness of the physical object when it is psychically established through the mediation of the inner contexts which are already common.   The secondary conversion process holds for the whole context thus converted ; although in itself it would guarantee only a common system of inner meanings.   But the further conversion of the substantive terms of such a context, *already established as common by secondary conversion,* secures the actual external and physical control. The physical object might be private, indeed, before the common contexts are socially established.   But these contexts *include the physical terms,* which are then further guaranteed by actual sense-tests.   Thus confirmed as common by secondary conversion, these terms further prove to have direct physical control ; so that we

Commonness of Personal Body

is established after Secondary Conversion,

through Physical Control.

may say, " these are objects known by us in common *as bodies*."

Suppose, for example, two birds brought up in rooms exactly alike, each quite apart and unknown to the other. Could bird *a*
Illustration. have the meaning of furniture-in-common with bird *b*, if each bird were changed to the other's room at the same time each day ? Each might have a certain sense of common function and presence arising from odours or other stimulations fitted to arouse gregarious organic reactions belonging to birds ; what is called above " psychonomic commonness." And it is conceivable that each might have the beginning of a dualism between furniture and bird-self in which the self would be largely the bird's own organic shape.[1] But either of them could have the meaning " furniture the same for the other bird " only by some experience in which a common conversion of meanings had taken place between them as birds ; and bird-self, as in some sense a class-meaning, had developed over against things, also a class meaning. Indeed the commonness of physical things as bodies can come only through experience of *commonness and privacy*, the element of privacy attaching to the sphere of mind in which meanings are unshared and unconfirmed.

This is only to confirm the position taken up on an earlier page,[2] to the effect that the final separation of mind and body
Reached by comes through an act, imitative or other, by which
the Motive the same content of inner life is found to be in two
of Separation
of Mind and bodies at once.   If the one inner content *is* attached
Body.   to both bodies, it *may be* detached from each. The reverse reading of the situation is now the motive to commonness of meaning. If a content *may be* determined *as the same in two minds*, it *is* controlled by *a common external body*. The sameness or commonness of inner determination, found in secondary conversion, gives the cue to the oneness of the physical thing itself.

The essential meaning of this for the theory of knowledge—a matter to which we must return—is that the control found to be

---

[1] A good illustration of this organic self has presented itself to me recently. My parrot " Tuck " was in a rather small cage, and as his tail was long and stiff he could not set his swing going freely without striking beak or tail against the side of the cage. He then rapidly fell to swinging sideways by pressing hard on one foot and then on the other till the swing took on a side-to-side movement ; and seeing that his " organic self " was so much *thinner than it was long*, he got a full swing in this way. This is now his confirmed habit. I think his meaning " Parrot-self " is of something about a foot long but only three inches thick !

[2] Vol. i, chap. x. § 3.

" foreign " is now re-established and confirmed within the move-ments of contents themselves, in that aspect wherein they are " common." The integrity of selfhood, as a developing mean-ing, implicates *not only other selves, but also other things-in-common that are not selves*.

50. We have now arrived at a point of view from which we are able to see in their mutual settings certain of the more special truths pointed out in the discussion. No less than three of our separate formulations, two of which have already been stated, fall together in this one result. First, the formulation of the secondary conversion move-ment as a form of mediate control (vol. i. chap. iv. § 6) ; second, the formulation of persistence as " recurrent sameness " of the com-mon type (vol. i. chap. viii. § 3) ; and third, the formulation of the sense in which the meaning of " reality " in the substantive mode is common (a position made out in the later discussions of vol. iii.).

This unites such Partial Truths as,

As to mediate control, it is, it will be recalled, control exercised not immediately upon an object, but indirectly or medi-ately through a secondary context by conversion or otherwise. The process through which common meaning is secured by conversion into another's context at once establishes that second context as one of mediate control of the meaning. My opinion lacks control until it finds it through yours to which I make appeal.

(1) Mediate Control through Another's Context, and

51. As to the second of the formulations mentioned above— that whereby " recurrent sameness " may take on inter-psychic form—that too is an aspect of the commonness of secondary conversion as now made out. The meaning of " sameness after absence " requires a recurrence after an interval during which the persistence of the object when absent is presupposed. It is evident that of the cases that may occur one is that of recurrence to the same person's mind directly, and another is that of its indirect recurrence *through the experience of some one else*. In this latter case, the event is then brought over into the first person's experience by secondary conversion. The second event, in short—that in which the recurrence consists— may be a context in a consciousness foreign to that in which the meaning is to mature. This widens re-markably the range of confirmation through persist-ence ; for the sphere of confirmation *becomes, for each observer, the experience of any or all*.

(2) Persistence through Recurrence

in a Context in another Mind.

52. The formula of substantial persistence takes on therefore, as is made out above (vol. i. chap. viii. sect. 12), the form of common meaning generally. Whatever is found syndoxic is by the fact of inter-psychic conversion also found substantial in one mode or another, so far as in either or any of the persons having the experience, an original coefficient of substantial existence is active. For example, A and B find themselves in agreement as to having seen the light of a lamp-post burning on a certain corner. This is equivalent to a secondary conversion of either A's or B's memory into that of the other, giving rise to a syndoxic meaning in both or either. The only question remaining is whether the existence belonging to the thing seen, which either's memory invokes for the substantive part of the experience, is that of the coefficient of direct conversion. Here it is a physically existing thing, the lamp-post ; but it might be an event, a logical demonstration, or any other meaning whose final conversion is in a world controlled by a distinguishable coefficient of existence, open to common inspection.[1] Either mind may on occasion supply this.

So Common Meaning becomes sign of Substantial Existence.

Illustration.

The result is that the common moment of meaning becomes a sort of *Who's Who* of ready reference generally. So far as it is reflected in the individual's own sense of competence in judging, so far the "social register" merely confirms it ; so far as personal process is not so sure of itself, the social register is drawn on for "copy" or confirmation. The result is the education of the judgment toward that full independence and self-reliance which finally characterize it.

Commonness becomes a "Who's Who."

§ 7.   COMMONNESS THROUGH DISCIPLINARY ENFORCEMENT

53. The additional factor in the entire process of transfer of meaning from the social environment to the individual's mind is that called above disciplinary enforcement. It is also a factor well recognized in current discussions. The entire body of tradition and social heredity is to be learned

Disciplinary Enforcement

---

[1] In fact such a situation is sometimes appealed to as proof of such worlds of existence. If for example two persons agree in reporting independently the same apparition, the "psychic researchers" claim this as proof that it is not an apparition but a thing in a sphere of actual experience of either or both. Of course the fallacy of this is that a common meaning might result from common functions, interests, or motives merely, as is recognized above, with no control in a sphere of external reference which one of the person's processes could mediate for the other.

by each individual, and society stands ready to see that he learns it as soon as possible. Hence through certain recognized aids, language, play, art, obedience, the contexts of established social recognition are hammered into the plastic surface of the child's mind. Obedience is the explicit, and suggestion the implicit channel of such discipline and instruction.[1]

as producing Commonness of Meaning.

The result is enormous abbreviation and economy in the process of learning. But apart from such saving it is doubtful whether this enforcement adds much in any further or characteristic way in the progression of common meaning. True, the child becomes more docile and accommodating; but he may readily lose as much by his lack of self-assertion and independence. What he learns by enforcement he must make his own by the essential processes of assimilation; so far as this is not done the lessons are not incorporated into the body of the meanings he is prepared to exploit. So far as they are thus assimilated, they are subject to the same progressions in further development as his independently acquired meanings. He must make them none the less habitual in his ejective and recognitive functions, and schematic in his experimental and accommodative functions. The only net gain, apart from the growth of actual information through obedience—a gain which is, as I said, enormous—is the modicum of regulation and restraint that comes from standing constantly in the limelight of criticism, and submitting to social sanctions in case of disobedience or stubborn failure to make due progress.

This shortens the Learning Process,

but does not remove the need of Assimilation,

as of other Meanings.

§ 8. COMMONNESS OF " APPROPRIATE " OR " SYNNOMIC " MEANING

54. IV. With so much notice of the transition effected by secondary conversion we may pass on to consider the form of mature common meaning resulting in the substantive mode.

In the Substantive Mode,

Here we have the beginning of the " appropriate " or " proper " object : a meaning that is becoming synnomic although not yet fully logical. Its features are those characteristic of the substantive mode proper, in which the dualism of mind and body has hard-

Common Meaning as becoming Synnomic,

---

[1] Of course the student to social theories is reminded of the theory according to which the essence of the social bond is " constraint."

ened into its later quasi-logical form, giving two substantive classes or groups. Its characters as quasi-logical are summed up in the statement that the class-meaning is that of a schematic or "assumed" context, when looked at as instrumental to further progress, and a pragmatic or "presumed" context, when looked at as what is established and recognized.
although not In both these respects, the meaning, whether of mind **General,** or body, is not yet fully general.[1] Not logical judgment but "practical judgment" is the term that sets forth the nature of the function, if we make the concession of using the **but** term "judgment" in the latter sense at all. A better **Pragmatic.** designation of the meaning, in that respect in which it counterfeits a true general is found in the term "pragmatic," as defined in the Introduction (chap. i. sect. 9).

55. The peculiar advance in commonness in this mode is that which attends upon the progression into the dualism of **Advance is** substances, an advance due in general to the processes **seen in the** of *habituation* accompanying those of accommodation. **process of** **Habituation.** Accommodation does its work, as pointed out just above, through imitation and discipline, these being essentially processes of acquisition of common contexts ; habituation in turn contributes the strain whereby the synnomic colouring begins to attach to such contexts. The processes of habituation come in at once—they are always at hand—to fix and refine the gains made at every stage in the development of meanings.

Recognizing the validity of the law of habit as given in the books on psychology, we may say that it operates in the **Meanings of** realm of common meaning in a way to alter the char- **Common and** acter of the distinction between private and common **Private** **become** meaning : it is no longer that of *the distinction between socially confirmed and unconfirmed meaning, but that between appro-* **Appropriate** *priate or suitable, and eccentric or unsuitable meaning.* **(Common)** **and Eccentric** This is the important transition in common meaning **(Private).** from the merely confirmed or catholic to the synnomic, each being in the sense already defined syndoxic.

---

[1] It is extremely dangerous to draw lines, and I do not mean to declare that consciousness actually reaches this full dualism of mind and body without at the same time having the "general" meaning that functions in judgment. But it is still possible to treat a mode as developing on to completeness without complicating the case with the shadings of meaning that spring up as prophetic of a later mode. The distinction is genetic rather than chronological.

56. The matter may be best approached from the point of view of our earlier distinction between inner from outer persist-

The Effect of Secondary Conversion: Persistence. ence. The outwardly or physically persistent was found to be a sense-object found recurrent after absence. Inward or mental persistence, on the other hand, attaches to all inner contents considered as held together in a controlling inner function. The complication arising when conversion into the contexts of others' minds is actually resorted to, shows itself in the meaning of persistence. We have to ask in what sense *common meanings as such are persistent* ? The answer to this question will aid us also in further discussions, since not only is the persistence of common meanings a mark of their synnomic force, but it is also a character of what we are later on to denominate truth.[1]

The persistence of meaning as common is not simply that **Persistence of Common Meaning is of a new Sort.** of physical objects, for commonness attaches to objects which do not physically persist. Further-more, such persistence is not merely that of images in a mental life, for such images often persist when not common. Accordingly, in the common meaning which attaches to *both types of objects*, we have to seek *a persistence of a new sort or mode*. We may call it the persistence of meanings that become synnomic, or briefly "synnomic persistence." It brings in the second and mature stage in the development of synnomic meaning.

57. If, to begin with, the common meaning is one that is convertible into another's context of thought, it must have the coefficient of persistence attaching to that other's inner life. I cannot confirm my result by yours, for example, except as you **It presup-poses other Minds as persisting.** are continuing there, a thinking self. Yet the "you" of conversion is not a specific singular "you"; it is the presumptive "you" of the class "minds." That is, the persistence required for conversion is that of the substantive term "mind" in the dualism of mind and body. Minds must persist, in short, in their characteristic way, if I am to *be in the habit of resorting* to them for continuing confirmation of my own meanings. The persistence of a world of minds becomes, then, as soon as I reflect and judge, a *presupposition* of my judgment.

The dualism involved is a contrast meaning. The bodily

---

[1] See chap. xiii. § 8.

object is really persisting in its own way as the mental also is.

and also Persisting external Objects   The persistence of the synnomic requires common body terms as well as common mind terms to the extent that persisting minds implicate persisting bodies ; although, as we have seen, the bodily commonness is taken up and mediated or reported through the mind term. We may say, then, that the persistence of synnomic meaning either **into which the Meanings are Convertible.** actually requires, or has the presupposition of, secondary conversion into mental contexts which are (1) *themselves common to minds* and also (2) *in part reconvertible into physical or other external common objects.*[1]

58. Let us take, for example, as a case of such commonness, the statement, " They say Napoleon lived in Elba some time."

Illustration.   This is a common meaning—" they say." It persists as being convertible into meanings of historical record, tradition, etc.   These are *contexts of thought* which must themselves be common to historians and others ; and further, the presupposition is of Napoleon, Elba, the entourage, etc., are historically actual things, *common objects to those who lived to see and report the time, place and event.*

The reassertion of a synnomic meaning, therefore—that is, the assertion of its persistence as truth—requires the presupposition **Presupposition of Acceptance in Common as Common.** of its *former acceptance as common to minds having their own persistence* and also the presupposition of the *sort of persistence and commonness for which they in common accepted it.*

59. If we call the persistence already given in the meaning entertained by the different minds whose consent is presupposed, **"Aggregate"** " aggregate persistence "—in the case given, the common report of the historians, based on original testimony—then the new shade of meaning of persistence reflected in the individual's acceptance and assurance is its " syndoxic " counterpart.   He presupposes the historians' common acceptance of the presupposition of adequate common testimony.   In other words, he presupposes agreement among the historians, and they in turn presuppose agreement among the eye-witnesses.

The force of this is apparent—say, in one's own acceptance of such an event.   My meaning is one, of presupposition, not

---

[1] By the persistence of common meanings is meant their persistence as meanings ; not, of course, their mere persistence as events in a consciousness.   These latter, as events, might be purely eccentric, or private.

of testing; of acceptance, not of investigation; of habit, not

The Indivi-
dual's Pre-
supposition.
of accommodation. The necessary conversion processes have taken place *before the meaning reaches me.* The ground of my acceptance of the historical statement as persisting and true is that it shall have secured this commonness for competent minds.

60. If, however, I be myself engaged in research in history and wish to open the question of testimony, my meaning

But it may be
questioned
is then at once erected as merely schematic. I ask, has it the persistence of common meaning of the sort called testimony upon which other historians have proceeded? By this process I may disprove its commonness in certain ways or degrees—a procedure which illustrates the essential factors in the meaning.

Suppose I find a statement in Froude only; I then say, this may be inexact. That is, Froude's report alone does not guar-

and Dis-
proved,
antee the commonness requisite to the persistence of a mental context, a truth; but it still does not follow that Froude's presupposition of adequate testimony may not be well-founded. If then I go to the archives and find reason to think Froude *not only alone but also mistaken,* then the last

and lose its
Commonness.
vestige of commonness, and also the last claim to any sort of persistence as truth, vanishes from the statement.

61. We now have also a clear distinction of the two sorts of privacy. Objects of a physical sort, for example, when seen only

Two Sorts of
Privacy.
by one observer, who has not yet taken his meanings up into the secondary conversion stage, are private in the sense of unshared. Yet they have that "psychonomic commonness" which the function itself may impart to the meaning. Of this sort of privacy too are the "selective" meanings or appreciations which are not judged about, but directly experienced.[1] But such objects, when thought in common, acquire the persistence of mental contexts, and so lose their privacy.

On the other hand, again, there are images which fail

(1) The Un-
shared and
(2) the
Eccentric.
of the secondary conversion, even though they seem to get the primary. These are read off as private in the sense of inappropriate or eccentric. The N-rays are now taken by many physicists to have this sort of

[1] It is in this sense of unshared psychic process that the term private is used in the classification given in vol. i. chap. vii. § 27.

private or unconfirmed meaning. The X-rays, on the other hand, have come to be common and persistent scientific meanings. The N-rays may become so—and are so to the group of men who confirm the phenomena—as soon as the common obser-vation is repeated under well-controlled conditions.

To sum up the general position—we pointed out (1) the move-ments through which a sense of personal *competence arises and asserts itself in the individual's judgment*, giving the lie, in a sense, to its own social origin and support (the conclusion stated in sect. 47 above). We now find, however, (2) that this same function deals with a *content under presupposition of commonness and persistence*. In these two positions, there is presented not only a genetic account of the social factor in judgment, but also an analysis of its import and intent to the individual.[1]

62. But the question now returns upon us : does this fully ac-count for synnomic meaning ?—meaning reached without actual **Does this** social control, but *appropriate as having the common* **fully account** *intent ?* How does a function capable of being **for Synnomic** **Meaning?** merely private have more than private competency ?

I reply—by reason of the two-fold presupposition of the ex-position given above ; that is, by the growth of the dualism by which the private is also established.

The " appropriateness " comes with the sense of the *mutual-* **Its Persist.** *ity of the persistence meaning* ; *this is the ground of its* **ence is its** *claim to be worthy of common consent*. The child finds **Claim to be** **Common.** his objects fulfilled and supplemented by your contexts; so he holds his objects as contexts to fulfil yours. If *his* persist because *you* confirm *them*, *yours* persist because *he* confirms *them*. In this he is right and the object is *appropriate*. This reading of your contexts is perforce an ejective reading of his own thus already fulfilled. So far forth as your objects are not yet read as being fully formed, *either to him or to you*, the whole context in question remains schematic and assump-tive. And if fully formed and not thus confirmed, but, on the contrary, found lacking in confirmation, then they are private.

The result then is that all the habitual, the socially experienced

---

[1] It was pointed out in my *Devel. and Evolution*, chap. xvii., that from the objective evolutionary point of view the psychophysical organism has " reproduced in its own platform of determination the very criteria of selection at first enforced only by the environment " (p. 259). The analogous result of social life in educating personal judgment is also intimated there.

and formulated, is persistent and common. It is synnomic.

Other Knowledge is Private in the Sense of the Unconfirmed. All the once-present, untested, experimental matter of new accommodation is neither substantively persistent nor common. It is not private in the sense of eccentric, although it may be private in the sense of unshared; and most likely it is in a more undeveloped stage of commonness. Often it is in a transition stage, confirmed as to its substantive parts, in question as to its transitive parts, yet asserted with the prophecy of self-assertion by the youthful conquering hero of the drama of life, to whom the universe of knowledge is not too great a prize. Most of the " epics of the nursery " are of this sort : tales of real persons doing unconfirmed or impossible things.

63. Synnomic meaning is, therefore, a normal character of knowledge in the late quasi-logical and logical modes, when **Synnomic vs. Schematic Knowledge.** read as recognitive rather than as selective meaning. Whatever is accepted as mind is appropriate object of all minds; and so of bodies; if an object be so far determined as to be body and not mind, body it is to all minds. So far as it is problematic, it is neither common nor private ; for the problematic is in its essential meaning selective, an assumption, and is not yet determined in any way that establishes common acceptance or the lack of it.

§ 9. *Judgment as Synnomic and Universal.*

64. V. The next step forward is now directly in our path. We must ask how any other meanings—those not thus sealed **Judgment makes all its Meanings Synnomic.** with the "common" seal—fare when judged. This question is already answered in the demonstration that *all judgment is syndoxic*. The taking up of a meaning in the process of judgment acknowledges or rejects it ; even private meaning, so far from being neglected, is affirmed in the characteristic judgmental way. The meaning, not before common, *is made so by judgment*. For the judgment adds those marks which make experimental meanings general, and experience as such objective, to all thinkers.

65. It remains to say here also that the meaning " privacy," like all other meanings, takes on the sort of commonness that **Privacy as a Common Judgment.** judgment confers when privacy is itself asserted of a subject-matter of thought. So the synnomic character of appropriate meaning, which before excluded the privacy of eccentric process, now floods over the entire

H

field of reflective meaning. Only that can be object of judgment—even the meaning of privacy—which is taken up as content of experience and so made common to all.

We may summarize the results of our exposition in the following succinct statements.[1]

66. (1) Commonness may be purely of the "aggregate" sort, and may not enter into the individual's meaning at all : this is the sphere of *functions which are private or unshared* **Summary.** *from the observer's point of view*, such as the common baying of the moon by two dogs as I observe them.

(2) Commonness as intent may arise simply from common function : it is *the mere commonness of common action*, as of the dogs' baying of the moon in each other's hearing.

(3) Commonness begins to be cognized, and with it privacy, when there is *perception of aggregate process among individuals* : the commonness illustrated by introjection, as of a third dog who observes two other dogs eyeing the same bone. This is the germ of syndoxic meaning.

(4) Commonness as specific syndoxic meaning arises through the "secondary conversion" of one mind's context into that of another. *The commonness attaching to transitive relationships* is of this sort, as that which comes to the child by imitation of another's action. *Commonness here is that of catholicity or prevalence.*

(5) Appropriate commonness attaches to meanings which, though in one mind, *are held as appropriate to all* ; it matures in the quasi-logical dualism of body and mind. It is synnomic.

(6) The commonness of judged meaning is always synnomic by virtue of its generality as universal, particular, or singular. *Commonness here is that of universality.*

(7) *Privacy* is not a psychic meaning until the contrast-meaning of syndoxic commonness, is reached. Private meaning, from the psychic point of view, is either what is found to be *ineligible* to common process, "the unshared," such as a purely selective meaning in a prelogical mode, or what is due to *eccentric* process in contrast with the "general," "universal" and other meanings of the logical mode.

---

[1] Other conclusions, reached as corollaries from these, appear below: that selective meanings are not exhausted as recognitive content but remain unshared (chap. xiv. §§ 4 ff), that this covers personal meanings as such (chap. xv. §§ 3, 4), that semblant meanings are selective meanings treated as if common (a matter for further examination in vol. iii.), etc.

The further pursuit of this progression into the hyper-logical modes, where additional interesting meanings arise—notably that of the "universality" of aesthetic meaning—is reserved for the third volume of the treatise.[1]

§ 10.   Commonness and Privacy as Presuppositions

67. Remembering our definition of presupposition in the theory of meaning, we may now describe commonness and privacy
As Pre- in terms of that definition. A presupposition is a
suppositions sphere of reference in which a meaning is controlled : the external, the inner, the humorous, the semblant, etc., are presuppositions each of its own characteristically determined contents.   In what sense and degree can commonness and privacy be looked upon as such presuppositions ?

This topic is interesting because it involves a line of distinctions of meaning that cut across the distinctions of existence and reality in which the presuppositions of judgment are cast. The important distinction here is that between commonness of *content* and commonness of *function*, with which we have already had to do.

---

[1] It is now apparent to what an extent discussion may be rendered futile by the failure to distinguish the common meanings called "social." Royce, in claiming a "social" strain in our knowledge of the external world seems to mean in the main our *judgment* of that world, as a persisting world.   So far it is true.   But then he seems to pass to the view *perception* would be impossible without common experience ; this is in my opinion not true.   Another writer, Dr. Bush, puts forward a "social" criterion of difference between "the physical and the mental" ; but for judgment, both these meanings are "social" ; as substances, mind and body are again both "social," but in a different sense ; in memory, they are yet again in another sense "social" ; and the only mode at which both are not "social," that is in some sense "common," as we are using that term, is that of bare projection, in which they are not differentiated.   If one means by not-social, "eccentric," then only certain mental things are not-social; but if "unshared" be meant, then all psychic happenings are together unshared, while their *meanings*, both minds and bodies, may be equally shared !   Do we not talk to one another about "minds" with a perfectly intelligible common meaning ?   The only sense in which such a criterion of the mental would hold is that in which *as a sphere of reference* it is *immediate* ; but that sort of privacy, as being "unshared," does not hold of experience of "the mental" as subject-matter of judgment.   See Royce, *Studies in Good and Evil*, VIII., and *Philos. Review*, Nov. 1894 ; Bush, *Journ. of Philos.*, II., p. 561; and cf. Stratton, *Psychological Bulletin*, January 15, 1906.

It is evident that a presupposition of inner existence may
related to those of Judgment. attach to the commonness of synnomic content, as in the judgment "memory is true to the past," and also as well to the privacy of eccentric function, as in "I have an odd fancy." But the fact that we do not, in our judgments, express such differences explicitly—although of course we may do so—seems to place such intents of meaning on the plane of presuppositions.

An illustration or two will suffice to show that this is really the case. On the one hand, we may cite judgments of common content with the presupposition of privacy ; and on **Illustrations.** the other hand, judgments of private content with the presupposition of commonness. The judgment, "the chairs get in my way," asserts the common meaning, chair, with the presupposition of a sphere of privacy, my personal action, within which I am restricting the predication about it. The judgment, on the other hand, "man fears pain," is one of private content asserted as holding in pain-experience, a sphere common to human life.

68. We are able also to set forth how far the spheres of existence or reality coincide with those of commonness or **Do "Common" and "Real" Presuppositions coincide ?** privacy. It will be remembered that all judgments are synnomic ; they all presuppose the " appropriateness " of their subject-matter, whether the meanings which make up that subject-matter have each for itself a common or a private presupposition. That is, judgment always presupposes eligibility to common consent, even when it asserts something to be private. Much more evidently does it presuppose it if it asserts something to be in some specific sense common.

Taking this latter case first, we may say that judgments which presuppose reality of some sort, that is, spheres of existence, **Reality judgments always have Common Presupposition ;** presuppose commonness also. Evidently everything except what is not eligible for repetition in conscious process (generally the " unshared ") or for " secondary conversion " from mind to mind (the " eccentric ") is in some sphere of control in which sharing and conversion processes are essential factors : these are just the spheres of existence or reality which judgments presuppose. These spheres are not only open to common recognition, they have been constituted by a series of common recognitions. All reality, then, as a presupposed meaning, carries the additional

presupposition of commonness of the sort belonging to its
sphere. Even the sphere of privacy, for example, presupposed
in judgments of private function, is common in the sense that it
is " aggregate " to different individuals having each his private
inner life.

69. While this is true, however, such a relation between
the two presuppositions is not reciprocal. Commonness attaches to all reality, but reality does not attach to all commonness. The commonness that attaches to a reality as a sphere of
control is commonness of content or meaning *in that sphere*, not
alone commonness of the process itself ; but the presupposition of
commonness of *process* attaches to all judgments whether they

but the
reverse is
not always
true.

presuppose reality or not. Judgments whose contents
are placed in a sphere of partial belief or possibility,
or in a sphere of unreality, still have the presupposition of appropriateness. My judgment, " sea-serpents are
mammals or fish," presupposes your consent to my proposed
disjunction, but leaves you free to differ from me in what sense
we may take sea-serpents to be real or unreal. It is this difference that justifies the distinction of the terms " truth " and
" opinion." Truth, having reference to reality, must be common

"Opinion"
may be "com-
mon" but still
"untrue."

if it be true ; opinion, being a matter of function, may
be false although it be common. Put more tech-
nically, we may say that the universality of truth
guarantees its. eligibility for common acceptance, but common
acceptance or catholicity does not guarantee truth.

70. This leads then to the case that best illustrates the
range of privacy as a presupposition. The commonness of

Presupposi-
tion of
Privacy.

judgment extends to all judging function, but not to
the contents in certain specific cases. These cases we
have found to be two, the " unshared " and the
" eccentric " meanings. The reasons for this have also appeared. The unshared is the psychically immediate : that which
is referred to no mediate or remote sphere of control. The
eccentric is that which is so fugitive, detached and meaningless
that it is taken to be without control.

The latter, the eccentric, always has the presupposition of
privacy. What is not controlled, *prima facie* does not have

The "eccen-
tric" as
private.

that control which is open to inspection and reciprocal formulation in a common meaning. There is,
however, along with this, the presupposition of the
commonness of the judging-function, by which its privacy is

declared. Such meanings issue in judgments of "unreality" as
described above. While judgments of reality declare common
meanings, judgments of unreality, on the contrary, declare private
meanings. When I say "Life is real, life is earnest," a particular
common sort of reality is meant, that of human life ; but when
I say "Such is my dream," no further question of its sort of
unreality arises ; the presupposition is that of eccentric process.[1]

71. The "unshared" has a privacy presupposition of a
different sort. If an unshared experience remained simply
fugitive, detached, and evanescent there would be no further
question about it ; but much of the unshared—the whole life of
appreciation for instance—does not so remain. It is organized
in the "funded contents" of the history of consciousness, whereby
there arises what is known as a continuing and experiencing
mind. This becomes also a sphere of control, the subjective,
which has its own marks of reality. The individual personal
The   history of the man becomes for him "the great un-
unshared.   shared " ; but its construction as a "real," together
with other minds, in a sphere of "mind," removes from it the
property of being unshared and makes it common by secondary
conversion. So far, indeed, as the events of my past history
are contents of the reality we call mind, they are generalized
becomes as   materials. It is thus that you in turn treat your history
judged,   as that of a mind. So far as judged "real," therefore,
Common.   the contents of such an "unshared" life are common
as all generalized meanings are. They are taken up and made
contents of judgment.

There remains here, also, therefore, as in the case of the
eccentric, only the function, the immediate unshared process,
As   that is private. It is this that constitutes each person
immediate   a "singular" individual. So while as sphere of reality
it is Private. or control, mind is as common as any other such
sphere, yet as psychic or subjective function, it is a private
meaning.

[1] It may be asked, indeed, whether the "unreal" is not a sphere
having a certain sort of commonness. And it may be so described when
itself taken up as an objective and abstract meaning (see sect. 73 below).
But to make a specific judgment of the unreality of a given psychic content is to declare it to lack any further reference than that to the psychic
life which the corresponding *judgment of reality* renders. So far as a
content lacks reality it fails of just those marks by which it could be
reached by common process ; it is then "eccentric" and private. Cf.
chap. ii. §§ 3, 4.

72. We reach the conclusion, in short, that the presupposition of privacy of judgment is always one of function : either eccentric **Immediate** function in which, it may be, a quasi-common meaning **Function** proves to be deceptive, or normal function as imme-**always** **Private.** diate event and meaning. This leads us again to the position, already worked out on an earlier page,[1] that the inner sphere, the inner process as such, is the second and final presupposition of thought. But here it is a presupposition of privacy ; there it was a presupposition of objective meaning. The solution of this apparent paradox will bring us to the end of this series of transformations of common meaning.

73. We said in our first series of distinctions of common meanings (vol. I, chap. vii. §§ 3 ff) that any meaning reached from the psychic point of view might be made " aggregate " to an observer, who took the psychological point of view. For instance, I may think of you and him as each thinking with the presupposition of privacy of process. I then make your privacy-**It becomes** presupposition part of my subject-matter, which is **when judged** objective and common. It is thus that the pre-**Common.** supposition of privacy, like any other, may be made predicate of an existential judgment in which just that *lack of control in any sphere* may be made sphere of thought or " universe of discourse." The sphere of the unreal becomes something to talk about and even to predicate. This only confirms our earlier conclusion that unreality may be the presupposition of privacy ; and that the unreal is always private and fugitive process.

74. Our conclusions, therefore, regarding the relation of reality and commonness as presuppositions, are as follows :

(1) As to meanings which are subject-matter or contents of judgment, reality and commonness are coincident and inter-**Conclusions:** changeable presuppositions. Whenever one asserts **on Reality** **and Common.** or presupposes a sphere of mediate or reflective con-**ness.** trol, the meaning is universal and synnomic.

(2) As to meanings which are of the nature of functional intent or process, the presuppositions of privacy and unreality may both be present, but they do not always coincide. The presupposition of absence of mediate or reflective control does not in itself determine the content as eccentric and unreal. There is the further possibility—

(3) That the presupposition of private process may be part of that of inner or subjective reality, since the processes of

[1] Chap. ii. sects. 19–21.

" functioning " of inner contents, by tertiary and secondary conversion, extends to contents having this presupposition.

(4) The presupposition of reflection itself as a sphere of control characteristic of the reality " mind," results from the objectifying of the intent of functional meanings which are psychically immediate and private.

Our conclusions, further, regarding the general presuppositions of different sorts of commonness are as follows :—

On Commonness as Presupposition. (1) Synnomic or " appropriate " commonness is the presupposition of all acts of judgment, and of all contents controlled in reflection.

(2) Catholicity, or syndoxic meaning of the " actual " or prevalent type, is of the nature of further " assumption," [1] beyond the intent of judgment. It is, however, an attribute of knowledge in the late pre-judgmental modes.

(3) Privacy is the mark of personal and of " eccentric " process. It is a presupposition only in judgments of privacy.

§ 11. COMMONNESS AND PRIVACY AS ATTRIBUTES OF KNOWLEDGE

75. If we ask finally the broad question how far commonness and privacy are attributes of knowledge, our results allow a wide generalization.

It appears that commonness of a form that knows no privacy is a primary character of all knowledge. It later on *makes its own privacy*. It has a series of guarantees, from the sense *Commonness is primary* mode to the logical. Beginning with the commonness of common or gregarious function, it is reaffirmed by secondary conversion, by imitative absorption, by disciplinary enforcement, by ejective re-reading, by the necessity of generalization, by the rise of the dualism of mind and body. In all these great stages it is a normal and indispensable factor of meaning. Then it embodies itself in reflection in a way that makes judgment its conscious expression and its indubitable witness.

In short commonness is the original, privacy the secondary and derived character. The " presumption " of knowledge is not indi-

---

[1] It illustrates the general fact that either commonness or privacy may be made " assumptive " as a " postulate " of any context of thought. The distinction between presupposition and postulate is developed in the next chapter.

vidualistic. Such a statement of it is mythological. There are
Privacy is not a lot of individuals each having his own private
secondary. meanings which are somehow to be brought into a common system. On the contrary, there is a lot of common meaning which is to be reinterpreted by each individual as his own, and possibly, his private possession. The result here is the same— and the urgent need of seeing it is the same—as that which a similar genetic study has lead to in the case of the problem of social individualism.[1] *The individual*, I have said in effect elsewhere, *is not a social unit, he is a social outcome.* He is a result of *refined processes of social differentiation.* If he makes himself a social unit over against society, he becomes eccentric and anti-social, and his damnation is sure. So of knowledge. *It is not a private possession; it is public property.* It begins common, stays common, claims to be common, enforces its commonness. No knowledge confined in one private head, re-peated in other private heads an infinity of times, would ever be-come an organic system of common knowledge. It must already, in its constitution, reflect its social origin and fitness. The single item of knowledge, as a private self-contained thought of a single
Privacy an thinker, is the result of *refined processes of cognitive*
Outcome. *differentiation. The private thought is not a cognitive unit, it is a cognitive outcome.* The thought that claims the isolation and absolute lack of common control of an individual unit, is read off as eccentric and unreal and its damnation is no less sure.[2]

[1] Cf. the writer's *Social and Eth. Interpretations*, chap. ii. § 6.

[2] This general result opens up a singular relation between the two great conversion processes I have described as " primary" and "secondary " respectively—a point already intimated in the matter of persistence (in sect. 51 of this chapter). Both may be interpreted in a view which makes them cases of a larger movement. Primary conversion is *inter-modal*, a context of a later mode as converted into the control of an earlier, as a memory into a precept. Secondary conversion is *inter-personal*, one person's context is converted into that of another, my memory checked by another's. But *each conversion is both* ; for the " other person " of secondary conversion is my object or context, and the control thus se-cured is really *inter-modal* as between my memory and my present ex-perience. Again the original control of primary conversion is an experience to me, a person, and the inter-modal conversion of my memory is that of one personal whole of experience into another. One gives a commonness of the inter-personal which is inter-modal, the other a commonness of the inter-modal which is inter-personal. And so again do we reach the in-alienable right of any *confirmed* knowledge to be common ! I find my

The result is, in my opinion, one of the corner-stones of any valid or effective epistemology. Commonness is a presupposition of all reflection that reaches reality ; it is, in characteristic form, also a presupposition of all knowledge which deals with objects as existing or as having any describable form of cognitive content and subsistence.

lower modes of confirmation, say those of sense-perception, to be supplied by an *animal*, my pointer, *just as well* as by myself; and I expect my judgments of reality in those modes which he can apprehend, say the physical, to be true for him as for me. On the contrary, also, I take his experience of reality—say his " pointing " of a partridge—to be convertible into my judgments; and as a result I bring down the bird ! The logical aspect of this identity of the two modes of conversion has been adverted to above (§ 8, note). See also the account of " Community " as a character of Propositions (chap. ix. § 5) and the section on " Difference of Discernibles " (chap. xiv. § 9).

Chapter IV

ACKNOWLEDGMENT OF THE PROBLEMATICAL AS DISJUNCTIVE

§ 1. Presupposition, Assumption, and Postulate

1. The positions reached in the preceding chapter involve the recognition in the logical mode, as elsewhere, of meanings that are not fully determinate or definite ; they are on the way towards definiteness. In the progress of conception there is always the forward as well as the backward look, and the drift toward further determination always gives colour to the meaning, as does also that backward reference already embodied in the context as part of the subject-matter of judgment. So evident is this, that we have been able, in arranging the modes of judgment with reference to the belief involved, to distinguish clearly the great class of meanings called "problematical" for which there are recognized propositional forms ; and also to distinguish two sorts of such meaning, differing from each other just in the mode of their indeterminateness. The disjunctive judgment, as embodying alternative meanings, is indeterminate as to the inner relations of the content, a mode of meaning expressed in the proposition by the words "either-or." But, on the other hand, there are judgments and propositions which embody "contingent" meaning, in which the relations of content are determinate, as expressed by the dependence sign "if," while the whole meaning is still indeterminate as to the sphere of reference in which it, *as a whole*, may or may not be accepted. Both sorts of indeterminateness, of course, leave the meaning open to further development and interpretation. In the one case, the disjunction is dissolved by the progress of experience ; in the other case, the lack of belief is relieved by a process of further judgment. The disjunctive passes into the assertorial, with the presupposition before present to the

Two sorts of Indeterminateness.

whole meaning, and the conditional passes into the assertorial, by acquiring a similar presupposition, with the relational meaning before present. Each adds to its determinateness by definition in that respect in which it was before lacking.

In classing the two meanings, the disjunctive and the contingent, together, however, as problematical, we have already

Indeter-
minate (1)
Content and
(2) Control hit upon their common character as being each in some sense indeterminate. It now becomes our task to work out more fully the differences between them, and show the characteristic modes of judgment and proposition in which these meanings are actually used. In the one case, there is *an indeterminate content of determinate acceptance*, in the other, *an indeterminate acceptance of a determinate content*. The first of these we may further describe as *judgment with presupposition* : as, for example, "whales are either mammals or fish " ; and the second as *judgment with postulation* : as, for example, "if sea-serpents have gills they are fish." It will appear at once what this difference means and especially how what is now called " postulation " differs from what is already familiar to us under the term " presupposition."

With reference to the general attitudes involved, it is evident that we are dealing here with the special cases, arising in the logical mode, of the fundamental difference between " acceptance " and " assumption." The table given in chap. i. § 4 sect. 11, may be consulted.[1] The presupposition is an attitude of *logical acceptance*, the postulate one of *logical assumption* ; both having reference to the sphere of reality or existence in which the meaning has or suggests a control or fulfilment.

2. The presupposition is that determinate sphere of reference and control which attaches to the whole disjunctive meaning.

(1) gives Pre-
supposition. It may be physical existence, newspaper report, fancy, it matters not. It is the sphere which is accepted and acknowledged as that in which the disjunction stated in the subject-matter is finally to be resolved. I may well say, " let us look up whales and see whether they are considered fish or mammals." I acknowledge a sphere of information—the authorities on the subject—by reference to which the uncertainty may be removed, and a statement reached in assertorial form. This then is the presupposition of the meaning.

3. On the other hand, the judgment " if sea-serpents have

---

[1] See also the larger tables given in the Appendix.

gills they are fish," asserts a relation of coincidence between two meanings, which holds if and when the sphere of reference is established. It leaves quite outside my intention any demand that you agree with me in finding such whales in any accepted sphere of existence. All I mean is that the context "gilled-sea-serpent" includes the marks of "fish," be that context in a sphere still to be determined. It does not presuppose a sphere; it postulates one. It may have different postulations in different minds, which nevertheless accept the contingent relation between the terms of the subject-matter as common to their several thoughts.

But this meaning is not finished; no meaning is. It is, as we saw the disjunctive meaning also to be, a pausing place, an eddy, (2) **gives** so to speak, in the flow of psychic process. And as **Postulate.** soon as we ask into what it develops, what the next stage of meaning is into which it issues, of course we find the answer in the further progress in that respect in which it is indeterminate. The question in mind back of the statement about sea-serpents is, what is the sea-serpent?—are there such creatures?—I should like to solve the problem one way or the other. I conclude that the sea-serpent is a fish, physically realized in the Atlantic Ocean! This at once brings in a sphere of reference, a sort of control, a "real" intent, which is now a presupposition. But the subject matter was constituted without this so long as some reality was merely postulated for the meaning—merely set up as itself an experimental and instrumental meaning to subserve my further research. Instead of a given existence, charged with problematical content, as in the disjunctive, here we have the given relational content charged with a problematical reality. This element of meaning—reality set up and treated in a schematic and assumptive way—is called a "postulate." Such meanings are variously described; as "objects with postulates," "thinking with postulates"; or the content itself is said to be "postulated": just as, in the other case, the real reference is said to be "presupposed."

4. The difference between the presupposition and the postulate, is, it is plain, one that we have taken occasion to **Difference** characterize in other modes. The presupposition is **between Pre-** a meaning determined in the process of individuation; **supposition** it is that of a definite class or control. It is general; and the cases are particulars under it. In the judgment "fish have scales," the presupposition is a sphere of physical existence

which is a sort of real control ; and all fishes exist in this sphere and illustrate it. Fishes are particular physical existences.

The postulate, however, is not a general meaning with reference to the content for which it is postulated. The place of the
and Postulate. case as a particular in the class is not yet accepted nor believed. Its postulation is for the purpose of forwarding the movement whereby the case is to be finally assigned to its class. As soon as I become convinced that the reality is thus or thus, then and then only is my judgment wrapped about with a belief presupposition extending to the entire related subject-matter. When Columbus sailed westward he *postulated* a world in which certain astronomical and geographical relations held. Luckily he found a patron willing to postulate it with him. Since his discovery, however, all sailors *presuppose* the world he postulated.

This may suffice at this point for the description of the postulate.[1] We will return to it later on. It is a schematic or assumptive control meaning.

The two cases in which logical meaning involves, in its further determination, a process of essential schematization
Quantity having been sufficiently distinguished, we may take them up one at a time, inquiring into the forms in which such meanings embody themselves in judgments. The schematic meaning of the alternative type that is embodied in the disjunctive judgment, shows the varieties known in formal logic as judgments having extensive "quantities." In considering them we shall therefore also be working out a theory of Logical Quantity.

§ 2. DISJUNCTIVE MEANINGS WITH PRESUPPOSITIONS : SCHE-
MATISM OF THE PARTICULAR AND OF THE GENERAL

5. The point of view from which disjunctive judgments, such as "coins are either gold or silver, etc.," take on differences
It involves Disjunction. of quantity, expressed by "all," "some," etc., has already been suggested. It will be remembered that we pointed out[2] the case of disjunction by "exclusion" or exhaustion in which the alternatives exhausted the entire range or extension of the judgment. "Coins are gold, or silver, or

---

[1] The "Postulate" as a meaning is treated in chap. v. ; its interpretation in the theory of reality is reserved for vol. iii.

[2] See above, chap. ii. sect. 47.

copper " is such a judgment. It will be evident, from a little further thought, that all disjunctions divide the meaning, although all do not exhaust it. For every case of individuation in the logical mode is an act of assigning a particular to its appropriate general meaning or the reverse. We may take the point of view of the meaning of the particular, and say, for example, "this gold object is either a coin or etc."; or we may take the point of view of the general meaning "coin," and say "coins are gold or etc." The general meaning coin is not only not inconsistent with the further determination in the case of each coin, but it is the whole meaning within which the range of the terms of the disjunction is to be determined.

This is indeed only to recognize over again the fact that a meaning which is disjunctive as to its parts and inner relation- **within a** ships, may yet be determinate and general as to **General.** its control and belief. Given the general meaning "coin" the further determination is as to which of several sorts of coins this or that is to be.

From yet another point of view, the issue is the same. The act of generalization goes out upon some character or mark present in certain cases. Other characters or marks may serve also for the development of other general meanings. The meanings thus established do not coincide but cluster about and overlap the particular case each for itself. All coins are "some silver," "some gold, etc., objects"; "silver objects" is a general meaning which claims some "coins," no less than does "coin" claim some "silver objects."

Within this general characterization, however, variations of meaning arise which it will be well to distinguish. We will consider the two modes in turn, and then inquire into their relation to each other.

6. I. It is evident that we may consider the case in which the general class, the subject, is so far determined that the **Definite** entire extension is exhausted by the sub-classes into **Alternation.** which the cases are distributed. A good example is that just given, "coins are gold, or silver, or copper"; there are no coins, no cases, to be added to the extension of coin after all these sorts of coin are told off. This is the case called disjunction by exhaustion. The meaning is one of "definite alternation."

The schematic or problematical character of the meaning lies entirely in the further determination of the single case as falling in one or other of the alternative sub-classes. This may be symbolized by the following diagram (Fig. 3), in which the entire extent of the concept is exhausted by the areas in which the sub-class meanings overlap with it.

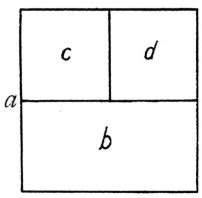

Fig. 3.—Definite Alternation of Particulars. "This *a* is *b*, or *c*, or *d*."[2]

7. Remembering that this is a case of schematism only with reference to the particular, the particular alone being indeterminate, we may distinguish another case, which also involves an indeterminate and schematic particular. In the case just given the alternation or disjunction is between established meanings or classes, into which the entire extension of the subject is divided. There is the other well-marked case in which the extension is not thus exhausted by established meanings, but certain of the sub-meanings that might be set up are still to be arrived at. The determination to be achieved is not that of assigning a case to one of certain already given meanings, but of finding the classes in which cases actually occur. For example, the judgment " some books are red," leaves it open to discovery or further determination what other colours books Indefinite may be found to have. Here the meaning is one of Alternation. " indefinite alternation." It may be symbolized in

<hr />

[1] Cf. the earlier sketch of prelogical alternative meaning where certain of these forms are mentioned (chap. ii. § 8). The treatment here is from the point of view of logical quantity.

It may be added that it is not intended by these diagrams to introduce a system of graphic representation, or to modify those already in use. The figures are intended simply as aids to the understanding of the text.

turn by the following figure (4). The entire circle *a* includes that of the *b*'s, and also various other possibilities, as yet undetermined, in one of which the given case is to fall. ·

It is of the nature of indefinite alternation that the number of the alternatives, as well as their character, may be undetermined. I may say, " it is a lighthouse or a ship or something else," introducing any number of " or's." And I may find the indefiniteness so unqualified that I am not able to formulate even one of the alternatives, as in " I wish I could make it out—what is that light ? " Here the mere class " light " is given, and the entire further determination within the class fails. This is the case of pure interrogative meaning in the logical mode, as is pointed out below.

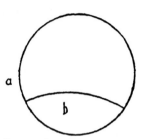

Fig. 4.—Indefinite Alternation of Particulars. "This *a* is *b* or something else."

8. We have recognized so far, therefore, from our present point of view certain cases of the embodiment of a general meaning in a disjunction, of which the alternatives take on the following modes of indeterminateness. They are cases of what is called above schematism of the particular.

Schematism of the particular :

(1) Disjunction by exclusion or exhaustion, called definite alternation of the particular : as in " a railway signal is blue, or green, or red."

(2) Disjunction as indefinite alternation of the particular: as in " a railway signal is blue or some other colour."

9. II. It was intimated above that the problematical aspect of a meaning may attach not to the particular, but to the general

Schematism of the General.

aspects which it presents. The characters of the single cases may be well made out ; and the question for further determination may be as to the one or more general classes in which the sub-classes or particulars are to be placed. " Whales are either mammals or fish " is such a meaning. It assumes a definite set of marks common to cases distinguished as whales ; and the schematic use of the meaning is to determine the class-meaning in which whales are found.

This is not an unusual or forced sort of judgment ; on the contrary, it is one of the greatest instrumental value in all actual processes of discovery. It is the type of experimental meaning

I

by which knowledge is essentially advanced. In the schematism of the particular, the general meaning is internally enriched by the instrumental use of those particular meanings by which it can be interpreted ; here the particular relationships are clarified and added to by the schematic use of the alternative general interpretations in which they give promise of further development.

We may call this the " definite alternation of the general," and symbolize it in figure 5.[1] The large circles *b* and *c* represent the general classes in which the objects of the small circle *a* may fall. In words, the proposition takes the form " *a*'s are *b*'s or *c*'s, it may be either," or " I don't know which."

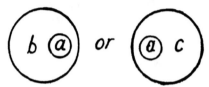

FIG. 5.—DEFINITE ALTERNATION OF THE GENERAL. " *a*'s are *b*'s or *c*'s, (it may be) either."

In contrast with this, there is " indefinite schematism of the general," in which the class meaning is not held down to certain alternatives. It may be illustrated by Fig. 4, provided the circle *a* be taken for the entire sphere of existence within which *b* or other general classes might fall.

Summarizing, therefore, our results under this heading, we have the following :—

Schematism of the General :—

(1) Definite alternation of the general, as in " whales are either mammals or fish (one or the other)."

(2) Indefinite alternation of the general, as in " knowledge is of reality or of images (or of we know not what)."

10. III. Considering the two sorts of logical schematism comparatively, we may recall a distinction already arrived at on an earlier page.[2] We saw that a disjunctive meaning **Exclusive and Indefinite Disjunction.** might be of what is called the " exclusive " type on the one hand, or, on the other hand, of a character more

[1] The word " or " may be omitted from this diagram if we bear in mind that we are dealing with a disjunction in which the presence of *a* in both *b* and *c* cannot mean the assertion that " *a* is *both* *b* and *c*." Cf. the remarks made in chap. ii. sect. 47 (3).

[2] Above, and also chap. ii. sect. 47.

properly called "indefinite." "Signals are blue or red or green'
is a case of exclusive alternation ; a signal can be only one of
these colours ; the others are excluded. This case is one of
"definite alternation," in the interpretation of the particular.
But there is also exclusive disjunction in the case of indefinite
alternation ; as in the judgment, "this signal is blue or some
other colour." If it is found to be blue, then any other colour
is excluded. Furthermore, in the case of the indeterminate
general, there may be exclusive alternation, as in, "whales are
mammals or fish," or indefinite alternation, as in "what are
called sea-serpents are mammals or some other natural kind."
It is evident, therefore, that the assignment of exclusive or indefinite meaning to a disjunction is not the same movement
as that of the determination of general and particular. Both
the general and the particular may be either definite or indefinite in their mode of exclusion.

The solution of the matter from our present point of view is
interesting, for it shows that indefinite exclusion is simply
Exclusion an additional element of indeterminateness, involv-
requires a ing a repetition of the schematism with reference to
further
Schematism. the determination of the relation of the sub-classes
or meanings to one another. The only case in which this relation
of the sub-classes is definitely established and determined is
that of disjunction by "exhaustion" ; for there the division
proceeds by classes which do not overlap but supplement one
another within the extension of the whole meaning. This case
is only one possibility, however. The classes brought into
alternation within the subject-meaning of a disjunction may
vary also with reference to their range or extension *inter se*.
When I say "he is foolish or mad," I do not mean to exclude
the reply, "he is both."—as has already been said in our
earlier reference to this case." [1] I accordingly have, *in quite
the same sense as before*, a real schematism ; a meaning used
instrumentally for the determination of the possible overlapping
of the sub-classes which my original disjunction established.
Schematic The circles (*b* etc.) in the diagram of indefinite al-
Alternation. ternation of particulars (Fig. 4), while fulfilling the
condition that they cut the circle of the subject-meaning (*a*),

---

[1] Above, chap. ii. § 8, sect. 47, where indeed our present result is suggested. A good actual case is that of a mute who may be deaf, of whom
one would say "he is either deaf or dumb." The chances are that he
is both, his dumbness resulting from his deafness.

may also cut each other, or coincide with, or lie outside of, each other. See the diagram (Fig. 6) for this case, called "schematic alternation or disjunction of the particular."[1]

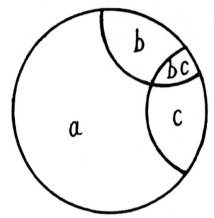

FIG. 6.—"SCHEMATIC ALTERNATION (PARTICULAR)." "*a* is *b* or *c* or both (indefinitely)."

11. An additional case on the side of indeterminate general meaning appears among the cases of schematism of the general ;

Inclusive general Alternation. it is the case in which the disjunction expressed is not of the exclusive type. The judgment "mammals are either terrestrial or aquatic" does not exclude the possibility of cases which are amphibious; that is to say, the

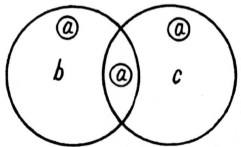

FIG. 7.—SCHEMATIC ALTERNATION (GENERAL). *a*'s are *b*'s or *c*'s or both (indefinitely).

---

[1] Schematic in the sense that the relation of the classes of the alternation itself is uncertain, as well as the assignment of the given case to one or more of them.

genus "mammal" allows either indifferently or conjointly. "Knowledge is either of reality or of images," permits a theory that knowledge is of reality although also of images. In short, the circles of general meaning of the diagram given above for general schematic meaning (Fig. 5) may themselves cut each other, although both contain the subject term which is asserted subject to the disjunction. See the accompanying diagram (Fig. 7) for this case, known as "schematic general alternation."

§ 3. LOGICAL EXTENSION AS QUANTITY

12. Interpreting disjunctive meanings strictly with reference to the movements of belief, and inquiring how the differences of inclusion, as between general meanings terminating upon the same particulars, are embodied, we come upon the question of extensive quantity. We express the entire meaning "coin" as related to other general meanings contemporaneous with it, by "some," "all," "most," "few," "only," etc. Certain of these variations have been recognized by the formal logicians in their descriptions of quantity : as in "some coins are silver," "all coins are metal," "this is the only pewter coin." It will be profitable to look into these differences from our present point of view.

As a matter of fact, we find our acknowledgments of content taking form according as the process of generalization has found confirming instances of the kind of control which the germinating general expresses. The process by which the individuation as general and particular proceeded in the first place, is reaffirmed in the inclusion of new cases not before covered by the meaning. This is the process of increasing the extension or denotation of the whole meaning or subject matter.

On the other hand, change comes in intension in the sub-classes, by the accretion of marks in the growth of experience. Cases of newly observed characters occur more or less frequently. The relation of the whole meaning or general to the sub-classes or particulars—both its degree of certainty and the balance of uncertainty—it is the function of the disjunction to express. The judgment "I have observed a black man," passes after additional experiences of the same sort into, "a few men are black," then into "some men are black," "every other man I see is black," or "half the men are black," and becomes "many," "most," or "all the men here are black." The attitudes of acceptance here terminate

Quantity (margin)

and its Varieties. (margin)

upon the distributive or quantitative aspects of experience : hence the term " quantity " attached to the varying linguistic forms in which these judgments are embodied. The distinctions of formal logic recognize three such determinations, based, as our own also are, on relative determinateness. " All," expresses the case of determinate character attaching to each of the particulars of the class-meaning ; " some," the case in which there is a disjunction as between indeterminate parts of the whole number of cases ; and " a " or " one," that in which the determination is of a single case only, all but one being either determined by exclusion as not intended or left indeterminate. Omitting " all " and " one " for the present, as being fairly unambiguous, we may distinguish further well marked attitudes of belief within the meaning of " some," that is, attitudes terminating upon meanings embodying differences of quantity as extension.

13. In the range of logical thought, there are certain great quantitative variations of meaning, which are the basis of the objective method called statistical, and to which we *Judgments of Possibility,* attach the meanings " probability " or " improbability." The distinctions of probability depend directly upon the attitudes of relative expectation and belief, which we are now making the principle of our research. Granted a state of mind which recognizes a problematical meaning as one of " possibility," we then say that such a schematic meaning may be further defined as more or less " probable." The disjunctive judgment is one of possibility, whatever the quantity of it may be ; and the meaning thus open to further determination in quantity is that expressed by the term " some."

There are two relatively unambiguous meanings in quantity however, which claim more determinateness than " some " : *and Probability,* meanings that carry belief that a relation is " more likely " or " less likely " than not. These meanings are expressed by " most " and " few." " Most " renders explicitly the meaning " more than half," and " few " the meaning " less than half " with equal explicitness. The former is a " probable " judgment ;. the latter one of " improbability," with reference to the issue of a particular case. " Most crows are black," " few crows are white," thus embody quantitative attitudes. The expectation is that any unobserved crow will probably be black, and that it is improbable that it will be white. Calling these respectively judgments of " probability " and

" improbability," we may set them down as extensive quantities which are less vague than " some."

While there are in our language forms and indeed single words which render such probable and improbable meanings, and distinguish them from each other by a certain reference to a midway point in the division of quantity, yet that point itself is not thus hit off by a convenient linguistic form.[1] We may express such a definite equal division into halves by various phrases : " about half," " an equal part," " an even chance of," etc., are such expressions of half-and-half quantity. It would be interesting to analyse the motives that enter to determine problematical judgments in the forms " most," and " few," or leave them in the more indefinite form " some." No doubt the quantity " half " is less frequent, because it suggests, if it does not require, an exactness of measurement or observation not necessary in ordinary discourse. One would have to recognize also, in any adequate account of the matter, the many more irrelevant influences which warp, bias, and in general determine belief, as coming in to impart to the quantity expressed a shading one way or the other away from the neutrality of an exact division. It is exact theoretical neutrality, of course, that we appeal to in tossing a penny or throwing the dice.

If we call the judgment which embodies alternative meaning a " judgment of possibility," indicated verbally by the quanti- and Impro- tative sign " some "—of which the limiting cases are, bability. as we shall see, " all " and " one "—then the alterna- tives represented by " most," " half," " few," etc., may be known as " judgments of probability." Any problematical or alter- native meaning is possible ; and all such meanings have relative probability.

If we distinguish (as above) the judgments " few," " less than half," etc., as " improbable," and those of " most," " more than half," etc., as " probable," we have a scheme of relatively definite terms. " Probable judgments " are those of rela- tively wide extension, " improbable judgments " those of relatively narrow extension, and " possible judgments " those of indefinite extension. As examples, we may give the three judgments, " most mammals are terrestrial " (probable), " a

---

[1] In French and German the terms " plupart " and " viele " have connotations of " more than half " ; and there are the terms " un peu " and " plusieurs," " ein Wenig " and " einige " (less definitely), on the side of " less than half."

few mammals are aquatic" (improbable), "some mammals are amphibious" (indefinite). Relative extension is here understood as a determination within a class, within which it implies a disjunctive meaning.

14. The two cases left over, those commonly called "universal" and "singular," also have interesting interpretation **Universal and Singular quantified** from our present point of view. It will be remembered that the movements of belief, as terminating upon more or less determinate contents, are the ground of distinction ; and that these movements vary according as different quantitative meanings are embodied in the judgment. The two cases now to be considered are those of the belief which embodies the greatest possible extension of the subject-matter on the one hand—the "universal" judgments, in "all"—and the least possible extension—the "singular" judgments, in "one" —on the other hand.

At the outset we find it possible to distinguish both these cases from those which do not thus embody a quantitative meaning or intent although verbally expressed in the same forms. There are judgments of the form "all S is P," which might as well be expressed in the form "S is P." The question may be raised indeed as to whether such judgments are entitled to the quantitative "all" at all. So with "singular" judgments. A single individual may be made subject-matter of a judgment, which nevertheless does not intend to say or to mean that it is a single case. These distinctions are fully confirmed **and un- quantified.** by our present investigation. There are judgments, universal in form, that are not quantified, as well as those that are quantified ; and there are also both unquantified and quantified singular judgments.

15. The quantified universal is the limiting case of the judgments already described as relatively wide in extension. The **The Quantified Universal.** widening of the extension from "many" to "most" or "nearly all," finally exhausts the class within which the case falls, and thus issues in the meaning "all." It is the judgment based on increasing acquaintance with instances, each of which illustrates the relation in question. "Induction by enumeration" is a superficial way of thus widening extension by addition of cases.[1] A more profound case is that of the normal growth of a conceptual

[1] It is not the only or the most important sort of Induction (see chap. xi. § 2, for the full discussion of Induction).

meaning by generalization. It serves to express meanings that are synthetic or predicative, the range of overlapping of two class meanings, subject and predicate, becoming relatively wider until the whole of the former falls within or coincides with the latter.

Such a judgment is, therefore, a quantified universal, since its meaning is one of extension. It may always be fairly interpreted as the answer to a question which embodies the relative indeterminateness of a schematic meaning to the questioner. " All mammals have skins " may be taken as answer to the question whether skins are found on mammals, and if so on what part of the mammal class. The universal aspect of the judgment has its characteristic meaning as being one of the alternatives which, until the judgment in " all " was formed, represented a real disjunction.

16. All universal judgments, however, are not of this sort. Some are not judgments of extension at all, although ex-
The Unquantified Universal. pressed in the same linguistic form. Such judgments state a relation in the subject-matter quite apart from any schematic or problematical use of this subject-matter. For example, the judgment " virtue is praiseworthy " may be rendered by the expression " all virtues are praiseworthy " ; but the enumeration of virtues is not what the original intends. Such a judgment does not lie at the limit of relatively determinate meanings with respect to quantity, that is, to the number of cases observed or for any reason accepted. Its intent is not to answer the question how many virtues there are, and how many of these are praiseworthy. It is, on the contrary, a judgment of the intensive rather than the extensive sort. It is also opposed to the quantified universal in that it is not synthetic, but analytic ;[1] it is reached by an analysis and expansion of the meaning virtue, not by a process of experience of new cases. Judgments which issue from definitions, judgments that are symbolic and selective, judgments embodying axioms and self-evident meanings, are in this sense unquantified universals. The symbolic use of a triangle, with all the judgments passed upon its constitution and inner relationships, have no reference to the quantity of triangles, nor do they raise the question of the liability of some to escape the

[1] That is, in itself ; the question how far its result may enter into a system of implication that can be called " synthetic," is to be discussed later on.

formulations reached. The difference is one on which, as we find later on, two forms or modes of logical implication rest.

The contrast of meaning in the two universals is brought out when we say that the unquantified form, if considered as answer The two go to a question at all, is not answer to the same question with different as is the unquantified. My assertion, "virtue is Questions, commendable," does not suppose you to be inquiring how many virtues—few, some, many, most—are entitled to commendation, as is the case with the judgment, "all mammals have skins"; but rather, what is the meaning of virtue, wherever it is found?—how is virtue constituted, no matter whether one or many cases of it be looked at?

A similar contrast appears between these two meanings when we inquire as to their negatives. If I say "some mammals have and different not skins," I express a negation of the quantified Negatives. universal, "all mammals have skins": but for the unquantified universal of the form "virtue is commendable," the negative is not a judgment of different quantity, or one that quantifies the subject at all, but one which denies the relation asserted; we have the negative judgment, "virtue is not commendable."[1]

17. A similar distinction appears also in the case of the judgment known as "singular." It is commonly treated in the logics as the case of most restricted quantity; or Singular may be of the universal of a most restricted subject-matter. quantified The relatively narrow quantity of "some" reaches its limit in the restriction to "one." This is certainly a true interpretation of many singular judgments. Their intent is to embody the restriction of the application of the predicate to just the one case. I may say "this coin is pewter," meaning that I am not prepared to recognize any pewter coins but this. It is the case reached as the lower limit of the scale of which the quantified universal is the upper limit. As one follows the relative range of extension from wider to narrower, he passes from "all" to "most," "many," "some," "few," "very few," "one." Such a judgment gives answer to the question how many, and is thus a true quantified singular.[2]

But in the sphere of singularity also there are meanings that

[1] For further treatment of the "essential universal" see chap. x. § 5 and chap. xi. §§ 3 ff.

[2] On modes of quantity, as illustrated by the singular, see chap. xiv. § 8.

are not quantified. The judgment "your act is commendable " **or unquanti-** is such a meaning. The subject matter is the single **fied.** act. But the question it answers, if it be considered answer to a question at all, is not how many of your acts are commendable, nor how many acts like this you perform. It is rather the assertion of a relation between the terms of the subject-matter. Its denial, too—" your act is not commendable "— is not quantitative with reference to the logical subject[1], but intensive.

Our method thus enables us to detect in the two forms, conventionally called "universal" and "singular," essential differences of mode in the matter of belief. Either may or may not embody that intent of disjunction which quantification of the subject embodies. Only those cases of each which do so embody disjunction fall under the type of function called in this work schematism ; for only that meaning is schematic which proceeds upon a relative lack of determinateness, and issues through experimental processes in a relatively greater determinateness. Both the universal and the singular may be limiting cases in a scale of relative indeterminateness ; and as such they are charged with experimental meaning.

18. If this be true, it follows that it is only as thus considered that the universal and the singular are different judgments. **As unquanti-** " All mammals have skins," and " this mammal has **fied Universal** a skin," are different as respects quantity. But so **and Singular** **are the same.** soon as the quantitative difference is removed by employing judgments which exclude it from the intent of the meaning, then the difference between the judgments lapses. " Such deeds as yours are virtuous," and " your deed is virtuous," express, so far as neither is quantitive, exactly the same meaning. A relational content may be expressed, therefore, either in universal or in singular form without ambiguity, in cases in which extensive quantity is tacitly or explicitly eliminated. Formal logic is therefore in this case justified in considering the singular as a universal.

19. It is possible now to show that two distinctions made in the foregoing treatment turn out to have the same meaning. We distinguished between the quantified and unquantified

---

[1] Both here and above this statement is restricted to the "subject." for there is an important sense to be explained below in which all negation quantifies the predicate (chap. viii. sect. 9, 1).

Schematism of Universal and Singular is Quantification. universal and singular, and also between the schematism of the general and of the particular. It now appears that the schematic general, when we examine its nature more closely, is of the character of an unquantified universal meaning used hypothetically. The judgment, " whales are mammals," so far as it is schematic— that is, meaning " whales are mammals, are they not ? "—is a schematism of the general term " mammals " ; and so far as it is universal—meaning " whales have the marks of mammals " —it is unquantified. A clearer instance is that given above— " virtue is praiseworthy." So far as there is any doubt of the praiseworthiness of virtue it is a schematic general ; but in that respect in which it is universal, it is unquantified. In meanings of this sort, however, the relation of schematism to quantification comes out ; the relation, namely, whereby schematism of the particular involves quantification. To schematize particulars, as in "some coins are silver," "are coins ever pewter ? " " a few coins are gold," " this coin is gold, silver or copper," is at once to quantify the judgment. This is only to say that a schematic particular is always of the character of a disjunction.

§ 4. INTERROGATIVE JUDGMENTS

20. The attitude of belief in what is indeterminate within presuppositions may become itself a matter of explicit statement. **Interrogation.** Of course, this may take the form of a direct statement of belief or of doubt. Doubt is expressed in the judgments of possibility already described ; ignorance is expressed by its own direct assertion. Yet in the interrogative, ignorance and doubt have a further form of expression which brings the judgment of ignorance within the schematic employment of a positive subject-matter. In the interrogative judgment there is not simply a statement of a subject-matter as an *ignotum*, as in " what metal this coin is I do not know " ; there is besides a series of meanings in which a relative indeterminateness is schematically embodied. All the schematic or disjunctive meanings of the logical mode may be interrogatively rendered. The two great classes of such meanings are those called above " schematism of the general " and " schematism of the particular." For instance, in the question, " what is this ? " or " are whales fish ? " the general class meaning is indeterminate, and the predicate, used schematically, is varied all the way from the suggestion of a single class, as in " are not whales fish ? " through

explicit disjunctions, such as " are whales fish or mammals ? " to the cases of meanings barely suggested or intended, as in " what sort of creatures are whales ? "

If we arrange such judgments in the order of their respective quantities as embodying belief from high probability to mere possibility we have this series :—

(1) " The whale (that is the whole class) is a fish, is it not ? " —corresponding to the quantity of high probability expressed by " most," in " most marine animals are fish."

(2) " Is the whale a fish ? " corresponding to the quantity " as likely as not " expressed by " some."

(3) " The whale is not a fish, is it ? " corresponding to the quantity of probability expressed by " few."

(4) " What sort of a creature is the whale ? " corresponding to the quantity of mere possibility.

Similarly, the interrogative may be the embodiment of the schematism of the particular ; and this may vary from the suggestion of a single possibility, as in " is not this coin silver ? "— through various disjunctions, as in " is this coin silver or gold ? "— to a vague suggestion of a predicate, as in " what metal is this coin—copper ? "

If again we arrange these meanings in the order of their respective quantities, as embodying belief, we have the following :—

(1) " This coin is silver, isn't it ? "—high probability.

(2) " Is this coin silver ? "—as likely as not.

(3) " This coin is not silver, is it ? "—improbability.

(4) " What metal is this coin—pewter ? "—possibility.

The meaning that is purest as logical interrogation is that in which there is simply a given general class, and no further information. The question seeks more definition. " A light ! what is it ? " is such a meaning.

The essential movement of logical interrogation, therefore, is that of schematism. Its only possible interpretation is from **Schematism.** the point of view of belief *determined upon* a more or less *indeterminate* subject-matter. It therefore falls quite naturally within the series of interpretations which our present mode of treatment makes possible. It is, when logical at all, an attitude toward a logical subject-matter ; that is, towards a subject matter already logically determined with its own presupposition. In cases in which such logical determination of the subject-matter is not mature, the attitude is one of the

simple schematism of the prelogical modes. The question
mark which we may discern—assuming Darwin's authority for
the facts of the figure!—in the rigid horizontal tail of the dog
as he approaches an unfamiliar rival that is also a possible
ally, is the legitimate forerunner of man's developed logical and
linguistic query, "is the stranger enemy or friend?" To the
dog there is problematical dog-meaning ; to the man there is the
logical disjunction, "friend or foe, which?" The instrumental
function of interrogation as "proposal," in its linguistic and
social rôles, is given further treatment below (chap. vi. §§ 4 ff.).

§ 5.   Quantification of the Predicate

21. It follows also that we are in sight of another topic which
has had more or less cursory and unsatisfactory discussion since
The Predi- Hamilton's treatment of it ; the topic of the quanti-
cate is fication of the predicate. Do we ever mean by the
statement, for example, "some men are black," anything
definite or determinate as to how many black things are men?
The series of quantitative indications "some," "most," "few,"
"one," etc., are actually used to qualify the subject ; how are
those meanings expressed in which the intent is to qualify the
predicate by a similar series of determinations as respects
quantity ?

We do not say "some men are some black things" ; what
we do say is "some black things are men." But in this the term
not usually men has lost its quantitative mark, and we now have
Quantified. to ask about it as predicate the same question that we
asked about black things when that term was predicate. There
are here two interesting questions involved. First, why it is
that it is the subject and not the predicate that is verbally
quantified, and second, why it is that both are not quantified.
Why is it that we do not usually say either "most crows are
some black things," or "crows are some black things."

22. The answer to the first question is found, I think, in the
fact that quantification is a means of embodying a disjunction,
The Sub- and disjunction is a means of the development of
ject is the knowledge through schematism. The intention of
Developing
Meaning. the judgment, "some coins are silver," is the disjunction between cases of coins of different metals. Now such
a disjunction can be stated only by the use of a subject-matter
which is determinate as far as possible, not itself also indeterminate. This requires the quantification of the subject. The

progress of the meaning, that is, is one in determination beyond that already reached ; this is possible only by the disjunctive use of the determination that is already reached, expressed by the quantitative sign attached to the subject.

Further, the choice of subject-matter furthers the experimental development of meaning. If it be the interest or purpose to

It is made Schematic

develop what has heretofore, let us say, been the predicate term, then its relative determinateness and quantity must be taken as point of departure for a new act of schematic rendering of it. This brings about the reversal of the terms. The predicate becomes subject just by the need of developing its meaning through a disjunction in which a profitable schematism is secured.

This is seen in all vital and profitable intercourse. If I say to you "some men are black," it does not advance my know-

in Intercourse.

ledge for you to reply "some black things are men." On the contrary, the motive of assertion is to secure your acceptance or modification of my statement by a judgment which accepts my disjunctive meaning or alters the quantity of my subject term. You say, " yes, they are," or " yes, a few," or " yes, most in this community "—all aiding my knowledge as to the subject-matter selected and made schematic in my original statement. If, on the contrary, the subject taken for statement had been " black things," then that would have been made schematic subject, and the further determination secured by working out the disjunction would have attached to that.

23. In regard to the second question—that as to why both subject and predicate are not quantified—again the answer is

To quantify Predicate is unfruitful,

that this would not be profitable, since it would schematise both terms and leave no fixed meaning with reference to which further determination could be secured. If, for example, I say " some men are some whites," the entire meaning could be advanced in either of the two ways mentioned already ; through the schematic use of " men," in which case the disjunctive force of " whites " is not utilized, or by the schematic use of whites (by making it subject) in which case the disjunctive force of " men " is not utilized. The only further way that profit could accrue would be by an accretion of meaning to advance the determination of both the " some " quantities at once ; as in the judgment, " most men are few whites." This would involve the actual discovery of two new things at once, the greater relative fewness of men among the white things, and the greater relative someness of whites among men. This is of course possible, but it is very unlikely. Such a doubly quantified subject-matter would serve to distract attention, dissipate interest, and render the process of schematism by disjunction ineffective. It would really require the carrying on of two different processes of experimentation at once.

24. It is evident, however, that what has just been said applies primarily to the schematism of the particular, that is, to

but possible. the case in which the disjunction arises in the interpretation of a single case as under a general meaning. " Some coins are silver " raises the disjunction between " silver " and " some other metal " for the determination of any given coin. It is here that quantification discloses the disjunction upon which the schematic process proceeds. If we ask the question as to the quantification of the predicate in judgments which schematise the general, there arises a somewhat different problem.

For example, let us take the judgment, " these counters are coins or toys." Here there is a disjunction between the two

It occurs in general meanings, " coins " and " toys," with which
Schematism the given objects are experimentally charged. The
of the subject is unquantified ; its range or extension is
General. not in question nor is its further determination in quantity intended. What is stated is true of one, some, or all the counters. The entire intent of the disjunction is to divide the extension into two alternative and possible classes, " coins " and " toys." There is no escape from the conclusion, therefore, *that the predicate is quantified*. It is equivalent to saying " some of one of these classes are identical with these counters." It is the intent of a judgment that schematizes the general class to quantify the sphere in which the presupposition of belief functions. It seems to be as plainly understood as if the " some " were actually expressed. I say, " they are most likely coins," meaning " among coins there are many such objects " ; or, " they are hardly coins," meaning " among coins there are few such objects while among toys there are many." Note the difference between " some of these objects are coins," and " these objects may be coins " ; one quantifies the subject, the other the predicate.[1]

---

[1] It may be said in reply to this, that " A is most likely B " is equivalent to " most A's are B's." And no doubt that is true when there is no alternative class of C's in mind. But when such alternation is in mind,

25. Our general conclusion, then, is that the *schematism of the particular* involves the quantification of the subject in all its modes, including the quantified universal and singular; while the *schematism of the general* involves the quantification of the predicate,[1] joined with a subject that is unquantified even though it be in the form of a universal or a singular.[2]

§ 6. LOGICAL QUANTITY AND EXISTENCE

It is not my purpose to discuss the exact sort of presupposition that attaches to each quantity of judgment; but one of the major controversies in the topic may be cited and briefly passed upon.[3]

26. It is argued that the universal judgment, "all men are mortal," does not carry the implication that there are such things as men; the universe of discourse simply supporting the relation asserted between man and mortality. On the other hand, the particular judgment, "some men are mortal," is said

---

the intent is not to say how many A's are B's; but to say that there are relatively more B's than C's that are A's; that is, that the whole class in which all A's are included is larger than the B class, and its extent and character comprise other cases: in this case toys as well as coins. The general class, therefore, the predicate, is quantified in respect to the disjunction between coins and toys.

[1] On the sense in which negation quantifies the predicate, see chap. viii. § 5. sect. ix.

[2] We are not concerned to ask how far these results may be utilized by formal logic in the way of supplementing its traditional moods and figures, though something might be said. It may illustrate the possibilities of the case, indeed, to present the following syllogism, made up of particular judgments in both premises and conclusion, which is valid though not recognized in the usual treatment of quantity. If we allow " most mammals are terrestrial," it does not follow that " all " are or are not " terrestrial." If, however, we also allow, " some mammals are aquatic," we then have premises for a valid conclusion which is also particular. The syllogism then is:—

Some mammals are aquatic.

Most mammals are terrestrial.

∴ Few mammals are aquatic.

Such a syllogism enlarges our information, and the conclusion is reached by the union of the two premises. It is a common and fruitful mode of argumentation in inductive science, and has its exact formulation in the theory of probability, which assigns to " most " and " few " exact numerical values.

[3] See Keynes, *Formal Logic*, 2 ed., § 119. and Ladd Franklin in the writer's *Dict. of Philos.*, art. " Proposition." III.

to imply the existence of men, since it requires the inspection of some men to justify the assertion. A good [1] case is that of Dr. Ladd Franklin : " all Philadelphia lawyers are liars ". This, it is said, allows the meaning, " there are no lawyers in Philadelphia," while " some . . . are liars " does not.

This position cannot be maintained in this form, I think. The presupposition is that of a control-coefficient of the sphere in which the relation asserted holds. Now we do not change this coefficient, nor do we presuppose it in different senses, in the two " quantities " of judgment expressed by " some " and " all." In " all Philadelphia lawyers are liars," I mean, " presupposing such men " ; and in " some Philadelphia lawyers are liars," I mean " some " of the " all " of the same presupposition. The apparent difference of implication in the two judgments arises by reason of an altogether different psychic movement, one spoken of on an earlier page. The universal form may be used for a *schematism of the general meaning*, of which the final control is *still to be determined* ; it is this shading of meaning that seems to allow—and often does allow—the absence of " real " implication, because in this the subject is not quantified. This form quantifies the predicate, and opens the control-sphere to a disjunction of modes of existence. The particular judgment, on the other hand, by its limitation of the assertion to " some," is problematical only of the particular ; the general meaning is categorical and not of merely schematic and alternative import. The particular of necessity presupposes a control which establishes a form of real existence.

Existence is presupposed in Quantified Judgments.

We may say, therefore, that all quantified judgments do in the same sense have a presupposition of existence ; but that schematic universals do not, because they are not quantified. The exact parity of all quantified statements is seen as soon as we take cases in which the ambiguity as between problematical and assertorial general meaning is removed, as in such judgments as " virtue," or " these acts of virtue," or " this act of virtue is praiseworthy." In all of these, the actual realization of any such act is not presupposed.

This may be generalized in the statement that there are no specific differences of implication of existence attaching to the

---

[1] Good, that is in the sense of being favourable to the view in question, since it is based on an enumeration of actual instances.

different quantities of judgment ; the apparent exceptions are unquantified. Even the singular judgment has no constant presupposition ; it also may be unquantified. When the singularity is of the " imported " or selective type, fulfilling a special interest, it is existential, as is true also of universal selective judgments. " John Anderson is my jo John " and " I shall eat all the oranges " are both existential in their presupposition, and equally so ; because both express selective and appreciative meaning. But a singular that is " essentially " so, a single item of recognition, may exist or not. The inn-keeper who says, " the guest in No. 10 is drunk," is no more nor less a liar if there be no guest in No. 10, than is the one who says, " some of the guests in my hotel are drunk," or the other who says " all the guests in my hotel are drunk," when there are no guests in any of the hotels. Lacking other grounds of belief, we should be equally deceived by each of the three statements.[1]

It does not differ with Quantities.

The extreme statement of the position that I am now criticizing is one that follows quite logically from the view that the presuppositions are different for different quantities ; namely, the statement that all existential judgments are in their import particular. It is mistaken, I think, because it makes particularity, and individuation as particular, the test of existence. Why may not all of a class exist ?—and why may not such a meaning be verbally expressed ? The proper mark of distinction is quantification, not particularity. All judgments whose subjects are quantified presuppose the existence of their subjects— that is the correct formula and the adequate doctrine. To ask " how many " is to presuppose " some." [2]

---

[1] That it is a matter of quantification appears from the strengthening of the existence meaning when a real disjunction is introduced. If the hotel-keeper wants to be absolutely sure that the emptiness of his house will not be suspected, he should say " some of the men are drunk "— for why should he except female guests if there are none ? It would be a much more effective " bluff " for a boy who had no marbles to say " all my glass marbles are in my pocket," than " all my marbles are in my pocket."

The general question of the " existence import " of propositions is treated below, chap. ix. § 2.

[2] This is consistent with the distinction sometimes made between " real " and " enumerative " universality in logic. " Real " universality attaches to what I have called above the " unquantified universal."

Chapter V

CONTINGENT MEANING WITH POSTULATION

§ 1. POSTULATION AND IMPLICATION

1. The distinction already proposed between the Presupposition and the Postulate will be readily recalled. In tracing out the modes of quantitative judgment, as embodying disjunction, we have raised as well, in a preliminary way, the question of "postulation." The schematic assumption of the general class, which issues in a quantified predicate, implies a certain alternation of control modes. But the character by which we have distinguished the postulate from the presupposition is that in the former the control has not yet hardened into a presupposition but remains, in some degree, problematical and subject to assumption. Whatever the relations may be which are asserted in the subject-matter of a judgment, this subject-matter may be quantified in its general aspect alone, that is, in its predicate, and in interpreting such a meaning the process of schematism becomes one by which an alternation arises between different control modes. For example, the judgment "virtue is praiseworthy," may allow of such a schematic reading. The meaning may be, " in whatever sphere virtue may exist, or wherever an act may be depicted which is virtuous, the relation between this virtue or this act and praiseworthiness is to be recognized." In short, we may *postulate any control we please*, life, fiction, humour, semblance, it matters not ; *in any postulated sphere*, " virtue is praiseworthy." This is true of meanings of the " contingent " type, as " if *A* then *B*," or " *B* if *A*," or simply " *AB*." The contingent relation is one of logical dependence within the given or assumed control.

The difference between this case and that treated already as disjunction is noteworthy and interesting. The contingent meaning postulates a control, the disjunctive presupposes it. The former means " both A and B wherever either A or B may be found " (whatever sphere is *postulated*) ; the latter means " A or B, one or the other, whichever is found " (in the sphere *presupposed*).

The force of postulation is not removed from a whole of implication when there is a disjunction within it. In the judgment A or B is C, such a whole is set up as true whatever sphere may be postulated for C.

2. Instances may be given, however, to illustrate a further and rather subtle distinction, which has to be made in the interest of clearness. This distinction is that between " schematism of the general " as discussed in the earlier chapter,[1] and postulation, as now defined.

The schematism of the general, as in the judgment, " these articles may be pennies " may be interpreted as suggesting further determination of the general with reference to the particulars. It does not raise any question as to the sphere of existence of the general in its appropriate control. On the other hand, such a judgment as " anything that cuts is a knife " is true, in whatever sphere such a relation may be supposed to occur. In the latter case, there is room for postulation, the sphere is not fixed and presupposed, it may be this or that.

In short, not only are there the two instances of logical schematism cited in the discussion above, there is another. There are first, the case of the indeterminate *particular*, the motive of the judgment being the assignment of a general class to its particular cases ; and second, the case of the indeterminate *general*, the motive being the discovery of the class to which given cases belong ; and third, the case of indeterminate *existence or control*, the motive being to find the sphere in which the general-particular meaning itself gets its fulfilment. *To this last alone is the term " postulation " to be applied.*

A third case of Schematism

3. When we look at the difference between the last two cases a little more closely, we find in it the root of a distinction of great

---

[1] Chap. iv. § 2, of this volume. In actual life, the mind stands ready to construe a developing meaning in whichever way the schematism may prove fruitful. For example, the meaning " this article may be a penny " motives the further scrutiny of the coin, which may result either in the identification of the case as a familiar " penny," or in the widening of the " penny," meaning to include an unfamiliar coin.

importance in theory of knowledge and logic—that between
" postulation " and " logical implication."

The ground of the difference is a very fundamental one.   The
postulate is in its nature an assumption as to the final reading
of that control which is later on called " reality."   Implication,
on the contrary, is the system of related or contingent meanings,[1]
taken for itself, apart from the assumption of a sphere in which
Implication it may be found to hold.   We are to see later on what
a body of   the nature and limits of implication are in this sense ;
Contingent
Meaning.   here we may simply point out the relation of these
two modes of meaning to each other.

§ 2.   The Presupposition of Belief—an Implication

4. The place of " presupposition " proper, considered as an
aspect of meaning, with reference to implication and postulation,
may now be pointed out.   It illustrates the distinction of the two
Control may be last-named meanings, for the control which a system of
"Implicated." relations presupposes is, as will appear fully later on,
part of its body of implications.   If I say " mermaids are green,"
I presuppose the sphere in which mermaids are to be looked for ;
and this is an implication of fact about mermaids.   It may rest
in the background, as presupposition of my belief in talking about
mermaids, or it may be brought out in the existential statement
" mermaids are found in the Atlantic."   *So all presuppositions
are of the nature of implications.*   They are part of the intent of
the judgment, of its subject-matter ; they may themselves be
taken up and made subject-matter in appropriate existential
statements.   But as long as the sphere of existence is still in
question, still problematical, so long the postulate suffices to
give a schematic or assumptive control to the subject-matter.
I add " if mermaids exist," or " postulating a sphere of existence
for mermaids," or " wherever we find mermaids "—" they are
green."   It then becomes clear that judgments may be construed
either as *implicating or as postulating*, as *presupposing or as
assuming*, a control sphere.   A further intent of question then,
it is plain, may attach to judgments called " conditional," and
meanings called " contingent " : the question as to the control
postulated or assumed.

Let us look at the following examples.   In the judgment
" if it rain, you will get wet," I mean that your getting wet from

[1] The characters of contingent meaning as implication are summed up
in chap. xi. § 3, below.

this cause implies the existence of a world of rain which is the "presupposition" of my statement. The relation is asserted subject to this given presupposition of existence. But suppose I hear the same judgment at the theatre. I now say the scene is " realistic " ; the characters actually look wet. But the world **Conditional** of rain is now a postulate of the play. The related **Meaning** meaning " rain-wet " indeed remains for my thought **two-fold :** what it was before. But the word " if " may serve to convey a two-fold meaning. It serves to convey an implication, a presupposition of real existence ; but it also serves merely to suggest a relation, the control being left for further postulation or assumption.

5. This two-fold reference of a conditional or hypothetical[1] statement is, I think, peculiar to it, and constitutes it a most pregnant form with reference to the divergence of the two types of meaning now in question. It may be put in this way : the conditional asserts a relationship of terms within a whole of subject-matter ; but in so doing it may leave problematical or schematic the sphere or world in which the related whole is to be found. The content is one of contingency or dependence, an implication ; but the control may be left subject to postulation. Of course, the whole may be judged with a definite presupposition, and that presupposition is then not itself hypothetical ; on the contrary, it is then capable of being brought out in an existential statement which is in form not hypothetical but categorical.

In a word in the presupposition we have *the acknowledgment of the contingent* as holding somewhere, while in the postulate we have *contingent acknowledgment* of what may hold somewhere.

In postulation, therefore, the mode of existence is still undetermined. We have found an intimation of this already in the discovery that universal assertorial judgments may be **Postulation is** unquantified. As unquantified, they have the force **of Existence** not of disjunctive but of contingent meanings. The judgment " virtuous acts are praiseworthy " has the force, not of " some virtue is praiseworthy," but of " wherever virtuous acts occur, they are praiseworthy." That is, such a universal statement is made not with the implication of uncertain quantity within a given existence, but with the postulation of a sphere of existence for a given relation. The full meaning of the

[1] In the sense of the " hypothetical proposition " of formal logic.

hypothetical " If *A* then *B*," is " *A* is *AB*, if there is any." The
first clause " *A* is *AB* " shows implication ; the second, " if there
is any," shows the further reach of postulation.

§ 3.   The Postulate a Selective Meaning

6. The sort of " reality " or existence postulated in this case
or that depends, of course, on the sort of objective subject-matter
set up.   Postulation is not indiscriminate nor capricious.   It
is an intent which embodies the selective meaning attaching to a
content and suggests a further mode of assumptive interpretation.
All that we have found out in our earlier discussions of the sort
of meaning called " schematic " may be now recalled.   The
recognitive context is charged with the further meaning which
the fulfilment of our selective interests or purposes require.   It
thus becomes an instrumental and practical device
for furthering belief.   It becomes in the logical mode
the means of carrying on and extending the range of
implication.   As far as it secures results which advance the
system of implications already made out or allow further presuppositions consonant with them, so far it is a fruitful resort
in this mode as in the earlier ones.   Under other than theoretical
interests, it ministers to their proper fulfilment, as in playful or
merely fanciful postulation.   For example, the higher mathematics is riddled with new postulations—new supposed universes
in which different axioms are treated as holding.   For such
postulations to be of value they must be capable of so attaching
themselves to the train of logical implications that they have
a chance of being finally justified as presuppositions.

For example, there may be postulated a space in which parallel
lines meet.   In consequence, a changed set of implications,
resulting from the substitution of this postulation for the usual
plane-space presupposition, are built up, giving interesting
relational constructions.   So long as the postulate is retained—
the proviso that parallel lines meet—any such set of
implications may be said to hold.

But the limits of postulation are overstepped if I go on to
say " parallel lines are praiseworthy."   This postulates a universe
in which some peculiar excellence or worth attaches to parallel
lines.   This admits of no further development, it introduces
what we call below logical " irrelevancy."   The set of implications

Postulation must be relevant.

Examples.

involved in the geometry of space of parallel lines is not affected one way or the other by my choosing to praise parallel lines. The postulation must be of such a character that it may be carried out in the relational system already given as a context of meanings ; so that there is a possibility that, knowledge being what it is, the postulate may be established as a presupposition underlying a similar system. All this is involved in the theory of schematism as we have already developed it in earlier connections.

The relevant postulate is, therefore, more or less remotely a function of the subject-matter to which it attaches ; it is of the nature of the prospective and schematic reading of a present system of knowledge, and anticipates its further development and organization. It is never a sheer guess, never an utterly indeterminate act of assumption ; it is always of the nature of a judgment of possibility, which aims at being resolved into one of probability and finally into one of that conviction in which belief with presuppositions finally comes to rest.

7. Its essential character withal as selective and experimental must not be overlooked. If it were merely an extension of the recognitive or relational context, it would be already established either as an existential predicate or as a presupposition of belief. In fact, it is neither of these. It is that selective and preferential interpretation which seizes an alternative and develops it. Its
It is Experi- attachment therefore to one form of implication rather
mental. than another yields the satisfaction and fulfilment of a selective interest. One individual, having a certain body of interests, finds it reasonable to postulate disembodied spirits to explain a set of mysterious facts. On this postulation he works out a set of implications from the facts. The " vision " you saw must be the " ghost " he saw, the voice of the ghost is the voice of his father, etc. All this is so far forth for him not only the organization of the facts by the postulate—so that he says this hypothesis explains the facts—but it yields to him also the satisfaction of his selective interest in postulating the ghost. The terminus of the selective interest yields also the fulfilment of the theoretical interest of tracking out logical implications.

8. This fulfilment of the two motives in the one object is what we have found also at lower stages of mental development. It is by this union that knowledge is essentially and vitally advanced. Mere recognition would be stationary, its objects bloodless facts, its implications those of a static system of relations,

were it not for the human interest, the selective and restless
Union of prying, that schematizes and postulates ahead of the
Motives in accomplished truths.   It is thus that new possibilities
the result. are developed and brought to the test.   We found
it so in the schematism of mere detail and also in that of larger
class meanings, both arising together in the interpretation of
concrete situations within a given world of presupposition.   We
now see that the further unifying control is to come out of
the same sort of mental procedure.   Given class meanings and
their relational implications, wholes of subject-matter, then there
arises the schematism of the further union of classes in con-
trol-modes, for the more inclusive interpretation of experience.
What, is finally asked, is the control that fully allows and develops
all the implications of all sets of truths, together with all selective meanings ?   This inquiry leads on to the postulation of
" principles " by the ontologist.

Chapter VI[1]

THE DEVELOPMENT OF LOGICAL MEANING : PREDICATION AND INTERCOURSE

§ 1. THE DETERMINATION OF THOUGHT IN A SYSTEM

1. The foregoing description of logical meaning from the point of view of the belief embodied in the various forms of **The Motives give** judgment, leads naturally on to the inquiry as to its development. We have seen, in our broad survey of the genesis of the logical mode, certain motive principles at work for the establishing of logical content or subject matter. It is, of course, the continued action of these motives that carries on the movement, in the logical mode itself, by which its meanings are added to and extended. We may, therefore, in taking up the problem of the development that logical meanings normally undergo, recall to mind the essential movements already recognized.

(1) In the first place, it may be again pointed out that logical meanings constitute a context of thoughts. The prelogical meanings of all sorts, the individuated contents **a Context** established by processes earlier than explicit judgment, are taken up in the organized system of experience which is the objective thought-world of the thinker. It is first of all the thinker's experience, controlled in the inner processes of judgment and acknowledgment, whatever further reference or confirmation it may have as being true to or cognizant of " reality."

(2) In the second place, we may recall the outcome of the discussion of common meanings in the logical mode, to the effect **that is Common,** that all judgments and hence all thought-contexts are common in the sense of being " synnomic " or " appropriate " for the acceptance of all competent judgment

---

[1] A large part of this chapter has been printed as an article, called " Thought and Language," in the *Psychological Review*, May, 1907.

·everywhere. The belief of the individual, as determined in an act of judgment, is for him the expression of the belief of the larger world of personal selves. Apart from the question as to whether other individual thinkers do or do not at the time agree with him, still, in giving his belief, he is constituting a subject-matter to which, by the essential movement involved, others are expected to give their assent. This has been made plain in an earlier passage.

(3) In the third place, again, this common character and meaning of the subject-matter of thought was found to rest genetically and prelogically upon a process that is both social and experimental : the process described in our earlier discussions under the term " secondary conversion." We found that the context of knowledge, considered as a confirmed and established body of data, was in very essential ways due to the recognition and use of the contents of the minds of one's social fellows. Before it is judged, knowledge, as so far common, is syndoxic. All but the original substantive parts of experience—the parts found directly convertible into the hard coin of persisting and recurring fact—is actually set off from the fugitive and private images of fancy, through this secondary and essentially social conversion process. It was in the further development of this motive, it will be remembered also, that the marks of knowledge as general, universal, and even singular were derived. The conclusion that knowledge—in any mode that is not sub-personal and so sub-social[1]—is a " social outcome rather than a private possession ", summed up our results in the matter.

through Social Conversion.

We should expect, as has been said above, that the development of the context of thinking would be by a process continuous with that of its origin ; that is, that accretions to the body of experience would be effected in the way that earlier acquisitions had been made. And this appears necessary when we remember that no material is available at all except that which has passed through these simpler modes. The new thoughts are always also sensations, memories, images or other such meanings thereupon found available in the development of the selective motives by which thoughts as such are constituted. There is, therefore, no extension of the context of thought except as the judgment is further determined upon mean-

It is judged

[1] Even the low-grade knowledge of the perceptual mode is shot through with the quasi-social meaning that we have called " commonness of common function."

ings, by its one characteristic process.[1] This process is, as has been said, both social and experimental. Its social character has been already worked out ; its experimental character, within the social mode of control, is to be treated just below.

(4) Finally, we may point out, in addition to the foregoing, a character of thought which has not as yet been adverted to ; **in Linguistic** one that fixes genetically both the social motive and **Form.** the experimental motive as now put in evidence. It is the *linguistic character* of thought. Thought is a system of predications or assertions, capable of being embodied in a more or less explicit system of symbols for purposes of interpersonal communication. The genetic relation of speech and language to judgment will be found to give striking confirmation of the point of view developed in the consideration of logical meaning, to the effect that judgment is in all cases common or synnomic.

§ 2. THOUGHT AND LANGUAGE

2. The old problem put in the question, " Is thought possible without speech ? " has no real significance except so far as it is **Thought and** set genetically or from the point of view of the com- **Language.** parative origin and development of these two great functions. But from such a point of view it takes on considerable significance. The current theories which deal with the topic from the side of language make out, each from its own class of data, certain plausible positions, which may be stated as introductory to our own treatment of the problem.

3. (1) *The Personal or Dynamic Theory.* This theory is based on the interpretation of " expression." It finds some sort of symbolic **Expression.** representation necessary as soon as the meaning to be expressed *becomes general or abstract*. The symbolism of gesture language, pictographic writing, etc., precedes that of vocal utterance and conventional phonetic written signs. It would seem, indeed, that if expression is to develop from a purely ejaculatory, demonstrative, or other mainly concrete stage to one of general or abstract meaning or import—that is, if it is to express something *imported*, something additional to the bare concrete common content of present experience—there

[1] This it may be remarked omits those apparent extensions which are due to thinking as such, that is to deduction and reasoning : these are treated below as elucidations rather than extensions of the thought context (see chap. xii.).

would have to be a vehicle of a sort intentionally symbolizing this additional meaning. For example, a savage could not respond to or express the meaning " man," *as suggested by but not limited to* " this man," except through the use of some sign of this further intent. Theoretically, of course, any sort of conventionalized indication—act, posture, sound—might have been selected for this function in the processes of development ; but we find the function in which it has been embodied to be speech. Speech issues in a system of articulate vocal symbols, together with the special development of the same symbolism embodied in writing. So much may be said on the personal side ; the side of personal expression as such.

For the purposes of linguistic theory, this may be called the " personal " or " dynamic " point of view. It recognizes the fact that the person is the source of new accretions of social meaning, and the dynamic movement of such meaning is made possible only as the results of personal thought find adequate and appropriate expression. It considers language as a live thing, flexible in its growth with the development of thought, divergent and varying in its comparative systems of symbolism. It gives a comparative philology, and aims at the genetic solution of linguistic problems in terms of psychological meanings.

Dynamic view of Language.

Evidently, therefore, this point of view is in its own province most important. But the further question as to the conservation, the conventionalizing—in the large sense, the socializing—of meanings, whereby they show themselves more than personal, and in an important sense also less than personal, is equally urgent. This question may be put sharply thus : how can a system of symbols serving as expression of a dynamic movement of personal thought, also serve as the embodiment of established and conventionalized social meaning ?

This inquiry has direct enforcement from the side of the psychology of what is called " intercourse." There is no purely " personal " intercourse ; all intercourse is in its constitution inter-personal. Its intent is to be understood as well as to find expression. It becomes necessary to enlarge the theory of expression to make its unit one of *common meaning*. The lowest functional term of expression is in some crude sense " intercourse "—the development of common meaning. Turning therefore to the theories of language reached from the social side, we find in them a second type.

Intercourse involves

4. (2) *The Social or Static Theory.* The theory of common symbolic meaning would seem not to find its problem in the first instance in personal expression. Its problem is not how personal meaning could become common in its expression, but how a conventionally common meaning could be the vehicle of genuine personal experience. Would not any system of symbolic meanings become, just by the rigidity and static character that its social fixity would impart, unavailable for personal purposes?

Indeed, the function of language, we are told by the static theorists, does not extend to the expression of what is personal as such. It comes to reflect personal interest only **Common** by being first of all conventional and common. The **meanings.** demand of intercourse is for a symbolism to express meanings already understood and accepted. It is only by social generalization that a meaning can become eligible for linguistic embodiment at all. Witness the fact that feeling and impulse, so far as they are not thrown into descriptive form as knowledge, cannot be given common linguistic rendering. Music may be cited : what does music express? Only so far as a meaning has taken on a form that gives it currency in society, can it be rendered in intelligible speech.

Upon this type of theory a view is based which makes language a static, stereotyped system of forms. The classics, being no **Static** longer living and growing but dead, offer the models **Theory.** of literary form. Any current modes of speech and language that do not fit into these models, fall so far short of the instrumental adequacy that facile social intercourse demands.

5. While stating these two types of theory in this extreme contrasted way, I do not mean that advocates of them in just **Two lines** this form are to be found ; but the antithesis presents **of Research.** a fair contrast of attitude and spirit. Especially does it appear in the method of research that the schools respectively adopt. The men who look upon language statically are critical rather than genetic in their method. They study types rather than comparative forms. Given the perfect models in which the human thought movements have once embodied themselves, say in classical Greek, and philology becomes the criticism and application of these models. Essential variations in model, reflecting racial and temperamental character and essential differences in intent and spirit in the actual development of cultural meaning—resulting in a variety of comparative modes maturing in

common—all this they find it difficult to take interest in. The other school, on the contrary, having in view just the final point of origin and departure of all social meaning, the thoughts of the individual, make just such comparative variations all-important.

6. The line of solution would seem to lie in the distinction already made in the remarks on expression : the distinction **Intent both** between meaning on the one hand that is singular **Dynamic** and in some sense private, and meaning on the other **and Static.** hand that is general and universal. Just as there is a sphere of personal experience that is ineligible to common and symbolic expression, so there is a sphere of common and public experience that is ineligible to strictly private uses. In their range, in short, personal meanings and social meanings greatly overlap but do not coincide. Consequently, there is the requirement all the way along that the symbols of conventional expression be as far as possible flexible, in order to embody the accretions to personal experience ; and on the other hand, that they be fixed enough to embody the habitual and conventionalized meanings of historical and common experience. This requirement is embodied in the view, now fast gaining ground, that language is a growing organic thing, relatively satisfactory for the epoch and the group ; but by no means containing or requiring a system of fixed and stereotyped meanings.

Moreover the development of the appreciative or aesthetic consciousness is, all the while, working out new systems of symbolism for the more recondite meanings of personal intent and ideal fulfilment. The arts are such semi-socialized and in turn socializing systems of symbolic meaning. Their rôle is seen, in connection with the more conventional symbolism of language, in the various forms of conscious literary art. These *just by being acceptable as art*, are also more adequate as embodiments of personal meaning.

7. These two points of view may serve to guide our further thought. On the one hand, we must find the process whereby **Both meet in** personal experience may be rendered in the symbolism of common intercourse ; and on the other hand the process whereby the same symbolism, although of necessity fed by the progress of personal experience,[1] may nevertheless

---

[1] This states in a different way, and in so far reinforces, the position maintained in another place, that the content of social meaning must be cognitive, must be knowledge, since only cognitions are general and common (see *Soc. and Eth. Interps.*, chap. xii.).

preserve and embody the fruits of social and historical tradition.

If we assume, as a matter of fact, that the requirements of such a system of symbolic meanings are normally met in their **Language.** linguistic embodiment, we have then to analyse further the situation in which such meanings are in vital and effective use ; and the modes of intercourse that embody such developing meanings will also interest us from the point of view of the genetic progress of thought.

§ 3. THOUGHT AS LINGUISTIC MODE

8. We should expect to find, if our earlier positions are well taken, that thought, logical meaning of whatever grade, would take on a linguistic mode, an actual social form. Both of the great characters of logical meaning *require it.*

One of them has already been seen to be effective in the sketch just given of the two great points of view current in the theory **Synnomic** of language ; although expressing personal meaning, **meaning.** language must still be socially organized. This hits upon just the relation of the personal or private to the common strain in all logical meaning. The character of logical meaning as being at once personally judged true, and also acknowledged as appropriate for common acceptance—this is just the character we have found. It is denominated synnomic. The transition from pre-judgmental to judgmental meaning is just that from knowledge which has social confirmation to that which gets along without it. The meanings utilized for judgment are those already developed in their presuppositions and implications through the confirmations of social intercourse. Thus the personal judgment, trained in the methods of social rendering, and disciplined by the interaction of its social world, projects its content into that world again. In other words, the platform for all movement into the assertion of individual judgment—the level from which new experience is utilized—is *already and always socialized* ; and it is just this movement that we find reflected in the actual result as the sense of the "appropriateness " or synnomic character of the meaning rendered.

This requirement, signalized as the common or synnomic character of the linguistic embodiment of thought, may be called **as Common** the "habit " aspect—the funded, conserving, retro- **or Habitual.** spective, general side of meaning in the logical mode. Evidently it is this that the static theorists of language have in mind. Language must embody meanings that are estab-

L

lished and common. They are personally available only so far
as the individual can use this kind of meaning, that is so far as
his meaning *is already synnomic*. If our theory, however, discovers that all personal judgment embodies such meanings, then
we may simply say that this function, language, *is the normal
and appropriate embodiment of individual judgment no less than
of social meaning.* It is the vehicle by which *social stuff is personally rendered.*

9. The other aspect, however, is equally real. It may in
contrast be called the " accommodation " side—the side of
It is also   growth, accretion, development of personal meaning
Personal,   through the resort to language as instrument and
means. Of course, it is evident that both the general and the
schematic, the retrospective and the prospective, the belief and
the doubt, the assertion and the assumption, must be capable of
characteristic linguistic embodiment.

It is upon this requirement that we find the dynamic theories
of language dwelling in turn. They recognize the fact that
and Dynamic.   thought would be killed, both as personal instrument
           and also as representing social values, if its vehicle
were stereotyped and unchanging. The symbolism of language
must reflect the mode of development and growth peculiar to
the progress of thought.

Now the development of thought, as we are to see in more
detail, is by a method essentially of trial and error, of experimen-
Through   tation, of *the use of meanings as worth more than they
Schematism   are as yet recognized to be worth.* The individual must
use his old thoughts, his established knowledges, his grounded
judgments, for the embodiment of his new inventive constructions. He erects his thought as we say " schematically "—in
logical terms, problematically, conditionally, disjunctively—
projecting into the world an opinion still personal to himself, as if
it were true. *Thus all discovery proceeds.* But this is, from the
linguistic point of view, still to use the current language ; still
to work by meanings already embodied in social and conventional
usage. And the result, what of that ?

10. The result is now the essential thing. By this experimentation both thought and language are together advanced.
Language   Suppose the new meaning is not confirmed in the
and thought   way suggested, the old terms do not fully define and
are advanced. limit the connotation that actual trial justifies. Language then grows to fulfil the demand of the developing thought.

It is accomplished, it is plain, by no situation that compels language to be private *or* public *instead of both.* As tentatively suggested the meaning is rendered *as if common,* in common speech ; the new form it takes on, while now become common as meaning, is still the individual's personal thought as well. Language grows, therefore, just as thought does, *by never losing its synnomic or dual reference : its meaning is both personal and social.*

11. As soon as we recognize these two essential motives in the development of thought, a profound meaning is given to the

Conclusions.

question of the relation of language to thought. It is not one of our principal topics : and only so much as directly concerns our present interest may be ventured upon. But there are certain statements whose truth now appears, and which bring from the side of language direct confirmation of our view of the origin and nature of synnomic or judgmental meanings.

(1) It would appear that language is the instrument of social habit, in the sense that it conserves and stores up as a social

Language embodies Social Habit.

heritage the accretions to common meaning. And this appears not simply as a fact, but by reason of the principle that *only in language* are the available elements of personal experience and meaning socially stored and rendered continuously available. It is the register of tradition, the record of racial* conquest, the deposit of all the gains made by the genius of individuals. In terms of our earlier discussion, the social " copy-system " thus established reflects the judgmental processes of the race ; and in turn becomes the training school of the judgment of new generations. Not indeed would I say that linguistic models and linguistic study as such have any such pedagogical importance ; that is just the fallacy of our present-day instruction, that makes a fetish of language as such. But every day linguistic intercourse, *language performing its vital rôle,* is thus important. Linguistic study is instrumental, a means to an end ; the end being admission to the storehouse of meanings and models of racial judgment, which literature in all its forms serves to mediate. When language is made an end—except of course in that department of research in which language is itself the content—it becomes a form that is eviscerated of its filling and meaning, much as thought is eviscerated of its content and so loses its meaning also when we leave out of account the essential movements of personal belief.

(2) In speech, the function by which the content of language is actively rendered and interpreted, the accommodation side of thinking is given its chance.   Most of the training of the self, whereby the vagaries of personal reaction to fact and image are reduced to the funded basis of sound judgment, comes through the use of speech.   When the child speaks, he lays before the world his suggestion for a general and common meaning ;   the reception it gets confirms or refutes him.   In either case he is instructed.   His next venture is now from a platform of knowledge on which the newer item is more nearly that which is convertible into the common coin of effective intercourse.   The point to notice here is not so much the exact mechanism of the exchange—secondary conversion—by which this gain is made, as the training in judgment that the constant use of it affords.   In each case, effective judgment is the common judgment ;   and there grows up the ability to make such judgment effective without the actual appeal.   This has been made plain already ;   here the object is to point out that it is secured by the development of a function *whose rise is directly ad hoc—* directly for the social experimentation by which growth in personal competence is advanced as well—*the function of speech.*[1]

Social Accommodation by Speech.

In language, therefore, to sum up the foregoing, we have the tangible—the actual and historical—instrument of the development and conservation of psychic meaning.   It is the material evidence and proof of *the concurrence of social and personal judgment.*   In it synnomic meaning, judged as " appropriate," becomes " social " meaning, held as socially generalized and acknowledged.   The dictionary is the register of private judgment become social.   Written language, literature, is its institutional and traditional side ;   speech is the schematic and personal rendering of its intent, its accommodative side.[2]

[1] The first and more superficial criticism of the reader here, as elsewhere in these genetic discussions, is one which raises the question as to whether speech is the only function by which this is secured.   We are asked whether a child who is deaf and dumb does not become a competent thinker.   Certainly he does, in this measure or that, according to the case, which is only to say that the rôle normally played by speech may on occasion be taken up in a less effective way by some other functions having a content capable of the symbolic reading that usually attaches to language.

[2] This confirms the position taken in the work *Social and Eth. Interps.*, in which the method of social organization is found to be imitation ;   for not only is language the embodiment of generalized cognitive content ;   it is also, as functional in speech, imitative through and through in its

§ 4. The Development of Thought through Intercourse : Predication

12. The view of thought now briefly indicated justifies certain positions regarding the form in which the import of an item of
Intercourse knowledge may be expressed when embodied in such
as "Elucida- a vehicle as language. On the surface it appears that
tion." the entire import of such an item varies with the setting in which it is developing. The interest at work may be of this or that sort according as this or that group of meanings, ordinarily called a " topic," is being pursued. This in turn varies with all the dispositional or other tendencies or motives coming to consciousness in the individual. The content itself, so considered as a subject-matter of thought, has relations, discovered or not discovered, in a larger whole of meaning. For example, the item horse may have very different shadings of meaning developed according as I am conversing with a horseman, a naturalist, a dealer, or a veterinary surgeon. In each case only those ramifications of intent that are relevant to the common interest of the parties to the situation are elucidated and further advanced. If we consider that phase of the situation that concerns the

method of learning and propagation. It is only through an imitative *method* that a generalized common *content* can arise.

This view enables us to see that language is instrumental to the development of both personal and social meanings. What linguisitic theory needs, in fact, is better psychology : a psychology that shows the artificiality of the dualism of private and social meaning that the opposed theories assume. If it were true that there were no concurrence—no identity—between the movement of individual thought and that conventionalized in language, then not only would a theory of language be impossible—language itself would be impossible as well.

This is one of the topics in which a view of judgment that justifies the essentially common character of its meaning renders service in a field of more remote interest. If the demonstration of the social genesis of the individual's judgment be sound, philology will have a basis for the solution of one of its great problems.

Another fact known to psychologists and philologists alike has an interesting value in the light of our discussion : the fact of " internal speech." Recent investigation shows that it is not a mere by-product —our having words " in our minds " and " on our lips," when engaged in silent thought, reading, etc. (cf. *Mental Development*, chap. xiv.). It is rather the incipient stirring up of those social and symbolic equivalents of thought, that vocal rendering employs. The normal development of thought and speech going on together, the functional processes are not separable. The intended psychic meaning can only come up when its symbolic vehicle is incipiently stirred up with it.

person for whom a set of relationships is already established
as a whole of subject-matter, then the form of linguistic expression he employs is motived by the interest of what we may call
" elucidation." You *elucidate* to me the fuller import of what
you understand. The motive to intercourse on his part is in
this case not discovery, not the extension of the system of meanings, but the imparting of it to another—literally its *elucidation*
to one who has not yet, it may be, fully thought it out under the
same set of relevant interests.

13. On the other hand, supposing the interests to remain
the same, the attitude embodied in the use of the term, sentence,
or other linguistic unit, may be not elucidation but " discovery,"
not teaching but learning. And, of course, on the surface this
may seem to require no active resort to speech at all. But such
a statement, as being in any sense a final account of the matter,
would be very superficial. The process of development of a
system of logical meanings is never one of passive reception or
even of relative inactivity. The growth of logical meaning in
the hearer is by a series of judgments. The process is one of
individuation of more or less familiar meanings in new constructions or contexts, through which the self receives
Requires Thinking in the Hearer. in a new impulse to its assertion of inner control. The
understanding of a statement, or a series of statements
in detailed discourse, may be seemingly complete for each step ;
but the elucidation of the speaker may vary in effectiveness for
the hearer all the way from a mere glamour of familiarity or
formal correctness, through varied stages of piece-meal, fragmentary, and semi-detached judgmental wholes, to that complete response of the hearer's logical interest that unifies the
entire set of relevant items. How the more superficial sorts of
comprehension of a subject may be possible is subject of remark
further below ; here it may suffice to say that when they are thus
superficially received, it is pseudo-thinking ; it gives meanings
that remain in large part either in a mode not yet judgmental,
or so habitual as to be under mere reality-feeling, or again they
are mere material for effective schematic use in this way or
that when judgment upon their further relevancies is actually
achieved.

If genuinely receptive, the attitude of the hearer is, indeed,
It is "pro-posed" one of continuous thinking. His selective interests are
not so much taxed when the relevant information is
directly supplied to him ; but the meanings suggested to him

are, in the first instance, merely proposed, assumptive, experimental. Each item added to the whole requires assimilation by some process complementary to that whereby, in the contrasted case, he tests in the social environment the meanings of his own suggestion. There must be a means, personal to the hearer, of testing the content of a thought proposed to him as valid, just as there must be a means, social in its nature, of testing the personal hypotheses put forth by the individual. Both of these processes are made effective through the medium of the common function, speech. The one sort of testing, the appeal to the socially established context of common meanings, as represented by authority, has already been discussed ; the other, that **Predicative** whereby the socially [1] problematical or schematic **in Form.** meaning is confirmed by appeal to individual judgment, is still to be treated of. The unit in which such items of meaning are cast, for either of these forms of confirmation or for both, is now to be inquired into : it may be called the *unit of linguistic expression.* It is what is ordinarily known as a *Predication*, or a *Predicative Meaning.*

§ 5. MODES OF PREDICATION : ELUCIDATION AND PROPOSAL

14. As soon as we take into account the entire situation in a case of intercourse of any kind, we find certain points of view from **Both** which the same meaning may be considered. There **Speaker's** are always at least two persons to the situation, and **and Hearer's** **points of** if we distinguish these persons as " speaker " and **view.** " hearer," we have the two personal elements marked off. Each of the persons is either already in possession of the judgmental meaning or he is not. If he is, then he is in rôle, if not in fact, " speaker " ; that is to say, the meaning is that which he might utter in place of the actual speaker ; and whatever term we apply to the function of expressing this meaning, it may be put down as applying to his *act of participation in the situation.* On the other hand, there is the point of view of the one to whom the intelligence imparted by the proposal is in some sense not already his meaning, but is an addition to it, or a modification of it. He is the " hearer "—no matter how many of him there may be ! The shadings of meaning involved may

---

[1] " Social " in the sense of suggested *to a hearer* by whom it is to be ratified. Of course all social acceptance is constituted by an aggregate of such individual ratifications.

be distributed under this two-fold division—*the speaker's mean-ing and the hearer's meaning.*

The next thing that occurs to us to note is that each of these persons, speaker and hearer, may have in his mind either a **Each is two-** meaning that he believes or a meaning that he **fold.** questions ; either a " logical " or a " schematic " meaning, a " presupposition " or an " assumption," may underlie the relational subject-matter that constitutes the pre-dication. And there must also be supposed a form of correlation between these two types of meaning, considered as being in a situation in which the speaker and hearer get the same subject-matter at the same time—as indeed they must, lest intercourse lose its commonness and so be futile.

15. This analysis when pursued exhaustively gives the fol-lowing cases :—

(1) Belief in the subject-matter on the part of the speaker, and predication that serves as elucidation of this subject-matter : **(1) "Elucida-** this we may call *predication as elucidation.* If this is **tion."** accompanied before the predication by belief in the mind of any actual hearer, the meaning to him is also one of elucidation, for he might have been the speaker.

(2) Question in the mind of the speaker and predication that in some form proposes something ; this we may call *predication* **(2) "Pro-** *as proposal.* If it be met by belief in the mind of the **posal."** hearer—belief already formed—it is to the hearer not proposal but elucidation ; and he in turn may proceed to eluci-date the proposal of the questioner. If, on the contrary, the hearer joins the speaker in erecting the subject-matter into a schema of problematical meaning, his meaning is then also one of proposal.

There are therefore four possible cases : (1) *Proposal*—(with) *Proposal,* (2) *Proposal—Elucidation,* (3) *Elucidation—Elucida-* **Four com-** *tion,* and (4) *Elucidation—Proposal,* in each case the **binations** meaning in the mind of the speaker standing first. Imagine, for example, a teacher teaching his class. The pupil says " A continent is really an island, isn't it ? " (proposal), and the teacher replies either " yes " (elucidation)—giving case (2)— or " look in the dictionary and see " (proposal)—case (1). After looking up the dictionary, both pupil and teacher may say, " it is an island, as we thought "—elucidation with elucidation, case (3)—or the teacher may say, " I still question what you read "—elucidation with proposal, case (4). It must not be sup-

posed that " elucidation—proposal " and " proposal—elucidation "
give the same situation ; they do not. The former is the situation in which there is exposition with reference to which the
hearer has not arrived at an assenting judgment ; the
latter, on the other hand, is the case of a question met
by an elucidating response. The latter is the more
fruitful situation, genetically, since it results in actual development of meaning in the mind of the questioner ; giving a third
term of elucidation, and if this be also stated, the progression becomes "proposal—elucidation—elucidation." The other case, that
of elucidation—proposal, is not of this fruitful issue, unless it be
followed by a further elucidation by the first speaker, and then
an elucidation also in the mind of the hearer ; but this latter
pair of terms brings in one of the other situations mentioned
above, that of elucidation—elucidation.

of Elucida-
tion and
Proposal.

Put in general terms, we may say first that a statement of
belief may be met by acceptance or by question, and second,
that a statement of a question may be met by a belief
or by a joint question. The instrumental utility,
and with it the genetic justification, of these four cases of predicative meaning, is now to be taken up. In each of them we will
see that predication, and with it all use of logical meaning, *is
in some important sense experimental,* when once the social point
of view essential to its full interpretation is taken up.

Belief and
Question.

§ 6. Predication as Experimental Meaning

16. It would appear on the surface that if logical meaning is
to be common, and thus socially available for intercourse, its
forms must be those by which on occasion the enlargement of the range of acceptance could be secured.
The forms of predication then would be *ipso facto*
instrumental to the production of further judgment and belief.
But certain considerations force themselves upon us which forbid
so easy an instrumental interpretation. We have seen that the
growth of knowledge cannot be entirely personal and private ;
the necessities of social life, which are also personal,
forbid. But it is equally true that the securing of
common acceptance, and the enlargement of the body of inter-
personal acknowledgments, cannot go on alone, as being the
entire fulfilment of the rôle of knowledge ; for the individual's
judgment is all the while the norm of what is established as

Predication
as Instru-
mental.

Social
Utility.

knowledge, and without individual consent there is no social acceptance ! The propagation of a thought in a social set can only be by the intrinsic adoption of the thought by the individuals of the set severally. Any other process would make not common knowledge but common hypothesis or proposal, with no relatively final solution or elucidation in knowledge. In such a case the final criterion to the individual thinker would not arise in his own processes of selective thought, but would be a calculus as to how many of the community already accepted it. Catholicity would take the place of what we call reasonableness or validity.[1]

There is in short the attitude toward society expressed in the sentence, " *I believe,* therefore have I spoken "—the attitude

Personal Belief.

of conviction, *coelum ruat*—as well as the attitude, " I would believe, help thou mine unbelief "—the attitude of social acquiescence. And we should expect that besides the evidently instrumental character of the appeal to society, there would be a corresponding instrumental appeal of society to the rules of individual thought. Put in terms of pre-dication, this would read—social proposals require individual elucidation, and individual proposals require social elucidation. The very development of knowledge, if it is to issue in a system of what we may call " truths," requires that both these forms of confirmation be present all the while.

Apart, however, from further theoretical discussion, we may point out the fact that as expressive of attitudes toward mental objects, meanings reach the poise and equilibrium of knowledge only through a two-fold elucidation. The belief of the speaker is still *to invoke that of the hearer* ; that of the hearer *is again submitted to the judgment of a second hearer,* when the former becomes speaker. The judgment of the individual is forever fed by the return wave from the circulation through the social tissue. On the other hand, the social set are never all convinced, and the outriders of society must be subdued to the informing and reasonable elucidation of the dominating individuals.

[1] In terms of the discussion of " community " below (chap. ix. § 5, and chap. xiv. § 8) the intent " by whom " would replace the intent " for whom."

A sort of social pragmatism might be constructed along this line, by reinterpreting—as we have—the individual's judgment of reasonable-ness back into the field of social acceptance, the " hole from whence it was digged."   But this is just what current pragmatism finds it difficult to do, since much of its development is on the basis of the reconstruction of experience in the individual for control by personal action.   The point is taken up again below, chap. xiii. § 2 in the discussion of " Truth."

17. The process of formation of what we call " truth " is, therefore, a continuous and dialectic one. Apart from the de-
Two Sides of Truth. finition of the term truth, and the justification of its use for a body of subject-matter constituted as logical content—apart from such details, which are to be treated of later on[1]—we may say that there are several sorts of truth. A predication which a thinker elucidates is true so far as it is not ineligible to the hearer's elucidation and belief ; but it may still actually be mere hypothesis or proposal to the hearer to whom the elucidation is to be addressed. Again, a matter of social convention, of confident social elucidation and advertisement by acclamation, is true in so far as it is not ineligible to, not mere proposal to, the judgment of any individual thinker ; for the same item is perpetually subject to the sharp-shooting of the more expert intellectual marksmen to whom the social judgment looks for its reconstruction and direction. There are two sides to the dialectic, two poles around which the web of truth must be stretched ; and until both sides be compassed and both poles surrounded, truth is unfinished.

From the instrumental point of view we discover, therefore, two sorts of schematism or proposal ; and it is a result to which our discussions now directly converge that both are never finally banished—that *thought, and with it truth, remains in one sense or the other experimental to the last.*

18. This would seem to take no account of one of the cases mentioned, that of " elucidation—elucidation," the case in which
The Extreme Case. both speaker and hearer are on familiar ground, and the intercourse is mainly the stating of agreements. Is not this, it may be asked, a case in which the aspect of proposal fails and the experimental character of thought does not appear.

On the surface such is the case ; but there are other considerations which lead us again to reinstate the proposal intent that seems on the surface to be absent.

(1) In the first place much that is called intercourse is not at all on the plane of thinking as strictly defined. We have
Double Eluci- dation may be (1) pre- logical already pointed out that there may be a play of contents cast in logical form—especially in linguistic form—that does not arouse the questioning attitude, because it also fails to arouse the judgment attitude. The gloss of reality feeling, the glow of familiarity and recognition, the smoothness of habitual function is upon it, and the intercourse

[1] See chap. xiii.

is merely the exercise of social function. The intercourse of cronies, gloating over common images of memory, that of the garrulous, exhibiting the trophies of former days, the argumentation of dreams and of the court-fool playing upon words or conceptions, are all types of intercourse in which the vital spark of belief has been extinguished behind a dull screen of presumption or presupposition. Given such a basin of uncritical acceptance, the fish of cognition—images, memories, words—may swim and play in it at will. All this is to be read off as not indeed experimental, not proposal, because it is also not logical, not judgmental.

(2) There are, however, other cases concerning which the inquiry is of far greater moment. There come at once to mind or (2) universal. two types of possible predication which seem to be entirely given over to elucidation, and to have no experimental or problematical character or intent.

19. In the first place, there are those empirical truths which are universally accepted, being not only appropriate for acceptance, but also actually acceded to in the judgment of all. Without stopping to argue whether there are any such truths, let us assume that there are, and ask in what respect they still have experimental or instrumental character.[1]

Evidently the aspect of elucidation may extend over the entire field or sphere in which the belief presupposition lies. The first Case. That is, the speaker and hearer may have a common presupposition of the control sphere in which their common acceptance holds. If, for example, we say, "the planets move in elliptical orbits," and elucidate the statement by a demonstration in terms of the geometry of plane space, this elucidation once made is then accepted by all competent minds. There is then a presupposition within the sphere of plane space, in which the relations thus elucidated find their real reference. So with any sphere of reference. We say "Newton established the law of gravitation once for all," presuming the cosmos of nature as it is ; or "mermaids have green scales," assuming

---

[1] It may be said, indeed, and with force, that such truths are impossible since the demand for actual catholicity could not be fulfilled. There would always be further intelligences to which the truth would have to be proposed and administered. Once admit the pedagogical reference of linguistic predication—the informing of the uninformed—and at once the continuity of racial tradition and culture comes in. All truth as linguistically embodied is " proposal " for all the generations yet unborn.

the common sphere of report, humour, folk-lore, superstition, or what not, in which the statement will "go."

But this being the case, we have, it is evident, also limited the sphere of reference of our elucidation just by establishing it. **Elucidation** There are other controls not invoked, when this or **within Belief.** that one is invoked. We shall see later on that even a judgment of identity, that most fundamental sort of elucidation, is essentially limiting over and against the exclusions it makes. There is, therefore, with each of the presuppositions of our positive belief, also the limitation of the reference of the statement, so that the judgments of possibility still arise as to its further extension to other spheres. The elucidation is indeed a set of **Postulation** implications within the common presupposition ; but **involved.** the presupposition is itself beset by further relationships that rest in the limbo of postulation.

20. This may be brought out from a somewhat different point of view. It will be remembered that we found all sub-**Reality is** stantive classes, all different control spheres, to be **Assumed.** essentially contrast meanings, arising progressively as the matter of experience is differentiated through use. The growth in real reference is toward the union of these classes in meanings of larger intention. There is the constant unification of reality, with the differentiation of existences.[1] Now a given set of implications may be established within a sphere of existence, while its place in the larger whole of reality remains a matter of assumption and postulation. From the point of view of the larger inclusion, the meaning cannot be one entirely of elucidation ; although from the point of view of what is actually established, within a sphere of controlled meaning, it may be.

21. The further case is that with which "real logic " is principally concerned—that of those synthetic predications which **A priori** appear to be altogether independent of experimental **Truths.** process either for their establishment or for their application. Historical theories deal with the " à priori," the " primitive," the " innate," the " constitutive," the " normative," the " regulative," etc., of a score of names—truths so-called that are beyond the range of proposal, because they constitute the presuppositions not of this content here or that there, but of all logical and reflective process as such.

[1] See vol. i. chap. x. § 9.

The discussion of these principles is to follow in another place. Here however we may suggest a line of least resistance. In the **They are Pre-** first place, we may at once grant what the à priorists **suppositions.** mean by calling such principles native, constitutive, etc., to the extent of saying that they are *presuppositions* of any predication in which they enter. Whether they are, as we are arguing, themselves genetically derived individually or racially, or whether they come simply by a gift of favour of Dame Nature, they are still the presuppositions of positive cognitive constructions. Granted this, our further question then is, do they have the intent to propose or postulate, as well as to categorise or elucidate ?

In answer to this question, we have to say that they do : that they are experimental in their reference and intent—instrumental and of the nature of proposal—in two ways.

(*a*) They are, whatever their origin be, presuppositions of typical modes of experience—rational, ethical, aesthetic, etc—as Kant long ago found. The ideas of the reason are not the same as the postulates of aesthetic judgment, nor the intuitions of the moral life. The whole of experience is broader than the sphere of presupposition of the merely rational. So also the rules of conduct are not available for the solution of the antinomies of pure reason. All such norms, rules, principles, are presuppositions of special types of meaning in the development **They involve** of experience as a whole ; and the extension of any of **"real" Pos-** them beyond its functional sphere of implication is not **tulates.** part of its elucidation. There arises then a *comparative morphology* of meanings, a final synthesis of interests, in which each set of presuppositions in one field becomes available in its neighbour's field only by postulation. Kant postulated the universality—the " real " universality—of the rules of the practical reason ; and thus secured results which did not, however, for a moment re-establish for experience as a whole the competence of the ideas of the reason, for these were presuppositions for pure reason only.

(*b*) Again, we are here called upon to inquire as to the presupposition of experience itself : the sphere of judgmental **Reflection** control within which all meanings with their special **as Postulate.** presuppositions are possible. Before saying that any set of principles are final—are pure elucidation—having no reference to further realms of unrealized and possible control, we have to ask whether the sphere in which they apply may not merely postulate reflection or experience, and not of necessity presuppose it. We ask whether the implication of reflection is the only one that will satisfy the especial interest involved. To illustrate, the materialist, for example, may say : yes, my belief presupposes my thought, but it also presupposes a control foreign to my thought. The adjustment of their respective claims is postulation : the final control may be reflection, but it also may be matter. You may presuppose experience for what experience is, but when you make experience a presupposition of the whole of reality you are proposing or postulating something more.

Summing up these two positions—both of which are to be argued in detail in our discussions of "real logic"—we may say :—

(1) Whatever is a presupposition of any limited sphere of control or existence, becomes a postulate when given application in experience beyond that sphere.

(2) The presupposition of experience itself, as a dualism of subject and object, or of reflection, is that of a limited **Conclusions.** mode of "real" meaning, and so it *becomes a postulate when used to interpret all reality as such.*

There is, therefore, even in those modes of predication illustrating "elucidation—elucidation," no final meaning free from experimental intent in the form of further proposal.

22. These two considerations, which suffice to establish the point that no knowledge is finally established as true for elucidation only—having no intent of proposal or **Illustrations.** reference to some more or less remote control—may be briefly exemplified in two special cases. *Singular meaning,* on the one hand, and *private meaning,* on the other hand, may be cited.

Singular meaning, as we have seen, renders that which is left over, after the processes of generalization have done their **Singular** work—whether it be the singularity of "essential" **meaning as** marks, or that of immediate and "imported" appre- **Proposal.** ciation. Now the motive to the elucidation of universal meaning arises actually only in the interpretation of a concrete situation ; that is, it is motived in the construction of a singular experience. There is evidently no passage, *before the act,* from the universal to the singular ; it comes by getting an actual experience of the singular. In all vital thought process, therefore, the universal elucidation or system of implication is instrumental to a proposed or hypothetical immediate experience, and is contingent upon it.   Just as we must say that a singular *presupposes* or *implicates* a general or universal meaning, so we must also say that a general or universal *assumes* or *proposes* a singular. Otherwise the meaning is abstract, empty, and dead.   " Form without content is empty."   While therefore there are, as will appear below, systems of purely abstract and theoretical implication—" deductions " from universals—still the life of thought always comes back for its justification to that sphere of limited control in which the particular case displays its marks of concrete singularity.

23. So, too, with the marks of privacy. The presupposition of judgment, of implication, of elucidation, when taken in
Private Meaning as Proposal. its breadth, is that of reflection ; all thought is controlled in the inner life.   The possibility of private meaning, whether it be that of mere fugitive psychic process, or that of appreciation of worth, is within this presupposition.   But such meanings are not reflective meanings ; otherwise they would not be private, but common.   The sphere of the private, therefore, is still that of proposal, hypothesis, postulation in its final intent.   Judgments of mere eccentric privacy postulate a world of " un-reality," over against those established " realities," which are the presuppositions of belief.[1]

24. Proceeding now to isolate the typical cases of proposal involved in situations of intercourse we find them to be two.
Two Modes of Proposal. First, there is the attitude or intent of question *in the speaker*, of proposal or assumption of something *he himself does not yet believe or presuppose* : this is the attitude in which the individual explicitly appeals to social conversion in order that his schematic context may be confirmed for his own acceptance and judgment.   Second, there is the attitude of question in the hearer, the audience, the public, in presence of the elucidations of the speaker : this is the attitude in which the social set, the general intelligence, waits upon the judgment and predication of the individual that the final availability of its meanings may be assured.   In the former case, there is the question, will it work in the whole of society ?—will it bear the

---

[1] This appears also in worth experience as such ; many impressionistic and pathological emotional experiences, which find no cognitive or other relational grounds and judgment, can only postulate them (cf. chap. xiv. §§ 4 ff.).

social test ?   In the latter case, there is the question, will it work in the individual's system of established beliefs ?—will it bear the test of competent private judgment ?—is it reasonable ?

These are the two tests always present in the determination of new matter in the system of meanings in the logical mode—**Two Tests.** *the two tests of truth.*   They are the test of *commonness* and the test of *reasonableness,* both being aspects of the intrinsic intent of all logical predication.   They are the poles of reference of logical meaning in its growth, as first " syndoxic " or " held [1] in common," then synnomic or " judged as common," and finally " catholic " or " judged in common."   The " reasonableness " of the synnomic is just that " appropriateness " attaching to a meaning *whose social intent faces both backward as already accredited and forward as still to prevail.*   A further word on the relation of these two tests to each other.

25. First, it should be borne in mind that we are here not concerned, except in certain secondary ways,[2] with the commonness of mere catholicity as numerical measure of ac-**Test of Commonness** ceptance ; but with that more profound ingredient in knowledge whereby, in its very formation, the individual judgment intends a common meaning.   The judgment of the individual once formed is necessarily to him a common judgment : it is synnomic in the sense of our earlier discussions.   But the experimental method of growth of the faculty of judgment in just this synnomic direction, both racially and in each individual, requires a series of situations in which the proposed or schematic meanings of the individual have first the syndoxic character " in common," and so pass into judgments.   The simplest case, of course, is one of fact in which the individual is not already possessed of the requisite information, and awaits the elucidation—the narrative—of another.   He then, with this increase of syndoxic information, forms a judgment of his own that is synnomic.   Thus arises a judgment of fact, the report of the other taking the place, by the operation of social conversion, of his own appeal to fact.   Before such an appeal, or the reception of the equivalent information, his opinion would have been schematic and assumptive.   It is this case, in which

---

[1] That is, "assumed" or "presumed" in common in a mode short of judgment.

[2] See below, § 8.

the accretion to knowledge is a matter of fact, whether reached by direct or by social confirmation, that has given rise to the description of this test as the "test of fact."

In the more recondite operations of thought, the essential appeal is the same. It is for that informing element of content or meaning, derived through the common context of socially established fact, that brings out the synthesis of judgment. The individual resorts to some source apart from his own ready-formed context of meanings, used by him hypothetically, to the world of fact in the larger sense, through which his assumption may be grounded and his belief justified. The essential redistribution of meanings that constitutes the process of assimilation of the proposed data to the body of experience, now takes place. In the result, the item is assimilated, and the context of believed and grounded items is so far enlarged.

or of Fact.

26. The other test is different in its nature; but being a real test, it is equally instrumental to the development of thought. It is that of items proposed for social acceptance, but awaiting the judgment of the individual. It is the appeal to the "reasonableness" in which the competent thinker renders his synnomic meanings.

Test of Reasonableness.

I have said above that this resort to the formed judgment of the individual is necessary to social acceptance—the acceptance of grounded social judgment. "Commonness" in the simpler senses of that term—the meanings of "common" short of the syndoxic [1]—such commonness may exist without logical bearing of any kind. There may be mere social aggregateness. But the passage from what we may call social proposal—rumour, contagion, plastic imitation, etc.—however aggregate it may be, and however socially diffused into the status of logically common meaning, is always through the mediation of the judgment of individuals. All "social meaning as such," and all "public" meaning resting upon it, are subject to the test of "reasonableness" to the individual thinker. Social commonness, in short, rests upon individual acceptance or "reasonableness"; while individual acceptance as "reasonable," has its roots in social commonness. The test whereby the social proposal, the aggregate or relatively catholic meaning, becomes one of genuine logical character, we therefore call the

Appeal to individual Judgment.

---

[1] See vol. i. chap. vii. §§ 5 ff.

" test of reasonableness " [1] as contrasted with " the test of fact." [2]

27. The factors involved in this two-fold dialectical movement may be shown by the following diagram. It should be remembered that it is the progress, or determination of meaning from proposal (assumption) to elucidation (belief), that is in question, and not the development of pure implication or elucidation as a body of related contents already fully determined. The term " truth " is used in the table in a way that anticipates a later discussion.

Diagram.

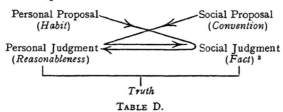

Personal Proposal (*Habit*) — Social Proposal (*Convention*)

Personal Judgment (*Reasonableness*) — Social Judgment (*Fact*) [3]

Truth

TABLE D.

[1] I take the term " reasonableness " as covering the general mark of knowledge wherein it satisfies and fulfils theoretical or logical interest from C. S. Peirce. As popularly used it has just the ambiguity of confusing the two phases of attitude we are trying strenuously to separate, *belief* and *assumption*. We say we believe a thing because it is " reasonable " or *proved*, and also that we assume a thing because it seems " reasonable " or *likely*. It is by a transition of attitude, rather than by a change of content, that knowledge and hypothesis are distinguished. A definite set of implications are reasonable, grounded, believed ; a set of assumptions not believed but only proposed, are also reasonable, but *only so far as they tend to lead up to belief*. It is to the former intent, that of actual acceptance, that I shall apply the term. On " reasonableness " as mark of meaning, see below, chap. x. § 1.

[2] It may be recalled that in the treatment of " Selective Thinking " in another place (*Devel. and Evolution*, chap. xvii.), I worked out certain tests from the individual point of view, calling them respectively " test of fact " and " test of habit." The test of habit is what is here, from the psychic point of view, recognized as personal proposal. In order not to repeat what is said fully there, I may simply call attention to the treatment in that place of (1) the " platform " or level of determination of systematic meaning from which all new items are selected as assumptions, and (2) the resulting theory of truth as that which having passed the " gauntlet of habit " or assumption, then has to submit to the test of fact. Truth in the realm of empirical discovery, then, is what is in this two-fold way selected. What is now added is the point that the hearer, society, does the same : society brings back its " assumption " as mere social proposal or habit to the test of individual endorsement as " reasonable."

[3] The socially established meaning may always be classed as " fact " since as established control or test of the individual's meanings it has essentially that rôle.

28. The point of interest just here does not reside in the further explication of either of these tests ; it resides rather in the statement that no predicated or judged knowledge is ever free from that instrumental and problematic reference which one or other of these tests would further fulfil. Either that which is reasonable is still to be elucidated for some mode of acceptance, or that which is generally accepted is still to be proposed for individual confirmation as reasonable.

All Predication instrumental.

The process of intercourse, therefore, to be all that it is for thought, requires that elucidation should perpetually fulfil the demand set by the correlative function of proposal. The social reference of thought is all the way along prospective as well as retrospective : prospective, in that it presupposes a proposing society for which further elucidation is necessary ; retrospective, in that it incorporates in its own competent judgment just that strain of commonness which only an earlier 'social confirmation in its own case could have produced. Put differently, we may say that if, at any point, truth can be considered finished and absolute, not subject to further growth, but only capable of repeated elucidation, then at an earlier stage it might, *for the same reason*, have been so considered, and its present stage would not have been attained. And so on all the way down the line of racial progress. But, on the contrary, the elucidations of one generation only bring out the proposals of the next ; the elucidations of society, the proposals of the man of genius. And in both cases the extraordinary thing is that in the proposal that requires a new platform of elucidation, the table is turned upon the thinker who makes his knowledge final. The judgmental content must be " set " as final, seeing that it is common, synnomic, retrospective and in so far also legislative for all intelligences ; but the newer gauge of reasonableness, on the one hand, or of fact on the other hand, once thrown down with its claim to a new finality, the process of vital reorganization again goes forward. The older truth loses its presuppositions or finds them restated in a new set of postulations.

Prospective.

29. It is not in order at this point to indicate the bearing of this result in a theory of knowledge considered as epistemology. We are later on to consider which of these tests is the more fundamental. The whole matter is here one of genetic adjustment of motive factors in a whole function. If one care to select one aspect of the whole, and

Implications for Epistemology.

say " thought, being experimental and instrumental and prospective, is pragmatic through and through " ; very well, so it is, from that aspect of it—the aspect of accommodation, discovery, development. But if another select the other aspect and say " all thought is retrospective, a platform, an organization, a social and common meaning, having its relational forms and rules of predication, a matter of habit and theoretical worth "—what is to prevent his doing so ? But both are partial, both abstractions. Knowledge is a specific organization, within whose subject-matter characters appear and develop that fulfil the theoretical interest without which no elucidation, predication, *language*, would be possible. But again, knowledge is an adjustment, motived by a pragmatelic and embracing interest, without which no theoretical organization or meaning could ever have been developed. No good social psychology, and no epistemology based upon such a psychology, will long be content with either of these partial and fragmentary interpretations.[1]

30. We may now go on to consider in more detail the two sorts of intent called in the foregoing account " elucidation " and " proposal." But we should carry with us all the while the conclusions now reached to the effect, (1) that all elucidation, all predication that is really judgmental, all inner organization of thought in a system of implications, has been developed with constant reference to proposals to which it is the reply and elucidation, and (2) that all instrumental reference of knowledge, all discovery, all postulation, all practical insight through truth, are possible only on a basis of established judgmental content whose adequate theoretical elucidation it

Summary.

---

[1] It may be said here, and has been said to me by a thinker who calls himself a " pragmatist," that we are still in the entire process dealing with a development for which the movement of cognition is instrumental : the development of psychic activity or function as such. To this I do not object, if we include *objective meaning* with function ; although when I come to think it through I find the result very far removed from what is usually called " pragmatism." The whole development, on the basis of our results is a social development, a larger social order, and with its postulation goes the contrast meaning, also postulated in the logical mode, of a non-personal and non-mental order, an environment. A dualism thus persists and will not down—a dualism whose implications forbid a return to any sort of subjective interpretation of *the reality implicated by thought,* any interpretation which confines it to what is relatively organized in the individual's habit. The solution is to be found only in an experience that is not indeed *a-logical,* but *super-logical* and immediate in its mode—to anticipate our discussions of " Real Logic."

presupposes. The ground of both these statements may be re-called in a sentence—namely, *knowledge is common property, not an individual possession.* Individual judgment not only presup-poses universal acceptance, it also seeks to acquire it. Truth is fitted always not only to *satisfy somebody's theoretical interest, but also to stir up somebody's curiosity and practical impulse.*[1]

§ 7. THE CONCURRENCE OF PERSONAL AND SOCIAL THOUGHT

31. Language embodies, if our general position be true, that stretch of cognitive meaning that is both individually accepted Concurrence save in mere Private Meanings. and socially rendered. It shows the concurrence of the two points of view from which the development of thought may be observed. Moreover, so far as the individual's psychic life is looked upon as one of relative isola-tion from his fellows, as a centre, that is, of personal and subjective meanings, the stream of his personal development merges concurrently into that of the social whole in those mean-ings which he can render by speech. His other meanings, the purely selective ones, the appreciations, and the partly-conative ones, the sorts of intent that fulfil his personal interests and purposes, together with the purely private ones of the fugitive sort that never acquire social validity—all these lie outside the sphere of intercourse and fail of exact linguistic rendering.[2] We

---

[1] This genetic process of building up a competent individual judg-ment, asserting its individuality over against the social body which is its very *fons et origo*, is seen to be a phase of the " dialectic of personal and social growth " developed in detail in my work *Social and Ethical Inter-pretations*. It is there shown that the consciousness of the personal self is formed and becomes relatively self-asserting, as over against society, by a process of imitative assimilation and ejective re-reading of social material, so that the individual is " *a social outcome, rather than a social unit.*"

[2] It has been interestingly shown, however, by W. M. Urban that there is a sort of " appreciative description " whereby such meanings may be indirectly suggested by verbal description (*Philosoph. Review*, Nov. 1905). It would appear quite possible to arouse in another an appreciative state like one's own by the use of indirect symbolism or description. We have the general resort to the " commonness of common function," to produce common experience. It has been pointed out above that music and other expressive functions do excite meanings that are common though less definite than those of language. They serve to convey a certain " de-scription of appreciations." There is thus a great tract of meaning, partly personal and partly social, lying between the two extremes of privacy and logical commonness.

can, indeed, imagine modes of social expression—we have them possibly in the crude quasi-linguistic symbolism of some of the higher animals—in which this concurrent rendering of meanings at once in private intent and also in common social acceptance has gone very little way. A society with only gesture language would have little such concurrent development ; and one with only pictographic signs would be relatively rude in respect to the development represented by written language.

The principal and striking thing about language, however, as thus being both personal and social vehicle of thought, is **Thought not** its testimony to *the falsity of any individualistic theory* **Individual-** *of thought.* Thought must be social in order to be **istic.** adequately personal, as we have seen : language summarizes and demonstrates this necessity. The gradual development of language shows the impulse and necessity for intercourse both as pedagogical instrument in the hands of society and also as vehicle of the individuals informing and reforming work in society.

§ 8. CATHOLICITY

32. We are now in a position to state an opinon as to the place and importance of that relative amount of actual common **Catholic** consent usually known as "catholicity." Under **Meaning is** various phrases such as "universal acceptance," **Aggregate.** "common consent," "belief by all"—*semper, ubique, ab omnibus*—it has had a certain place in epistemological theories, albeit not a fixed or unambiguous place. The most general and indeed the quite valid distinction in the matter is that between catholicity, as thus described, and universality considered as an intrinsic aspect of the meaning. All may or may not accept a meaning that is universal in the sense of holding without exception within its sphere, or valid in the sense of being worthy of acceptance by all. The distinction is that made in our discussions between common meaning that is appropriate or synnomic for all thinkers and common meaning that is syndoxic or aggregate, as actually accepted. An aggregate meaning is one held by an aggregate of individuals ; a synnomic meaning is one worthy to be accepted by any individual. It is the "aggregate" meaning to which the character properly called catholicity attaches.

33. Our earlier discussions give us also a clue for estimating the rôle and place of catholic meaning ; indeed we have now only

to sum up certain positions already made out. Its place is in
It arises by Secondary Conversion. that plane of development of knowledge at which confirmation is by a directly social conversion process.
The child in seeking confirmation may not yet be
capable of effecting a judgment that will, when once formed, be
self-legislating for all thinkers and consequently synnomic. On
the contrary, his control processes may be much more unorganized.
Each item is a fact for itself, to be confirmed by some one else.
But its relative aggregateness comes to give it more than mere
personal force. Especially in the urgencies of practical life does
this appear. Conduct here and now depends upon the proper
" sizing up " [1] of a present situation ; and for this sizing up the
aggregate percept or memory is safer and richer than the merely
personal. The search for aggregate meanings is therefore a
genuinely fruitful impulse, and its results have a real instrumental
value.

This is substantially the state of things—though the account
of its later phases would not be so simple in its terms—all the
Leads up to Judgment. way up to the actual appearance of judgment. The
commonness of knowledge is simply aggregateness
or catholicity, being thus syndoxic in the individual's meaning,
until it becomes synnomic in judgment, when the 'processes of
generalization, ejection, and sembling—all the complex motives
that converge to the act of judgment—give new character to
the common intent. The fruitage of all the social discipline,
both individual and racial, is reflected once for all in the individual's self-determination as a subject. judging its experience.
Then it is no longer necessary to him that any living creature
should actually agree with him in the movements of his belief.
His knowledge is then no longer merely catholic in its intent.

34. Another way of looking at the case affords us a like
result. It will be remembered that in discussing the tests that
Transitive Events are Aggregate. arise in the development of thought through intercourse, we found it necessary to distinguish what we
called in a large sense the " test of fact " from the
" test of reasonableness." Now the former is sometimes indeed

---

[1] Or in the usage of a group of present-day writers, the " control " of the
situation. But " control " is here more than ambiguous : it is just as
true that the situation " controls " both the thought and the conduct.
In so far as the individual finds a meaning to *acknowledge* and *conform to*,
the situation " controls " him. What is meant is simply the interpreting
of the situation with view to the guidance of conduct. See the discussion
below, chap. xiv. § 1, of the different conceptions of " control."

a test of fact in a literal sense ; it is an appeal to a control system read as outside the individual's inner psychic process, a literal appeal to sense or memory data, a real conversion into an original mode. Further, we have also found that for the "transitive" parts of the presented context, the "events," no direct appeal to personal sense-experience—or to first-hand experience of any kind—is possible ; the actual resort is to another's inner context of perception or memory. This is only another way of saying that the motive is then to try to establish aggregate or catholic meanings, to ascertain the real and actual agreements among individuals.

The other test, found in the logical mode—the test of reasonableness—may not be in any way invoked. The establishment of a matter of fact may be a question of aggregate testimony, and whether one or more accept the fact is of the essence of its credibility. "In the mouth of two or more witnesses, every word may be established."

35. There is another sphere also in which aggregateness or catholicity is of importance, and for the same reason. It is that **Private Ap-** of relatively private meanings of the appreciative type. **preciations also** Such meanings being those of personal interest and **Aggregate.** purpose, there is no direct process of rendering them in terms of predication : that is, of making them socially synnomic in their essential force. Accordingly, they rest, in the matter of social value, largely where prelogical meanings of the recognitive type also rest—in the aggregate stage. It may not be possible to argue about tastes, but it is possible by indirect description and relevant action to influence it—by example, by insistence, etc. It is thus that art "criticism" may carry the mass ; not indeed by criticism, or reflective judgment proper, but by suggestion, by setting up copy for unreflective imitation. The movements of public and private taste—in the large sense—are massive movements of aggregate or catholic expression of what is after all personal and not in any more inherent sense common.

36. All this may be summarized for our present purposes by saying that catholicity is instrumental in its function to higher forms of commonness ; and that this function is subserved when **Catholicity** the schematic, problematical meaning passes over **is Instru-** into judgment. We might use the term "quantity" **mental.** as measure, in the one case, of the number of individuals agreeing about a thing, and in the other case of the number of cases of the thing about which they agree. The

former is not extensive quantity, as the latter is, when the meanings are judged.

Our conclusion, therefore, is that mere catholicity may be a pre-logical character of knowledge. Its logical rôle is considered below.[1] It has indeed its continual and important influence upon our processes of thought—upon the conclusions we reach—because so much of our knowledge is shot through with problematical and appreciative elements in which aggregate opinion has its proper place and its influential rôle. But the injunction of the reasoner to his adversary is "dare to be a Daniel, dare to stand alone!" And the adversary perforce replies, "I know no allegiance, but to truth; with me passion plays no part."

It is quasi-logical.

---

[1] See chap. ix. § 5, where two sorts of " community "—as the " common intent " of a judgment may be called—are distinguished : community " by whom," and community " for whom " the meaning is rendered in judgment.
There is, indeed, the point of view from which catholicity enters into the determination of logical thought. The social proposal that has not yet stood the test of individual confirmation and elucidation is cor-related with the individual proposal that has not yet received social en-dorsement. It would seem that both depend upon progress in actual acceptance or relative catholicity. It matters much to a political party or to an executive committee sitting upon important business, and still more to a criminal on trial, how many of the citizens, committeemen or jury respectively, agree on the measure or verdict. The effectiveness of a proposed legal measure, the policy of a government, or the life of an in-dividual on trial depends upon and reflects the relative " quantity " of persons as spoken of above. But this is only to say that the number of agents or thinkers who agree conditions or supplies the essential con-firmation *that issues in social judgment*, just as, at the corresponding stage in individual thought, the number of agreeing persons is reflected in the training and establishment of individual belief. The essential point is, that it is as assumption of proposal as *instrumental to the development of judgment* that catholic quantity enters, not as part of the synnomic intent of that judgment after it is once constituted. Once the legal " judgment," the verdict, the truth is reached—no matter how it was conditioned—then lack of catholicity or general consent does not affect it either in the legal realm or in the logical. See chap. xiv. § 8, for the exposition of " quantity " in community.

Chapter VII

THE DEVELOPMENT OF LOGICAL MEANING :
PREDICATION BY THE TERM

§ 1. The "What" and "Why" of Predication

1. Having now discussed broadly the rise of that form of meaning to which the word predication is applied, we may go on to examine its usual and normal forms. It will be remembered that we have found two correlative aspects attaching to all predication, those of "proposal" and "elucidation." The preceding chapter brought out the proposal aspect strongly, showing the instrumental and experimental force of all predications when viewed in the larger social or common rôle which their linguistic character and origin impart. It would then be our further purpose to discuss this in detail. But as we also found that the proposal is necessarily stated in a "schematic" form—as an assumption, or supposition—the only way to get the hypothetical force of a predication is to understand the "schema" or context that is taken as framework for the intent proposed. There is always the schema or outline body of meaning chosen as appropriate vehicle for the elements of meaning proposed. This schema is the platform of past "reasonableness," from which the new hypothesis is to make good its subsequent "reasonableness." It becomes necessary, therefore, for an adequate analysis of logical meaning, to consider the modes of established predication as being, in the first instance, so much matter given for elucidation.

Our most promising method of procedure would seem to be to take the various modes or stages in the development of predication, and to ask of each in turn as to its structural or recognitive meaning, its "what"—that is, *what it now means*, as an item of contextuated and socially available information. The "what" is the subject-matter of judgment. Having determined this, we may then enquire into

Two aspects of Predication.

The What of Elucidation.

the instrumental use of such a meaning : the " proposal " that the meaning when considered instrumentally suggests or intends. This latter we may call the question of the " why " of a mean-
The "Why" ing : the for-what-purpose or end, personal or social,
of Proposal. the meaning is available for experimental treatment. If we use the phrase " selective thinking," as we have above, for the entire process whereby meanings grow in the logical mode— the process of " systematic determination " sketched in the pre- ceding chapter—then we may say that every given meaning is both predication *as* elucidation *of* a proposal, and predication *as* a proposal *for* elucidation.   It is as his elucidation that the believer proposes it to another ; it is as proposal that the questioner brings it to the hearer for his elucidation.

We may then go forward by this method. In each case having discussed the meaning taken for investigation in the form in which it is individuated for personal belief, we may then show that this meaning and function are not final, but that the reference of the subject-matter, as schematic and instrumental to further belief, is equally and necessarily present. The theoretical " what " is then supplemented by the prag- matic " why," all through the progress of knowledge.

§ 2. The Progression of Predication

2. Looking broadly at the progress of thought from the rela- tively simpler to the relatively richer modes of organization of its
Extension. meanings, we find available the general distinctions and terms current in the traditional logic. It is clear that the mode of logical meaning as such involves what we have called " individuation as particular and general." This type of relationship is necessary to constitute the subject-matter a judgment. With this go the meanings " universal " and " singular." All these are now to be characterized as elucida- tions, seeing that they take on linguistic or other symbolic em- bodiment in predications. With these we find corresponding instrumental meanings or proposals for acceptance. This, follow- ing customary usage, we may call the meaning and mode of Generalization. It has the logical mark of " extension " or " breadth."

The other mode of " quantity " of logic is called " intension." Here we find similar questions. The intension of a
Intension. meaning, its intensive or qualitative marks, may be considered either as definitely acquired and determined, on the one

hand, " set," so to speak, a matter for predication or elucidation ; or, on the other hand, as proposal, as instrumental to further acceptance. The development of Abstraction in logic, considered as change in intension, presents both these problems. The theory of abstraction must therefore go with that of generalization.

3. These two modes of meaning, taken together with any other characters attaching to logical content, constitute aspects **The Term.** of what is usually, from the psychological point of view, called Conception. The resulting meanings themselves are known as Notions, and as units of linguistic and logical meaning, Terms.

The embodiment of logical meaning in general and abstract concepts may be called the first great stage or mode in the progression of such meaning—the Conceptual Mode. As linguistically embodied—that is, as normally constituted—it is the earliest and most fundamental sort of logical elucidation.

Our first topic therefore, is, the Term, General and Abstract.

A further characteristic movement at this stage of the logical progression is that whereby singular meaning is reached. As a form of logical individuation it presupposes general meaning ; but as a term its intent is not general. This mode we may call that of singularization, and the meaning the Singular or Proper Term.

4. Next we find a sort of elucidation in which the demands of linguistic embodiment, and with it the evidently social charac- **The Pro-** ter of thought, become more explicit and emphatic, **position.** in the statement of the meaning in a sentence or proposition. In this mode, the meanings or terms are disclosed in a form which holds them in relative separateness or relation within the entire conceptual meaning. The Proposition is a second stage in the progression of elucidation ; and constitutes another topic.

In treating the proposition we shall have to consider also the fundamental " Qualities " of logical meaning, Affirmation and Negation—and any others besides that our method may suffice to discover.

5. A third stage appears in what is ordinarily called Reasoning, or Argumentation, with its essential motive, Inference. **The Argu-** In inference two or more relatively separable units **ment.** of conceptual meaning are elucidated as related within a larger whole. The elucidation consists in exhibiting

and developing relationships through a process of mediation. It shows a further growth of conceptual meaning in organization. All the later and seemingly more complex forms of logical meaning known as Argument or Inference, are elucidations in which one or more of the simpler modes are present.

6. If now we apply the term Implication, as we have above, to the mark of logical meaning, whereby it " hangs together " as organized, or systematically determined—including both the system of explicit contents and the underlying presuppositions of belief[1]—then all the modes of elucidation become *methods of developing implication.*

Implication.

We are now able to throw together as follows the modes of implication in their genetic sequence—

> Implication : its Modes—
> I. *The Term.*
> II. *The Proposition.*
> III. *The Argument.*

§ 3. Conceptual Meaning : the General Term

In our earlier discussions the genetic theory of general meaning was somewhat fully worked out. A summary of these discussions may be given here as introductory to the discussion of the later stages of logical implication.

7. (1) It will be remembered that individuation of a content as in some form general and particular is the method of origin of logical meaning as such. The redistribution of meanings whereby the subject-self is set over against objects of experience constitutes the mode. It issues in the attitude of acceptance which is the act or function or judgment ; and the subject-matter on the objective side is a relational whole wherein the relation of particular to general within the whole becomes itself object of thought. Only as thus treated, that is as in a context of inner presence and control, a context of personal experience, can particular cases have that standing which gives them also the intent of generality. All this has had full justification in the foregoing chapters.[2]

Logical
Meaning,
General

(2) A further result appears also, namely, that which relates

---

[1] It is these elements of presupposition, indeed, that the word often suggests, the implications being relations and bearings that are not explicitly brought out. But even then the implications are such only because they are capable of being brought out in explicit form.

[2] Vol. i. chaps. x., xi.

to the meaning called universal. The universal meaning attaches
and not to the general aspect as such nor to the particu-
Universal lar, but to just the relation in which the general and
particular aspects of the meaning are intended. The relation
between the particular " this horse " and the general " horse "
is universal : the case means what all cases that sustain and
justify the use of the term also mean.

8. This being in brief the standing of general meaning, considered as subject-matter of the logical mode of judgment, it remains to ask how it takes on those further characters now found
to attach to logical meaning : the characters of " commonness "
and linguistic form. For we have found these characters normally present in logical meaning.

The commonness of general meaning follows indeed from
its character as being subject-matter of judgment. For as we
and found in our discussion of judgment, it has always
Synnomic. the sort of commonness called synnomic. It carries
the meaning that the issue of the judgment is appropriate to
any competent judgment and hence might be ratified by it. If
it be true, therefore, that the general-particular meaning is
content of an act of judgment, constituting its subject-matter,
then the synnomic character must attach to such meanings.
They must be worthy of acceptance, whether or not they be
actually accepted. We have seen that no logical meaning
need be universally accepted. The sort of commonness attaching to a general meaning is therefore simply that of the commonness attaching to judgment. Here we may at this point leave
the subject, appealing to the conclusiveness of the earlier discussion.

The additional point that remains for our notice is that
which concerns the linguistic embodiment of general meaning—
It is embodied " linguistic " being used not as necessarily excluding
in Terms. other forms of symbolic embodiment that may be
more or less available socially, but as being the most highly developed and general. This introduces us to the logical meaning
of the term, as such.

The term, as used in grammar and logic, is that linguistic or
other symbol in which a relatively fixed and separable unit of
The Term. social meaning is embodied. It is a socialized item
of knowledge : a meaning crystallized verbally for
social purposes. The further question is, of course, as to the
process whereby such a meaning takes on this form.

9. The answer, so far as general meaning is concerned, is near at hand ; indeed it is involved in what has been said as to the linguistic or symbolic embodiment of logical meaning as such.   The motive to such embodiment was found to be just the rendering of personal meaning in a form which constitutes it at once judgment to the person and proposal of intelligible meaning to the group.   The meaning that remains private to the person is not judgment ; nor is it socially available.   But as soon as that redistribution takes place that constitutes such an item a judgment in the individual mind, so soon, and by this act, it is elucidated for social acceptance :

The Term names the Meaning. that is, it is in its form appropriate for any judgment process.   The term as such, if we confine the word to the symbol, is the name given to this meaning. It is differentiated in some characteristic way, usually linguistic, from other terms which also present aspects of judgmental meaning.   In language, such a term as " man " stands alone for this socially general aspect of the meaning ; while a pronominal or other index, as in " this man," " a man," etc., is used to render the particular or singular aspect.

Apart from linguistic detail which shows great variety, our point simply is, that the essential reference whereby alone judgment as synnomic meaning arises, suffices also for its linguistic embodiment.   Only as thus embodied, is its common meaning and force held and subsequently advanced.

10. As bearing, however, upon the subsequent advancement of such a meaning, another result of our discussion may be **It also proposes.** recalled.   Advancement is always by proposal ; although there is elucidation made by the speaker, such elucidation erects a proposal in the mind of the hearer. Either speaker or hearer or both must use the embodiment already given in the term as the thought-platform from which fruitful experimental advance is achieved.   We are thus led to the final interpretation of general meaning wherein it appears as the first stage in the larger progression of implication.

We should therefore ask two questions concerning any general meaning : (1) what does the term elucidate ? and (2) how does **Two Questions.** it propose ?—for we have claimed that it is the rôle of all predication as linguistic embodiment of logical meaning to perform both these functions.

11. In answer to the first question, it may be pointed out that any term whatever elucidates the relational context which

constitutes it a general, particular, or universal meaning. I point
Elucidation to an object on my table and say to my child "pen";
of context. it is clear in just what ways I am elucidating to
him the meaning of the object.

(1) I inform him that he sees a *real thing* : this by the implication of the *control* or sort of existence *presupposed* in our
Its Control common perception. This comes up for explicit
discussion later on[1] where the presupposition of
reality as a mode of implication is treated of.

(2) I inform him that there is only one proposal that has the
sort of confirmation that my perception and judgment can give,
Its Common- i.e. that embodied in the *common connotation of the*
ness. *word "pen."* This then elucidates the meaning as
general.

(3) With the foregoing elucidation of meaning, I am still
holding the child's thought simply to the percept ; that is, I am not
Its Gener- talking about pens in any mode other than that of
ality. actual existence here and now. I might of course do
so. I might playfully suggest by tone of voice, say, a semblant
class-pen, using a match-stem, or a pencil, for the content of it.
Or I might point to a vacant spot and say " pen," only to excite
a fugitive and placeless image or schema to embody my meaning.
But these I do not mean : I mean the actual object. It then
becomes a *particular, a case of the general*; I intend " this pen ";
and the term " pen " is thus further elucidated. I might state
the entire meaning conveyed by the term thus : " Here is a real
object which is one of those things known as pens."

Such then is the elucidation contained in the general term.
It embodies in a *vocal impulse and symbol the entire general-
particular meaning*, performing its personal and social office all
in one.

12. In what sense, further, we may now ask, is it a proposal,
a problematical meaning, a schema for further determination
and development ?

In this sense, I think. It is never uttered or thought as an
accomplished logical meaning, except with the character of
Question of appropriateness to judgment everywhere and always.
Proposal Its meaning as general is final, retrospective; but
socially speaking it need not be catholic. Is knowledge ever entirely
justified of its social generality ? This is a question we have

---

[1] In vol. iii.

N

already discussed. We decided that there is no knowledge of the type "elucidation-elucidation"; no knowledge finally established both for the speaker and for every possible hearer. The **as Postulate.** presupposition of a limited control carries with it the postulate of a universal control within which the application of the meaning may be revised. With reference to the working out of such a postulate, the given context may be used schematically as proposal for further discovery in two directions, both of which have already been noticed.

First, the elucidation itself opens the meaning to social criticism. The presupposition of synnomic commonness may **Proposal to Hearer.** be directly challenged; its claim to secondary or social conversion disputed. One never lays bare his thought without the *arrière pensée* that defence may be necessary in the face of difference of opinion. I may call the other person a "fool" when he trespasses upon the reserved ground of what is to me a universal meaning; but by so doing I may shut off from myself the chance of profiting by his wider information, and so of giving my own conclusion very essential revision.

Second, there is always the reading of the meaning primarily from the point of view of the hearer; for it is just my motive in **Also as Information.** speaking to inform the hearer. That is, I must also recognize the *unfinished character of his judgmental process* and allow for its issue in judgment. My judgment, in short, always legislates consent, but that it fully secures it is a further postulate; that is, it cannot presuppose it. The actual variations of social generalization, of catholicity of thought, are manifold; there is teacher and taught, genius and dullard, informed and ignorant, reasonable and prejudiced; and the socially available and socially current item of knowledge must have its adaptableness to the latter's judgment as well as its adaptedness to the former's—in each of these contrasted pairs of persons.

13. It remains, however, true, as is said in an earlier connection, that a general meaning as such is always retrospective; **The General as retrospective.** it is final for the judgment that constitutes it, and in this respect it is not problematical. So far, therefore, as its linguistic embodiment and use do require its taking on schematic form for further experimental determination, it is either for those intelligences that do not yet judge it to be general or for application in a sphere of postulated control. Its proposal intent resides in its suitability for progressive redetermination in some new mind or in some new sphere. To all those in whose

minds it is a true general, its rôle is already that of elucidation.[1]

As a matter of fact, the intent, whether it be in the form of a presupposition of accomplished belief, or of a proposal for experimental solution, is usually made more or less clear by one or more of the accidents of verbal discourse, such as intonation, gesture, context, etc. In this way, a relatively unambiguous intent is communicated in the actual use of the term and its social utility adequately subserved. In written texts, the punctuation is in the same way an even more conventional aid to the rendering of the intent. "Et tu, Brute" may be rendered vocally or by print as an exclamation, as interrogation, or a statement of fact.

§ 4. Conceptual Meaning: Abstraction

14. In what is called abstraction we have a development of

---

[1] A difficulty, which amounts to a real embarrassment in the discussion of certain topics, arises from the ungenetic character of common terminology: the application of the same term both to a process and to its result and often yet again to the subsequent process. "Generalization," for instance, is used both for that process whereby a general meaning is achieved and also for the general meaning after it is achieved. By this usage the varying intent of the meaning while the process is going on and then after it is made up is confused and obscured. Our distinction between the "assumption" of a meaning used as instrumental to the judgment—the meaning not yet general but instrumental to it—and the "presupposition" of the general itself, is quite lost. It is for this reason that, from the point of view of the intent and attitude involved, I prefer not to use the term generalization, but another—"schematization"—for the process whereby a meaning becomes general. This is the more necessary because we find the process of generalization proper later on to be one of real development of logical or general meanings—a matter of implication within a whole meaning of logical force—as developed below under the discussion of judgments of identity. In current discussions, under the term generalization, there is a playing fast and loose with different connotations, all the way from the process of reaching a general, to the general itself, and then to the process of argumentation with generals. The prime distinction—as I have constant occasion for insisting—is that between the schematic or assumptive meaning, involving an attitude of *question*, and the general or presuppositional meaning, involving the attitude of *belief*. Armed with this distinction, which alone gives us our psychological right to discuss logical topics at all—for without it, we cannot motive any continuous transition from prelogical to logical meaning—we thread our way through the genetic progress from platform to platform of objective construction. Our terminology must render these distinctions clearer, not obscure them, if we are to make any progress in our explanations.

another of the great modes described in our general discussion of
Selective   meaning.[1]   In the original differentiation of meanings
Meaning the by which the cognitive context as such is set off as
basis of
Abstraction. " recognitive," there also arises the more personal and
special mode of meaning called " selective."   It is that aspect
of the object which by its fulfilment or satisfaction of an interest,
disposition, or purpose, is by that fact relatively isolated or
selected. This has had illustration above. The dog's dinner-
plate was cited as an illustration of the type of meaning called
selective.   To him the mere plate, a round white object of visual
perception—what we designate the recognitive meaning—is as it
were only the suggestion, the mere framework of all that mass of
appetitive and personal meaning that gives the plate its fulfilling character with reference to his gustatory interest.   All
this is selective meaning or intent.   On the other hand, my
interest in the same plate, let us say, is that of an amateur collector of china.   I at once lecture the maid for having fed the
dog on a fine old Colonial Staffordshire plate.   The meaning of
the article, so far as its form is concerned, its presence as an
object of visual perception and common recognition, is in great
measure the same as the dog's ; but the selective meaning, the
aspect of its presence whereby it fulfils my interest, is as widely
different as is the collector's ceramic interest different from the
gustatory interest of the glutton.

This selective meaning, so marked from the beginning, as
embodying individual and personal dispositions and interests
active in determining the object, is the basis of the great movement in the development of meanings called abstraction.[2]

15. If we then, from the first and without more ado, call
this sort of meaning abstract, then we may state our problem as
that of tracing the development of selective meaning.

A little consideration will show in what sense such a meaning

---

[1] Vol. i. chap. vii.

[2] As is said in the earlier discussions, as soon as the distinction between these two types of meaning arises the very neutrality and steadi-
ness of the recognitive content becomes itself a matter of interest in its
own right. The interest of recognition, individuation, truth is thus
differentiated from that of special selective fulfilment, appreciative and
other. *So the rise of meaning is the rise of meanings.* Progress in the
genetic dualism of controls motives the contrast between the two types
of meaning ; but evidently, in so far as each is only a partial reading of
the entire meaning of the object, either alone is from the logical point of
view abstract—a point to be brought out fully below.

is from the start abstract. It is evidently so to that degree in
Beginning of Abstraction. which although separable it still remains an element of
a whole meaning. The whole meaning of any object
includes its recognitive context ; by that its presence
as content is secured. The personal interests, no matter how
urgent, do not normally determine the entire object. If they do
so abnormally then the object fails, just by not giving the satisfaction that the special interest itself aims at securing. Cases of
extreme desire for an object or end get their urgency from the
absence of the object, through whose establishment the special
satisfaction of the desire is to be secured. The rise of the selective meaning depends, therefore, upon the presence or thought
of the full object ; but it more especially includes that intent of
the entire meaning whereby it terminates upon and finds fulfilment in some restricted part or character of the object.

This indeed is the method of the development. The more
restricted appetite, disposition, or interest terminates on some
Abstraction a Fulfilment. mark or character of the entire meaning given by
cognition or recognition. This mark is by this move-
ment selected and held as fulfilling the interest at work upon
it. Such relative isolation of a mark, quality, or part of the
entire meaning is the " abstraction " of this part. It is then
rendered in our analysis and thought as an abstract meaning,
an " abstraction."

16. Finding this to be genetically the true motive to abstraction, we may consider its development through certain progres-
Its Stages. sions. Following our usual method, we will take up
in order " prelogical," " quasi-logical," and " logical "
abstraction for brief treatment. Our earlier treatment, in
various connections, of different aspects of selective meaning
will now stand us in good stead, and serve to shorten the present
discussion.

§ 5. PRELOGICAL ABSTRACTION

17. Recalling in rapid survey the progress of mental development before the rise of judgment, we find that selective
Early selec- tive Intent. or abstract meaning goes through certain interesting
modes. In the stretch preceding that degree of
psychic detachment that characterizes the relatively free and
uncontrolled images of fancy—through all this period the
place of selective meaning is substantially as described above.
There is a relative emphasis upon some aspect of a larger cogni-

tive whole, whereby its fitness to fulfil a special interest or purpose is established. The isolation of this aspect of the whole is only relative ; there is no positive individuation of the abstract meaning as apart from the whole in which it finds its appropriate context. This negative statement may, however, serve to point the question that now occurs to us, namely, as to how it becomes possible so to abstract a mark that the selective meaning comes to have a relative self-subsistence, and to be thought of as possibly present or absent in reference to the same content.

The problem thus stated suggests to us the motive to the further development. It is found in the semblant mode, already **Semblance.** described in detail and found to be in so many ways germinal in psychic development. Semblance is in this respect as in others pointed out, *quasi-logical* ; it shows at work the transitional motives through the operation of which the logical in the narrower sense is finally ushered in. We now turn, therefore, to semblant or quasi-logical abstraction.

18. We found in the first semblant mode, it will be remembered—in all the exercises of play—a certain loosening of the original control of the context, whatever the sphere **Conscious Abstraction.** from which the materials of the constructions were drawn. That essential contrast of meanings whereby the nascent dualism of inner and outer develops is now so far obliterated that any image may be cut from its proper anchorage and treated in " semblance." It is the intent of semblance to drop the *presumption* of this or that proper control— of this or that sphere of existence—and make the *assumption* of a different one. And the experimental method of further determination arises in this situation, and finds in it its first chance.

But it is evident that this assignment to a sphere of existence or control extends to any aspect of the meaning. The further **Assumed Meaning.** assignment of meaning is due to the selection arising in the development of the interest then dominant. The cognitive context, the bit or item whatever it be, is taken, within the sphere made semblant, as a schema or skeleton for the embodiment of a larger meaning, which it is merely assumed to have.

This it is evident both utilizes and enormously develops selec- **Selective Dramatiza- tion.** tive or abstract meaning. It utilizes those fulfilments already secured in two very interesting ways. First, we note that the rôle assigned to the thing selected for semblant purposes is itself a selective meaning. The soldier into which the broom is turned is "soldier" as the player understands and wishes him to be, not as he must in all details recognize him to be.   There is here a relative emphasis on certain characters of the real object that becomes possible from the alternative control that the present function allows.   And second, there is the further selective building up or dramatization of the semblant object and situation.   Here again the free material lends itself most fully to manipulation, to selection or elimination, under the growing sense of agency and competence of the individual who pursues the game.

And it also develops the abstract force of such meanings. For it requires their relative detachment from the recognitive framework as constituted in a "real" control.   The world does not admit black swans, sweet lemons, or lying clergymen, but the play does.   The license to imagine is the license to imagine *satisfactions, as well as facts* ; and to imagine any combinations of satisfactions with facts.

19. There is then here—and this is the important point—a growing isolation of the selective meaning.   The function is one **Meaning thus iso- lated.** that charges this or that schema of content with a further reading in the development of interest, desire, purpose.   The individual says, "let it be what suits me, sweet, white, etc."   Not that he thinks these meanings separately and brings them up to the object : that would require more developed abstraction.   But that he reads the object as possessed of the fulfilling quality, acts upon it as if the action were to find its proper terminus therein, and so more and more isolates his own selective intent.

No doubt this relative separateness of the abstract meaning would come and does come through the vicissitudes of earnest **Also by Active Life.** life as well.   All those experiences wherein the germs of negation, difference and unreality alternatively appear, would lead to the relative isolation of the marks or qualities to which they were pertinent.[1]   This gives a relative breaking up of the meaning-wholes whose original establishment was in a common control.   But the reason of it is the variation in the control of the whole that allows the relative loosening of the parts.   If the sweet taste is not there when the child tries a new sort of orange, it means that this mark, the taste, is more variable, not so regularly controlled in the whole meaning, as those other marks which continue to establish the object in his

---

[1] See below in this chapter, sect. 24, on "Erosion."

mind as an orange. If this be true then we should find the greatest progress made in that function through which the original control is most emphatically loosened and license allowed for the intentional manipulation of meanings. This is the case in the semblant mode, and so it becomes, I think, the great place for the early development of abstraction.

20. It is worth while, moreover, to cite the two cases, inasmuch as they present a real difference that our full theory of abstraction will have to recognize. It is a difference that the theory of selective meaning—worked out in worth-theory, ethics, etc. as well—must take fully into account. I mean the difference between an abstract meaning arising from the selective treatment of an item of the recognitive context, on the one hand, and one which embodies the intent of satisfaction or fulfilment on the other. It is evident that in the one case, we have a meaning that is selective of a primary recognitive content, while in the other, we have one that is not primarily of the nature of content, but of selective intent. And it seems clear, also, that we attribute these two sorts of abstract meanings to objects in different senses.[1]

Looked at even superficially, the distinction is plain and may be read in terms of an earlier one now familiar to us. The meaning, no matter what it is, is made up of content and intent, of framework and personal interpretation. The latter is what the selection in terms of personal satisfaction, interest, and desire determines. It is as such not part of the cognized content; it is either simply imputed to it, or actually read as arising through the process of inner control or participation. In the former case, this inner control factor is not differentiated within the entire meaning; the whole object as personal meaning is simply accepted as there. Later on, when the inner sphere becomes relatively subjective, the intent meaning becomes more and more "inner." The "tertiary" or selective quality falls away from the content. This becomes very marked in the play mode, and differentiates its results from the selective abstraction of elements of content or

---

[1] The distinction is one of importance for the theory of value, the worth-meaning being one that is "imputed" to or *imported into* the object as a "tertiary" quality, over and above those recognitive marks called since Locke, "primary" and "secondary" qualities. These latter we *recognize in* the object; the tertiary qualities we *attribute to* the object (cf. Urban, *Psychological Review*, March, 1907).

" real " fact. The child now recognizes his own initiation, his reading of values, as personal to him ; he consciously plays by sembling the objects with his own satisfactions. He does not attempt to turn these meanings into permanent recognitive contexts, nor expect his playthings to retain their dramatic rôles when he is not playing with them. This anticipates a truth about the world of values considered as worth-predicates. The value arises in the appreciation, the apprizement in the inner life ; and the process of abstraction is a movement that detaches this intent more and more from the object.

On the other hand, however, there are also the selective meanings which do belong to and remain part of the scheme *Case of Re-* of recognitive context as such. These are items of *cognition.* actual content even in the prelogical stages of cognition. It is selective meanings of this sort to which the intent of personal satisfaction and disappointment adheres. The difference is that, in the development of the entire meaning of an object, the mark or quality that gives the satisfaction or fulfilment is necessary to that fulfilment. The relative distinction between the satisfaction as a subjective experience, and the objective content that gives the satisfaction, is one of progressive contrast as the full meaning is achieved. Control of an external sort restricts the schema of content ; the intent to use this schema goes over to the inner life of the agent and user.

21. Further, this distinction serves, from the point of view of selective meaning, to motive the rise of logical abstraction as *Rise of* such. We have seen [1] that logical meaning is a re-*logical* distribution wherein all possible sorts and modes of *Abstraction.* meaning reach a common standing, a mediate control in thought or experience, from which their reference to their original spheres becomes again a secondary movement. This is the case with selective no less than recognitive meanings. For any meaning whatever may become object of thought and judgment. There thus arises, in the mode of judgment, the possibility of reading satisfactions and facts in a common context. The abstractions that are mere values, direct experiences, and those that are items of context, come to stand together as in a new sense abstractions, i.e. abstractions of thought, or logical abstractions.[2]

---

[1] See vol. i. chap. xi.

[2] That in certain cases this process does not exhaust the original

§ 6. Logical Abstraction : the Abstract Term

Having thus looked into the development of selective meaning in its progression up to logical abstraction, we may draw certain lessons from that development.

22. In the first place, we may at once say that logical abstraction as it is sometimes depicted is a formal and very largely a mythological function. We are told that from a given whole, a concept or object, the thinker intentionally isolates and considers one element of its meaning. This element, therefore, already formed as a meaning, is treated alone or abstractly. This is abstraction.

Usual View.

It is evident that this is the way that abstraction may proceed—provided the thinker is *already supplied with the abstract meaning*. For to take out a meaning as abstract is to have the abstraction already accomplished in mind. To say, " I will think only of the red colour of my coat," is to say that I *have already thought* only of the red colour. Otherwise I should not have known what mark or character I intended to abstract. In other words, this depicts *the use made of abstractions*—the purpose to select and utilize this or that abstraction—not the formation, the process of origin, of abstract meaning. On the contrary, such a process must be one whereby some aspect of a meaning *not yet abstract*—or not in the same sense, abstract—may become so. What is the genetic movement by which this meaning is isolated ?

It assumes "Abstract Ideas".

The truth of the matter then is that an abstract meaning is a selective meaning in course of development. It is selective in earlier modes before it becomes abstract in thought. Its relative isolation as a meaning of what is called logical " intension " comes through the gradual progression, as we have depicted it, from the prelogical and quasi-logical stages ; and its appearance as an abstract thought is the form the new act of selective thinking gives it when it is rendered subject-matter of judgment. In other words, it is not a judgment at all until it is an abstract judgment ; [1] *it is not selected for abstraction, but abstracted by a process of selection.*

It is not genetic.

meaning, but gives a "construct" or description of it only, is shown below, chaps. xiv., xv.

[1] We have already found this process illustrated in the rise of the abstract meaning " existence " which arises only by the act of judgment wherein the control-intent of a meaning is acknowledged. It is not a ready-made " idea " attached to a content (see vol. i. chap. x. sect. ix.).

23. Again, we are often told that abstraction is in some way a damaging process—that an abstract meaning is less real or true or fruitfully applicable than those that are not abstract. An abstraction is considered to be lacking in some element of logical value.

Now what truth there is in this depends upon the sort of mode of abstraction in question. All thought is abstract as

Is Abstraction "damaging"? such ; for it is a system of meanings that arise in the pursuit and development of personal purpose and interest. There are, it is true, two extreme sorts of abstraction. One is that which embodies a maximum of individual intent and preference, that which is set up as fulfilling, whether its context and control fully justify the anticipation or not. Such, for example, is the abstraction " perfection." It is a projection of what is properly called " ideal " meaning,— ideal mainly in the sense that as personal intent it is nowhere realized. Abstraction of this sort does lack the context of fact adequate to a presupposition of judgment and belief. But still as an intent meaning it attaches to contents in which corresponding general and particular meanings are also realized.

The other case is also an extreme : it is the limiting " theoretical " case in which the context of relationship is looked upon as fulfilling the interest of purely impersonal and independent truth. Such abstraction takes a thought-meaning out of its vital nexus or progression, out of the determining conditions of feeling, conation, and interest in which alone objects have their real presuppositions. Such abstraction, although motived by just that intent of neutrality that all common and reasonable meanings should possess, may be lacking in some of the elements of determination which all profitable thinking must include. The difficulty or defect of such abstraction is evidently its isolation or detachment from the complete whole of developing thought.

But between these two extremes lies the entire tract of meanings due to the actual movements of mind in reaching its

All meaning is more or less Abstract. knowledge of things. Its discoveries, its fulfilments, its elucidations, its proposals, all proceed under the vital selections which constitute meanings abstract. The very distinction by which truth can be set up independently of practice, is an abstraction which impairs the wholeness of the mental life. But on the other hand, the opposed contention that practise can proceed without recognition of a system of theoretical truths by which it is informed and directed, is

again an abstraction whereby a distinction of aspects, legitimate
within the body of the whole meaning from which they are
abstracted, is made to destroy the fabric of the whole.   The
motive to abstraction is, in short, one of the essential motives
at work in the development of knowledge just as the motive
to generalize is another, and the motive to idealize is a third.
But the resulting body of knowledge is, all the while, the progressive fulfilment and essential outcome of all these motives at
once.   All logical meaning is *general and also abstract and also
ideal*—and it is besides, in relevant and relative senses, *particular and concrete and true.*

24. The entire movement may be said to be one of *erosion*
and *accretion*.   A meaning is held for what it is, acted upon in
Process of   personal life and social intercourse, until experience
Erosion and rubs it down in some aspects of its full intent and
Accretion.   builds it up in others.   The child's general, derived
from old experience and labelled with an old name, becomes its
schema of assumption with reference to the less habitual and the
new.   Its meanings, both in their general application and in
their special and personal value, lose unessential marks and
acquire added worth, lose application here and gain it there.
Unlike the rolling stone, the current thought gathers as it runs.
I have illustrated elsewhere both these aspects—erosion and
accretion—with reference to the growth of conceptual meaning
in dealing with situations of fact ; [1] here the reactions to persons
may be further emphasized, since in the use of terms in social
intercourse the individual makes his appeal first of all to others,
and so checks-up and improves his meanings and his language at
once.   More particular detail on both these directions of growth
—narrowing by " erosion " and widening by " accretion "—
follows in the treatment of analysis and synthesis below. [2]

We may attempt, however, to show more positively the
relation of abstract to general meaning.   We find that so far
Abstraction   from being antagonistic or opposed movements, they
and General- are, on the contrary, complementary phases of any
ization.   and all thought process.   The contrasted aspects of a
logical meaning which they present are covered in logic by the
terms . " Extension " or breadth and " Intension " or   depth,

[1] See *Handbook of Psychology, Senses and Intellect,* chap. xiv. § 2, and
Social and Ethical Interpretations, chap. iv. § 1 (this latter dealing with
language as social instrument).

[2] See chap. ix, § 1.

both being called, especially since Kant, the " quantities " of judgments. The relation of Extension and Intension may be profitably considered from the point of view of the " terms " in which both abstract and general meanings are rendered.

§ 7. EXTENSION AND INTENSION

25. The discussion of generalization already conducted above may suffice to introduce the concept of extension.[1] In a **Extension as** broad sense, a general term is one that " extends " to **General** a wider or narrower range of illustrative cases or " particulars." For this reason, this range is called " extension " or " breadth." Its extent of meaning—its breadth or range of application to cases—varies and constitutes the distinguishing mark of a meaning looked at distributively or denotatively.

On the other hand, the idea of " intension " is readily seen to be broadly speaking that of relative abstraction. An object, **Intension** taken individually or connotatively, may vary in **as Abstract.** the marks or characters with reference to which it is selected or made up. I may mean " man " as illustrating " masculinity," or man as illustrating " humanity " ; and the special interest of the moment determines which I mean. If I mean " man the human being," the characteristic marks consist of all those characters which distinguish the human kind ; but if I mean " man the male," only those which characterize the masculine sex are intended. This is the difference in intension, the individual case being the same, and being indefinite as to extension, so far as my present reference is concerned. If we say that an act of cognition that includes more marks is " deeper " than one that includes fewer, then we may describe differences of intension as also differences of " depth " of meaning. And it is evident that the difference is determined by just the same movement of selection that we have found to issue in abstraction. The abstract meaning "humanity" isolates certain marks belonging to the larger whole of the human kind. As rendering this meaning the term " humanity " is abstract. On the contrary, " masculinity " is a selective meaning made up under a more special interest. Certain marks only of the larger whole of humanity are intended. The term " masculinity " renders this abstract meaning. Bearing all this in mind, we may ask as to the relation of extension and intension to each other.

[1] We have already discussed the extensive " quantity " of judgments in chapter iv. of this volume.

26. In general we may describe the difference between the two cases with reference to the classes which the meanings **Infra-class** qualify. Extension is a meaning of plurality and **Meaning,** particularity within the class defined by the intension ; it is, so to speak, an *infra-class* meaning. Its intent is not to ask how the class is constituted ; that is presupposed. Its intent is to determine the range of cases within the class. The intensive meaning, on the other hand, is an *inter-class* meaning. It intends just the determination of marks by which the objects are **Inter-Class** grouped in classes. Apart from the prelogical motives **Meaning,** —practical and other—by which objects are individuated in classes, we may say that the logical class is constituted by the recognition and acknowledgment of intensive marks

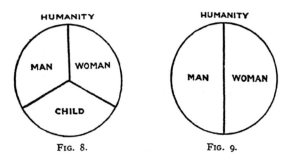

FIG. 8.   FIG. 9.

wherever they appear, in relative independence of the range or size or extent of the class.[1]

The diagrams (Figs. 8, 9) show the relation of the two sorts of meaning to each other. In Fig. 8, " humanity " has **Figures.** the three sub-classes " man," " woman," " child." If now the intension of " man " and " woman " be diminished, so that the difference is simply one of sex, regardless of age, we have Fig. 9, in which the relation of the " man-woman " classes has changed. They have absorbed that of " children," but the inclusion of all the cases within the class " humanity " has not been altered.

---

[1] This general view of classification we should have anticipated from our discussions of individuation (vol. i. chap. viii.). Individuation as general attaches only to particulars each of which is *eligible*, quite apart from other contemporary eligible cases. The relative inclusion of cases is a matter of their being each in turn eligible in its intensive mark. On classification see chap. xi. § 4, below.

27. It is an accepted statement of formal logic that breadth and depth vary inversely with each other : that an increase of Do Extension the range of cases to which a term applies requires a and Intension decrease in the number of characters selected, that is in the depth. For example, if we use the term " man " for the whole human race, thus extending its breadth to include women, we must give up the requirement that male characters shall be present, since female characters are now also permissible. That is, the definition in terms of depth must now omit all specification as to sex and this is an impoverishment of the intension. On the contrary, if we should diminish the breadth by limiting the meaning to " adults of the male sex," we would then have to include the further marks by which adults are distinguished from children ; this would increase the depth or intension of the meaning. This relation seems then to hold on the whole,[1] but from our present point of view we may raise certain interesting questions.

Assuming the method of growth of a meaning by generalization, on the one hand, and by abstraction, on the other hand, vary we may ask whether changing either or each of these Inversely ? requires a change in the status of the term in question with reference to the other. That is, can a meaning grow more general without altering its intensive or abstract meaning, and can a meaning grow more abstract without altering its extensive or general meaning ? Let us take up these questions in order.

28. As to the growth of a meaning in its general character or extension, two cases are to be distinguished. One is the case Enumeration. of mere enumeration, identification, or inclusion of cases not before observed. This is growth in extension in the sense of widened application through information as to the eligibility of cases to fulfil the intensive meaning. It is reflected in the " all," " some," etc., of quantified propositions.

Now it is evident enough that such an extension of the application does not of itself involve any change in the intension of Application the meaning : on the contrary it requires that the may change meaning be kept constant in this respect. To pass alone. from " six of these men are school-teachers," to " seven are school-teachers," requires that my intensive class meaning " school-teacher " remain the same ; otherwise the move-

[1] This appears in Figs. 8, 9 ; diminishing the intension of " man " and " woman " (as in Fig. 8) distributes the children in these two classes, and enlarges their extension (as in Fig. 9).

ment is fruitless. To those who accept the same definition of
school-teacher, that meaning is not altered at all in
intension by the discovery that there is present another
case. But there is another consideration, which arises from
our view of predication as involving both elucidation and proposal. We have to ask whether in this case the change really
involves any alteration of the extension of the meaning school-
teacher—any real process of proposal ?

But the
change is in

Evidently it does not ; both speaker and hearer already
accept the definition of school-teacher. In actual intercourse
the changed statement would indicate simply that the
observer had at first misapplied the meaning school-
teacher, or he would have included the additional case. The
range or extension of his *meaning* is the same ; the variation is
one of observation. If, however, a proposal is made to the
hearer to revise the extent of his meaning and include new cases
that *were not before eligible*, then there is really change in the
intension also. " Why must I include Mr. A., why is he eligible ? "
is now the question. This evokes the reply, " because he gives
private lessons." The effect on the meaning now is that the
hearer must drop from it the mark of teaching exclusively in
an organized school, let us say ; this is a loss in intension.

Application
strictly.

The test, therefore, is as to whether there is any real
change in the intended meaning elucidated : if not, then the true
extension is not altered by the mere telling-off or identifying of new cases. There is no change in the intension either, because all the while the meaning *intends*
to cover all eligible cases whether they have been actually discovered or not. We would not say that mistakes in the census-
returns of voters altered the extension of the term " adult-
male-citizen." But if it be *proposed* to include cases not before
intended, not before eligible—that involves changing the marks
of eligibility, which is nothing else than changing the intension.
Put succinctly, the question is : *is there anything proposed that
involves the reconsideration of the cases already admitted* ; if not,
there is no change in the extension, *no matter how many new
cases be found.*

No change
in Intensive
Eligibility

We may say, then, of this movement that so far as it is mere
identification of cases, mere enumeration, application, or repetition which *does not propose a revision of the meaning*, it increases neither the extension nor the intension. But so far as it does revise the meaning by proposing

No revision
of Meaning.

to include cases not before eligible, it changes both the extension and the intension. I shall call the extent of mere application or enumeration *breadth*, as contrasted with what is properly "extension." [1]

29. Another case is that in which the "speaker" is not merely elucidating a general meaning by enumerating or identi-

Case of Re-reading.

fying the cases thereof, but is himself *re-reading his meaning* by the interpretation of new cases. This, it is evident, is just the position of the "hearer" in the case already discussed. It is now a case *not of elucidation, but of proposal*. The meaning in course of development is brought to the facts not as a "general" but as a "schematic" or problematic meaning. Its progress is toward a new statement as general; it really grows. The case is broader than that already discussed, since it does not propose the acceptance of a definite additional individual—which requires the elimination or disregard of marks by which he was before excluded—but opens the broader question as to whether all increase in extension of this essential type, considered as real growth in general meaning, of necessity involves such an elimination of marks and a consequent contraction of intension.

In answer to this question we may cite a case in which increase of extension seems to carry with it increase rather than decrease of intension. It is the case in which there is contemporaneous growth of two general terms each carrying a certain intension and

---

[1] This is in accord with the corresponding suggestion (this chap, sect. 31) as to "depth," which is not new. It is important to make this distinction, not only on account of the use made of it in the theory of induction, but on account of the actual ambiguity that its disregard creates. Cf. the theory of "Information" suggested by C. S. Peirce in my *Dict. of Philos.* ii. p. 411. As I understand his view, in the case just given there is a change in the "information" of the entire meaning, or in the phrase of Duns Scotus, in its "extensive distinctness." It is well to have a term for this sort of variation in both its instances (the one here given and the corresponding variation in "depth" as expounded just below) and "information" is a good word for it. Peirce, however, seems to fall into confusion (loc. cit.) by identifying this case of "breadth" with real logical extension. As we will see later on (chap. ix. § 2), induction by "enumeration"— mere increase of information as to fresh cases—is not true induction in that it does not involve any new act of generalization. True induction involves change of intension as well as of extension. See the further note on the term "Depth," below, sect. 31 of this chapter.

With the position of this section the treatment of Keynes, *Formal Logic*, may be compared, especially his remarks on p. 39.

both so extended as to over-lap or mutually include each other.
In this case either term may be broadened to include
members of the other term and at the same time
acquire connotation or intension from the other term.
For example the term " whale " is extended, let us say, by reason
of a discovery in connection with its breathing apparatus, to
include certain animals before known as " mammals "; this
makes it possible to require of the meaning, as a class, that it
have other marks belonging to mammals, that is, that it be enlarged also in intension. The passage of the term " whale," to
over-lap the general class " mammals," or to be included in it, may
therefore, it would seem, increase both its extension and its
intension. It may acquire the intensive marks of mammals,
and also be extended to additional individuals.

May involve increased intension.

The essential question in the interpretation of this case and
others that might be cited seems to be concerning the nature of
the new information which leads to a change of extension. The question is, again, what new proposal is
suggested ?—what does the suggested change involve ?
The information may be such that the marks of intension are not
altered, as in the case of simple enumeration. This is the effect
on the class mammals of our illustration ; the whales, let us say,
are added to the class. There may come, however, through
such information, a real discovery that removes earlier misin-
formation, or establishes an inter-class relation bringing within
the term meaning (say the whales) a group of new individuals
with their class-intension.

What Proposal is made ?

30. By the rule of formal logic the intension of the term would
be diminished by ruling out any mark that before separated two
classes.

But the question arises, does the change always propose just
this and nothing else ? Is it not a matter of re-reading of the
whole meaning ?—of the cases already included along
with those now taken in ?—and is not the result
determined by the facts of the case ? In the present
case, the new proposal—to consider whales as mammals and also
to include new creatures as whales—may result in (1) leaving the
old intension of whales undisturbed, or (2) diminishing it through
the dropping of characters inconsistent with those of the mammals
now included, or (3) increasing it by the addition of the marks
going necessarily with the new cases. In actual experience the
first seldom happens, since both the processes involved in the

Re-reading may or may not change intension.

second and the third are at work and the result is a new reconstructed meaning. What the resulting balance of intension,
therefore, is to be is a matter of empirical determination. The
essential thing is that there be an actual change in extensive
meaning, not one merely of breadth of application ; this requires
a re-reading of the whole meaning for all the cases.

Viewing it in this way we are able to formulate the result,
in the terms of our fundamental distinction between elucidation
The result
what the
facts require. and proposal. If the new information really proposes anything new in extension then the intensive
eligibility of all the particular cases is to be re-read.
On the other hand, if the term be used strictly for elucidation,
then the new information simply secures its further application
to cases already intended by it, and no change in intension occurs.

31. Furthermore in this movement as actually taking place,
there is a necessary return upon the extension of the term, in
Does changed
Intension
involve view of the newly-read intension, and we arrive at an
answer to the second of our questions : that as to
whether intension can be changed without changing
extension. In the whale-mammal case, the return movement
is evident. It is possible that some of the old-time whales are
no longer eligible under the new rule of intension ; and they
must be dropped. Further research may also lead to the
dropping of some of the new mammal-whale-like creatures at
first admitted. So the question then becomes, what does the
new intension in turn propose as to extension ? If the meaning
be one of proposal, or of further instrumental use, then *only
the result can determine* whether such a changed intension will
apply to the same or to an altered collection of cases.

That the extension will remain unchanged is very unlikely,
for a reason analogous to that of the similar case of unchanged
changed
Extension ? intension in the reversed conditions, namely, that
motives to both increase and decrease are operative,
and the result is a matter of empirical re-reading.

It is to be noted, however, that here also, as in extension,
there is a possible sort of variation that raises no question of
Change in
Information,
only. revising the general aspect of the meaning at all ; a
case of added information in the matter of intensive
characters. In saying " John has a bad temper,"
or " all men are irritable " I do not change the extension of
" John " or " men " by adding a new intensive mark. This
case, like the corresponding one of increased application in

range or " breadth," yields readily to our interpretation. The increased marks are not added to the intension in a way that opens up to revision the old criteria of the class ; they do not propose anything requiring revision of extension. Following

Depth. a suggestion earlier made, I shall limit the term " depth " to this relative increase or decrease of information as attaching to a given concept, and confine " intension " to the essential marks that serve as differentia of the class.[1]

32. We are not interested in following out all the subtleties that have crept into the discussion of extension and intension ;

Intension as Proposal. our interest terminates on the general interpretation in terms of our distinction between elucidation and proposal—the attitudes of belief and question which are our guiding threads through all the questions of logic. The *proposal is the experimental aspect, the elucidation is the implication aspect* ; and here as elsewhere we find the meanings fruitfully interpreted from this point of view. Intension, no less than extension, is found to have both retrospective reference and force and prospective or instrumental intent. As retrospective it is subject-matter of accomplished judgment, having the presupposition of belief, fixed in extensive quantity, treated as part of a context of logical and theoretical meaning. As prospective, it is a proposal or hypothesis, assumptive in its " real " reference—a " schema " charged with meaning not yet acknowledged as of definite range and extent, but used as instrumental to further progress.

33. In a broad way, we may say that generalization, the application of a general rule, is genetically the attempt to fix, classify, and hold meanings. It is the reading of results

---

[1] See the author's *Handbook of Psychology, Senses and Intellect*, p. 274, together with the references given therein (especially George, *Lehrbuch der Psychologie*, pp. 499 f). The usage recommended here is as follows, adapting the terms denotation and connotation as employed by J. S. Mill.

		Denotation.	Connotation.
Quantity	..	Extension	..	Intension.
Information	..	Breadth	..	Depth

The term information as applied here is adopted as fit rather than as embodying the theory of information suggested by Peirce. I do not place " breadth " and " depth " as here used under " quantity " since they attach primarily and most characteristically to judgments that are logically " unquantified " (singulars and analytic universals).

already obtained in the development of personal and social interests. Its temptation is that popularly described
Résumé. as " hasty generalization " : the more superficial use
of such readings as fixed and final in situations that suggest
them. On the other hand, the failures and embarrassments
arising in the operation of this function are due to the rise of
meanings of the intensive sort which both claim and require
special rendering. This is abstraction—the isolation of special
qualitative aspects in situations already reduced in part by
earlier generalization. The process of development is then
furthered by the schematism, proposal, or hypothesis whereby
these newer and relatively isolated aspects of experience are
reduced. The new adjustment that renders the entire meaning
is then again a generalization. It reinterprets the contents as
particulars with a revised extension. Further abstraction again
becomes instrumental to further reinterpretation of experience ;
and so the vital process of organization goes on. Its forward
movement is tentative and experimental through and through.
But its results, read backwards, at each and every stage, are
theoretically true and final, in the control for which they are
established.[1]

§ 8. SINGULARIZATION

34. The individuation of an object as " singular " presents
a case in which the quantity of the meaning in extension seems
to be fixed while its intension is changing. My in-
Singularity. dividuation of my watch, or of my watch-dog, as a
single individual, does not forbid my finding out more and more
about the characters of the object. Those characters that make

---

[1] An interesting correlation comes to mind between this result and that
reached above in the discussion of disjunction. It will be remembered
that we found disjunction to attach to predications quantified in extension
as in " A's are either B's, or C's," the disjunctive force residing in the
schematic or " alternative " issue that is still undetermined. This aspect is
essentially an intent of " proposal " with reference to a further reading
that removes the disjunction. Now of the two main sorts of disjunction
we may say that schematism of the general —as in " these counters are
either coins or toys "—in a proposal *in intension* ; the objects are still
to be qualitatively defined and so the class determined. On the other
hand, the other great type of disjunction, schematism of the particular—
—as in " coins are gold, silver, or copper "—is proposal *in extension* ; the
objects are simply to be examined with reference to their distribution under
the given general.

the one object a watch, its reliability as a time-keeper, reveal themselves to me only gradually ; and those characters of the dog whereby he is entitled to a similar descriptive term change with his reliability when on " watch." So of any of the marks ; the single object may profoundly change its meaning for me.

At the same time, the case presents very interesting special features, arising in the movement by which singular individua-

Defined above.

tion proceeds. We may, therefore, recall the motives that determine a meaning as singular—motives pointed out in some detail on an earlier page.

35. It is usually held that the individuation of the singular presents no special movement of logical process. The singular

Is it Logical ?

is treated as merely a present object, having only that mode of meaning which constitutes it in some sense an individual.

But in reality, there is no prelogical singular meaning. To invoke it—as we have seen already in the case of abstraction—

It is not Prelogical.

would mean that one had already "made up" the singular as a unit before making use of it. Pro-perly speaking, what is called "singular" in the prelogical mode is in no full sense singular at all ; it is some one of those modes of " unity " already pointed out in the chapter on in-dividuation.[1] By these the logical judgment of singularity is being prepared for. So far as there is a meaning of singularity as such in the prelogical modes it is not one of cognition but one of appreciation : an object is a singular fulfilment, the terminus of an exclusive interest. But to fulfil such an interest it is not necessary that the object should have the marks of cognitive differentiation whereby only the one single thing will serve. We find that so long as the fulfilment may be secured the object may vary, provided it is taken for the same. Some other doll, not too different from " Jane," may serve as " Jane " in the child's affectionate interest ; while even the identical " Jane " will not serve once the idea of difference, or suggestion of change, springs up to inhibit the outflow of the exclusive and appre-ciative interest.[2]

---

[1] Vol. i. chap. viii. ; see also summary in chap. x. § 6, sect. 29.

[2] The actual recognition process here is that of class-recognition—involving the *a* elements of the attention, as given in the formula in vol. i, chap. x. sect. 31. The attention is not specialized upon the marks of singularity within the class, which would carry the corresponding judgment of identity and difference.

36. Another current interpretation of the singular meaning makes it a case of universal extension, equivalent to a meaning expressed in the form " all are." This not only accounts for it as a case of general meaning, but exhausts it in such terms.

From our present point of view, this is most superficial. To say that what I mean when I say " John is irritable " is that

It is not Universal in Quantity.

" A class of objects which, however, has but one case, John, has the mark irritability " is making sport of psychology in the supposed interest of certain economies of formal logic. On the contrary, what I do mean when I say " John is irritable," or " John is the only black man in the room," is something very different from this. Aspects of meaning are embodied which are quite new ; which though reached by the movement by which the general and particular are also reached, represents a very special determination. Indeed, as is said in an earlier place,[1] so special is it that instead of saying that the singular is the unit out of which general and universal meanings are built up, the opposite is true. It is only on the basis of the movement whereby general and universal meanings arise, and of the differentiations that they afford, that the cognition of an object as a singular and unique individual is possible. That is, it is only on the basis whereby the case has general and universal meaning, that it is given the singular meaning also. This appears in two ways which serve to introduce for the logical mode considerations analogous to those already advanced with regard to simpler modes of meaning.

37. In the first place, singular meaning may continue to be of the " imported," " imputed," or selective kind, already

It may remain Selective.

pointed out in earlier connections. In the logical mode, this appears as a judgment of " value," over against those judgments of " truth " or fact which give the subject-matter of thought reference to an outer control. If the experience remains, besides, one of immediate satisfaction or worth, then in that aspect it is not logical at all, but personal and private.

The rendering of a meaning as one of exclusive interest is always essentially of this type. The abstraction is of the sort just pointed out, the isolation of marks by some form of appreciation.

38. The same is true also of what we have called above the " essential " singularity of an object, that aspect whereby the

[1] Vol. i. chap. x. sect. 30.

given object is controlled as the only one in its sphere, as unique.

Essential Singularity not generalized. This means the presence of certain compelling marks in respect to which the process of generalization is resisted. It requires, first, a process of generalization of the wider meanings resident in the case in hand. It is only thus that the mark wherein the case is *not generalizable can be isolated*. This amounts to a process of abstraction as pointed out under that topic. The individual object under observation, *besides* fulfilling the meaning of particular under a general, and being an instance of a universal, has also some intensive marks whereby it stands as *not fully exhausted by these meanings*.

39. The result in both cases, then, is the same. There is the isolation of those marks of a whole meaning or logical subject-**The Singular is Special.** matter wherein that meaning is *not exhausted in its general, particular and universal aspects*. Just this relation of isolation is what is rendered in the judgment of singularity. When I say "there is only one Niagara," it is the relative uniqueness, or stand-off-ness, of this case as having marks over and above those by which it is classified with others. When I say simply "let us consider the water-fall Niagara," I am rendering not a singular meaning but a particular ; and when I say "there are other water-falls" I am using a general. These meanings are presupposed[1] in the rendering of the further judgment, "there is but one Niagara," but they do not exhaust it. Singularity is not rendered in a judgment of extension.

We thus see that singularity is indeed a special mode of logical meaning. The singular is not a unit, it is rather an out-**It is not general.** come at a specific stage in the development of logical process ; and as such it is a common, a relational, an acknowledged meaning. It is common since as judgment it is individuated as holding for general recognition and acknowledgment. It is thus open to public inspection. It is relational in the sense just brought out ; it implies general and universal meanings, the relational complex of the whole object. It is an acknowledged subject-matter, since it is only in a process of judgment that such a meaning is achieved.

These conclusions, we may go on to say, raise interesting points in connection with the place of this meaning in the pro-**Singular Predication.** gression of predication. It is evident that the modes of predication established for general and abstract

---

[1] These become, in the language of current worth theory, the "presuppositions," *Voraussetzungen*, of the attributed worths.

meanings that have no singular intent do not suffice. A singular meaning as such must have a vehicle whereby both its personal acknowledgment, and its common endorsement may have characteristic expression. This may be brought out in further detail.

40. First, we may say that the singular meaning is one in which the generalization in extension reaches its terminus and limit. The assertion, "there is but one Niagara," means that no generalization of waterfalls can go further and include those aspects wherein Niagara is thus unique. It is the case then of what would seem, from the point of view of generalization, not that of least extension, but that in which the meaning that serves as basis for the assertion is not one of relation between this and other cases under a general.

Singular object has least Extension

But second, we have to recognize also that the meaning is not only that which marks Niagara as a single case, but also that which allows the comparison with other cases necessary to establish its uniqueness. It is not only "the water-fall, *Niagara*," but also "Niagara, *the water-fall*." This gives the object all the intension of the class of meanings which its general aspects cover, as well as that which its singular aspect isolates. It is therefore an object having maximum intension.

and most Intension

41. So the question then arises—can a meaning of maximum intension, in the sense of unique character, have any logical extension at all? And the answer is that, properly speaking, it cannot. For it is of the essence of a particular meaning, not of a singular, that it be a case under a general. If in its singularity it essentially resists generalization, then its one case is not a particular. Or we may put the matter the other way, and ask whether an extensive class meaning can render the unique. This too we must answer negatively. For it is a class only as being a general, and there is no generality for that aspect of meaning in which the object is unique.[1]

But Singular meaning as such,

This suggests, in short, that singular meaning is not a meaning of logical extension, although it may for logical purposes be taken as a sort of limiting case of intension —the case that illustrates the increase of intension until it finally isolates the single object. But this, as I have shown, is not the method of its origin, nor

has neither Extension nor Intension.

---

[1] It may be truly said that the judgment of uniqueness establishes *a class of unique objects* ; but with reference to such a class the one object is no longer unique or singular, but particular.

does it reveal the core of its meaning. The singular is that which *objectively resists or subjectively eludes generalization.* It is motived by a process of special logical individuation. I shall, therefore, call the process " singularization." It requires, as will appear below, generalization in " community." [1]

42. The remaining question, that which principally concerns us here, is that of the place of singular meaning in the progression of thought ; in what respect is it a meaning of elucidation and in what respect one of proposal ?

At the outset we may say that a singular predication eluci-dates a content more fully than any other ; and this is only

Singular Object one of

to say that it has maximum implication. We see it in the fact that the truly singular judgment is reached only as the culmination of processes of general and

particular individuation. When I say " there is only one Niagara," and expect to be fully understood, I suggest a mass of relational meaning proceeding from " this water-fall only " (singular), to " this thing as a water-fall " (particular), and " water-falls like and unlike this " (general), together with " what-ever presuppositions of belief attach to our common reading of physical things."

Or put reversely, it requires belief in " physical existence," in " various types of water-falls," in the common marks of the " general meaning water-fall," and in those further

personal Elucidation

marks that in this case render Niagara " singular." As thus full of intent, it is the most difficult meaning to make catholic, although in its personal origin the least

difficult to construct ; for since it has but the one case, presenting marks for direct apprehension or valuation, it is, just in its singular aspect, remote from common inspection. The marks that resist generalization, as well as those that fulfil im-mediate personal interest, are, however, of all intensive marks most readily accepted and acknowledged by the one observer himself.

43. For the hearer for whom the elucidation is made, therefore,

but of Social Proposal

for the reasons mentioned, the singular aspects may be most hypothetical and schematic, stated as proposals

for the determination of his personal belief. The statement of another's apprehension or appreciation comes to him, as indeed does no other meaning, as a proposal for his own. The meaning is then to the hearer, so far as appreciative elements enter into its intent, the *least socialized and the most selective.*

[1] See chap. xiv. § 8.

We find the singular to be a meaning of great interest from the point of view of our main problem : that of the experimental determination of thought. For just *in that respect wherein the singular is immediate, concrete, and unhypothetical to the individual, in that respect it is mediate and problematical to others.* Its social confirmation is most difficult just where its personal value is strongest; for it is this part of the entire intent that general and universal meanings do not exhaust.

This introduces a remarkable antinomy in the interpretation of logical meaning ; it requires us, from one point of view, to treat knowledge by a line of criticism that desiderates a certain immediacy or first-handness which is at its best in the singular case. It is in the singular that personal belief realizes and justifies its presuppositions. It is the case that most nearly dispenses with further elucidation through general and universal meanings. But, on the other hand, the aspect of knowledge wherein the competence of judgment appears is that of commonness, social validity and acceptance. This is least realized in those aspects which are immediate, first-hand, and singular ; for such meanings, *requiring little elucidation, also give little* ; and the actual hearer, and in general the possible hearer, is asked to accept mere proposal with no further confirmation. Descartes' tests of clearness and distinctness for instance, and indeed all appeals to the immediate data of consciousness, are open to these two modes of estimation. It constitutes a real antinomy of judgmental meaning. What is " clear and distinct " as immediate, is private, appreciative, unelucidated in logical terms ; but validity for social acceptance is the ground and presupposition of appropriate or truthful subject-matter. How can judgment render both ? The most valid social judgments, taken strictly as relational content, are the least competent from the point of view of that sort of immediate acceptance that is independent of logical grounding ; and those most valid from the latter point of view, are those whose social confirmation and strictly logical grounding is most difficult and remote. This will be made matter of further discussion on a later page.[1]

[margin notes: Antinomy of Personal Singular — and Social General]

---

[1] See especially chap. x. § 6 and chap. xiv. §§ 3, 4, and 9, where it is shown that " essential " singularity yields to logical rendering through the judgment of " recurrence " in "community"; but that the " imported " singularity that springs from selective interest remains " a-logical " to the end.

44. Here we may cling fast however to the important result
that in the singular meaning the elucidation and proposal aspects
Conclusion. of the whole object come most sharply into contrast.
When I emphatically assert that "cucumbers are
deadly," I make a point that the hearer's own experience alone
can elucidate, a proposal to him as to the character of his future
experience. And when I say " this is Tige, my dog," I propose
for his observation those qualities that make Tige singular in
his marks. In either case I make an abstraction that escapes
individuation in extension [1] and all other processes by which
genuine singularity would be eliminated or obscured.

§ 9. THE CONCRETE AND THE ABSTRACT

45. The term concrete is defined by Adamson as follows :—
" To think concretely is to represent general relations as embodied in particular instances, and so to delineate the object
thought of after the fashion and with the determining details
of immediate perceptive experience. A concrete term is often
defined as the name of a thing." [2]

Taking this as a fair statement of the connotation of concrete
in logic, we find the same author, in the same place, defining
Definition. abstract as follows :—" A relative designation, implying the isolation of an aspect, quality, or relation
from the whole in which it is directly apprehended, and the employment of the isolated factor as the subject of an assertion."
He adds, " in Aristotle also appears the general mark of abstraction, as departure from the immediate data of sense." [3] Observing that this definition of abstraction is substantially that
which we have now justified from a genetic point of view, it
remains to see whether this author's rendering of the conception of the concrete is also sound.

If the general mode of meaning of the concrete is the opposite
of that of the abstract—one being the delineation of the object

---

[1] In view of the later result (see the references given in the preceding
note) according to which the singular is rendered as a general of " recurrence "—experiences of the one recurring object being equivalent to
different particulars of a general class—our conclusion here is one strictly
" in extension." " In extension " the *singular remains single*, although
" in community " it becomes a general of its own successive recurrences.

[2] The writer's *Dict. of Philos.*, sub verbo.

[3] In Aristotle the " concrete " is that aspect of meaning wherein the
" idea " or " form " is embodied in stuff ($\H{v}\lambda\H{\eta}$).

with " the determining details of immediate perceptive experience," and the other having the " general mark of departure
from the immediate data of sense "—then we should expect
to find concreteness attaching to meanings in the modes in
which abstractness also appears. That is, if relative lack of
A Contrast concreteness is abstractness, and vice versa, then
Meaning. " abstract-concrete " is a contrast meaning, attaching
to any content or subject-matter of thought. Or still again, if
concreteness attaches to objects relatively immediate as data of
perceptive experience, such objects being supposedly most free
from abstraction, then we should have to ask more positively
as to the consistency of this conception ; and as to the different
instances in which such concreteness is realized. On this point
certain relevant considerations emerge from our previous discussions.

46. In the first place, this general definition throws concreteness over to the content or relational side of a meaning ; for
Concreteness it requires an object relatively free from the
is Recognitive isolating process whereby selective meanings arise.
" Brown " as applied adjectively to my horse is concrete, since it is
part of the recognitive meaning given to a present object of
perception. " Brownness " is a selective or abstract meaning applicable to horses and other objects. If, again, I am talking
substantively of colours, brown is concrete, a given perceptual
meaning; and brownness, the character that makes it brown,
becomes the abstract meaning. This would seem to be a consistent interpretation, the concrete standing for that aspect of
a meaning wherein it is relatively more recognitive and less
selective.

In the second place, this would seem to be confirmed by
the requirement whereby common meaning is concrete, for
and Common. only a recognitive meaning is common. The concrete
is referred to as a sort of standard meaning, for
proof and demonstration, as embodying more directly the reality
and control of common fact. This makes it the basis of common
reference and appeal.

Yet, third—and here our variations begin to appear—the
requirement of directness and immediacy would seem to be
It may be fulfilled in certain cases by meanings that are most
Selective. selective. A pure appreciation, a personal fulfilment
attaching to a content, is, we should ordinarily say, the most
concrete of experiences. But it is also so abstract that it cannot be

placed in a setting of recognitive meaning at all. As directly experienced it is a phase of personal intent attaching to the thing recognized. If this be so, we have to ask which of these two criteria of concreteness, presentativeness with commonness of content, or directness with immediacy, is the final mark of concreteness. If the latter, then the relation of contrast between abstractness and concreteness would seem to break down.

47. This suggestion, which leads to a revision of the usual inverse relation between concreteness and abstractness is, on the whole, a fruitful one. It is only with reference to recognitive meanings—things, contents, presented data of common recognition—that the concrete is relatively not abstract. In the realm of recognitive and common meanings, the standard of control, conversion and final reference is the relatively un-selective, un-abstract ; here the least-remote, most-immediate, least-

The Immedi- discursive meaning is sense-experience. Here the
ate is concrete is common in that it is nobody's personal
Concrete abstraction. But this *does not hold for all experience*, for the whole intent of objects which embody *appreciations*, *selections* as well. These are, from the start, personal aspects of meaning which are, with reference to the content to which they attach, *most abstract*. But as immediate, direct, un-remote and non-discursive, they are *prime and unrivalled for concreteness*. It is evident, also, that from this distinction of points of view, the meaning that is most concrete as immediate experience to the individual thinker, is in so far private, and hence not concrete at all to any one else.

48. This distinction may be illustrated too from the interpretation given the " singular." We found that an object may
as is the be singular either because *it* insists on being so—by
Singular. resisting generalization—or because *I* insist on its being so, by my exclusive interest, whether it really be so or not. Now it is evident that concreteness attaches to both these typical meanings of singularity, but for very different reasons. The thing that insists on being singular is concrete because it is directly cognitive, presentative, relatively unabstract ; but the thing that I insist on finding singular is concrete because it is immediate to my selective and abstracting appreciation. One is common, the other is private. One is concrete because it is not abstract ; the other is concrete although most abstract.

49. The two cases, while requiring us to recognize two modes

of concreteness, also illustrate a fundamental distinction recently

Worths are both Concrete and Abstract. put in evidence by writers on worth-theory : the distinction between what may be called predicates of fact or truth and predicates of worth. The latter, the predicates of worth, are not objectively determined ; they are determined as termini of attitudes, of conative-affective dispositions. They are not therefore read as part of the recognitive context of the objective meaning, but as meanings of appreciation and intent. Their presuppositions include selective appreciations or worth attitudes. Hence if such meanings are considered concrete by reason of their *immediacy in experience*, there is no contradiction in saying that, as carried over and made predicates of the recognitive subject-matter, they are of all possible meanings most personal and abstract.[1]

50. Our general conclusion—somewhat embarrassed it is true, by the exclusively logical use of " concrete," which does

The Criterion is Directness. not allow for its usual popular meaning—is this. The criterion of the concrete is directness, immediacy, not cognitive particularity or " perceptiveness." Such directness, however, *in the case of cognitive or presented content*, is best realized by singular and perceptive experience ; in this realm, therefore, the concrete and the abstract are properly contrasted. But a peculiar double intent attaches to " abstract." Its criterion is selectiveness, fulfilment, with relative isolation for and by personal interests and purposes, which in the cognitive realm results in relative remoteness and mediacy, and so relative lack of concreteness. But in other realms of experience, such as worth-experience, selective meaning is most direct and immediate. Such meanings are both concrete and abstract, since in them the two criteria coincide.

To illustrate, what is my entire intent in saying " good oranges are always light yellow " ? The " light yellow " is an abstract

Illustration. meaning made relatively more concrete by being set in the perceptive context of real oranges. That is, it loses abstractness by gaining concreteness. But the term " good " expresses a different sort of intent : it suggests a direct but very selective and personal experience, not cognitive in character, but worthful, appreciative. As meaning conveyed to you, it is most abstract—a " tertiary " quality—hardly attached at all to the cognitive whole, " orange " ; but to me,

---

[1] They are called above " tertiary " qualities, as being but loosely and selectively attributed to or read into the objects.

and to you also when you eat the orange, it is most direct and concrete.

Bringing this topic, finally, into line with the development of our main subject, the experimental character of thought, we find certain things worth saying about the concrete term.

51. As terms, it will be remembered, that is as embodying matter of thought or predication, all meanings are in a sense abstract. They are relatively abstract in the degree to which the taking up of a meaning in the context of reflection makes it subject to a form of mediate control. It is made " remote " from the " directness " of its own appropriate control. It thus fulfils the mark of *logical* abstractness. But within the mark of abstractness thus imparted to all logical meanings alike, it is evident there are differences in the material used. I may think by means of abstract symbols, X, Y, Z, or I may think by means of symbols of colour, form, and smell ; the former are more, the latter less, abstract. Now when I think in terms of my private appreciative meanings, my material, though most abstract as original meaning, is as logical meaning most concrete. For it is least remote from that verification which my new personal experience may direct and control. The concreteness of *appreciative judgments as such*—that is, judgments that render appreciative meanings—is on a level with that of judgments of cognitive fact or sense-perception. Opposed to these, judgments are found so remote from their original control that they require discursive proofs. This latter requirement appears in such abstractions as " pure-sensation," " pure-experience," the " physical atom," the " biophore," etc. These are meanings from which the direct and relatively immediate " detail of perceptive experience " has been lost, and the abstraction cannot be confirmed by an appeal to what may be called a concrete situation in nature or the mind.

Worth judgments relatively Concrete.

For example, in " the orange is good," the goodness as a first-hand meaning is most abstract, but as judgment it is logically more concrete than the corresponding predicate in the sentence " the orange is atomic in constitution."

52. The logical intent of the concrete falls, as we should expect, on the side of the elucidation of meaning. We say to the " abstract " thinker—" give me a concrete illustration," " elucidate by citing cases." This means that the return to concreteness is from the less grounded and controlled to the more so ; from the proposal to the presupposi-

Logical Intent of Concrete and Abstract.

tion, from the schematic interpretation to the direct control. But this intent is, of course, quite relative. The meaning that is concrete with reference to further abstraction, is abstract with reference to direct realization. And the distinction of concrete and abstract, like that of recognitive and selective meanings in general, finds its most illuminating interpretation perhaps as furnishing another instance of the essentially double-faced—retrospective and prospective—character of all our meanings.

§ 10. RÉSUMÉ OF MODES OF IMPLICATION AND POSTULATION

53. We may now gather up certain conclusions already reached in statements which take us back to our fundamental distinction Implication between Implication and Postulation. Implication in Conceptual was defined as meaning so far fixed and reduced by Mode. processes of judgment that no hypothetical or problematic intent was left in it. Implication, in other words, is simply meaning by which belief, the attitude of acknowledgment in judgment, is rendered. Under this heading, we find two sorts of meaning : first, that which is subject-matter of predication, the content of thought ; and second, that which is presupposition of judgment, the control sphere in which the predication holds or is valid. Further, the process of predication, as dealing with any aspect of the whole of implication, is that of elucidation. Nothing can be elucidated but a greater or lesser system of implications. We have now traced this process in its first or " conceptual " mode, the logical Term.

On the other hand, we have found that knowledge progresses essentially by a process of schematism, a process whereby a given whole of implication is treated as not finished, finally judged, or, believed in isolation, but as having further bearings, relational ramifications of meaning not yet reduced to the body of implica-Postulation tion. This process has been called, in its characteristic and Proposal. logical form, Postulation. Postulation applies to the whole sphere of further question or assumption, the hypothetical control-aspect of any implication system. Taking form as definite suggestion or hypothesis in the mode of thought, it is proposal as over against elucidation. We say that this or that set of implications rests on certain accepted presuppositions, of existence, reality, etc.; but we also say that a given set of implications makes further proposals, or postulates a sphere within which the further quest of thought is to be prosecuted.

P

Within the larger modes or attitudes of implication and postulation respectively, therefore, we have those special predica-

The two Aspects. tions or proposals which a given meaning intends. These we have found to be, all through the conceptual movement of meaning, *correlative aspects of meaning.* The implication is never elucidated in its full meaning for actual intercourse without making a proposal for some one ; and a proposal cannot be made that is not based in a more or less definite set of implications which it also elucidates. This we have found to be fundamentally involved in the linguistic or other symbolic rôle of thought as mode of common predicative meaning.

These things being now fairly clear, we may point out a relation which comes to view in the foregoing, and at the same

Both developed in the Proposition. time serves to mark our further immediate progress. The processes called " induction " and " deduction," like the concepts of " generalization " and " abstraction," are indeed capable of the treatment usually given them from the point of view of inference in formal logic, of which they are considered the two contrasted modes. But they may be looked upon also, as further phases of the development of logical meaning ; as modes wherein belief and question, elucidation and proposal, are again rendered and advanced. These modes are here mentioned simply to suggest the general line of genetic continuity in which the Proposition is the next stage. To that topic, therefore, the Proposition, we may now turn.

Chapter VIII

PREDICATION AS PROPOSITION : LOGICAL QUALITY

§ 1. What the Proposition is

1. The proposition is that form or mode of predication in which relation is individuated as a meaning. This concise statement **An Abstract relational linguistic Meaning.** may be taken both to announce our programme of discussion and also to sum up our result. A further similar announcement is contained in the statement that the proposition is motived in the further development of abstraction. The fundamental ground of both these statements is found in the fact that relation is present in all logical meaning, and that only a process of abstraction can bring it out in a form of predication. Further, it is essential that relation should constitute a " subject matter " of logical meaning, and that there should be some form of socially available symbolism wherein this aspect of meaning is embodied.

Thus arises the proposition. It is the linguistic embodiment of the relational aspects of a conceptual meaning, made **It is Conceptual.** object of thought and means of intercourse. Whereas conception is a rendering of a whole meaning as intending the objective thing which the term connotes, the proposition is the statement of one or more of the relations which the concept holds together in " the thing."

2. Like all conceptual meanings, for that is what the propositional meaning is, this also must fulfil the functions of elucidation and proposal, elucidation, so far as the **It is Predicative.** meaning cites a relational whole as having issued in a predication of acknowledgment and belief ; proposal, so far as the meaning is one of further question and hypothesis, presented in predicative form for social or personal purposes. Following the method already employed for the earlier modes of predication, we may consider the proposition as fulfilling these two

rôles.   In the latter, we recognize the experimental aspect, the instrumental function, of the proposition.

§ 2.   What the Proposition Means : Content-wise and Control-wise

The proposition as now explained must be a predication clothed in linguistic form ; and we may ask in a broad way as to the characters of such formal predications.

3. It will appear without further debate that all propositions have two marks or characters which are essential, and from **Two Char-** which others may be derived.   In the first place, the **acters: the** proposition must have a content or subject-matter— **"What" and** **the "Where."** a " what " spoken about—and in the second place, it must have equally some sort of assignment of the subject-matter to a class, a sphere, an accepted mode of existence in which it appropriately falls—the " where," that is, in which the " what " is to be found.   Or, putting the distinction somewhat differently, in order to accept or believe anything, I must be able to say " what " it is that I believe, and also " where " or in what sphere —physical nature, fiction, rumour, art, etc.—I find it.   It will at once occur to the reader, that this is our old distinction between the " content " and the sphere of " control."

When we discuss a proposition, therefore, we must always distinguish the point of view from which it is a predication or **Belief-wise** logical meaning.   We may discuss the content, the **Meaning.** " what," without raising in any explicit way the question of the sphere of existence—the " where "—to be attributed to the content.   Or conversely ; we may ask, what existence, or control, we are presupposing, asserting, or finding appropriate to the subject-matter.   If we designate the former way of treating a proposition the " content-wise " or " relation-wise " way, then we may speak of the other as the " control-wise " or " belief-wise " way of considering it.   In the accompanying diagrams (Figures 10, 11) these two characters are shown by the two lines at right angles to each other.   S (subject) and P (predicate) are connected by the vertical line " relation-wise," but the meaning is controlled " belief-wise," as is indicated by the line so marked, as a single whole meaning SP.   Fig. 10 shows the meaning set up as proposal, suggestion, or hypothesis of the relation between S and P.

It appears now that when the proposal is accepted belief-wise, the content is asserted relationally (and when rejected, denied) as

Relation-wise Meaning holding in the particular sphere "where" the subject finds its control. For example, the relational assertion "whales are mammals" is established as soon as my belief goes out accepting this meaning "whale-mammal" as a whole, in the sphere, the "where," of physical existence. So the judgment is always one of positive acceptance or rejection, "belief-" or "control-wise," and this deter-

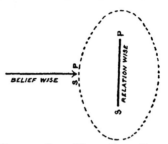

FIG. 10.—Proposition as Suggestion, Proposal or Assumption: the Relation of S to SP not yet judged.

mines the meaning as holding (or not holding) "relation-wise" in a "where-sphere" of some sort. This may be brought out by the further figure (11) which is an extension of that given just above. The positive act of judgment carries the whole meaning SP out into a sphere of existence, in which the relation between S and P is asserted or denied.

4. If we cared at this point to analyse further the intent suggested by these two conceptions, "what" and "where," as now explained, we should find certain very interesting correlations of our view with the distinctions of formal logic. This is done later on, when we are able to summarize as well discussions that are still before us. But it will aid us somewhat simply to suggest the great headings of such a correlation.

When we ask for the meaning of a proposition belief-wise, certain of our greater distinctions come at once to mind—the dis-

Other Characters mean How-much and By-whom tinctions due to relative determinateness of belief, embodied in modes of meaning as "assertorial," "problematical," "alternative," etc. These we may now call "belief-" or "existence-wise" distinctions, characters pertaining to

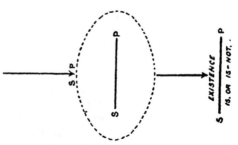

FIG. 11.—Proposition as Assertion or Belief, *after passing through the stage of Proposal*: S is (or is not) P, in an accepted sphere of control or existence.

the " where " of the propositions.   It is the character called
" Modality " in the logic of Kant.

We may also note the place of what is called " Quantity "
in logic, with which we have also had to do.   With the
" where " of belief goes the quantity, the " how-much "—some,
all, one, etc.   Quantity is thus an existence-wise intent.

Our discussions have also unearthed distinctions of another
sort, also marks of belief, or control—those of " commonness,"
" privacy," etc.   These too arise when propositions are looked
at control-wise.   They answer the question " by whom ? "
Logic never discusses this.   But I submit that psychologically it
is an inevitable and fundamental question, and its results are
also of the first importance for logic.[1]   I shall, therefore, include
it here as a character of propositions viewed belief-wise, and call
it the " Community " of propositions.   Community is a universal
character of logical meaning.   So there are the " where," the
" how much," and the " by whom "—Modality, Quantity, Community—of all propositions looked at *control-* or *belief-wise.*

When we come to take again the content or " relation-wise "
point of view, certain further characters appear, now to be
merely stated.   The fundamental matter to determine, on the
surface, is that as to whether the suggested relation is or is not
accepted, that is whether there is to be an assertion or a denial
in the given control.   This is the distinction of logic called
" Quality " ; to this our discussion of opposition was introductory, and the matter is to be treated fully forthwith.   But
besides this, logic recognizes—or Kant did, and that is about the
same thing, for the matter has been but little advanced since
Kant—the different ways in which a suggested relation may hold
or be accepted as holding.   It introduces really the question of
the " ground " or " grounding " of relations in a system
The "Why" of implication ; their relational " why." This we
and " For have to recognize and treat in detail.   The treatment
Whom " re- of contingent meanings has already suggested the
lation-wise.
basis of it.

Moreover, we have found a mode of meaning that brings up
the question of commonness of content viewed relationally,
that is, the question how far commonness, besides having its
belief-wise rôle, its control " by whom," also creeps into the
relational content itself.   Its question is " for whom ? "   All
judgment has this reference, as our preceding discussions have

[1] See the remarks and references given in chap. ix. sect. 44.

shown. So "community" is found to be also a character of propositions viewed relation-wise. And if we consider the two aspects of personal control together, the "by whom" and the "for-whom," the two characters may be described as "community-wise" characters.

If by characters, therefore, we mean marks from whatever point of view, control-wise or content-wise, they may be considered, we have, instead of the current Kantian list, Quantity, Quality, Relation, and Modality, the following :—

Question.	*Character.*	*Mode.*
Where	Modality	⎫
How much . . .	Quantity	⎬ Control- (or Belief)-wise.
By whom . . .	Community	⎰ ⎫ Community-wise.
For whom . . .	Community	⎱ ⎭
What	Quality	⎬ Content- (or Relation)-
Why	Relation	⎭ wise.

The special readings of which meanings are capable under each of these "characters" are to be given further along.[1]

§ 3. THE QUALITY OF PROPOSITIONS

5. Reverting to our fundamental position that every act of judgment is a belief—giving a meaning expressive of an **Belief Attitudes in Judgment** attitude toward a subject-matter—we find it necessary to refuse at the outset to subscribe to an exclusively logical interpretation of the proposition. By a logical interpretation I mean one which analyses the form without reference to the content ; one that recognizes the composition of elements, but *neglects the attitude toward the whole meaning*. The difference is one of no little importance, for, from the point of view of belief attitude, we have taken as the unit of the propositional meaning the whole subject-matter held up as fulfilment or intent of the attitude. So soon as we ask *what is believed or disbelieved or proposed* in a proposition, we see that it is a single meaning, a relational whole, a conceptual intent, which allows only the one matter, however varied its form of statement. This sets as the problem of our theory the progression of conceptual meaning from the simpler form of predication, the term, to the more complex, the proposition.

[1] See chap. ix. § 5, where a full table is given in sect. 42).

We come, then, to look upon the proposition as expressing an aspect of a whole meaning which the term as such does not fully bring out, although it intends it. One of the general motives to which the rise of this new mode, the proposition, is due, is that usually called " quality " as attaching to a predication—this " quality " arising from the success or the reverse of the elucidation of a conceptual meaning *in terms of its inner relationships.* We will find also that quality, as now to be defined, brings out also the experimental aspect of thought. We may begin the exposition of propositions, therefore, with the consideration of this character seeing that we have already developed the topic of negative meaning up to its passage into the " negative quality " of the logical mode.

"Quality."

§ 4. THE NEGATIVE PROPOSITION

6. In the development of the topic of opposition,[1] I pointed out the modes through which negative meaning develops. It is not necessary to recall the details here. It is only needful to remind the reader of the relation of logical negation to prelogical opposition, in order that the derivation of the meanings we are now to discuss may be made clear. This relation, as in all other cases of the passage of prelogical into logical meaning, is one whereby a meaning already prepared, is taken up in the redistribution of factors by which the process of judgment proceeds. In this case, the meaning that comes nearest to logical negation, and is utilized in it, is that of " cognized relationship " [2]—that mode of " relatedness " of contents in which the parts of a whole meaning have become so detached and ready to drop apart that just their *relationship in the whole* is a prominent element of the whole. For example, certain relationships of the parts of a familiar face are most prominent, giving the features of the face their characteristic meaning ; but there need not be any further isolation or individuation of the *relations as such*, apart from the whole meaning which constitutes the face an individual object. The face may be quite familiar because of these relationships, while nevertheless the relationships themselves are not taken up as subjectmatter of an act of judgment.

The

Prelogical

as Relationship.

The movement by which such a meaning is made logical is

---

[1] Vol. i. chap. ix. on " Negative Meaning."

[2] See vol. i. chap. viii. § 10, especially sect. 45.

one that seizes upon *relation as itself a separate and isolated*
Logical   *subject-matter of judgment.* It is no longer simply
Relation.   one of the marks of a larger whole of meaning ; but
it is abstracted for treatment for itself. As has been said in the
earlier place (vol. i. chap. viii. sect. 47) the terms which before
had the relationship as part of their meaning, now become in turn
elements of the meaning by which the relation as subject
term is illustrated.

Applying this to the relation of opposition, we are met by
certain interesting special features. The question arises—is
Not so with opposition, as partial or total exclusion, a meaning of
Opposition. relationship in the sense just explained ? Can we say
that there is, in a larger prelogical meaning, the relationship
of opposition which can be thus taken up as subject-matter of
thought? Evidently not in the sense given, and for the very
obvious reason, that the growth of prelogical meaning is in
terms of the positive inclusions by which the content is established and extended of exclusions, of the nature of opposition.

The individuation of an object as a unit, proceeds, as we
have seen, by contextuation. Hence all those motives and
processes of the development, by which meaning is simply excluded, add nothing to such an object. The object as made up,
however its development may have required opposition in its
various forms, would not present in its context relationships of
a negative sort. If this be true, then some other motive must be
looked for, for the rise of the meaning which is to furnish the
content of negative judgment. The question then is, whence
come the relationships of opposition which are isolated as subject-matter of thought in a negative judgment or proposition ?

Apart from its own interest, this question appeals especially
to us, as pursuing our present genetic method ; for we are in
duty bound to point out why negation should be present at all in
thought, if the constructions of subject-matter afford no inner
relationships of the sort required for such a meaning.

7. It will be remembered that we found the root of opposition
as mode of meaning, in a certain circumscription or limitation of
First Oppo- the cognitive content in the earliest objects of sense.
sition is   This we denominated " limitative " opposition. We
Limitative. then found that it was only through the germination
of special interests and dispositions, in the development of the
active life, that a more characteristic mode of opposition arose
through lack, embarrassment, disappointment, etc. It was seen

that through such embarrassments there arose exclusive classes. It was, moreover, by a development of this motive of exclusion, *as a rebound from attempted identification and active treatment*, that the meaning of relationship between wholes of separable meaning became more refined in the further progression of cognition.

This is the cue we now need. For it means that wherever we find negation, it is rooted in a limitation of a positive content, together with the exclusion of that which the meaning so limited does not assimilate or comprise. The motive through which prelogical opposition arose continues in force, in the transition to logical consciousness. This is recognized in a view already current, though not fully developed, in the discussions of certain writers.

Then it is Exclusive.

The motive is two-fold. First, logical opposition *is of the nature of an exclusion of positive elements of meaning through the establishment of a limitation* ; and second, like its prelogical prototype, it arises as *a rebound from the attempted construction of a positive*, or what is called in logic an " affirmative " meaning.[1] Let us take up these two positions in turn.

Failure of a positive.

I. The movement already described as that of proposal involves the erection or assumption of a subject-matter larger in extent or intension than that already covered by " elucidation." The meaning may be of either of the types " proposal-elucidation " or " elucidation-proposal " of our earlier discussion. The former is that of the movement called hypothesis, supposition, " schematism " in general. It may be actually addressed to a hearer to whom a question is put to secure information ; or it may be schematic only as instrumental to completely common or " synnomic " meaning. On the other hand, the mode " elucidation-proposal " brings out more explicitly the common reference of thought, inasmuch as it makes the motive to the predication the setting out or development of elements of implication, for the consideration and acceptance of the person to whom it comes as a proposal.

Proposal is made.

Now in both of these cases the negative meaning expresses

---

[1] Cf. in particular Sigwart *Logic*, vol. i. chap. iv., already quoted in this connection, vol. i. chap. ix. sect. 2.

The place of " privative " opposition, found to be also an original movement, appears also here, when the limitation is one of a selective kind. See below, § 8.

only the aspect of elucidation, not that of proposal. As a mode
Elucidation of meaning, *it is never of the nature of a proposal.*
by Negation. When I say " whales are not fish," I elucidate the
meaning whales ; I do not propose any new positive characterization of the objects. I am, therefore, either bringing out a
relation already established in a larger whole of meaning, or
I am informing some one else, answering a proposal possibly
made by him. This is shown by the fact that in the cases in which
the negative form is used, either for a hypothesis or for a social
proposition set up for consideration, the positive might be used
to convey precisely the same meaning. The forms " whales are
not fish ? " and " are whales fish ? " have—apart from a certain
expression of probability, which is an element of elucidation—*just
the same import.* Or put a little differently—assuming a present
state of uncertainty that justifies the proposal, it is possible to
express this uncertainty as well by saying " let us assume that
whales are," or " are not, fish." This fact is to my mind a con-
clusive proof of the correctness of the position that, as characteristic mode, negation is a *meaning of result rather than of suggestion.* When we ask such a question as " John is not dead ? " we
actually add the second, " is he ? " That is, we really mean the
affirmative form of question " is John dead ? " The negative-
seeming form of the proposal is only expressive of the added
expectation or hope that the answer may be negative ; but it
gives no negative force to the question.

If this be so, then the relation expressed by the negation in
order to be truly negative, presupposes a positive construction
Negative which is already embodied in a judgment; and the nega-
presupposes tive definition of this construction is motived by the
Positive. limitation and exclusion established by the positive.

8. Thus it is that the negative meaning gets its force by the
The exclusive removal of elements of content, which a positive
Relation is determination entails. The issue of a proposal, if in-
Judged. deed the proposal be a genuine one—one of real
problematical character as allowing a disjunction—has besides
the positive result also the negative. The whole meaning, by
restriction to its form of judgment of acknowledgment or acceptance, is also one of rejection. And there is here established in
consciousness an intent of relation which may be characterized,
when itself judged, as one of logical opposition. It is a meaning
whereby *the whole suggested or proposed resolves itself into two
terms asserted as connected in thought but not in reality.* The

separation of the terms is itself abstracted and made the subject-matter.

Another point follows from this ; it is confirmed also I think by the independent examination of cases. It is the point that
No Pro-   there is no independent progression in opposition as
gression of   such apart from the corresponding progression of
Negation
proper.   positive meaning stage by stage. The positive move-
ment—in the logical mode, the affirmative movement—affords the framework, and the negative statements are at each stage elucidations consequent upon them.

This being true, we are then led to ask as to the actual beliefs embodied in negative statements ; as to how the predications that take on negative form can be instrumental or experimental in the development of knowledge. Here we come upon certain points that extend the teachings of formal logic.

§ 5.   The Import of Negation : Logical Denial

II. Having now laid the foundation of our theory we may go on to show that in its import negation is of the nature of an unacceptable or rejected suggestion of a positive.

9. (1) In the first place, we may remark that one aspect of the import of a negative proposition is that it always quantifies
Negation   the predicate, whatever quantity the subject may
Quantifies   or may not have ; and further, that it gives the pre-
dicate a mode of universal quantity.[1] The statement that some or all of the objects of one class are not objects of another class removes them entirely from that class, so that all the objects of the second, or predicate, class are excluded from the former or subject class. This has been remarked upon above in connection with the question of quantification of the predicate.

This may be illustrated by any sort of negative statement :
" the cow does not give milk," " persimmons are not fit to eat,"
the   " some men are coal-black." In each of these cases
Predicate   of varying extensive quantity, the subject—singular,
universal, particular—is cut off from the whole of the respective predicate class, milk-giving, fit-to-eat, and coal-black things. These meanings are, therefore, taken in universal quantity ; and we can say, conversely, that all of each of them in turn is used as a not-P class.

[1] In making it always universal, it removes from it the marks of other extensive quantities as problematical and indeterminate.

The result of this is the establishment of an exclusion by the definite limitation of the predicate class. But the extension of the subject class is left indeterminate or not according to the quantity of the subject meaning in the particular case. We may write " there are A's that are not B's," or " there are A's that are outside the B-class," according as we wish to emphasize the non-B's or merely to exclude the B's.

by Limitation.

The result of this is that the negation does not present a suggestion, a proposal ; on the contrary, it reflects a decision, an issue, an assertion in a negative sense with respect to what was the positive suggestion, namely, that the A's were to be found among the B's.

(2) This, so far as the movement of belief is concerned, is to make the things outside the B-class, *the non-B's,* a positive meaning. This is the interpretation resorted to in certain logical formulations. Instead of construing negation as meaning that the A's *are-not* B's, we may turn the predication into an affirmative by recognizing that it establishes a class of things that the A's *are,* i.e. the *non-B's.* The negation then positively asserts the presence of the A's among the members of this latter class : thus, " some A's are non-B's."

It defines the non-B Class.

This again brings out the motive here assigned to negation. The only reason for stating the judgment in term of non-B's is to rule out the suggestion that the A's may be B's. This suggestion fails and the negation asserts its failure.

(3) The way is now open to the recognition of a certain instrumental intent or experimental force in negative propositions. It is quite impossible to develop further a meaning of definite and final exclusion—a meaning that arises simply to express the failure of an attempted construction of a positive sort—as an isolated negative meaning as such always is. This is recognized in formal logic in all the limitations of inference from negative premises, as set forth in the textbooks. To say what a thing is not is said to give you no inkling of what it is. It does not suggest a problematical or experimental reading for further research.

This involves Proposal.

10. But there is more to say. If first we construe the negation as intending the recognition of a class of non-B's, *things other than the predicate class,* then we find that the motive to the negation is the beginning of the definition of this further class—*the other things.* This is itself then liable to all the suggestions of further schematization, according to the sort of assumption it makes. In short, the fruitful force of the negative is due to its basis of

affirmation, not to its exclusion; and this is only to say, as we have already said above, that the negative is an obverse intent of a positive determination. The mark or character which determines the exclusion of the A's from the B's, in actual intercourse, is such because it also determines something positive about either the A's or the B's. This latter determination is capable of further development by the experimental use of the negation.

Illustration. Suppose, for example, I make the negative statement, "after-images are not memory-images," and suppose I say this in the progress of a research on after-images at a point when belief begins to be generated in this sense. My meaning is either, first, a definite conviction, in which case it represents a final meaning and no further experiments are necessary; or it represents, second, my growing conviction in this direction—a meaning to be developed by further research. Now how is such a growing conviction to be again advanced? Evidently by *further definition of that class of cases which are other than images of memory*. That is, my instrumental use of the egation is to secure further proof; to secure, in other words, progress toward the result that after images have acertain positive character. Its intent is the same, except for its elucidating force, as that of a proposal or hypothesis of a positive sort.

Negative based on a Positive. 11. These points give us, I think, the outline of a valid theory of logical negation which so far concerns the negative statement as embodied in a proposition. Every negative meaning is a predication arising in that stage of elucidation of meaning found in the corresponding positive. It is seen to be one pole of a two-fold abstract intent, predicated in a linguistic statement. This two-fold intent is what is meant by "quality": *whatever is positive is through limitation also negative of something else.* The positive is an affirmation of an inclusion which is also at once also an exclusion. Its inclusive aspect is rendered in the "affirmative" proposition; its exclusive aspect in the "negative" proposition.

System of Relations. From this it follows that negation finds its motive in a system of affirmative relations; it is part of a system of positive implications. The predication of such a set of implications involves the setting up of the negative as well as the positive relations; for by the negative the whole meaning is also elucidated. So the whole may also be set up as proposal. The exclusions are as positive in a relational whole as are the inclusions; and the use of the whole, even for purposes of further proposal, requires their actual statement. This is true even when we admit that the force of the negation as such, its import, may always be stated as incidental to the positive meaning in which it arises. The positive is *affirmation* ; the negative is *denial*.

Before going on to develop the several modes in which this general interpretation finds application, we may take up a matter which seems to be of some importance, and which requires further discussion in view of our own theory of limitative opposition, namely a possible third quality or mode of opposition called " Limitative." Kant, following Wolff, distinguishes three modes of quality, Affirmation, Negation, and Limitation.

§ 6. LIMITATION

12. In view of the use we have made of the motive of limitation, in the progression of negative meaning in both the pre-**Negation as** logical and logical modes, it will be instructive to **Limitation.** inquire whether we are thus coming into line with those who distinguish limitative opposition, under quality, from the qualities of affirmation and negation. In a sense, it may be said that we are thus supporting them by our genetic interpretations of the meanings involved ; but only with certain restrictions that forbid us to draw the hard and fast lines suggested by such a classification.

It is evident that the determination of a negative meaning as one of exclusion issues in a two-fold intent, as already ex-**Place of Pure** plained. It may be simply and only a cutting off of the **Exclusion,** subject from the predicate class. This in its purity, considered as a meaning isolated from any implicated relationships of the excluded term, is a case of simple elucidation. As thus considered, there would be no intent of defining a third class, the non-B's in which the subject term does fall. Waiving the question as to whether there are in the actual development of psychic objects any such cases, we may call it the case of pure or formal negative relationship. This type of " limitation " gives what is known as the " infinite judgment, the non-B class being everything whatever except B.[1]

13. But we have found that negation is motived by a posi-**The deter-** tive meaning, a proposal, in which an attempt is **mination of** made to reach an affirmative relation, in its own right, **Non-B class.** between the same subject and predicate. The failure

---

[1] It merges into the meaning of privation—a matter to be spoken of again below (in § 8 of this chapter).

of the attempt to do this is due to some actual determination whereby the affirmation is inhibited. Now this positive determination *sets a limitation on the B-class*, not by mere privation, but by a development that *gives content to the non-B class*. For whatever the mark is that forbids the inclusion of the A's in the B-class, it must be a positive mark of the non-B class. There arises, therefore, the intent, or if not a positive psychical intent, at least the implication, that the class of non-B's is such that the objects having this mark are in it. Here is a type of meaning therefore having the import " the A's are non-B's," which is not " infinite " nor purely formal.

This is reinforced by the fact that we do not usually make statements in a void—that is, without definite presuppositions of **Negation has** belief. On the contrary, intercourse is pursued within **Presupposi-** a larger whole of belief which justifies the exclusion **tions.** made in the negative statement. When we say, for example, "cottages (A's) are not palaces (B's)," we are not simply marking off from the B's an "infinite" world of things, about which we have no further information. On the contrary, the vital movement that our intercourse embodies takes place within the general presupposition of the existence of buildings otherwise much alike. It is because of some well-defined mark discovered or at least intended that certain of the buildings, cottages, are set aside in the pursuit of a present interest. The class thus excluded from the B's, therefore, the " non-B's," is definite enough—it is the whole range of buildings other than those called palaces. The form of statement is put negatively in pursuit of some genuine interest, and it leaves open to further investigation the place, within the class of non-B's, of cottages and still other buildings that also share the exclusion from palaces.

14. The requirement would seem therefore to be not only that such a meaning as that called " limitative " should be recog-**Limitation** nized, but that it should be made to stand out as the **real also.** positive ground of negation. It is not, however, the infinite or pure exclusion sometimes held as a logical quality different from the negative. The affirmative judgment expresses the inclusion of the subject class, the A's, in the predicate class, the B's ; and the negative expresses the exclusion of the former from the latter ; but this exclusion may be an implication by limitation from another inclusion, that of the A's in the non-B class, which limits the B class. In other words,

coming back to our original statement, the negation is a rebound of further abstraction from a positive determination.[1]

15. There are reasons, however, that compel us still to recognize actual meanings of the modes called "infinite" and "pure" exclusion. Granted such cases—and we are now to point them out—we have, indeed, three modes of logical quality, for which the term associated with the name of Kant may be retained; with the understanding, however, that the mode called "limitation" is to be restricted as is indicated above. It will appear that pure exclusion appears in the mode of meaning called "privative" in our earlier discussions.

Pure exclusion as Privation.

§ 7. NEGATION AS PURE EXCLUSION

16. We may take as point of departure the case suggested above as possible—the case of negation so "pure" of presuppositions, so isolated as to subject-matter, that the predication of exclusion does not advance any positive meaning in the subject class which can be taken to define the non-B class. Is there a meaning that tells us that A is not B, without telling us anything about the class non-B, further than just the fact that the A's are in it ?

Pure Exclusion

Such a meaning might arise, it would appear, in a type of thought so abstract that the relation of exclusion as such is isolated from any actual context of implication. This is the use made of the negative in formal or symbolic logic, where the mere relationship is the subject-matter, apart from what the relation means in the concrete linkage of terms. If we make the A and B mere algebraic symbols, mere X and Y, this sort of exclusion is secured, but at a certain expense.

In Symbolic Logic.

It removes the presupposition of belief in any sphere of existence or reality ; for in no sphere of belief are term meanings so

---

[1] What I mean by "rebound" is the consciousness of inhibition and snubbing that comes from a positive limitation. Put in terms of altitude, it is the *rejection* of a proposed connection of contents, brought about by the acceptance of a different positive connection.

A most vital rôle is assumed by limitation in the processes of "Identification" and "Induction," as is shown below (chaps. x. xi.).

As I write, I come upon this sentence in my morning paper, the *New York Times* (quoted from the *London Globe*) : "The American tariff makes it almost impossible for those not millionaires to overspend in foreign lands." This is a good case of the complications naturally arising in limitative statements.

isolated. The relation is considered a meaning whether or no illus-
It allows Postulation. trative instances of it are to be found. This throws the door open, however, for a free resort to postulation as distinct from presupposition. We may postulate any conceivable system of rules of procedure, of implication, any " laws of thought," in such a world of abstract relations. As a matter of fact, this absolute cutting off of the system from reality is not allowed even in such systems, for it would forbid the further development of the relational system itself. The presupposition of reflection and the maintenance of so much " reasonableness " as " consistency " at least requires, is necessary for the development of implication, however capricious the postulates may be under which the system as a whole is worked out.

17. It is worth while to note this, for it enables us to say something further about the sphere and value of the Aristotelian logic. It professes to be a science of the forms of logical relationship, considered as a system of pure implication ; and it all the while holds that its processes are those requiring no special presuppositions of belief.[1] It accordingly finds itself obliged to admit the relation of exclusion as a logical meaning, and negation as a mode of formal predication. This makes it impossible for it to distinguish, in any productive way, the spheres or universes in which this or that implication has any appropriateness.

But this is a procedure which the forms of speech do not permit. They are through and through filled with the presuppositions of this and that mode of existence and reality. Only a talking machine could rid vocal utterance of those shadings of intent which give the *nuances* of belief and question, explanation Limits of Formal Logic and command. Hence formal logic, to fulfil its rôle, should become entirely and radically a non-linguistic, symbolic discipline, an algebra. Moreover, " discipline " will be perhaps the most fitting term wherewith to characterize it ! For once cut loose from the presuppositions of normal thinking, controlled as reflection by reference of its matter, postulation has a free hand ; and who is to say how much or how little of the

---

[1] It is interesting that the extreme metaphysical or " logicist " writers, by a process of continued abstraction, get rid of the " presupposition " of actuality and reach somewhat the same " formal " result : so Spinoza's " definitio est negatio " and Hegel's " Sein gleich Nichts."

It is in reference to such a formal system that it is discussed whether the " infinite " judgment is still different from the " negative "—a further attenuation of distinctions within the attenuated !

regulation of actual thought is to constitute reasonableness or correctness in such a system of implications ? Why not, for example, postulate a system in which " A is non-A," and work out a " logic " under this axiom. The new mathematics which has been defined indeed as a symbolic logic of this kind, " a science of abstract relationships," entertains postulates that appear to do as great violence as this to what we ordinarily desiderate under the term knowledge.[1]

18. Another case comes to mind, however, when we cast about for meanings of the type called above pure exclusion— the case of meanings individuated as singular. We have already found the consideration of this mode of meaning of peculiar interest and importance, and here it again asserts its claim to special consideration. For it is evident that our general theory cannot apply without modification to a negative meaning involving singulars.

The denial of singularity, indeed, as matter of fact leads to nothing new ; for the exclusion puts the subject in the class of non-B's just the same : as in " Niagara is not unique," or "Niagara is one of many water-falls." It simply shows the inclusion of the particular case in a general meaning.

Again if we make the predicate singular, we reach a similar
Mutual ex- interpretation. To deny a class meaning of a
clusion of singular object is usual—as in " none of these men is
Singulars. John " ; they belong to the non-Johns.

19. The background of these cases is brought out when we recall the essential movement involved in singularization. It involves the isolation, whether by logical abstraction or through personal interest, of certain aspects in which the thing is singular, over and above those in which it is a particular of a general class. If this be true, then two cases arise. One of these appears in any state-ment which *denies anything of the singular* : it simply predicates negatively what is already implied in singularity ; that is, it simply reaffirms the singularity by stating one of the details of the exclusion that singularity means. The affirmative meaning, that is, that underlies the relation taken up for negation, is one
Denial of already covered in the essential movement that gives the
something singular ; it is not a new discovery, growth, or synthesis.
of a Singular It is purely an elucidation of the positive singular meaning established by privation ; and it partakes of the nature

[1] This is not to say, of course, that higher mathematics and symbolic logic are not in their own province beautiful and worthful endeavours.

of the failure of an attempted assertion of generality as the original judgment of singularity also did (see chap. vii. § 8).

The other case of the two is that which involves some altogether new mark or predicate, which is found also not to attach to an object already for other reasons found singular. In this case we have the mode of limitative exclusion : there is a movement of determination of the non-B class.

The negation, accordingly, by which the singular is denied of some other meaning or some other of it, is of the usual type ; the cases in which either of the terms is not a singular admit the usual construction.   The only case of the negative rendering of singularity, as a distinct movement of predication, is that of the *mutual exclusion of two singulars inter se.*

20. This will appear also from the following consideration. In the recognition and assertion of essential singularity we have a movement that already partakes of the nature of opposition.   The singular marks are those that resist generalization ; and this leads to a meaning that is in its intent *not what the general is.*   As a singular individual, John is in so far a *super-man* : the attempted use of the general meaning " man " as exhaustive of John thus fails.   If this be true then to deny singularity of anything is only to remove this motive of negation, and to assert generality.   But this is not enough when a singular is denied of a singular.   There then arises a further movement whereby a relation of exclusion between *two such super-man characters* is asserted.   It would seem to go beyond the ordinary predication which asserts or denies a general.

Denial of Singularity.

When we actually employ singulars in both terms, saying, for example, " John is not Harry," we strike upon a certain " logic of singulars " to which our former explanations do not so evidently apply.   It would seem impossible to construe the assertion " John is not Harry " as the failure of the attempt to take Harry for John ; for the reason that both are already individuated as singular.   Each excludes any other case by the terms of its individuation as unique.   Moreover in saying " John is not Harry," we do not mean to place John in an indeterminate class of non-Harrys ; on the contrary we mean to assert that he is a determinate, single, and unique person, as is also Harry.[1]

[1] There are, no doubt, cases in which " John is not Harry " means to deny a proposal whereby a certain " Harryness " was suggested as belonging to John.   But in that case " Harryness " is a general, a meaning broader than " Harry," and we are no longer dealing with a strictly singular predicate.

21. We accordingly reach—to sum up—the following cases of negative singular propositions.

(1) *The denial of singularity itself ;* this amounts to the assertion of generality. The singular motive is removed. " Niagara is not unique " asserts that " Niagara is but a particular case among waterfalls."

(2) *The denial of something of a singular ;* this is, like any

Three Cases negative of limitation, the failure of a positive, and is due to information about the non-B class. But under this head we reach the special case :—

(3) *The denial of a singular of, or its exclusion from, another singular.* This does not remove any earlier motive to "singularize " (as in the first case above), nor does it assert or define a general class (as in the second case). Its intent seems to be that of pure exclusion.[1]

22. This has its most evident illustration in cases of what we have called " imported " or selective singularity, the uniqueness

Imported Singularity as Negative of the object being that which it gets in its rôle of fulfilling an interest or purpose. When we say " this taste is not that of oranges," we add nothing whatever to the orange meaning nor to that of the non-orange class ; that is, we make no discovery beyond that of mere non-applicability of the orange taste. But we do reassert negatively the singularity of the taste as an immediate experience. The result cannot be said to come from an attempt to make the assertion " this taste is that of oranges." If the attempt is made, it indicates that the new taste is not individuated as singular, but remains still vague and more or less undetermined.[2] If the taste has already been judged singular—that is, as not any other taste including that of oranges—then of course the assertion that it is not orange taste is nothing new. It is then purely and only elucidation of the singular meaning, with no compensating advance of knowledge such as usually accompanies negation by limitation. As elucidation to another, it is a case of " appreciative description," spoken of again below (chap. xiv., sect. 16)— the attempt to convey a meaning by indirect means. One might say, " the taste suggests oranges, but it is not the same." This

[1] It is my purpose here to say only so much ; the further interpretation of the case follows below, under " Opposition of Singulars " in § 10 of this chapter.

[2] As, of course, in the mind of one who asks whether the taste is that of oranges.

cannot be called the failure of an attempt to judge it to be orange taste.

The other case of singularization—the case of essential singularity, or of the recognition of essentially singular objective **Essential** marks in the object—is not so evidently open to this **Singularity.** construction. Yet it is true, as is argued above, that in individuating such a meaning as singular, the door is already closed to its further development by negation. It may grow in concrete definition, in "information" as to intensive character, but not in a way that modifies its singularity. From this point of view, therefore, any denial with reference to it must be only the reassertion or elucidation of its singularity.

23. The question then arises why such predications are made at all—those, say, of the extreme type, singular denied of singular, such as John is not James—if they represent **Motive to** only elucidation of meanings already completely made **negative** up. This opens again the question of the use of **Singulars.** propositions in intercourse. The answer is that such predications are made with reference to a proposal in the mind of another who has not yet made up the meaning as the first thinker, the speaker, has made it up. This has been referred to just above. In this connection we may point out certain further considerations relative to what is called "limitative" quality.

§ 8.   DOUBLE LIMITATION

24. We have found that, apart from certain singular propositions, a negative statement always implicates something about the class that limits the predicate—the class non-B when the predicate is B. This may be further illustrated from the presence in language of what are called negative terms. Such terms **The Nega-** carry the negative force as part of their essential **tive Term.** connotation, and in their use it is clear that the predication asserts something about the class that limits the corresponding positive term. For example, in "man is immortal," "this fact is immaterial," "sweet cider is non-alcoholic," "his temper is ungoverned," we have statements in which the predicate is of this negative sort. It testifies to the reality of the movement in the mode of quality called "limitation," for it shows the actual demand for terms to render this sort of meaning.[1]

---

[1] The use of such terms, indeed, often gives negative form to a proposition of positive or affirmative force. For example, "John is unkempt" has a positive meaning ; as has "John is careless," in which the affix

This being the case, it occurs to us to ask whether the same mode of limitation as applied also to the subject gives any characteristic logical meanings.

This has been maintained. The view that limitation in the sense indicated extends to the subject is attributed to Boethius.[1] **Negative Subject or Non-A.** Such a meaning would be in the form " non-A's are B's." On the surface, this seems to hold, for the negative terms just spoken of serve their turn as subject as well as predicate. " The unregenerate are damned," " immortality means more than the absence of death," are such predications.

25. The implication is in fact quite real. There is no reason that a non-A class should not have something said about it, nor **Limited Subject** that such a meaning should not be fruitful. And we find in language certain propositional forms, not considered by the traditional logic, in which such meanings have special rendering. " None but the brave deserve the fair " is a

---

" less " is formally negative. These variations have important bearings, since they extend to the use of negative forms of various sorts to express positive meanings ; and in some cases, unless properly understood, they would seem to call for a revision of our interpretation of negation. For example, such judgments of observation as " John has no hair " would seem to present obstacles to our view that negation arises from failure of attempted assertion. But as a fact, such propositions are not negative. " John has no' hair " means " John is bald "—a positive fact of observation or information. If we give a real force of *denial* to the judgment then we must ask *what it is that is denied* ; and that leads to the recognition of a proposal that is positive in its intent, such as " I suppose your brother John has full hair," to which the reply is, "No, John has no hair." The term "unreal" is a notable negative predicate of positive significance (see above, chap. ii. § 4).

[1] See also Bradley, *loc. cit.*, pp. 111 ff. Mr. Bradley's objection to " the use of non-B as an independent class " seems to lay too much stress on the " independence " of such a class. It is not independent ; it is *being determined all the while* as a class just by the rise of those " marks in A which exclude B," made by Mr. Bradley the ground of negation. So also of the non-A class, determined by the marks of B. The interpretation of the case of " marks in A that exclude B," is to be given later on ; it raises the question of " contradiction " as a direct or immediate fact. I find (below, chap. xi. § 5) that there can be no such thing as direct flat-footed contradiction between contents as such. It is always a matter of relative lack of synergy or synthesis in the active processes by which constructions of content are controlled and limited *inter se*. As appears in . our present discussion, apparently " pure " exclusion—exclusion not resting upon a motive of limitation—is always to be interpreted as *privative* in its force.

statement about the non-brave—they do not deserve the fair. This is a negative rendering, under the form of a limited subject, of the affirmative meaning " only the brave deserve the fair." So " all but the wicked will be saved " is a proposition in which an assertion is made of the non-wicked—they will be saved. This is a predication about a limited subject.

This sets in evidence with greater emphasis the truth of our general position regarding logical negation ; the position that

Confirms reality of Limitation. recognizes the mode and motive of limitation. It is, moreover, possible to carry it out in further detail. We should have to recognize the possibility of the negation of a negative or limitative term, whether that term be subject or predicate or both. These three cases are illustrated by the following : " Man is not immortal " (equivalent to the form " A is not non-B," or " man is mortal," and illustrating the logical rule that two negatives give an affirmative), " immortality is not predicable of man " (equivalent to " non-A is non-B," or " mortality is a mark of man "), " the unfaithful have no claim to be considered not responsible " (equivalent to " the non-faithful are not among the non-responsible ").

26. The fact should be noted, finally, however, that in all these modes of judgment or proposition, certain presuppositions of

Presupposition of a restricted class. belief are usually present, and that these presuppositions condition the range of the limitative meaning. When we talk about the unfaithful, the immortal, the irresponsible, etc., we do not intend an infinite, boundless, inchoate, or indeterminate class of objects. The term " infinite " usually applied to such predicates is, therefore, very inept. The motive to predication is always to be found within the range of a wider class-meaning whose control is presupposed. The instance given above—" the cottages are not palaces "—may be cited here again to illustrate this general truth. It may be said that every system of implication that is profitable for the advance or elucidation of knowledge, implicates a presupposition of belief in the sphere in which the relations predicated, whether affirmative or negative, find themselves. Of course such a sphere of reference may be wider or narrower ; it may be the restricted sphere of a concrete situation ; or it may be the entire universe of thinkable things, of logical meanings. The former case has its extreme illustration in singular predications ; the latter—that of the removal of all bounds to the non-B class, save that of reflection itself—introduces us to the further consideration of a sort of negation already spoken of in its earlier modes, that of Privation.

§ 9. PRIVATIVE NEGATION: WILL TO BELIEVE

27. The description of the extreme cases of exclusion in the foregoing section may have recalled to mind the discussion of privation given in the treatment of prelogical opposition.[1] It will be recalled that in privation a content is stripped of rela-

The Privative "not other." tionships in a way that leaves indeterminate the " other " of the privative, " this and not other." Instead of the definite exclusion " this and not that," it reads " this and not anything else," the force of the privation being in the indeterminate range of the " other " or " anything else."

This, it will now be seen, allows us to assimilate to such privation the case just mentioned of pure exclusion when it is itself negatived, as in the proposition " A is not non-B." Non-B so far as no positive determination of the class is intended, is here an indeterminate other to B, and in making the assertion we are declaring " A is nothing else than B," or " A is B and B only." The meaning then is simply AB, treated privatively.

This case though actual is not frequent, since, as said above, it represents pure exclusion,[2] and that is not the usual motive to

The Imperative Privative negation. On the contrary, the motive is usually the positive determination of the non-B class, which implicates the exclusion of A from B. It may serve, however, to bring to our notice a case of actual privation in which a different motive comes forward, and asserts a more or less evident influence in the determination. It is the motive of selective interest or will-to-believe, by which a new phase of " semblance " is introduced. The imperative proposition shows

[1] Vol. i. chap. ix. §§ 4, 6.

[2] In import, such a meaning is, but for its wider sphere of reference, the same as that of the universal double negative " no A is not B," and this is equivalent to the privative " A is nothing but B." In limitative opposition, as opposed to privative, we have, " There are no ' Robins ' in America that are not Thrushes," which is equivalent to "American Robins are nothing but Thrushes." This case illustrates well the limitative motive in negation. The statement arises not from interest in thrushes but from finding that the American so-called " Robin " belongs in the not-English-Robin class (being a red-breasted thrush). The use of the double-negative as cited above (the denial of a limitative in order to reach an exclusive meaning) is clear proof of the reality of the limitative.

it most plainly, whether in form affirmative or negative; the proposition, " let A be B and nothing else." Here the " nothing else " is privative and indefinite; the non-B class is anything-whatever-but-just-B. But it is evident that this does not arise by an attempt at affirmation of a definite predication; it arises, on the contrary, by a special individuation of A, under the lead of a selective interest or purpose; and the motive to the privation is the fulfilment of this interest.

28. We shall have to recur to this again in the detailed consideration of the higher semblant or aesthetic consciousness. It is one of the extraordinary privileges of such consciousness that it can arrive at a selective inclusion of contents, without definite exclusions. But here it is simply our purpose to point out that this is not logical negation; that is, it is not negation resting on actual implication of content.[1] For just in so far as the intent is a selected and semblant meaning, it is not yet a judged content; it is rather a schematic content, not yet believed or acknowledged; it is of the nature of proposal, not of implication or elucidation.

Will-to-Believe. The function of the " will-to-believe," so far as it carries the meaning forward beyond its actual grounded text as assured judgment, is to read-in a preferential intent, a personal schema, a proposal. It is not subject-matter of judgment until it becomes both common and logical as sustaining the relationships of particular and general. The larger function of this movement in the logical mode, therefore, is the instru-

It is not Logical. mental one, over and above whatever logical force its content may have. So long as such meanings remain in the phase of personal purpose, will, or intention, they are essentially private, unconfirmed, and hypothetical; but so far as this function, just by its rôle as motive to proposal and research, leads on to further discovery, its quasi-logical and instrumental value is very great.

The distinction should be made very plain, however, between the two sorts of personal interest that appear here—interests not generally distinguished in the more popular discussions to which the will-to-believe doctrine lends itself. Such a predication as " let it be thus and so " may be made with the intent *to discover whether it really is thus and so*. It then motives the advance of knowledge by the regular methods of discovery and

---

[1] It is the extreme case of " modality " considered as that character of judgment in which the element of *determination by an act of personal belief* is reflected. Cf. chap. ix., sects. 36 and 42.

proof. But on the other hand, the same sentence may embody the intent *to have it thus and so whether or no.* In this latter case there is the force of privation—" it shall be nothing else "—which is a personal and forced judgment based on private preference, lacking in grounds of belief, and expressed in the imperative mood. It is the former alone, a schematic and instrumental affirmation, an experimental meaning, a proposal entertained tentatively and for purposes of research, that is fruitful and logically of value. The latter, on the contrary, is an attitude of obstruction, private ownership, dogmatism, and prejudice. *It is will to deny.* Its value, as pointed out by its exponents, resides in the negative results, the rejection of alternatives, the concentration of purpose, the rousing of activity—all on the side of the life of conduct and individual achievement—rather than in any contribution it may make to the body of reasonable truth.[1]

It is Schematic.

§ 10. OPPOSITION OF SINGULARS

29. It remains to point out that here, in the privative mode, we have the explanation of the mutual exclusion of singulars treated of above as " pure exclusion " (see § 7 of this chapter). One singular may be denied of another not from motives of attempted assertion, or of limitation, but from the mere recognition of the terms as singulars. This involves the question as to why in each case the object in question is found to be singular. If it be because the object is determined in the pursuit of a special interest or purpose, then evidently the denial to this object of any predicate is due to the movement of privation just described. The original individuation is privative, and the particular predicate denied is already included in that general act of privation. This case, therefore, clearly illustrates privative negation.

If, again, it be the other type of singularity—the singularity of essential objective marks—we must, if the motive to exclusion is to be discovered, go again back to the ground of the singularity. This we have seen to be limitation. The individuation of a singular object limits the content thus determined. The

---

[1] Its place appears also in the social and ethical fields, where judgments of worth are of the " imputed " or " personal " sort, the content itself being largely personal attitudes. One may *make* " truth " or " reality," in the ethical sphere, by taking active part and being strenuously " in it," by precept, exhortation and example.

process is one in which the movement of generalization fails to exhaust the object. This is true of each of the singulars when brought into connection as subject and predicate. The negation, therefore, in this case, is an intent simply to recognize this double limitation. Its assertion in a proposition is largely mere emphasis. As a further result, it depends, it is true, on the earlier movement of limitation, but it states the result as a relation between the two singular terms.

The sense in which double singular negation is an exception to the view of negation developed above is plain. It goes back on the one hand, to privation, so far as it involves imported or selective singularity. Essential or objective singularity, on the other hand, goes back to the motive of limitation by which the singularity was originally established. It does not explicitly require an attempted affirmation, because it is not experimental or fruitful. It is merely a recognitive and emphatic mode of assertion of a positive.

§ 11.   ACCEPTANCE, DENIAL AND REJECTION

30. A somewhat different view of negation is held by those who identify negation with the rejection of a content, this rejec-
Rejection. tion being looked upon as a movement opposed to that of acceptance and acknowledgment. It is held that rejection is as fundamental as acceptance ; and that the consequent act of denial is equally original with affirmation. This, it is evident, controverts our view that negation is a movement arising through a positive determination limitative in character. It finds exclusion as such to be the fundamental form of negation.[1]

Such a position is defective, I think, in its identification of negation or denial with rejection ; and it is similarly mistaken in
It is not root identifying acceptance with affirmation. The rôle of
of Negation. *affirmation with negation or denial* is not the same as that of *acceptance with rejection*. Acceptance or rejection is an attitude toward a whole of content, whereby its control in this sphere or that is recognized and acknowledged : I accept mermaids in fiction, I reject them in the world of physical fact. Affirmation and denial, on the other hand, are matters of relation between items of meaning *within the whole accepted or rejected*. I affirm or deny that mermaids are green, *within the presupposition of the sphere in which my acceptance has established mermaids.*

[1] Cf. the able article by Prof. Ormond on "The Negative in Logic," in the *Psychological Review*, vol. iv., 1897, p. 231.

It is an affair of contextuation, of relationship, of linkage of parts within the whole, not one of acknowledgment, control, or belief-attitude with reference to the whole.

31. It may be said, however, in reply to this, that I affirm or deny the control itself, and to deny is to withhold belief ; **Rejection is** and both of these statements are true. But still the **of Control.** line of distinction just made is not erased. For with reference to the first statement we may say that the presupposition of belief as acceptance may itself be made part of the relational content, as we have seen. We then predicate the sort of existence that our belief has established, and deny a different sort. That is, the implication of existence *comes to be part of the system of relations* that may be affirmed or denied. I deny that mermaids exist in one sphere because I have accepted them in another sphere.

So also with the other point suggested, namely, that when we deny one thing of another we accept or reject the whole mean-**It is of a** ing that the relation proposes. This again is true ; **Sphere.** but in so doing it is the *relation* that we accept or reject *as holding or not* in a sphere already accepted. The acceptance of the sphere is not what is up for proposal, but the affirmation or denial of the relation *within this sphere.*

In other words, affirmation or denial is always relevant to the relation of one thing to another, that is what it is all about ; **Denial is of** it is always a matter of inclusion, exclusion, predica-**Relation.** tion, attachment or detachment, this-ness and other-ness, etc., of relatively separable meanings or terms. It is therefore the treatment in judgment of a relational subject-matter within a sphere or world of acceptance or presupposition. To render a rejection in terms of denial or negation is to make the sphere of acceptance or rejection itself a term, and to ask whether the relation of this meaning to the one affirmed or denied of it holds in a still larger whole of implication.

This has been intimated, indeed, in our earlier discussion of opposition in the prelogical modes. We found relationships of **A Prelogical** limitation, difference, privation, etc., developing in **Distinction.** various modes of meaning ; even where the self was not determined as capable of acknowledging or rejecting by an act of judgment. The attitude of dissatisfaction, re-bellion, rejection, etc., is very real; but such an attitude does not remove the object as a cognitive construction. It simply serves to differentiate it as being what it is, that is, to assign

it an appropriate sphere.   Now in the logical mode these differentiations serve as basis for the relationships in the context which
affirmation and negation are to render ; and the rendering is
always within the control already established and presupposed.

One of the roots of logical negation, therefore, is to be found
in those early lines of *limitation* with differentiation, exclusion
Root motive and inclusion, etc., which are developed into relations.
is Limitation. These the judgment takes up and renders by affirming
the inclusions and positive relationships, and denying where these
fail.   To do this, it is evident—as is argued in detail above—
is to recognize that certain combinations fail upon the positive
establishment of others.   The only live issue that would
" put-it-up " to belief, so to speak, is a positive proposal ;
and the successful issue establishes relations of exclusion and
denial as well as those of affirmation.

§ 12.   Modes of Quality

We find, in conclusion, as the result of those detailed discussions of which the genetic development of opposition has been
the principal problem, that the modes of quality to be recognized
are somewhat as follows.

32. There is, first, the root of all opposition found in the
limitation of a cognitive field.   This develops positively by the
(1) Limita- extension of that field by inclusion with its further
tion. exclusions by limitation.   This process, genetically
very early, is reinstated in the movement of the logical mode,
where the development of affirmation is by both inclusion and
limitation.   Inclusion resets the limits, and this limitative relation is rendered in a judgment of denial or negation.   Genetically, therefore, the mode of limitation motives the distinction
of quality as affirmative and negative.

But the limitation may be selective as well as recognitive.
The content of cognition may be one of privative determination
—the intentional exclusion of *whatever else there is except*
(2) Privation. *what is then and there selected.*   There arises then a
form of opposition quite original in type, known as privative or
imperative negation.

Finally, both of these types of negation—the sort of exclusion
that rests on limitation and the sort that rests on privation—
(3) Exclusion. are formally applied to meanings individuated as
singular.   In singularization, a meaning is individuated, for either reason, as exclusive.   In the mutual exclusion of

singulars we have the extreme development of opposition. It secures the isolation of terms from their relational setting and their treatment as " single " atoms to be combined and recombined by the characteristic operations of thought. It does not present a new form of negation, however, since its function is entirely that of elucidation and emphasis.

These general conclusions may be shown to the eye in the following table, which is designed to be read from left to right as presenting the genetic progression of opposition as it issues in logical quality.

Recognition
Selection $>$ Limitation $<$ Affirmation $<$ Exclusion
(Privation)   Negation   Privation

TABLE E.

Chapter IX

THE PROPOSITION : ITS IMPORT AND CHARACTERS

§ 1. ANALYSIS AND SYNTHESIS. ANALYTIC AND SYNTHETIC PROPOSITIONS

1. The two great modes in which the proposition renders the meanings of terms have been long since distinguished as " analysis " and " synthesis," the two forms of statement being called " analytic " and " synthetic." The distinction has become, on the one hand, one of the truisms of logic, and, on the other **The Distinc- tion.** hand, one of the most knotty problems of philosophy. The general distinction turns upon whether the full statement in subject and predicate merely analyses the meaning already present in the make-up of the subject—as in " the book has a red cover "—or whether it effects the synthesis or joining to the subject of a meaning, the predicate, now for the first time attached to it—as in, " the coal of the anthracite fields is very hard." The distinction would seem to turn upon the interpretation of the subject term : that is, upon the question as to whether in judgment there is a function of joining two distinct meanings together, or only one of recognizing parts of what is already constituted as a single larger meaning.

2. This question, it will be remembered, we have already fully discussed. Our conclusion [1] was that the subject-matter of judgment—now rendered in a proposition—is *the whole meaning intended by the statement.* Its essential import is the relation between the logical subject and predicate, as set forth in the **Analysis** proposition. Accordingly, from the point of view of this whole meaning, the proposition is in all cases an analysis, in the sense that it is impossible to render a relation which is not individuated as a single meaning holding the two terms in one. On the basis of this truth we reached the " conceptual " view of predication.

[1] See chap. ii. §§ 1, 2, 3.

Now it is evident that such a view answers very well for analytic propositions. We are safe in saying that my statement " the book has a red cover " is analytic ; for had I not already seen the book and individuated it as a single meaning, I could not have made such a statement about it as a book. But there would seem to be a difficulty in so accounting for judgmental contents which seem actually to adjust, in a relation, meanings before remote from each other and disconnected. " Caesar was the conqueror of the Gauls," for example, would seem to be synthetic ; the feat of Gaul-conquering is apparently added to the thought of the man Caesar.

This difficulty, troublesome as it has always been to the theory of knowledge, admits, I think, of ready solution from our present point of view, which distinguishes between elucidation and proposal, and recognizes that while all predication is eluci-

Analysis is Elucidation. dation, still most predication is also in some sense proposal. The analytic aspect of the proposition is, even when superficially viewed, that of elucidation. This we may set down as requiring no further argument. When I say " my book is the red one with the ink-blot on the back " I am elucidating the meaning " my red-ink-marked-book," as it already stands in my mind. This is clearly analysis.

Moreover, I think we may convert the statement and say that there is no elucidation that is not of the nature of analysis : that nothing can be stated in the elucidation of a meaning except what in some sense presents an analysis of that meaning.

3. But it will be at once asked—have you not made all actual judgmental content subject-matter of elucidation ?—and have

Synthesis is you not said that all implication, indeed all predication, is of the nature of elucidation ? To which we must reply—we have. How then, it is asked, can you identify elucidation with analysis without shutting out synthesis altogether ?—do you mean to say that there are no synthetic judgments ?

Yes, this is what I do mean to say, in the sense that there are no judgments that are *synthetic only*. The general ground of this assertion—apart from particular grounds on which we will

never found alone. proceed to justify it—is this : it is impossible to state, predicate, " propositionize," or otherwise express *what is not conceived*, and the expression of what is conceived *is of necessity analytic of that conception*.

How then are we to construe those statements that do not ex-

R

press old implication, but on the contrary embody new information —matter not yet grasped as conceptual and relational meaning ? Calling such statements synthetic we may divide them as follows :

(1) Synthetic meanings, of the nature of proposal.

(2) Judgments with synthetic intent, or proposal force, over and above their established subject-matter.

(3) Propositions synthetic in form, but problematical in force.

(4) A mass of what may be called " mixed synthetic intercourse"—all that body of information, predication, elucidation *ad hoc.*, proof, discussion, etc., the motive of which is the development of knowledge for somebody or other.

4. Besides these meanings, all of which embody elements of proposal, we have left over only (*a*) analytic judgments which explicitly express their whole conceptual intent, including the ground upon which the elucidation proceeds, and (*b*) analytic judgments which rest upon presuppositions not thus fully expressed, but still intended.   If we cared to use terms which invite one of the current genetic fallacies pointed out above, we should say of these latter that they involve " implicit implications," corresponding to the explicit grounds of implication given in the judgments first mentioned.   Evidently both of these classes are admittedly analytic ; we will find however that these also do not finally free themselves from elements of proposal.

Proposal is present.

5. We may now proceed to cite cases under the four heads given above and show that they are synthetic only so far as they *intend further proposal over and above the established analytic content.*

(1) Synthetic judgments so-called are often synthetic meanings of the nature of proposal.   This covers all propositions not fully accepted, but " suggested " for acceptance.   Such meanings are those pointed out as instrumental throughout all the development of knowledge ; as the schematic rendering of a content, they are prelogical or pre-judgmental.   In the mode of judgment, it is, as we have seen, the incubating stage of elements of general meaning.   It is synthetic just in that it adds meaning or intent beyond the content present in the schema. It is an intent of selective semblance, hypothesis, future fulfilment—something that the mode in which it occurs finds instrumental to the further handling of its situations.[1]   It is one of

Cases of Synthesis

---

[1] What I call, all through the course of mental development, " schematism." See the " Introduction " to this volume, and also chap. x. §§ 4f. of vol. i.

our chief positions that such accretions to meaning are not yet fully logical, for they are not capable of that retrospective reading which the general and universal characters attaching to particular cases allow. Inasmuch as the act of judgment requires the distribution of the elements of a meaning in the relation of general and particular, with the acknowledgment of what is so constituted, the aspect of meaning still in the stage of proposal or hypothesis is not yet judged. However expressed, the meaning is modified by a "may be" or a "suppose." This, it is clear, rules out many of the quasi-judgments called synthetic ; they are not judgments at all. While synthetic as meanings, they are still not subject-matter of judgment. They are judgments only when they assent to actually accepted subject-matter, which may be restated in terms of analysis.

(2) This state of things extends into the logical mode; there are meanings quite logical in content and form, which have, besides, a further intent to suggest or assume something beyond the accepted content. Of such a character are the propositions **Proposal Intent.** given in an earlier place to illustrate disjunctive and contingent meanings in all their variety. A disjunctive judgment, particular or general, is always logical in respect to the fact that it asserts the entire disjunctive meaning ; but it is schematic, intending a proposal, in reference to the final solution of the alternation suggested. Looking at the entire meaning in this way, we find that the body of logical implication involved is analytical ; while what is synthetic is the element of proposal which still remains problematical.

For example, "coins are gold, or silver, or brass" analyses the meaning "coin"; but its element of synthesis is the suggested determination of the nature of the single coin. This is problematical, not yet rendered in the judgment itself. So also the proposition "these articles are coins or counters," gives an analysis of the whole meaning, but suggests the stated solutions as both possible. A similar interpretation may be given to many other propositions ; there is a body of implication liable to lucidation by analysis,[1] together with a proposal of further synthesis.

So with the contingent. It is a meaning whose relational content is established, and it is the motive of the judgment to assert

---

[1] It is shown below, in the discussion of reasoning, that the analytic content may be used as a premise, either categorical or hypothetical, for the further advance.

this analytically; but the control, the grounding of the entire meaning, is left problematical and schematic. Here again the matter that is judged is analytical, the part that is synthetic is not judged as elucidation, but set up as proposal.

For example, "if A, then B," asserts analytically the dependence of B upon A in the entire meaning AB; but it does not assert that the meaning so made up, the meaning AB, is actually realized or accepted as existing anywhere : that is, that there is a synthesis of the terms A and B except as a proposal made in thought.

(3) There are cases of propositions clearly and undoubtedly synthetic in form, and also clearly assertive, but which however, on closer inspection, reveal a problematical intent. The things to be proved—the "postulates" of mathematics, the "assumptions" of science, the "hypotheses" of research—are all expressed in the categorical form of statement, although, both in motive and in actual intent, they suggest a synthesis rather than assert it. The utility of this becomes evident when we remember that the resources of expression are not confined to explicit statement, but include the auxiliary modes of gesture, intonation, punctuation, vocal emphasis, etc., by which the modifying doubt or assumption is imparted to the form of words.

(4) In intercourse as we find it, all these motives are found mixed and unsorted—a very riot of beliefs and questionings. And the only guide to interpretation at all fruitful is found in the truism put at the head of this paragraph— *no one can express what he has not conceived*. He may conceive it in either of two ways and for either of two purposes—either for and as elucidation and belief, or for and as proposal and question. If he has conceived it, then no matter how he puts it, as believed or as proposed for belief, it is analytical of his conception. In this he is the " speaker " of our earlier account of the situation in all intercourse. On the other hand, if he be the " hearer," and the thing come to him from another for his acceptance, or for his investigation, still he must understand it, put it together, schematize it in a whole meaning : and this meaning is then the subject-matter of whatever judgment he makes. He now finds it possible to judge, predicate, acknowledge, only the relationships within the entire intent of the construction. To say that he has judged one thing true of another is to say that he has conceived and accepted the entire meaning which the assertion or denial sets up. The conceptual make-up of the meaning is, therefore, the genetic and

logical presupposition of the judgment. And the explicit relational statement renders in more formal terms the meaning already embedded in the whole.

6. Whatever, therefore, is really still in the sphere of synthesis belongs to that side of the proposition which is assumptive and hypothetical, not to that side which accepts a sphere of existence. The issue in judgment, giving the propositions called synthetic, is the acknowledgment of the growth of the concept to any stage **Further** of accomplished relation. In other words—coming **Judgment.** close to the actual movement—the proposal, which is synthetic, motives the redistribution of elements whose issue is a new stage of conception. The judgment is the belief side, the mediate control, wherein this new distribution is held up objectively and analytically.

In short, we come here yet again to the distinction that will not down, the distinction between the processes of exploration, trial-and-error, proposal, by which syntheses are suggested and tested ; and those of belief, predication, implication, elucidation, by which the accepted syntheses are exploited. This latter is retrospective, analysing, ratifying, acknowledging, **Judgment** finding theoretically true. It proceeds upon the other, **as Belief.** the synthesizing, experimenting, proving. And it is only confirmatory of this distinction to find here also that belief deals with presuppositions and established references, while proposal deals with novelties and syntheses.

7. We see, therefore, that of the entire judgmental intent, the two aspects called above elucidation and proposal are always to be distinguished ; and that while the matter of elucidation, the content proper, presented as acknowledged and believed, is **is Analytic.** analytic, the proposal, the intent set up for further confirmation and acceptance by either of the parties to the intercourse, is synthetic. It is then a fair conclusion to draw, when we recognize the presence of the matter of elucidation as such, that *all judgment is analytic.*

8. But the great problem of predication, considered as a dual and relational meaning, again forces itself upon us ; and we recall the terms of our former solution of it. We found ourselves obliged to recognize the movement, within the context of thought, **As instru.** whereby relationships are established and developed. **mental.** The instrumental aspect of thinking is that of proposal, experimentation, assimilation of meanings to one another and to the whole context of experience. The " selective thinking "

is as real as the acknowledging or recognitive thinking. If it be true—as we have claimed—that there is no judgment or predication that entirely fails of the proposal force, no meaning strictly of the type " elucidation-elucidation," then our analysis of the cases given above not only shows, as we have said, that all judgment is analytic, but also that *all judgment is synthetic*. From the point of view of the relations in the entire content of the predication—the whole subject-matter of thought—the judgment is analytic ; but from the point of view of the manipulation of relatively detached and formed terms or class meanings, the judgment is as clearly synthetic. We feel, therefore, here the need we have felt before of doing justice to both these aspects of the developing movement of predication.

it is Synthetic.

9. The great inclusive distinction that points the way is again that which we have found between acknowledgment as control function and predication as content or relation function. It has just served us in making out the larger meaning of the aspects of judgment known as quantity and quality. It appears again below in our interpretation of the existence reference of propositions, as has already been intimated above in the discussion of the existence force of quantity. It is the fundamental distinction between the function of acceptance, acknowledgment, belief, terminating upon a content as such— *the reference of such a content to its appropriate control*—and *the development within that content itself* of the enlarged context of predicated and implicated meanings. *The former is synthetic, the latter analytic.*

Distinction of Control and Content.

As soon as we apply this distinction with any pretence of thoroughness, we find that the distinction of analysis or synthesis is one of point of view. As acknowledged contents, assertions, wholes of conceived and established meaning upon which belief is fixed, all judgment is in its nature analytic. Of this aspect it is true that we can assert only what we have already conceived. Of course we cannot acknowledge or believe beyond what we apprehend. So every judgment, in so far as it is a vital belief—either asserting or presupposing existence—is of necessity the bringing out for predication or implication of relationships present in the whole thus accepted.

Analysis of Content.

This is the point of view of logical quality. Quality is *par excellence* relational. It deals with the linkages of meanings, all

on the level of objects of thought : the relation-wise reading
Analysis is shown in the diagram given above.[1] Thoughts, logical
in Quality. meanings, float like cakes of ice, and bump together,
stick one to another, repel and exclude each other, all on the one
moving surface, regardless of conditions of depth, which are the
presuppositions of another dimension at right angles to their side-
wise movement. All the patterns that they form are logical,
rendered as affirmations, limitations, negations, exclusions,
privations.

But all the while there is present also the other dimension,
the in-and-out, subject-object, belief-acceptance, judgment-atti-
tude meaning sustaining and controlling the whole. This is the
existential or quantitative aspect of propositions. As we have
seen above, all quantified judgments have the existential reference.
" To say ' how many ' is to presuppose ' some.' " The movement
of quantity is itself just the explicit reference of the meaning as a
whole to its control or existence sphere, regardless of the further
statement of, or intent to develop, the relational content of the
predicated system.

10. The burden of our story is the emphasis on this latter
aspect, on the tracing of genetic progressions, on development, growth, expansion of the system of established thoughts :
the selective aspect of thinking. All this is proposal, assumption, treatment-as-if believed—but without explicit reference to
Synthesis that assumption or actual statement of it. It is always
of Control. present ; intercourse proceeding by *any real genetic
movement* is impossible without it. Here is the intent of judgmental meaning to project its proposals, to make its enlarged
suggestions, to build up its semblant hypotheses, to reason out
its quasi-logical systems of implications.[2] *All this is a matter
of synthesis :* and in this aspect all judgment is synthetic.

It becomes then a question of actual intent : of quantity
or existential reference, of assumption, of synthesis, on the one
hand, and of relation and analysis, on the other hand. I
accept or reject *this or that, as a whole*, a synthetic meaning proposed for my belief in a sphere of existence or fulfilment ; but I
affirm or deny *this or that, as a relation of analysis*, be the sphere
that our intercourse presupposes what it may.

11. We thus reach, I think, both a further application, and
also an important confirmation, of our fundamental recognition

---

[1] See Fig. 10 in chap. viii. § 2 sect. 3.
[2] On the synthetic force of Inference, see chap. xii. § 3.

of the double reference of all judgment : its control reference and its relation reference ; its subject-object dualism and its individuation of meaning in a related context. The consideration of the two great problems of logical interpretation, the problems of quantity and quality, has driven us back to this distinction [1] ; and now we are able to correlate them in a further interpretation that seems to explain the logical distinction between analysis and synthesis. The matter of prime moment, as all our discussions of prelogical and also of quasi-logical meaning taught us, is after all, the question *how the attitude felt as inner control crystallizes into a self, believing and judging a whole synthetic meaning, and how the objective content, the what, takes form in a system of related contents.*

This is the vital genetic movement. It is the synergy of minor dispositions and interests which constitute the self a subject. For this self the thought is synthetic, the achievement selective, the truth novel. But as to the relational whole, spread out as a detailed context, that is an analytic display of the entire meaning grasped by the synergy of the·self-movement.

12. We may also note here another correlation that breaks in upon us quite unexpectedly. We may ask the purely " synthetic " theorist [2] how a negative judgment is possible. From a purely synthetic logical point of view this question admits of only one answer : a negative judgment is impossible, it is meaningless. For how can a denial as between two things be a

Negation denies Synthesis. synthesis of them ?—or how can a synthesis deny one of its own terms ? From the point of view of logical quality this is unanswerable. But if we take the quantitative or existential point of view, we find that it is just the movement of synthesis that *motives the denial.* A suggested affirmation that runs " up against " a snag in the shape of a real growth in meaning, a positive condition of fact—this issues in rejection of the whole attempted synthetic meaning. To reject *SP* belief-wise is to deny *P* of *S* relation-wise. *A proposal doesn't work.* What is impossible when construed in terms of content

---

[1] We shall find also that the interpretation of the other prominent characters of propositions, " Relation " and " Modality," turns upon this distinction ; see § 5 of this chapter.

[2] A purely synthetic theorist would, I suppose, be hard to find, and yet such a position is that of the formal logic of term-meanings : two quite separate terms are *brought together* in a proposition, and a third *is added* and so *united to the first* through the syllogism. See a typical presentation of this view, in Dr. Ladd Franklin's article, " Proposition," in the writer's *Dict. of Philosophy.*

is after all very real in terms of belief. The resulting negation, while synthetic as to the *proposed* whole which is now rejected, is analytic as to the relationships of the proposed but rejected whole.[1] That is, as proposed the meaning is synthetic, but not negative ; as rejected it is negative, but analytic.

I submit that this general relation is true of any negative proposition whatever. If it is a case of exclusively quantitative, that is to say existential, import and is plainly synthetic, it still establishes a meaning capable of being rendered in an analytic proposition of denial. " Some men are black " implies existence ; it quantifies and limits the term " men," and so suggests cases that are not black but some other colour, say white. The analytic negation " some men are not white " is a negative rendering of the quantitative synthetic proposition " some men are black." That is, the positive synthetic growth is always on the side of the affirmative or " proposal " reference.

The other extreme meaning for our interpretation, a purely analytic and qualitative one, such as " the face includes eyes, nose, and mouth " cannot be denied without resort to a proposed existential reference by which a positive and synthetic import of meaning is secured.

When indeed we asked, in a broad way, how a negative meaning was possible, the reply was, by the rejection of a proposed synthesis.

---

[1] I have pointed out in another place (*Handbook of Psychology, Senses and Intellect*, 1st Edition, p. 293), that from the point of view of strict logical exclusion, there could be no such thing as a negative analytic proposition ; for nothing could be analysed out of a concept, to be used as predicate in a statement of what is not in the concept. But from the psychological point of view of denial, as issuing from the positive growth of a concept, either by increase or decrease of marks in a positive way, a negative statement may render an analytic judgment. The passage referred to is as follows : " A negative analytic judgment in logic is impossible, simply from the fact that that which is denied of the subject cannot result from an analysis of it ; thus the proposition ' birds are not parts of trees ' cannot be called analytic. Yet the negative analytic judgment is possible when looked at from the side of the psychological movement. It is by the analysis of our judgments that the accidental is discovered and rejected by negation. For example, the child first observes trees with birds, and it is only after he has seen trees without birds, that he can rectify his notion tree by depriving it of the birds. In this case, the very origin of the negation is found in the necessity of an analysis and rectification of the notion tree. The rejection of a synthesis covers all negative judgments in logic." This is true even when, as in the case given above, the proposition expresses the result of an analysis. It is the rejection of a proposed synthesis which was perhaps formerly accepted.

" American statesmen are not corrupt " rejects the proposal that attaches corruptness to American statesmen. But why is the synthesis rejected ? As the result of an analysis of the conceptual or relational meaning " American statesmen." The proposed synthetic whole, whether accepted or rejected, is then rendered analytically as a relational content.

13. In brief, therefore, we may say that every proposition is analytic, inasmuch as it embodies a larger meaning toward the relationships of which the knower has taken up an attitude of All proposi- acceptance or rejection. The whole meaning, analysed tions into the terms of the relation set up, is what the predication means and intends.

Equally also, every proposition is synthetic, inasmuch as it is the affirmation or denial of a whole meaning whose parts are united in a characteristic relation. As constituting a new whole of related parts the synthesis is real ; as setting are both. forth the related whole that the belief attitude accepts or rejects the analysis is equally real. The entire function, of which these are aspects, is judgment.

Here then we have a confirmation of the view of judgment worked out above. It is a movement which by a redistribution of contents relates objective meanings in a context of reflection (synthesis) *and also* segregates the subject or control over against the entire context of reflection which is set forth in a system of related details (analysis).[1]

14. The actual processes of analysis and synthesis have already been described. They are continuous with the processes of " accretion " and " erosion " of the prelogical modes.[2] A meaning already entertained is simply put to use, erected for the treatment of experience as it comes. The larger wholes of Processes of habitual schematization and habit are fitted upon the Analysis and new events as they occur in practical life, with varying Synthesis. degrees of success. The crude meaning " man," for example, is revised and toned down, loses irrelevant marks, finds its salient features brought out—all this is analysis. It is rendered in judgments and propositions in which the new items of meaning thus secured are held apart from or within the whole constituted in thought. On the other hand, accretions come by information, experiment, all sorts of proposal and hypothesis ;

---

[1] Diagrams illustrating this movement are given in vol. i. chap. xi. sect. 15 (figs. 2, 3).
[2] See chap. vii. §§ 2 ff.

active accommodation processes embody the issue of practice. Meanings before isolated are thrown together and fitted into a larger whole of assimilation and implication. All this is synthesis. It goes on by a ferment of change in the body of knowledge itself. It is the growth of the " ice-field " both in extent and in configuration. And both, analysis and synthesis, are actual all the while. The body of knowledge yields the richer analysis, the larger system of implication, as the synthetic processes are effective and accommodative in the rounding out of the mass of contents. The two are obverse sides of the one great movement of selective thinking, continuing as it does the processes that motive generalization and abstraction. And we are to see that the same dual motive issues further in the great modes of reasoning known as Induction and Deduction.

§ 2.   THE EXISTENCE IMPORT[1] OF PROPOSITIONS

15. It is by a further explanation along the line of our principal interest that we are now led to the consideration of another of the debated points of logical theory—the question of the sort of existence or lack of existence intended by this or that proposition. It may be a good way to get at the matter to connect it with what we have just been discussing—the acceptance or The Existencerejection of meanings by an act of judgment, when the Reference. existence import is explicitly asserted ; and from this to approach those more obscure cases in which it is more open to question. This will lead us from the " existential " judgment as such to the judgment that seems to have no existence reference attaching to it. There are such extreme cases ; judgments that seem indifferent as to the existence of their subject matter.

16. As to the existential judgment, we have seen that the reference to existence may be made either as a presupposition Existence or as a predication. The act of judgment that estab- as Presup- lishes a content for thought always acknowledges the position. control in a specific sphere of existence. This is, indeed, just what we have found existence to mean—the specific sphere in which control and conversion may be found. To accept an object as physical means to believe it one that may

---

[1] The word " import " used logically is fairly equivalent to the term " intent " as we use it for meaning generally ; import is the intent of logical meaning, connoting over and above the exact relation of terms used as subject-matter, the additional suggestion, assumption, remote reference, presupposition, etc., that are *imported* into the bare statement.

be converted into the co-efficients that sense-perception gives. So also in other spheres. Now where this remains simply a reference not actually asserted, it is what we call a " pre-

Existence as supposition " of belief. But this intent to acknow-
Predicate. ledge existence may itself be made subject-matter of predication ; in this case, we have the existential proposition. This is, so far, plain sailing. The existential judgment is one of affirmation or denial of the sphere of control already presupposed in the acceptance of the subject-matter.

When, however, existence is not thus explicitly affirmed or denied, we have to ask in what sense it is still presupposed by the various propositional forms. Going through the different sorts of judgment, we should find in connection with their respective form and contents, indications as to what sort of presuppositions of existence they severally intend.

17. Our first great indication is afforded by the ground of the distinction between logical " quantity " and " quality," as it shows itself in the two attitudes of acceptance and affirmation. The quantitative aspect of a judgment is the acceptance aspect, its belief-wise aspect. The qualitative aspect is its affirmation, its relation-wise aspect. The relation between acceptance and affirmation may be put thus : to affirm one thing

Quantity of another is to accept the whole meaning that the
means affirmed relation sets up. This is in turn to presuppose
Existence. a sphere in which this whole meaning—the entire related content—has the characteristic control that justifies the affirmation.

We may accordingly say that all quantified affirmative propositions presuppose existence whatever the quantity be—a conclusion anticipated above in the discussion of quantity (chap. iv. § 6).

Again, considering rejection and denial in the same way, we find that to deny a thing or meaning is to *reject it from a control—not to reject the control.* The control of the subject-matter is

Also when presupposed, and the predicate term is denied because
Negative. the relation does not hold *in this control.* The exist-
ence sphere of belief is the same, whether the content be affirmed or denied. This is exactly the same result as that reached in the case of the affirmation : *there is the acceptance of a control.* The affirmation is the acceptance of the sphere in which the predicated relation holds ; the denial is the rejection *from the accepted sphere* of the proposed or suggested rela-

tion. Both presuppose in the same sense, the acceptance of a sphere of control or existence.[1] So far as denial means rejection, it is simply the rejection of the suggested content from the sphere in which its proposal would place it. This presupposes the acceptance of the sphere ; otherwise the denial would be meaningless.

This leads to our first general position, namely, that affirmation and denial stand on the same basis in their reference to a sphere of existence ; *both alike make reference to it.*[2] Denial rejects a relational content from the sphere ; affirmation accepts it in the same sphere.

18. But it may be said, does not the denial of a relation reject any sphere in which it might hold ? I at once answer, no. The denial is always made with reference to the positive determination of the subject-matter ; the control sphere of the content meaning is always presupposed. When, for example, I deny that " angels **Denial is** marry," I do so *for and within* the sphere which the **acceptance** conception of angels presupposes or suggests—that **of Existence.** of mythology, eschatology, or religious legend. But I may still say that "in reality," in the " Kingdom of Heaven," in dreams, anywhere else than just in the one connection presupposed, they may marry. To deny that avarice is in the long run economical, is not to assert that it may not be economical in some other moral and economic order than that of our present practical life. " John has no hair " does not forbid my imagining,

---

[1] It follows from this that "disbelief" is a form of belief—belief in a sphere with reference to which the proposed content is not accepted. There is no assertion of " un-reality " in general ; it is always a specific non-existence that is asserted. "The opposite of belief is doubt. . . . Disbelief is equivalent to belief in something which negatives that which is disbelieved " (The writer's *Handbook of Psychology, Feeling and Will,* p. 157).

[2] This disposes equally of two wide-spread logical views ; one that particular quantity implicates existence while universal does not (discussed above, chap. iv. § 6), and the other that affirmation implicates existence while denial does not. I use the word "implicate" rather than "imply," since to imply existence would be to involve an *affirmative* existence meaning, while to " implicate " existence would only involve a *reference to existence*—to a sphere of control—of any sort—whether affirmative or negative. For example, in the question " are there black swans ? " existence is implicated, but whether it is to be implied is what is in question. To say that the negative does not "imply" existence—in the narrower sense of affirmative implication of existence—is simply to state that it is negative—which " goes without saying."

dreaming, joking, hoping John into a condition of greater hairiness. I do not reject a sphere in which John may be a perfect Esau. In denial, in short, as was said above, the essential presupposition is positive not negative ; its negative force comes through limitation, not through direct exclusion. Here we have a further consequence of that point of view.

19. We have now greatly simplified the question. We have now to ask—is there any judgment, any proposition, that does not have, as part of its import or intent, the presupposition of some sort of existence ? Or put negatively, can a proposition be made, and not be meaningless, which does not accept a sphere of control in which its related content holds and may be found, or in which it is asserted not to hold and not to be found ?

Is all Judgment Existential ?

Here again we may abbreviate discussion by recalling our earlier results. In arranging judgments with reference to their embodiment of belief, we found that there are no effective judgments that do not refer the content mediated by reflection to some original control. When this remote or direct control was found lacking then that called " mediate," the control of reflection itself, is invoked to take its place. Reflection has its own co-efficients, its own existence force, as a realm of positive realization. The inner world of thinking is a sphere of actual existence. To speak of a thing's being valid in the organization and control of the life of reflective thought is to give it a very definite sort of existence reference.[1]

Yes;

But we found also a still further case. We found it necessary to recognize the sphere of the merely psychic as a region of the disorganized, fugitive, unreal. The psychic as merely fanciful is the region of the uncontrolled, the fatuous, the weird and invalid. Its character is such just in that it escapes not only the presupposition of immediate or direct control, but also that of the mediating processes of reflection. The images of mere fancy, the fugitive dreams of sleep or waking life, are lawless ; they mean nothing but just their detached and naked psychic presence.

only the Uncontrolled is unreal,

20. Here then are three possible cases. It is only of the second of them—normal judgment, that is not explicitly existential—

---

[1] Later on (chap. xiii. §§ 2, 4) it is shown how the body of thought detaches itself as a consistent and self-contained system of truth, presupposing, however, the " mediate " control reference.

that the question of existence import can arise at all. Of the
third, the fugitive content, we may say that it can have existence
meaning only as it is reduced to the second : that is, only as its
images *are made content of judgment* and so assigned to the
sphere of the inner life as one of positive control.   In this
It may be way they may acquire a definite existence reference.
mediated. Your dream is a thing, a something—even when you
pronounce it a fugitive thing or something, an unreality—when
you refer it to the general flow and make up of your inner life.
You express its meaning when you say that it does not *make good
in the life of thought ; but you then presuppose the life of thought.*
Even the denial of its validity is the assertion of the control
sphere of reflection.

But as clear as it is that existence beyond the merely
psychic *is not intended* of the fugitive—so clear *is it intended* of
what is in any way remotely controlled. Though mediated by
thought, the original control is presupposed, no matter what the
mode of predication.

21. There remains then only the question as to whether there
The merely is any sort of reflective or judged content that has no
Logical further control than that given in its own constitution
as reflection. Or put differently—does all reflective content
have to come through an earlier control which in turn is mediated in judgment ?—or, is there logical process of such a formal sort that it has no specific content whose control requires
reference to existence ?

Clearly to ask this question is to answer it negatively ; it is
plain that reflection cannot get along without the control that belongs to it. For reflection is itself one of the sorts of
is existent. control mediated by each act of judgment.   The content of any act of reflection presupposes the subject-object
relation as a specific mode of control. And whatever aspect of
meaning the particular proposition taken for examination may
bring forward—abstraction, generalization, singularization, affirmation, negation—still the sphere in which such a mode of predication is constituted is there as part of the intent or import of
the proposition.

22. We reach then a second general point, namely, that *all
Existence propositions have an existential reference*, understanding
sphere by " existence " any of the spheres of realization in
which the whole meaning or intent may be accepted, questioned, or denied.

This appears indeed negatively from the attempt to deny such a reference or presupposition. To deny existence is always to assert belief in the non-existence of the postulated meaning in of the non-existent. a specific sphere. But this requires the presupposition of the sphere from which the postulated content is excluded, as we have already seen.

In what sense then can we say that a content does not exist ? To this we may reply in the terms of popular usage.

(1) When we say a thing does not exist, we generally mean that it exists only in the thought of the thinker ; that is, that it has no further implication of control than that of the judging function itself in which it occurs.

(2) We may mean that it is put forward schematically, as a proposal for determination ; and that its existence is still a matter to be determined. *It has not yet been found to exist.*

The latter is the more fruitful case for our further theory, and receives full discussion in the next chapter. Most of our judgments—those having contingent and disjunctive intent of all kinds—still await confirmation through processes of further control. We find that judgment, viewed with reference to the ideal of final and complete confirmation, never lacks such experimental intent. And while of such meanings we may say that they may or might exist, here or there, consistently with the presupposition of normal reflection, still their further adoption and ratification, as holding in some further sphere, remains to be decided. Here there is introduced a line of considerations pertinent to the question of the tests of different modes of acceptance, to which we must return.

Existence of the Problematical.

23. The conclusion of our study so far, however, is that apart from the fugitive vagary, the uncontrolled image, the typically "unreal," all judgments equally, whether affirmative or negative, intend existence of some sort. To deny external existence is still to presuppose it as a sphere, and also to presuppose internal organization in a context of reflection, which is also a mode of actual existence.[1]

Conclusion.

---

[1] It is a corollary of this argument that the "commonness" of judgment implicates existence ; for to be common is to presuppose other minds, and the sphere of existence of the other minds is but an enlargement of the circle of reflective process. Another point is that the commonness of judgment extends not merely to common function, but to "appropriate" and synnomic content as well. So that a judged content implicates a sphere of existence that is open to common inspection and confirmation.

§ 3. THE FORMS OF THE SIMPLE PROPOSITION

24. Coming now to consider the specific forms that predications take on in the proposition, we are greatly aided by the discussions already presented above. The modes of judgmental meaning have been distinguished [1]; and we should expect to find propositions expressing these types of meaning in characteristic form. These modes were, it will be remembered, " assertorial " on the one hand, and "problematical," in a large sense, on the other hand. Understanding by the assertorial a mode of accepted meaning em-**The various** bodied in an assertion relatively free from question, we **meanings** need not now distinguish such statements with respect **embodied in** **Propositions** to quality, that is as affirmative or negative. The same is to be said also of problematical meanings and statements ; they may express a problematical meaning either affirmatively or negatively. So we have on our hands two great types of propositions ; those which embody a determinate and accepted meaning—determinate in content and accepted in judgment— and those which embody a meaning relatively indefinite in one or other of these aspects, being either indeterminate as to content or *sub judice* as to acceptance. The first class, the assertorial meanings, we find rendered in " categorical " propositions. The second class offers two alternatives, as has been already indicated : either the content is determinate within an indefinite control and belief—giving a " contingent " meaning, embodied in a " conditional " proposition—or this content is indeterminate within a definite control and belief—giving an alternative meaning embodied in a disjunctive proposition.

This it will be remembered is in outline the set of distinctions brought out above. What is here added is simply the naming of the propositions in which these modes of meaning are respectively rendered. Putting them in a table, we have—

TABLE F.

Meanings.	*Propositions.*
1.—Assertorial.	1.—Categorical.
2.—Problematical.	2.—Problematical.
A. Contingent.	A. Conditional.
B. Alternative.	B. Disjunctive.

25. An interesting further problem is at once suggested, both by the tenor of our present investigation, and also by the emphasis

---

[1] See chap. ii.

given it in current discussion—the problem of the comparative force of these several forms.   There are many discussions **Which is Fun-** written from a logical point of view, inquiring which of **damental?** these forms is the fundamental, the *Ur-modus*, so to speak.   The problem, quite apart from its popularity, lies directly in our way, since it is by a genetic or longitudinal investigation that our inquiry proceeds, and the comparative motives and functions of the several types of proposition should be clear to us if our earlier results have been full and correct.

26. We have, indeed, certain data at hand for the answer to the question.   The conditions of the rise of logical meaning are **A matter of** those of judgment, which is the coming of belief and **Belief.** assertion.   There must be a certain categorical force *in any proposition whatever* that embodies judgment ; there must be *an acknowledgment of something*.

But it is equally plain that such a judgment may be an acknowledgment of *a whole of very indeterminate or problematical details*, or of *details of a very indefinite or problematical whole* ; and further the acknowledgment may be of a detailed whole along with observation or question as to the *sphere of control* in which the acceptance holds good.

That is, assuming the amount and sort of determinateness that motives and justifies the act of judgment itself, we may distinguish the following sorts of indeterminateness still possibly attaching to the meaning rendered in the judgment.

(1) Indeterminateness of problematical content within a presupposed or determined sphere of control.

(2) Indeterminateness of control of a given or determined content.

(3) Determinateness of both content and control.

The order of genetic development is, I think, that given in this enumeration.   The modes of meaning arising under the conditions that early experience of judging copes with, are those which reduce appearances to classes, which eliminate alternatives, while **Content is** securing increasing confidence with view to action. **relatively** All this is *in the sphere of alternative or disjunctive* **determined.** *meaning*.   Suggestions of meaning, schemata of selective rendering, actual resort to conversion processes, immediate or secondary, all show this essential movement from the ambiguous, the problematical, the risky, to the definite, the fixed, the safe.   Of course there is the categorical strain, the presupposition of existence in a sphere of fact ; but this is the criterion of judgment itself; it may be a mere presumptive intent. In order to be fully categorical the meaning of a proposition should be free from alternative suggestions; that is, the intent rendered by the proposition should forbid disjunction.

The first form, therefore, that judgment takes on as a proposition is *problematical*. It intends either the proposal of a (1) The Dis- general class for the interpretation of the particular junctive. case, or the proposal of a particular to illustrate a general class. In each case the meaning is alternative and disjunctive in type, having the presupposition or presumption of the sort of existence or control in which the whole experience or situation is developing. It motives the further movements towards contingent and categorical propositions.

27. The second phase seems to be that which we recognize as *conditional* or "contingent" in its type. It, again, like the disjunctive, has its natural place in situations in which a meaning is made instrumental to discovery and action. All the regular (2) The Con- series of items of knowledge—the associations, the ditional personal mediations, the social linkages, the mechanical sequences of life and fact—all lend themselves to the larger contextuation by which the alternations of disjunctive meaning are dissolved. The "this or that" yields, by the tracing of dependences, to the establishing of "this with that," or "if this then that." The "if" of the contingent "if A then B," invokes all the items of actual knowledge whose present support may guarantee one of the earlier alternatives and so dissolve the disjunction. This again is a movement within an accepted sphere of belief.

28. Finally, there comes that mode to which both the earlier ones are instrumental : the full conviction of what is both *established in sphere and grounded in content, the categorical*. In very truth its intent is settlement, stability, determinateness ; absence of alternatives, contingency, hypothesis. As a motive, a factor, (3) The a strain of meaning, it is present all the while in the Categorical presuppositions and presumptions upon which the whole judgmental movement proceeds. But in the vital progress of meaning, especially in its linguistic mode of development in which the common and social intent is normally to the fore, the element of proposal, of prospective reference, of indeterminateness is there to give the meaning an experimental force. Of course, as a mere form, the categorical may be bent to any use— from the confidence of intellectual laziness, to the show of social

" bluff "—but as a typical meaning, having a characteristic intent, the assertorial is rather an ideal to which both the disjunctive and the contingent are instrumental.

29. Various of our special discussions indicate this—were it worth while to cite them in detail. The negative assertorial we have seen to be a rebound from an attempted affirmative, the latter being a proposal of essentially disjunctive or contingent force. Such an attempt results in both a categorical (and limiting) affirmative and a categorical (and exclusive) negative. Again in the case of the singular, we find a meaning established as most fully assertorial, but it presupposes processes of experimental generalization whose intent is to exhaust the object ; and only where hypothetical generals fail so to exhaust it, does the categorical singular succeed.

In short, we may say, indeed, that while judgment *as an act* is in its intent of acknowledgment and assertion essentially categorical ; yet *in its content or subject-matter* the categorical mode is the end-state or ideal of the process. It is intro-Giving a duced and motived by experimental processes. Progression. Earlier disjunctive or alternative readings lead on, through stages of wider associative and relational contingency, to points of equilibrium or rest. The issue of any such progression of meaning in categorical form is then, although categorical with reference to the assimilated and interpreted matter, at once again and continually made disjunctive, schematic, and instrumental with reference to the further control of experience.[1]

§ 4. ELEMENTS OF THE PROPOSITION : TERMS AND COPULA

30. We have already discussed the presence of terms in the proposition. We found that, considered relationally or analyti-

---

[1] A brief analytic treatment of this topic is to be found in my *Handbook of Psychology, Senses and Intellect*, chap. xiv. ; it contains conclusions which the present discussion goes to enforce. Other discussions are cited there ; here I may refer only to the characteristic remarks of Bradley, and the full discussion of Sigwart, in their respective *Logics*. Mr. Bradley's view that the disjunctive is made up of two hypotheticals has been adverted to above (chap. ii. sect. 47, 2, note). The " categorical basis " that he finds underlying such propositions (*loc. cit.* p. 122) agrees with my own presupposition of existence ; but this belongs to the *belief-wise attitude*, not to the *subject-matter taken relation-wise*. We cannot say that a categorical proposition comes first, for that would be to isolate it as a meaning, while as " basis " of the problematical forms, it is not isolated but presupposed in connection with a further subject-matter.

cally, there are always two terms or term meanings entering
into the entire subject-matter of judgment when rendered as proposition. But we have also seen that,
when considered conceptually, that is, as a whole meaning or
subject-matter of acceptance, considered that is synthetically,
the two terms go to make up one. " S is P " has two terms, S and
P ; but what is judged or asserted is " SP," a single conceptual
meaning. The terms, therefore, are those smaller units or parts
of the entire meaning which stand in relation to each other,
when the entire meaning is acknowledged or asserted.

The Terms

We have seen further in what sense existence becomes a
term. The meaning acknowledged as a whole carries the additional intent or presupposition of belief in a sphere of existence.
This aspect of the whole, no less than the more recognitive and
relational aspects, may be set up for assertion as a term ; and
the judgment then declares the entire meaning " SE " in the
form " S is E " (" men are existing," or " men exist "). The
procedure is strictly analogous to that mentioned above.

The additional element of the proposition, considered as a
linguistic form, is found in the connecting verb " to be," in one
of its forms, such as " is " or " are." The question
then arises as to the force of this connecting word,
called the " copula."

The Copula.

In general, we find that whatever the linguistic form of the
proposition may be, we can reduce it to the form " S is P."
" Mammals breathe," " Caesar crossed the Rubicon," " Let all
creation sing "—all these may be so reduced, for the purposes
of formal logic, by introducing a verbal noun for the predicate.
This carries the force of the verb over to that term ; and then
" is," or some other part of the verb " to be " becomes copula.
" Mammals *are* breathing animals," " Caesar *is* the man who
crossed the Rubicon," " All creation *should be* singing," etc., are
renderings of the propositions just cited. This shows that the
content-meaning as such, the subject-matter or relational whole
which enters into the predication, may be *exhausted in the statement of the terms themselves*. The something made subject
may be considered a consistent mass of meaning, a term, and
the something predicated of it another. What then remains
over for the copula ?

31. The same question emerges if we approach the matter
in another way—from the point of view of analysis. Taking the
whole meaning " SP " as exhausting the subject-matter, and

rendering it analytically so as to relate P to S within the whole, what then is there left over, that may still find embodiment in the copula ?

(1) In the first place, we may say negatively that the copula does not express the relation which it is the intent of the proposi-
Copula is nottion to declare.   The relational intent is just what is
relational. expressed in the predicate term.   For example, the proposition " the dog is fierce " is equivalent to " the dog is fierce-dog," the motive to the assertion being that of saying that the meaning " dog " passes into that of " fierce-dog."   So " the sun melts the snow " is equivalent to " the sun is snow-melting-sun."   In other words, the object of judgment is to assert a related whole ; the predicate suggests the relationship *before* it is judged.   If it be true that the predicate already renders the relation, then the copula does not have that rôle.   Suppose I say " salt resembles sugar," I mean to place salt in the class of sugar-resembling-things.   Here the relation of resemblance-to-sugar is the predicate-meaning.   It is what I assert of the salt.

(2) More positively, we may say that the copula does render the additional intent of the act of judgment, over and above the mode of relation which the predicate establishes.   This intent appears in two very essential aspects of the proposition.

(a) The judgmental intent to *refer the content as a whole to a sphere of existence*—its belief-wise intent—*is rendered in the*
It is Ex-   *copula*.   The meaning " SP," whatever relation be
istential.   suggested by P, remains a suggestion merely, a proposal of schematic meaning, until the belief " S *is* P " is pronounced.   The willingness to say " S is P " at once provides the reference of the whole " SP " to its appropriate sphere of control ;   there is the acknowledgment of its existence in that sphere.   Of course this intent may be rendered in other ways.   An exclamatory, an impersonal, a merely gesticulated assertion may have the assertorial force ;   but the normal linguistic vehicle in a great many languages, is the verb " to be," with the *essential connotation of that verb maintained*[1]—namely its connotation of the existent.   The existence reference always present in a judgment finds its place in the copula of the corresponding proposition.

We may say, therefore, that *the copula expresses in all cases*

---

[1] Of course the reverse argument might also be pressed, to the effect that the use of the verb " to be " in so many languages as copula proves that existence is the meaning rendered.

the existential reference of the proposition, whatever the mode of that reference may be; that is, in whatever sphere or universe of discourse the control of the subject-matter may be found or intended.

32. The only case that might be cited as questionable from this point of view is the explicitly existential judgment itself. How can the copula express existence in this case, when existence is already expressed in the predicate ?

This case readily yields to our analysis. Generally, the separate copula is omitted from the statement. It is not needed in the judgment of existence. " Mermaids exist " explicitly cites the mode of existence in the predicate accepted. But as soon as the judgment takes on synthetic form, the existence being in any way not altogether or assuredly given in the meaning as a whole, then the copula comes back to express the added reference to existence, as in " mermaids *are* existing," or " mermaids *do* exist." This means that existence, like any other term-meaning, may be merely proposed or suggested, and a sign of actual realization is needed when that meaning is to be asserted as a fact.

The Judgment of Existence.

33. (*b*) We are thus led to the second aspect of meaning intended by the copula—that which appears when the proposition is considered belief-wise or synthetically. The copula *is the sign of synthesis*, not, as is ordinarily or commonly stated, an expression of relation. The synthetic movement, as we have seen, is just the genetic movement— the change in the entire meaning whereby it gathers new elements. " The dog " passes into " the fierce-dog," " the sun " into the " snow-melting-sun." Now we have seen that it is the function of judgment to render these stages in the progression of conceptual meaning. When my meaning " dog " grows with new experience into " fierce-dog," my motive in the predication is just *to assert this change*. I wish to elucidate the fact, to inform and warn my neighbours. The motive to the synthetic assertion is the actual development of the meaning. This then is what the copula does—*it joins together the earlier and later stages of the developing meaning*. I say to my neighbour, " the dog Tiger has passed in my thought and should also in yours into a fierce dog " ; that is exactly what I mean when I say to him simply " Tiger is fierce." " Tiger has become, or has been found to be, fierce " is the full meaning.

Copula is Synthetic.

The copula then, considered from the genetic, the synthetic,

the belief-wise point of view, *is a sign of progression*. It
A sign of Progression. renders the progressive aspect of logical intent. It
becomes the linguistic equivalent of the assertion,
" I have found this so and propose it to you."

34. We may go on to say, moreover, that these two aspects
of the import of the copula are always present, both of them.
The Copula Essential. They are, as I have said, aspects attaching respectively to the analytic and synthetic, and these two
modes we have found to reflect the essential readings of the proposition, relation-wise and belief-wise. In all cases, then, we
may confidently say that *the copula is the root meaning of the
proposition qua judgment*. It hits upon what distinguishes an
assertion, a judgment, a belief, a presupposition from a proposal,
a suggestion, a schema, a hypothesis, an assumption. By
it the mode of meaning characteristically logical is put into the
proposition. It renders at once both the existence reference and
the advance achieved by the act of acknowledgment.[1]

§ 5.   THE CHARACTERS OF PROPOSITIONS

35. Still considering the proposition as a form of predication,
we are now able to suggest the main characters attaching to its
Propositions as Answers various forms. The modes of function whereby the
content is assigned to its real control, and the accompanying assertion of relationship within the sphere of control,
are our two leading threads in assigning the meanings of propositions to their respective classes of intent. When we do so
consider them, and ask what characters represent these distinctions in the forms that propositions actually show, we find
our path plainly marked out before us.

It will be remembered that we went so far in an earlier discussion as to suggest the chief modes of meaning shown by
propositions ; [2] here we may proceed to fill in the scheme there
indicated.

The " sphere " of belief of the proposition, looked at control-
wise, was found to have three modes of intent, expressed in

---

[1] It may be recalled that it was suggested above that a special symbol
should be adopted for the fact of progression and the sign ((was
adopted, the meaning being " becomes," as in " the dog ((fierce-dog."
Our present conclusion fully justifies this ; for it finds the meaning of
" becoming " present in the " is " of the copula.

[2] Chap. viii. § 2, " What the proposition means."

answer respectively to the questions "where ? "[1] " how much ? "
to certain and " by whom ? " ; and the content intended, in
questions. turn, shows " relation-wise " three modes, answering respectively the questions "what ? " " why ? " and " for
whom ? " Each of these modes gives to the proposition a
characteristic meaning, whether it be explicitly brought out in
verbal form or not. They recognize the forms found by Kant
and the formal logicians generally, and add certain others—
notably those placed under the heading " community," which
has not heretofore been recognized. We may now take up
these modes of meaning in turn, showing how our earlier
discussions of the nature and growth of predication allow of
the renderings now discovered in the various forms of proposition.

36. (1) *The "where-reference" of Propositions, or the Belief-
Reference : logical, "Modality."* This is that universal character
of judgmental meaning whereby it refers to the sphere in which
the assertion holds explicitly or in presupposition. We have
already described this reference in detail, in the chapter on
" Acknowledgment and Belief " (chap. ii. above).

It has also been pointed out that judgments make the where-
reference in different ways, according to the adequacy of the
(1) The content to excite belief, and the consequent relative
Where? of determination of belief upon the content in question.
Modality. If the subject-matter is definitely acknowledged, its
relational aspect admitting no reservation or ambiguity, it is
" assertorial," the meaning being " actual " ; if its reference as
a whole requires further determination of the content itself or
of its assignment to a sphere—and so has an alternative strain—
then it is " problematical," rendering the " possible." Differences
in the problematical, resting upon different sorts of indeterminateness, give judgments of different forms reflected in the disjunctive
and the conditional modes of " Relation " (see sect. 40 below).

Besides these there are no further modes because there are
no further variations possible in the act of reference itself. It
either asserts from two-fold assurance—assurance of both control and content—or from only one, leaving the other indeterminate and alternative. Thus the variations discussed in detail
in earlier passages are rendered in propositions.

Moreover, we have recognized two forms of assertorial meaning, both making positive reference, but each having its own

[1] " Where " may always be converted into " in what sphere ? "

peculiar motive : that of recognition or "indication," and that of selection or appreciation. These forms usually have different linguistic embodiment. They may be called respectively "recognitive" (or "indicative") and "imperative."[1]

A peculiar shading of meaning arises as soon as the content takes on the complexity of a system of implications, so that logical "dependence" and "necessity" attach to the relation asserted. Such a judgment may be called "implicative."[2]

Another way of making an existence or control reference is not to assert it, but to question it. This gives the "interrogative" form of proposition. But as this meaning is one of assumption rather than of belief, its judgmental standing is compromised. We may, therefore, in drawing up the following table of judgments of modality, place the interrogative in brackets, as being only quasi-judgmental. In cases in which it expresses doubt as to one only of the aspects of the meaning distinguished above, it becomes alternative, a force reflected in the relational content as disjunctive or conditional.[3] We have therefore the following :—

The several Forms.

---

[1] "Imperative" because the final ground of assertion of all selective and appreciative meanings is simply, "I say so," "I report it," "I require it." Prof. W. G. Hale (as cited in the next note) has pointed out this distinction within the interrogative, as in "what is it ? " ("indicative interrogative ") and "what shall I do ? " ("imperative interrogative "). The "imperative," so far as logical, and not merely "will-to-believe" (see chap. viii. § 9), renders what is "actual."

[2] The Kantian "Apodeictic" or "necessary" judgments are covered under the Imperative and the Implicative, the "necessity" in the latter case being that of logical dependence, to which we will return later on. The distinction of the two modes "Imperative" and "Implicative," indeed, enables us to point out the two cases called by students of syntax "subjective" and "objective" necessity (cf. Hale, "A Century of Metaphysical Syntax," *Proceed. St. Louis Cong. Arts and Sciences*, vol. iii. pp. 192 ff). Kant gives little recognition to "subjective necessity "— seen in what I call "imperative meaning."

The other Kantian modalities, "Actuality" and "Possibility," fall under our "Recognitive" and "Alternative" respectively. The need of revision of the Kantian scheme of modalities is seen in its confusion of belief attitude, or modality proper, and relational content or implication (on its reflection in the philological field, notably in the treatment of grammatical "moods," see the paper by Professor Hale, cited just above).

[3] Professor Muirhead suggests to me that "the interrogative of investigation should be distinguished from that of mere personal doubt." I think the distinction goes with that just indicated between "objective" and "subjective necessity ": in investigation, the *uncertainty* is objec-

Modes of Modality or Belief-reference—

1.—Assertorial { Recognitive. / Imperative. / Implicative. } Actual } Necessary.

2.—Problematical { Alternative. / [Interrogative.] } Possible.

(Chap. ii., iv.) [1]

37. (2) *The " how-much" of Propositions : logical Quantity.* In respect to quantity, our treatment has mainly recognized **(2) The "How Much":** and justified the results of the traditional logic, reaching the three modes known as " universal," " particular," and " singular." We found, however, that the singular is a peculiar mode of logical meaning, and has a special significance not usually recognized. This recurs again and again in our work and is to be the starting-point of certain of our discussions later on. We may follow the usual arrangement of logical quantities, as follows :—

Modes of Quantity—

1. Universal.
2. Particular.
3. Singular.
(Chap. iv.)

38. (3) *The " by-whom" of Propositions : logical Community* [2] *of Control.* Still adhering to the control-wise or belief-wise

tive in its grounds (going back to a system of objective truths) ; while in personal doubt, it is subjective, being a phase of a movement of belief. This distinction, indeed, like the other, illustrates my contention that *modality* proper is an affair of belief, while " objective " certainty and contingency are matters of logical *relation*.

[1] In each of these tables of characters of judgment, the chapter of the work is given in which the meanings indicated are discussed in detail.

[2] Of course this and the mode of " community for whom "—and modality too, if one be consistent—are not logical at all to those who define logic strictly as science of formal statements as such, *whether or not they be held by anybody.* But a " logic " that once departs from a purely algebraic or symbolic system and admits any shades at all of material reference, existential import, or variations in modality, finds no stopping-place until it exhausts *all that the proposition means and intends.* The meaning " for whom "a statement is true is just as real and vital as the meaning " to what " it applies and " why " it does so. And I think it will be evident before we are done that theory of knowledge has suffered grievously from the restriction of its logical foundation to purely formal and impersonal relations. For instance, the whole question as to whether a statement is a judgment, or merely a hypothesis or proposal, is involved in the intent " by and for whom " it holds (see sect. 44 below.)

aspect of meaning, we find another intent in the requirement
(3) The Community "by whom." that some functional process be responsible for the reference to the control in question. This is embodied in the judgment itself in the degree of implication of more than the one judging self. It does not necessarily go over to the question as to whether the content as such is fit for the same treatment by others, but only intends its implication to be one of actual processes. It is a mode of community-wise implication, the sort of community that attaches to control as such. Our earlier treatment of " commonness " of meaning leads us to distinguish the following modes :—

Modes of Community of Control—
1. Private.
2. Aggregate.
[3. Catholic.]
(Chap vi. § 8, chap. ii. and chap. vii. of Vol. I.)

The mode of catholicity is placed in brackets since, while making a real determination in community, as number of individuals " by whom," it still does not add to the intent of the term " aggregate " except to carry it to its limit. There is a sense in which the " aggregate " is not " private," but there is no sense in which the " catholic " is not " aggregate."

Considering now the other great aspect of judgmental meaning, that which finds its expression relation-wise or content-wise, we have certain characters to point out.

39. (4) *The " what " of Propositions : logical Quality.* The first relational character to be mentioned is that de-
(4) The "what": Quality. scribed in logic under the name Quality. We have discussed it above. Its modes correspond to those of acceptance or rejection, reached from the side of belief, reducible as we have seen under the heading of " modality " to *acceptance and question.* For the relation-wise meaning we find the two great modes of " affirmation " and " denial." The development of the mode of denial is, however, as we have seen, a phase of the larger movement of opposition, in which there are the two fundamental movements of " limitation " and " privation." The formal " exclusion " of term-meanings *inter se*, as found in logical denial, issues from these developmental motives, which persist in their own right along with explicit exclusion.

Under quality we have therefore the following :—

Modes of Quality—

1. Affirmation.

2. Denial $\left\{ \begin{array}{l} \text{Limitation.} \\ \text{Privation.} \\ \text{Exclusion.} \end{array} \right.$

(Chap. viii.; also chap. ix. of Vol. I.)

40. (5) *The "why" of Propositions : logical Relation.*
Viewed relationally, the proposition shows of course the modes
The "why": in which relation itself may subsist. Here we find
Relation. those modes *within the content* which we have already
had occasion to point out as reflected also in modality. The
relation of terms in the content may be such as to call out
assertorial belief ; it is then a relation recognized and accepted.
The content is in so far an immediate one, inasmuch as its acceptance is guaranteed by its own co-efficients without further dependence or schematism. The attitude of mind being the
assertorial one, the proposition itself, considered relationally, is
" categorical."

On the other hand, the attitude may be one of problematical
acceptance, as pointed out above, and that for either of two
reasons. Either there is an alternation due to the indeterminateness of the content, a schematic relation called " Disjunctive " ;
or there is a schematism with reference to the sphere of control,
the schematism of the sphere being reflected in the " Conditional "
character of the relation to be accepted. Conditional meaning
may again be of the character of what is not yet relationally determined, a matter of discovery, called in our discussions " Hypothetical," being then only " quasi-logical," of the nature of
postulation ; or it may be an established relationship of reflection itself, an " implication," in which case it is a " Contingent " meaning rendered in an " Inferential "[1] proposition.
These distinctions have had their explanations in our earlier
discussions. We have therefore the following modes under
Relation :—

---

[1] I adopt this term at the suggestion of Professor Muirhead. The
term " contingent " used in the earlier discussions for meanings of
dependence (one term being contingent or dependent upon another) may
well be replaced, when the meaning takes on propositional form, by the
term Inferential. It corresponds to the case of modality called above
Implicative.

Modes of Relation—
1. Categorical.
2. Disjunctive.
3. Conditional $\left\{\begin{array}{l}\text{[Hypothetical].}\\\text{Inferential.}\end{array}\right.$

(Chaps. v., ix. ff ; also discussion of Modality in chap. ii.)

41. (6) *The " for-whom " of Propositions : logical Community of Content.* Finally, the character of Community shows itself also relationally. Not only is logical content controlled as judgmental subject-matter *by some one*, it is also controlled *for some one*. The implication of "appropriateness" for other process is independent of actual agreement with others at the time. This aspect of content or relational meaning is a mode of "Community" and gives the cases named in our discussions "personal," when the content is intended for the one individual only, "syndoxic" when it is controlled as sharable by others, and "synnomic" when it is judged as fit or appropriate for all logical process as such. We have, therefore, the following modes of Community of content :—

(6) The Community " for whom "

Modes of Community of Content—
1. Personal.
2. Syndoxic.
3. Synnomic.

(Chaps. iii., iv., and chap. vii. of Vol. I.)

42. If now we throw all these "characters" together in a larger table, we have a general view of the various aspects of intent that propositions may express. This is done in Table G (made up of the partial tables given above). In it I include also the developmental aspect of logical meaning as given in the term as well as the proposition, thus presenting a *résumé* of our discussions of predication.

Table.

TABLE G.

The Interpretation of Logical Meaning :—
I. *Conceptually, the Term.*
    1. General and Particular.
    2. Universal.
    3. Abstract and Concrete.
    4. Singular.
II. *Linguistically, the Proposition.*
    1. Control- or Belief-wise $\left.\begin{array}{l}\\\\\end{array}\right\}$ 3. Community-wise.
    2. Content- or Relation-wise

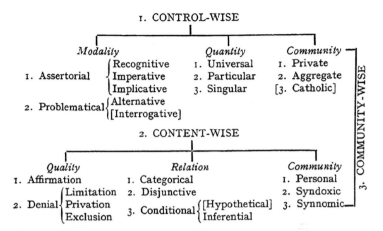

Our results may stand in this form for the sake of their correlation with those reached in the treatises on formal logic. We are not finally bound, however, by any demand for such a correlation, and the table just presented may now be taken as text for the suggestion of a more radical reduction.

43. The chapter headings cited in the partial tables above **Final Characters are two** show that in the earlier discussions of meaning from a genetic point of view we have reached our distinctions without recourse to formal logic at all. The positive rule of our procedure has been, that we discover the actual movement of belief and note the modifications of meaning that progressively justify belief and in turn embody it. That is, we have been dealing all the way along with control rather than with content. This appears in certain of our requirements, explicitly stated in their proper connections. First, we have set before us the problem of the instrumental or experimental character of thinking, its aspect of proposal as accompanying the aspect of established relation. This has led to the treatment of meanings as wholes set up in proposal for confirmation and elucidation—set up, in short, " schematically," " assumptively." Such treatment leads to our emphasis of the changing, growing, progressive side of meanings. Second, this has been carried further in our explicit attempt to interpret successive stages of meaning as " terms " or " concepts "—as larger wholes made the termini of acknowledgment and belief. Certain of our chapters have had the term meaning as their

sole topic. Third, we have found certain of our results justifying this procedure : synthesis attaches to the meaning in its
proposal and experimental aspect, analysis to its elucidation or
implication aspect.

Our present point, then, is this, that after all, two great characters of propositions are fundamental : one dynamic, synthetic,
developmental, the character of wholes as such ; the
(1) Modality of Belief and (2) Relation of Content. other static, analytic, the character of relations established within such wholes. So we may disregard all
the minor distinctions of characters that appear on the one side
and the other, recognizing that they all arise from the varying
ways that these two great modes of the subject-matter of judgment—considered as beliefs and as relations—interact and motive
changes in each other. We might subsume all belief-wise distinctions under the one heading of " Modality," taken in a large
sense and say that the mode of acceptance is one thing, and the
thing accepted is another thing. Then if we called the latter
" Relation," in the logical sense of the term we would simply
have rechristened, for logical purposes, our two familiar ways of
looking at meanings anywhere and everywhere.

Now in this, so far from leaving out the correlation with
formal logic, we strike upon the profoundest correlation, as
those modern logicians recognize, who say that all considerations of modality are to be banished from logic as a formal science,
and the rules of the science are to be only those appropriate to
a science of formal relationships.[1]

This is, in fact, the justification of formal logic. Its ideal
is a development of implication, apart from the material re-
Formal Logic ferences by which, in particular situations, the given
system of implications is controlled. Although in
our belief such a science must always fall far short of this ideal,[2]
still it is well to develop the theory of implications as far as
possible apart from the instrumental and existential references
of actual processes of thought.

[1] Note for example the criticisms made by Keynes (*Formal Logic*, 4 ed.
chap. viii.) of certain writers, such as Wolf, for importing modal considerations into the treatment of logical topics.

[2] We find the inevitable intrusion of the existential reference in discussions of logical quantity, logical denial, etc. One has only to look at
such discussions as Keynes' treatment of the existential import of propositions to be aware how artificial the requirement is that resort to modality
be always excluded.

44. There is room, therefore, for a treatment which explicitly reasserts the modal and existential force of propositions considered as embodying actual judgments. And it should not be surprising if this leads to results of interest if not for formal logic at any rate for theory of knowledge. The results of our discussions of "universality" (chap. x. sect. 25), of "singularity" (chap. x. sect. 30), of "truth" (chap. xiii. §§ 2, 9), and of "generalization in community" (chap. xiv. § 8) would seem indeed to bear out this expectation.

45. It is our task from now on, however, to treat mainly of Relation. This alone of the characters of judgment has not been **Theory of** already rather fully covered in our discussions. We **Implication.** will thus reach a theory of Implication, since the relational interpretation deals in the main with the determination and not with the control of the related system of thoughts. Yet we find that the first question that concerns us is the growth of the system of implications itself, and this brings up, besides, the working out of the law of growth by "trial and error" or selective thinking, which is in its main motive instrumental to discovery and practise. This appears in what is known as Induction. This is our next great topic. After that, the development of the inner implications of the system of knowledge, by processes of "mediate inference" or reasoning, comes up for consideration.

THEORY OF IMPLICATION: LOGICAL VALIDITY

Chapter X

IMPLICATION: JUDGMENTS OF IDENTITY

§ 1. THE MARKS OF IMPLICATION—REASONABLENESS

1. The foregoing general account of the forms of predication, the term and the proposition, has presented to us the thought-context as a related whole of subject-matter. Any such context, as we have seen, may be set up either as a judgment, or system of judgments, elucidating the whole intended, or as propositions in the literal sense of " proposals " for research and acceptance. We saw also that these two aspects of all predication may be considered as always present together. But they embody different attitudes of mind. The "proposal" is prospective, schematic, tentative, not yet accepted; the "eluci- dation" is settled, accepted, believed and held as matter of common knowledge. The latter presents a set of relationships sufficiently definite and stable, in their establishment and control, to be treated by what are called the " discursive " operations of thinking; that is, they are subject to various abstractions, linkages, readjustments, etc., to any extent that the individuation of the meaning as a whole may permit. This is the side of implication. It is the internal organization in which the achievements of successive judgment processes have issued. It is necessary now to ask how this organization proceeds, what the motives to it are, and what the larger or smaller groupings may be which the several

Implication a Related System.

---

[1] Being Part VI of the entire treatise on *Genetic Logic.*

members of such a system, be they terms or propositions, exhibit and allow.

The most general character of such a system of organized **Reasonable-** judgmental contents is what we often call its " reason- **ness.** ableness." By reasonableness, however, we do not mean any new or recondite property or mark suddenly taken on ; but on the contrary merely its natural intent as a characteristic content of thought. We do not find reasonableness attaching to mere feeling or impulse—we do not say that a headache or a hungry appetite is reasonable or unreasonable. This being so, we may now try to point out what such natural reasonableness means, and how it comes to be present.

This question allows a very definite and intelligible answer, when we ask our usual questions—the questions of determination and control. The content is reflectively determined and mediately controlled ; that is, it is a system of items held for reflection, and referable for conversion or confirmation to the earlier spheres **Mediate** of experience in which this or that " existent " thing **Control.** had its origin. So much is essential to its individuation as logical. The content must be thrown into the form of a related subject-matter under a control mediating its reference to another and more direct order of experience.

This means, it is evident, that in all cases such meanings are of the recognitive type, and that they are relatively stable and " given " for the purposes of the life of reflection. These two determinations, which follow as of course from the nature of the individuation of a content by judgment, allow us to define " reasonableness."

2. (1) The first thing to note is the recognition mark of logical meaning. The thought of a thing, the judged content standing as " that thing," is and must be recognized—both by self and for others—as the original meaning called the " thing." This involves a further stage in the progressions of " sameness " and " difference " of which the early stages have already been described.[1]

We found, it will be remembered, that the meaning " same," viewed negatively, passed through stages of " simply-same," " same-not-other," " same-not-different "—all movements by which the " same " content is progressively isolated by limitation, privation, and exclusion. With this development we found also a progressive definition of the object as positively the " same,"

[1] Vol. i, chap. viii. § 3, and chap. ix. § 5.

through various modes of persistence. Simple continuousness or lack of interruption called " present sameness," passed, when

Sameness as Judgment of Identity. represented by a memory image, into the persistence of existence called " remote sameness," and finally into the persistence of that which recurs in later acts of recognition, called " recurrent sameness." This last, sameness of the recurrent type, we saw, led up to the logical mode, since it supplied the relationship of cases of recurring common content and control that serve as content of judgment. That is, the positive " recurrent sameness " meaning gives also the negative judgment " not different."

The new thing that now happens in the logical mode is only what happens to all meanings when they are taken up in judgment. There is the isolation of *relation as such*, its individuation as a subject-matter. Both the movements just mentioned prepare for it—the negative movement, as the exclusion of " otherness " —and the positive movement as the determination of sameness. The issue is a *judgment of identity*. Given an object *that recurs, that persists in its recurrences, and that excludes all save these persisting elements of content*—that is just the subject-matter of a judgment of identity. Its meaning as identical, as one and the same, is what is now rendered in the judgment, whereas before it was only recognized or presumed. The judgment of identity or the function of logical identification, therefore, is simply *the recognition*, in the way we call " acknowledgment " in the logical mode, *of the persistent oneness of a given relational content*.

3. The operation of the negative motive is also to be observed. The establishment of samenesses proceeds all the way along by failures as well as by successes in the individuation of masses of

The Negative Factor. contents in units or wholes. There are constant rivalries and exclusions, as has been already pointed out, by which the relationships of difference and opposition arise. There is, therefore, always the negative over against the positive—a matter fully developed in the discussion of negation. Reasonableness, therefore, involves the maintenance of identities, and the corresponding exclusion of terms that are incompatible. The aspect of opposition arises along with that of identification, both being but aspects of the mode of individuation in judgment. The affirmative judgment is always in some form *an acknowledgment of identity*, while the negative is an assertion of the *failure of such an identity* to establish itself.

Summing up our result so far in view of the special problem of the character of logical reasonableness, we may say that any logical meaning or implication must be capable of statement as self-identical, both affirmatively and negatively. By this is meant that it is acknowledged as recurrently and persistently the same and not anything else. Putting it in an abstract way, we may say that the reasonableness of an implication-system involves the inclusion of what is recognized as identical, and the exclusion of what is repugnant or incompatible.

4. (2) There is a second motive, however, still to be considered : that of control. The determination of a content as the same is never in a void—save in the capricious and fugitive realm of fancy and in the realm of mere abstract symbolism and tautology. We do not think by " identifying " castles in Spain—constructions whose unreal character is but another name for lawlessness and irresponsibility—nor do we make assertions by repetition of the formula " A is A." On the contrary, the movement of thought is motived by actual reference to the normal control spheres The Control in which the objects thought of have their origin and establishment. We should expect, therefore, that the setting up of systems of related contents in thought—systems of implication—would reflect the control processes of their original constitution and use.

This, indeed, we do find ; and it introduces most important results in the realm of " reasonable " thinking. For we see that in each case, the bounds of application of a given system of relationships is limited to the sphere in which it is normally and properly controlled. We do not hold the inner life of thought, Various for example, to the rules of spacial extension and " Universes." quantity ; nor do we ask of objects of the physical world that they go about with us as our images do. All the coefficients, in short, of the respective spheres of existence are invoked, each for each, in the demand that the system of implications that they respectively support be " reasonable."

So there arise great spheres of what may be called appropriate or relevant implication : great " worlds " or " universes of discourse." The sphere of " semblance," for example, is a definite one in our thought, allowing linkages, relations, conclusions that we could not justify in the sphere of external causation. So the sphere of humour, the sphere of fiction, the sphere of abstract process, etc., each has its own logic of control which justifies a type of reasonableness holding for it alone.

Each has its "Logic"— in other words, its normal and relevant organization—in much the same sense that the universe of thought has its Logic.

5. When the content of any of these several spheres of control is made subject-matter of judgment it is thrown, it is true, into a

The Control
may be as-
serted.

common context with the whole of experience. All such contexts become parts of the content of reflection as such. So there is a reduction to the one process of judgment ; and the further question is—what becomes of those essential differences which render the several modes of content appropriate each to its own control alone ? This was answered in what was just said in the remarks on the recognition-mark of the object of thought. The marks of identity and repugnance, of sameness and difference, are the common marks of all logical content. The new and "mediate" control of judgment, while supervening upon that of the original sphere, still preserves the identities and exclusions of the original contents as constituted in their own realms of existence.

All this is simply matter of fact, to be confirmed by any one's introspection ; but it is fully confirmed also by the presence, as already shown in the chapter on negation, of the mode of quality, the sort of predication, called "limitation." Limitation is a mode of predication that reflects not the simple identity of

Limitation is
involved.

a content as judged "the same," nor the exclusion of another content as judged "not the same," but a further intent. It embodies just the discrimination we are now discussing—that between spheres of control, or existence, or reality, within which the different implication systems of the affirmative and negative sort are confined or limited.

6. To show this, we may recall what has been said about limitation. It is that aspect of predication—statable either positively or negatively in judgment—which acknowledges a " non-B " class. Now a non-B class may have two very different modes of constitution whose discrimination will bring us at once to the heart of our present topic. Non-B may embrace either " everything that is not B," or again, " a restricted lot of things that are not B."

In one case, for example, when I say "this cottage is not a palace " I do not mean to implicate a turnip, a gold watch, a mermaid, or a conceit from the mind of Shakespeare. But all these things are also not palaces. I might, indeed, in some other connection say with evident propriety of the cottage,

"Shakespeare had no such idea as this." But the true intent of
Restricted the limitative judgment, on the contrary, is to assert
Spheres. a relation of opposition only within a sphere or realm
of existence or reality or discourse having a certain presupposed
control, coefficient, and range of limitation. It has its roots
in "privation" in the Kantian sense, as denying something
that might well have been affirmed, of something naturally
looked for and found appropriate, of something relevant and not
disparate. In our own terminology, this is but to say that the
denial is limited to the same control, the same order, as that in
which the meanings were originally constituted. The logical
function cannot utilize the disparate to make up its predications.
"The apple tastes dark blue" and "the Matterhorn is jealous"
are not "reasonable" statements, because this need of relevancy,
of common control of the terms, is not met.

The other possible meaning of a negative judgment—that
given first above—is one that removes these restrictions and
makes a statement concerning the entire world of objects of
thought. It is the case mentioned before as "infinite" in quality. But we have seen that this is an abstraction; it has no
Not at large. vitality and no utility in actual thought. I never
need in actual intercourse to say that "cabbages are
not letters of the alphabet." Any conceivable motive for such
a negative meaning is wanting. There is a certain remoteness of
one sphere from another; and the very attempt to construct a
judgment holding as between subject and predicate is artificial
and meaningless. "Sugar is not high-minded" is not illuminating because it does not elucidate—nor does it propose—anything
that has or can have control as a single whole meaning.

7. We find here, therefore, on the side of the actual genesis
and maintenance of control spheres, a character positively reflected in the system of implications of thought. There is always
a presupposition of belief, circumscribed as a definite control
reference. Whatever I state, I state with this presupposition
common to the hearer and myself. Any system of implications
is wrapped about with this envelope of belief; and it may itself at
any time be brought out by an explicit existential judgment,
which will show that the mode of existence is the same for both
subject and predicate. Otherwise we say the statement is
meaningless, fanciful, irrelevant.

The character of reasonableness which this discloses is the
limitation to the restricted sphere which the two contents held

apart in the negative judgment may exhaust.   In the statement
" cottages are not palaces " my intent is to say that *among
dwellings* there are palaces and non-palaces, and that cottages are
to be classed among the latter.   This restriction is seen in the
limitation of the whole matter of implication to dwell-
**Exhaustion
or Excluded
Middle.**
ings or buildings ; this is the common presupposition
of belief under which the predication is made.   And
within this restriction, there is an exclusion of the non-palace
class, including the cottages, from the palace class, in a way
that exhausts the content of the sphere intended, the class buildings.
This is what is called in logic the mark of " exhaustion," or less
happily, " excluded middle."   Excluded middle is merely the
fact of exhaustion.   It has further treatment below in this
chapter (§ 3), and also in the discussion of Induction.[1]

But it should be remarked that such a character as exhaustion
or excluded middle holds only under the restriction entailed by a
definite presupposition of belief—a definite mode of control—
which constitutes the reference to a restricted sphere of existence.
It is not true, for example, that there is no third class as between
**Reference to
Restricted
Sphere.**
palaces and non-palaces if the restriction to physical
existence be removed.   For as soon as one begins to
allow his control spheres or " universes " to overlap
—as in play, for example—he can unite opposites, make third
classes, etc., and still talk about the results.   The drama is full
of this.   The character of " Wall," for example, admits of all
sorts of predicates that involve for their justification and development, the removal of one of the presuppositions of control—
either that of a physical wall or that of personal life.   But this
is a departure from logical implication as such ; the denials and
affirmations of valid implication do not attach to such constructions.

There is, therefore, a real motive of limitation, and a real
intent of exhaustion or excluded middle.   It is a meaning essential
to the judgment of identity, and necessary to that of repugnance
as exclusion.   It is a natural mark of reasonableness as attaching
to vital thought process, for it establishes the appropriate control-
reference to existence or reality.

We have thus derived, on the basis of continuity of genetic
motive from the prelogical into the logical mode, a view of reasonableness that gives it certain definite and fruitful characters.
All logical process fulfils its function, first, by the individuation of

[1] Chap. xi. § 2.

its content as identical and exclusive of what is incongruous or
Laws of repugnant in the sense given, and second, by the
Thought. limitation of its matter to those wholes of meaning
that arise in concrete situations of a definite and peculiar control.
These marks are hit off in the treatment of formal logic under
the heading of "laws of thought," stated in the formulas of
"consistency," "non-contradiction," and "excluded middle."
We may now look at these meanings a little more closely in the
light of our genetic results.

§ 2. Validity, Correctness and Truth

8. Before proceeding, however, to discuss further these
great marks of logical reasonableness, we may now name them,
both for the sake of giving headings to the principal discussions
to follow, and also to show the appropriateness of the terms
adopted as descriptive of the conceptions themselves. The mark
of the reasonable whereby it is a self-identical and consistent
Validity and content is what is known as *validity* ; the mark whereby
Truth distin- it is a meaning controlled in a relevant and limited
guished. sphere is its *truth*. An implication may be viewed
as one of *logical validity of relational content* ; and also as one
of confirmation and proof in the sphere in which the whole meaning has its relevant presupposition—that is, as *one that is true.*

Our two great topics for further discussion, therefore, are
these, validity and truth. The former is that which we now
turn to ; its full treatment of course would comprise a comprehensive exposition of the principles of formal logic.

Evidently, too, it is to implication as such that validity
attaches, that is, to the relational aspect of meaning thrown into
the form of predications. Our discussions are now to be focussed
upon this more logical aspect of relation.

9. These notions of validity and truth, which are still to be
discussed, belong in a series of analogous meanings arising
at the successive modes of cognitive development. The general
idea of something that is correct and justified in its own place
Modes of and mode is not confined to the logical. We find it
Correctness. also in the prelogical ; it attaches to images and constructions in general so far as they are confirmed each by its own
testing process through conversion or otherwise. If indeed we
take some such general term as "correctness," with the negative
"incorrectness," as generic, we find that each of the great dualisms

affords motive for the sort of variation that these terms connote. We may say that all mediately controlled contents—as, especially, memories—are more or less " correct " or " incorrect " when brought to the tests of fulfilment in their appropriate control spheres. This we usually express by saying that such images are " accurate " or " inaccurate." In the logical mode the corresponding character is two-fold, as we have seen just above. The relative success or failure of the construction to " make good " in a relevant sphere is its " truth " or " falsity "; but there is also the further relative competence and reliability of the content itself as an individuation of a relational meaning of sameness or identity. This is what we have called " validity " and " invalidity." So when we advance to the hyper-logical modes. There also the mediated content fulfils more or less adequately the meaning for which it is judged " fit " or " proper." Such variations are called " good " and " bad "; as in the aesthetically fit, which is artistically " good " or " bad," and the ethically proper, which is morally good or bad.

Accurate, Valid, True and Good.

These three stages of relative correctness are all modes of psychic meaning. Each springs from its own dualistic motive, and is an index of more or less successful mediation. An " accurate " meaning mediates the dualism of inner and outer ; a " true " statement, that of thought and things ; a " valid " conclusion, that of terms in a whole meaning ; a " good " deed or a " good " picture, that of fact and ideal. The last two, the logical and hyper-logical, are still to be explained.

10. The terms thus defined may be thrown into a table as follows :—

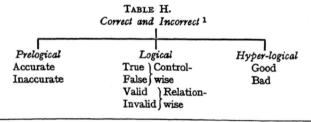

TABLE H.
Correct and Incorrect [1]

Prelogical	Logical	Hyper-logical
Accurate	True } Control-	Good
Inaccurate	False } wise	Bad
	Valid } Relation-	
	Invalid } wise	

---

[1] The general antithesis—no less than the special cases under it—is variously named. We often hear of " truth and error," and find both these terms applied to all modes of correctness. " Error," however, is, properly speaking, the defect of function which leads to " false " predication. " False " is properly the opposite of " true "; " falsity," of

The character of a logical content that makes it " correct " or " valid " and in so far reasonable is, as we have seen, the restating of the meaning of sameness in relational form. Its further development in the mode in which it is relatively simple, given as a single predication or logical unit, is first to be taken up. It appears in progressive judgments of logical identity.

§ 3.   IDENTITY, NON-CONTRADICTION AND EXHAUSTION

11. Recalling the positions now taken respecting implication, we may say that every implication is a system of more or less organized logical meaning.   The organization is a mode of individuation ; it proceeds by identifying the contents, and limiting their range.   Put in logical terms—every implication is a subject-matter identical with itself, different from or exclusive of any other, and, taken together with its contradictory, exhaustive of the sphere of control in which they are both found.   This suggests the procedure of taking up first the topic of identity and non-contradiction, treating these as obverse aspects of what is called in logic " consistency," and then turning to "exhaustion " or excluded middle.

The process of individuation whereby the " same " object of simple apprehension becomes the " identical " object of judgment has already been described.   The further exposition

Nature of Judgment of Identity.   may be introduced by a question concerning the constitution of the content of such a judgment.   This question may be put in this way—is the judgment of acknowledgment of the object itself, which constitutes it a subject-matter of judgment, all that its individuation as identical means, or is there an additional judgment of identity as attaching to the object ?   If the latter, what is the relation of the two judgments, and which of them is it that renders the meaning of implication ?

12 This question may be so stated as to suggest certain customary views and distinctions in epistemology ; and the solution also bears on these views.   We may ask, is there a " law of identity," a norm or standard of some sort, that comes to be imposed on logical process regardless of what the objective matter or content of the process may be ?   If that be true, then

" truth."   The relation of " accuracy " to " truth " is discussed in chapter xiii. § 1.

the mere determination of the object, its individuation as an object of thought, would not of itself carry this mark ; or more precisely, the object judged as such and such would also have to fulfil the law of being identical with itself. In that case the judgment by which the identity of the object with itself is established, is additional to the mere judgment of determination by which the object is constituted. Some such implication is made when a " law of thought " is invoked, even when no such explicit statement is advanced. The " law of thought " becomes in Kantian phrase " à priori," a " form of reason," with which the objects constituted by thought are invested. This lends itself, from then on, to the further view that the " reason " is a pure function of universals, which applies its formal principles to the otherwise unorganized and " unreasonable " objects.

What is the Law of Identity ?

13. Such views we are now in a position directly to combat. We find simply a judging function going on whereby thoughts, things, objects of experience, are judged as subject-matter of personal acknowledgment. This process is one of individuation. A meaning taken up as subject-matter of judgment is judged or acknowledged to have such a content and such a control, that is, to be *then always and for everybody the same. That is all there is to it*. It is thus *ipso facto* this identical object, by the very conditions of its determination, that is, by the fact merely of its recognition and logical acknowledgment. *It* is judged identical : it is not that identity is judged *of it*. Its identity is that aspect whereby it is acknowledged as *this object and not any other*.

To say, therefore, that there is a " law of identity " is simply to say that logical contents are always identified in the way peculiar to logical individuation. The identity of the content is that aspect of it whereby it is a stable and persistent meaning for predication. On each occasion of its use its meaning is what it is once for all established to be by the essential individuation of it as content of judgment. This we may, of course, abstract for the purposes of the theory of logical ground and validity, and state as a " law of thought " ; but it should be clearly understood that such a " law " is only a formula descriptive of a uniform process.

It is an Aspect of individuation

14. It may be asked, however, whether the individuation of an object of thought as logical does not go beyond the acknowledgment of the object-meaning and involve a judgment of the identity of this object. To this we have to answer that it does

have this meaning, but makes it an intent, an implication. It is of the nature of a presupposition of the mode of judgment itself. When a meaning is brought up into the context of experience, into the whole of reflection, it enters into the relationships of this system as a whole. It is no longer the isolated content or unit of its prelogical history, before it was involved in a context of thought relations. These relations become the setting of the item in the context of thought. The mark we call "identity," with its correlative exclusions, involves the linkage of sameness and difference in a larger related whole ; and the fulfilment of the essential marks of reasonableness again occurs in the larger consistency of the whole. A new item brought into the mind at any time falls into a related context whenever the relative identities and differences of its subject-matter establish themselves. It is thus again judged consistent with or fitted to this context, and is included in a larger whole of identical meaning. The identities and differences involved in any such case, however, are not made matter of explicit judgment, unless this be motived on occasion by the interest of the special process itself. They are now elements of the inner organization of the larger meaning whose acknowledgment as a whole the act of judgment renders.

Identity an Intent or Presupposition.

15. It is just in this fashion, indeed, that the body of implication grows. The identities of earlier judgment enter into the larger relational wholes of the later acts of similar acknowledgment. So that accretions come either from new discovery and synthesis or from new elucidation and analysis ; but always by the one process of making a more comprehensive judgment of identity.

Implication grows

The matter would seem to be fairly plain if we adhere to our genetic results. The mode of reflection is one of the establishment of a related context of items from different control spheres, all set up in an objective context of reflection. Anything taken up into this context has both its characteristic inner relationships which constitute it what it is, and its outer limitations, exclusions, etc., which make it not-anything-else. These relations, both within and without, now become interwoven in the whole body of experience ; and while the inner marks are those on which the individuation of the meanings as relatively separate proceeds, the outer are also there as implications in the larger wholes which reflection establishes by its continued acts of acknowledgment.

by Judgments of Identity.

The same appears also from a slightly different point of view—
that of the possibility of abstracting any relationship and making
it object of thought. The relationships by which content is
individuated in any mode go beyond the positive content already
established by limitation or exclusion. When reflection arises,
such relationships enter into the content or subject-matter of the
whole meaning ; and any aspect, any relation—sameness, difference, opposition, exclusion, limitation—may be taken up for
independent predication within any identical whole of meaning.
Thus those marks which are the differentiae, the characters, of

Identity may be judged. reasonableness, may themselves serve as subject-
matter of judgment. Identity and opposition, in
any of their phases, may thus be made subject-matter
of appropriate judgments. The case of identity, moreover,
when looked at as more than formal identification, involves a
certain combination of the two essential movements, positive and
negative, which give it further elements of import.

§ 4. IDENTITY AS RECURRENCE AND PERSISTENCE

16. A topic which comes within our ken in connection with this
matter of identity may be noted here as important for our later
epistemological criticism. It may be asked what relation a
Sameness and Recurrence, judgment of identity bears to the meanings of recurrence and persistence of the earlier modes. It will be
remembered that we were brought to the edge of this topic in
considering " sameness " of the recurrent type, and that at that
point we suggested a view of the relation established between
successive recurrences when rendered in the logical mode. This
question is now in order : the question as to how " recurrence,"
into which the persistence meaning of prelogical consciousness
resolves itself, is treated when taken up in the grasp of judgment.
This topic has been touched upon above, but it will repay us to
treat it a little more fully.

It is clear that the content of a judgment of identity must
render in some form the relation subsisting between recurrent
cases. For recurrence is the relationship in which, as we have
found, the material of the sameness meaning is given. " The
same " in the most developed prelogical sense—as we find it in
Rendered as Identity. the substantive mode—is the meaning arising when a
new experience suggests and fulfils an objective mean-
ing given on an earlier occasion. " This is my pen," is a meaning
of this type. It identifies the new experience " pen " by re-estab-

lishing the process whereby the meaning " my-pen " was constituted. If then we say that there is, in the substantive mode,
a meaning based on such recurrent sameness, we may ask what
the judgment issuing in the predication " this is my pen " adds
to this meaning.

Evidently it brings the meaning up into the context of thought.
It establishes the concept " my-pen " as general with reference to
the possible cases of the object's recurrence. To judge " this,
that, or any recurrence is my pen " is to use " my-pen-ness " as a
class predicate established for all appearances of the pen. This
meaning, therefore, is no longer a growing content, a schematic
meaning used as a hypothesis or problematical meaning to interpret recurrences ; on the contrary, it is a retrospective meaning,
made up on the basis of certain definite marks, and used to sum
up all possible experiences found to be particular recurrences of
it. The judgment of identity is a judgment predicating once
This is the   for all the intrinsic relationships by the recognition
Universal.   of which the meaning of " recurrent sameness " arose.
It thus becomes a " universal " meaning ; and as such it is discussed in the next paragraph (§ 5).[1]

17. This has its most important illustration in the meaning
of persistence whose early stages we have already traced with
some care.[2] We found the meaning " persistence " to have two
illustrations in the two great substantive classes, inner and outer
existence. Outer or external persistence, it will be remembered,
was found to mean " sameness-of-recurrence " of an object that
had also the coefficient of " sameness-when-absent " (called
" remote-sameness "). That is, an external object persists
The two   because it recurs and also has the meaning of an
sorts of   earlier remote persistence attaching to it. It has
Persistence.   persisted during the period when it did not recur.
Inner persistence, on the other hand, we found to be somewhat
different. It is the persistence of continuance, of movement,
motived by the active dispositional processes through which the
inner control asserts itself.

Now the interesting question at this point is as to whether
the judgment of identity issues in just the same meaning when

---

[1] As already intimated above, the objective aspects of singularity are
thus generalized for recurrent experiences, *as if* such experiences were of
different things or of different persons (cf. § 6 of this chapter, especially
sect. 30, and chap. xiv. § 8).

[2] Vol. i. chap. viii. § 4, and chap. x. §§ 1, 2.

dealing with these two modes of prelogical persistence. In short, do I judge myself to persist in the same sense and meaning that I judge my pen or table to persist ?

18. Evidently, in the first place, the judgment of identity utilizes those relationships already present in the meaning it renders. It cannot add to them ; it cannot detract from them ; it can only throw them upon the canvas of thought by an act of acknowledgment. We should expect, therefore, that the content of the two meanings, respectively, would differ somewhat as before, the new mode simply generalizing or universalizing the cases for logical purposes. The meaning of external persistence then becomes a meaning in which the thing is judged to persist in the variety of its own concrete cases, as an object under such and such control conditions : that is, as a recurring experience arising in a certain control-sphere—even when not recurring—in which at any time it might be again discovered. The external world—or better, *an* external world, whether physical, social, or other—is a world of persisting and identical externally controlled objects. This is, indeed, the necessary meaning ; for otherwise the distinction would be obliterated upon which reflection has proceeded in reaching the dualism of thought. For the same reason, also, the inner world persists in its own characteristic way—the way of inner persistence, not of outer. Otherwise again, the thought process would have confused the very dualism of meanings on which its own rise is conditioned.

The judgment renders both of these.

In other words—and this is the essential point—the act of judgment asserts a mode of control by which the self and its objects are set over against each other. In the object class there are both selves and not-selves, each of which is judged in its own way identical and persisting. These two sorts of objects take on each the meaning of its own original control. The self-objects are identified as having inner control as persons, inner persistence, thus illustrating the essential inwardness of self-hood ; the not-self objects as having outer persistence, that of the recurring type. The kernel of sameness or persistence meaning remains in each case what it is, though thrown into a form that generalizes the cases of it. The judgment renders this meaning by an act of acknowledgment.

Each persists in its own Mode.

19. The truth of this appears when we treat the judgmental subject-matter as a general and seek for its illustrative particulars. In the case of identity of an external object we have various

more or less mediate and remote means of confirmation. The easiest and earliest resort is, of course, to practical life ; the object fulfils its usual rôle. This is a mode of perceptive recognition : it may be called " identification by recurrence." Further there is also identification by testimony, by common appeal, by all that is involved in " secondary conversion " ; this is identi-

Shown in Conversion Processes. fication through "remote sameness." It rests the propriety of the sameness meaning upon the common result of various judgment processes. In the matter of inner identity, however, the procedure is not the same ; we neither wait for recurrence, nor do we ask our neighbours. We find in the immediately persisting and continuous mental life the experience that enables us to call the self identical. One involves the more or less experimental or "remote " process of establishing an identity, the other seems not to.[1]

§ 5.   THE JUDGMENT OF IDENTITY AS UNIVERSAL

20. We may now take up for further explanation the universal import of the meaning reached by logical individuation. It was suggested just above that in the progression into the mode of thought we should find certain meanings maturing to which we may now apply the term universal in a logical sense. The universal import attaches to the relation of the general to the particular.

It is not a new saying in our discussions that any relation may be made matter of logical rendering ; that any relation may be abstracted and set up as content or subject-matter of judgment.

The Logical as Universal. The " universal " intent of a meaning, like any other aspect of it is subject to such rendering ; and when an object is constituted in thought and judged " the same," those relations within the meaning which give it " general " and " particular " significance must appear in the new logical whole. The universal does appear in two ways, both of which carry further those shades of intent already suggesting universal meaning.

21. (1) In the first place when the logical relationship is interpreted in terms of general and particular, the meaning found universal is one that applies to *all cases legitimately covered by the general* ; that is to say, the general is universally applicable to

---

[1] This topic is carried further in the paragraph on " Identity in Difference " below (§ 1 of the next chapter).

its particulars.[1] This is the meaning of the universal from the point of view of the general.

From the point of view of the particular, on the other hand, the relation is differently formulated ; we say that the universal *admits of no exceptions*. Both of these aspects of universal meaning attach at once to the general-particular relationship.

Its Char-
acters.

For example, the general concept " horse " applies to all cases of horse ; and of horses there are none that escape interpretation through the general. These are the two ways of expressing the universal intent.

This rests, it will be remembered,[2] upon the movement of self-repetition of the meaning whereby the general is constituted. So far as the general is really established, that is, so far as it is a retrospective meaning summarizing a set of marks present in the particulars, so far it is no longer problematical with reference to any of those cases, but applies essentially to them all. If it be in any sense still hypothetical, or if it be used instrumentally for the interpretation of further doubtful cases, cases still *in futuro* in a logical sense, then it has so far lost its genuinely general character and is schematic and assumptive with reference to these cases. Generality, properly so called, is a relation established only with reference to cases subsumed under it ; it holds, therefore, of all such cases, since each is in its general character but a further repetition of the same meaning.

Based on
Repetition
of Cases.

This meaning is fully reflected in the universality of a judgment whereby the " sameness " meaning is rendered as identity. A judgment that identifies a meaning implicates its applicability to each of its own instances ; and we may say that all judgment that renders general meaning has the force of a universal. It identifies a case as *always and everywhere* carrying the very implication that the one instance used as subject-matter here and now is found to carry. This we may call, following certain logical writers, " essential universality." It is that intent of a judgment of identity that recognizes the impossibility of thinking a meaning as general without also implying that it is self-repeating for all cases in which it may be used at all.

Essential
Universality.

The same appears from the other aspect of universality—

---

[1] The intent of " necessity " before pointed out (vol. i, chap. x. § 5) as attaching to universal meaning is taken up below (in chap. xi. § 3).

[2] See the passage cited (vol. i. chap. x. § 5).

that in which it is a meaning that admits of no exceptions. As, from the point of view of the general, a universal meaning is one that applies to all the particular cases, so from the point of view of the particulars, no one of them can be excepted. So the individuation of the whole meaning as universal, in a judgment of identity, gives this result also—a relation admitting of no exceptions.

22. It will be profitable to stay a moment on this first case, in-asmuch as a current distinction separates it off from what is called " accidental " or " empirical " universality. By this latter is meant that force of a meaning which merely recognizes the **Empirical** presence of things together in fact, or in experience, **Universality.** but does not involve the demand that they be essentially and always together.

The distinction between the two cases is one we have already noted in passing, and one that recurs again in the discussion of the methods of reasoning. It is clear that what is called " acci-dental," " factual," or " enumerative " universality has the **Empirical** meaning of a judgment of identity, since the general **Universality** meaning even in such cases covers the particulars as far **is Disjunctive** as they are known. The difference, however, comes out just in this last clause—" so far as they are known." The use of a meaning for purposes of discovery, with the *arrière pensée* that further cases may modify it, throws it on the side of " proposal " ; and though no actual exploring process be pursued, still the intent allows that it might be. There is, in short, in such a meaning a *disjunctive force.* When we say " all under-graduates are crude," the meaning is clearly open to doubt as to the individual case. And even when we suggest a complete enumeration, as in "all school-teachers are underpaid," we clearly do not intend to say that there is anything essential in this relation. Admitting, then, that the difference is that there is a *suggestion of proposal or modification,* in the one case, the acci-dental universal, while the other, the essential universal, forbids such a suggestion, we may inquire further into the ground of the difference.

In yet another connection too we have come upon this dis-tinction. In discussing logical " quantity " we found it necessary to distinguish between two meanings both rendered, as logical **and** universals, by the form " all S is P." This proposition **Quantified.** may be quantified as in "all the books have red covers," or unquantified as in " (all) virtue is praiseworthy." Only the latter case, the unquantified judgment, motived not by discovery of more cases, but by elucidation of a whole of established meaning, has essential universality ; the former, on the contrary, intending a meaning that is growing, existential, and in so far alternative, is universal only in the accidental or empirical sense.

23. The root of the matter is to be found, I think, in the distinction between what we have described as " contingent " meaning, now asserting itself as logical ground or formal relation, which is analytic, and disjunctive meaning which is quantitative **Essential** and existential.   Implication proper, as involving the **Universal a** inner relationships of parts in a logical whole, is analytic. **meaning of** **Contingency** It establishes a related whole of meaning which is cut **or Ground.** off from its factual or material reference, and is so far not open to further development in a sphere of truth.   It is in such meanings that the experimental aspect of thinking hides itself behind the presupposition of competent reflection itself. The relations are those established within a complete and finished whole of content.   This is the intent called "logical necessity" : it is that isolation of a whole of meaning, within the presupposition of the sphere of reflection as such, which recognizes it as a system of dependencies and contingencies within the whole. This gives " essential universality " to these relations. Essential universality, therefore, may be called *the universality of logical dependence or ground.*

On the other hand, in accidental or empirical universality we have to recognize a different motive—one of material reference with view to discovery or proof.   The universality in this case is only so by indulgence or assumption ; it always allows its **Empirical, one** own undoing. The synthetic aspect of judgment **of Proposal.** appears in the realm of empirical and disjunctive meaning or logical modality, and the universal form is given to a disjunctive or alternative meaning for instrumental and personal purposes.   It would be only a slight change of terms therefore, if we should call this " experimental universality "—universality suggesting but not yet grounded in logical implication—seeing that *it is motived, not by elucidation and analysis, but by proposal and synthesis.*

24. It is an interesting fact to recognize that here, as in so many cases, the genetic progression is from the experimental or schematic to the logical or theoretical, from the assumption or postulation to the grounded identity or presupposition.   The movement of confirmation establishes the contingent relationship,

the inner dependence, the logical conditioning, and this is rendered in the judgment of logical identity.   The process, therefore,
is one not of further repetition of judgments as new cases arise,
nor one of judgment that attaches identity as a new predicate to
a made-up content already judged ; but one of a progression in in-
Progression dividuation, whereby the relations of fact are narrowed
from Empir- down and limited to that contingent form which may
ical to
Essential be rendered in a judgment of relative isolation in a
related whole.   This progression proceeds through the process
of induction which we are presently to sketch.   Here it may be
said simply that induction is the normal process of moulding
experience into its contingent and non-alternative form, so
that *the empirically true may be rendered as the logically valid
in the form of implication.*

25. (2) A second aspect of universality appears when we recall
the character of logical meaning called above " community "
—its character as being in some sense " common " or " social."

Our discussions have shown that an identical meaning need not
be " catholic," or actually prevalent, but that it must be " synnomic " or " appropriate " ; it must be *intended as fit to be prevalent.* A relation individuated as identical *is intended to be identical for all who judge ; a judgment of identity to be everybody's*
Common   *judgment of identity.*   There is more, then, in the
Judgment universality of the relation established between the
of Identity.
general meaning and its particular case than its
universal applicability ; there is also the *universal community
of its implication of logical function everywhere.*   This is one of
the leading results reached in this work.   The reference of the
knower to all knowers, of him who judges to universal judgment,
is as ingrained and essential as is the reference of the outcome
of judgment to all its cases.   And the interpretation of reasonableness on the side of implication must take into account the absence
and *impossibility of privacy or individualism of the subject-function,*
no less than the absence of atomism and eccentricity in the
body of the subject-matter.

By community of propositions, it should be recalled, is meant
that character whereby they implicate the appropriateness of the
meaning rendered for general acceptance.   This is an ineradicable
Its Commun- implication of judgment as such—an intent to render
ity : it is what is appropriate and fit.   It is necessary, therefore,
Synnomic. to inquire as to whether a judgment endowed with
universality of the sort described—the sort attaching to the

subject-matter or content—can dispense with some sort of universality also in the mode of community. Are all judgments, that is, universal in the sense of legislating their results for other intelligences ?

This question we have already answered in a general way. We found that all judgment as such intends to be synnomic or appropriate—fit for anybody and everybody. And in that sense it is *universal in respect to community*.[1] This we may call the " universal community " as correlated with the " universal validity " of the relations which the judgment renders.

26. We find, however, here as in the case of the content, a sort of variation as between the essential and accidental. If we say An Essential that it is the intent of a judgment to be universal Universal. in community, we must nevertheless admit that instrumental and problematical aspect of the social relation involved in intercourse which reflects the variations of actual acceptance or rejection. This appeared in our discussions of catholicity.[2] Relative prevalence reflects the proposal aspect of that which is still, in its essential force, synnomic assertion.

From this point of view, the meaning, however universal as a body of implication, becomes merely aggregate or relatively catholic. And within the mode of community, the distinction It is Aggre- holds, cutting across the similar one found to hold of gate when universality of content, between community as essen- Empirical. tial intent and community as accidental or empirical determination. The latter introduces into the reference to others' beliefs the character of quantity, which is absent from the essential force of the judgment as rendering a content fit for all cases of judgment.

27. This has its importance for, as we have already suggested, it introduces an *experimental strain, a problematical force, into all implication whatsoever*. The synnomic intent becomes an assumption, and no longer a presupposition, as soon as the mode of community is recognized that invokes for the meaning concrete judgment and actual acceptance. It must be submitted to the test of social prevalence as fact in order that its essential community may become effective in the actual development of knowledge in the larger whole of social intercourse.

From this point of view we come again to the position that

[1] See chap. iii. above, especially § 9. On variations of the content in respect to " quantity in community," see chap. xiv. § 8, ad fin.
[2] Chap. vi. § 8.

all logical meaning *when viewed in community*, even the universal of the essential relational type—the synthetic à priori if you please—is of the nature of postulation, experimental and instru-

This makes mental, both in its origin [1] and in its employment in

all Judg- actual predication. The development of implication

ments Ex-

perimental in of the purely deductive and discursive type is, as we

Community. are to see more fully below, always motived by symbolic and formal abstraction. Its place and rôle in actual thought, on the contrary, in that vital progression of meaning by which the growth of material knowledge is advanced, requires the return to the concrete and experimental. Only by constantly fulfilling this rôle can its own validation be secured.

Remembering that the mode of community is one of acceptance, belief, or inner control, and distinguishing the different forms of community as variations of control, we may throw our results at this point into relief in the following Table I, for the purposes of later discussion. It presents the conclusion that all universal meaning, considered from the point of view of community as control, *has the force of proposal.*

TABLE I. UNIVERSAL MEANING

1. *As to Content*—

Essential { Categorical in Relation. / Synnomic or Appropriate in Community (for whom).[2] }

Accidental { Problematical in Relation. / Synnomic in Community (for whom)[2] } Implication.

2. *As to Control*—

Essential } Syndoxic or Aggregate in } Proposal.
Accidental } Community (by whom).[3] }

§ 6. CLASS IDENTITY AND SINGULAR IDENTITY

28. Our genetic approach to the subject led us to discover the motive involved in the individuation of identity. It is the

---

[1] As to its racial origin, it is doubtless a crystallizing of what was found socially useful, a point made in a Darwinian sense by James (*Pragmatism*, Lect. v.) and by myself (*Devel. and Evolution*, chap. xvii.) and originally in a Lamarckian sense by Spencer (*Prin. of Psych.*, vol. i. p. 208).

[2] and [3]. These two modes of community are those already distinguished above (chap. ix. § 5), as answering to the questions " for whom ? " and " by whom ? " respectively.

rendering of the general and particular relationship. The
relation of general and particular within a whole
identical meaning is what is set up for acknowledgment.
If this be true, we have to ask the further question
as to its applicability to cases of singular identity. How can
a thing be judged " singular " and identical with itself, if the
meaning requires the relation of general and particular ?

How is a Singular Identical?

The answer to this question enables us to bring out, in illustration of the general theory, certain interesting further corro-
laries. Moreover it is a topic relevant to our theory of the singular.

There are, it is at once evident, two modes in which the judgment
of sameness, underlying the meaning of identity, may be determined. There is the sameness of *different cases within a general*
meaning, in which case it is the general that is judged
identical for all its particulars ; and there is the sameness
of the *recurrent cases of the one object* judged identical—
the identity of singular meaning. It is now our point of further
advance to say that these are really but one judgment, and that
they both illustrate the general theory laid down above. A
further striking sidelight upon the matter will come from our
doctrine of community. We may set forth these points in brief
preliminary statement and then proceed to expound them.

Cases of Generality and Identity.

(1) A judgment of *class identity* is the acknowledgment of
different objects as fulfilling the same general meaning.

(2) A judgment of *singular identity* is an acknowledgment of
particular recurrences of a single object as fulfilling the meaning
thus made general to these cases of recurrence.

(3) A judgment of *community or common identity* mediates the
two preceding meanings and shows their modal unity. It may be
interpreted either as the acknowledgment of a class of particular
objects under the same general, or as the acknowledgment of the
recurrence of one object for different acts of judgment, these
being from the point of view of community, *one and the same
thing*.

To these propositions we may now turn.

29. I. Class identity has been already discussed in some detail.
It is the case that issues in the universal meaning as respects
content or implication, whether it be " essential " or
" accidental " in intent. It was intimated above in
passing that this judgment is motived by the recognition of
a plurality of cases, interpreted as the recurrence of the general.
It needs, therefore, no further comment.

Class Identity.

II. Singular identity, like other singular individuations, follows upon identity as class meaning. It shows the two cases already distinguished in the treatment of the meaning of singularity.[1] An object judged particular with reference to its fulfilment of a class meaning, may not be exhausted by such treatment; it may also be found singular. This is either because it has marks left over that resist generalization, or because it fulfils a personal interest or purpose of a special sort.

Now both these modes of singularity are rendered by the judgment of singular identity. I may judge my dog or my pleasure to be " the same " through successive recurrences, although I at the same time render them as cases under the general meanings Singular " dog " and " pleasure." The appreciative, no less Identity. than the recognitive content, is taken up in the context of reflection and acknowledged as a singular. So far the rôle of judgment as individuation in a meaning of identity seems to be fairly plain and unambiguous.

III. In the intent of community or common identity, however, we come upon a development of extreme and hitherto unrecognized importance, as I venture to think. A judgment in community renders a meaning motived by the intent of commonness; it fulfils *both the foregoing at once* and comes to stand as *the mediation and consummation of the meaning of logical identity*. In its Common synnomic aspect, it renders a meaning which, as a body Identity of implication, is applicable to all cases of recurrence, mediates the cases I whether it be the recurrence of recurrent experience and II. to the same person or recurrence to different persons as given in the same or different particulars.[2] For as control, the recurring acts of judgment are indifferently either those of a process of private belief or those of an aggregate of such processes. The conversion processes by which synnomic control is established are essentially of the " secondary " or social sort : processes by which the private judgments make appeal for confirmation to the social fellows, or processes in which the socially accepted judgments make appeal to the individual's thought. Once given a synnomic meaning and its final establishing may be considered as being secured *by either process indifferently*. Thus it *renders both the personal and the social*.

[1] Namely " essential " and " imported " singularity.

[2] The different cases are explicitly brought out in the paragraph below (chap. xiv. § 9) in which the principle of " Difference of Discernibles " is formulated.

For example, when I say " virtue is praiseworthy," whether
I intend an essential or an accidental universal, I mean both that
the personal belief may be confirmed by social experience or that
the social belief may be confirmed by my individual experience.
And the same is true of a singular judgment such as " this is my
straw hat." The personal intent is rendered common by the
judgment of identity, just as in the class universal the common
acceptance is given personal rendering.

30. The case of the singular, therefore, when interpreted in
community, becomes a particular of class identity and universality ; while the case of the general becomes a meaning of personal
endorsement and ratification. In short, when the distinction [1]
between the one person's process and that of others is removed,
—as in all logical process it necessarily is—the recurrent appearance of one object is just the same as the recurrent appearance
of different objects : they are both simply *recurrent appearances*.

It follows from this that our discovery that the character
of community of judgment is intrinsic, is not only supported, but
gains further importance. In fact, it becomes impossible to
interpret judgment as a movement of progressive identification
without the recognition of such an intrinsic intent. The world
All identical of relation, of logical validity, *implicates the community*
judgment *of class identity*, whether this be motived by a
is general in
Commun- plurality of particular objects, or by the recurrence
ity. of the same singular object.

It follows that all judgment whatever, so far as it renders
implication, or essential universality, and not merely disjunctive
or schematic proposal of universality, intends a meaning of both
personal and social identity. And put conversely, all judgment,
so far as it renders implication in a whole of identical meaning,
is universal both in content and in the community " for whom "
that judgment is to hold.

31. It may be asked at this point whether this does not banish
singular meaning as such altogether from the logical mode.
Does not its interpretation as general destroy its singularity ?

---

[1] As matter of fact it is removed only on occasion. We usually
interpret the two cases differently because the recurrent experiences of
the same object are also " immediately singular " to the control process
of the personal mental life. This will be brought out more fully below
in chap. xiv. § 9, and in chap. xv., where the limitations of this mode of
generalization " in community " are pointed out.

In what sense can a meaning that is universal as respects community still be singular ?

To this it must be replied that it does banish singular meaning from the logical, if by the singular we mean a type of meaning that lacks community. For when a meaning of singularity is rendered in a judgment then precisely the marks that served to make it singular are generalized in one of the modes of community—as recurring in different experiences either for the same or for different persons. The intent of singularity which admits of no generalization has then retreated into the domain of direct appreciation or immediate experience.

The Singular remains Appreciative.

This may be illustrated without difficulty. Suppose I submit the statement " this is the only orange of this colour." By so doing I give the orange a meaning in community in two ways. I mean that you can find it the only one with me, or that I myself can find it the same one by repeating my experience of it. This is explained later, when it is shown that the identity extends to *successive appearances in one consciousness*, whether of one or of different objects (see the exposition of the principle called " difference of discernibles " in chapter xiv. §§ 8, 9). But in either case, I have made it a particular to a general of recurrence. If indeed I say " I find this orange to have a unique taste," I at least intend that I can again find it having the same unique taste ; and this I mean you to accept with me. The only thing that remains ungeneralized in community is the remainder of the original meaning, not rendered by the judgment, namely what is incommunicable about the actual quality of taste. This may still be singular either by the objective quality of the orange or by the imported quality of my appreciating interest. *This is just what evades the judgment.*

We have thus carried further the point that has already more than once forced itself upon us—namely, that the singular is a meaning that cannot be fully rendered in general and particular terms. As in the earlier place so here we are led to expect that this will later on be a stumbling block in the way of holding to a strictly and exclusively logical interpretation of experience.

It is true, nevertheless, that by our resort to " community," we have reduced the essential type of singularity, the singularity of objective marks, to statement in terms of the general of recurrence.

Chapter XI

MODES OF IDENTITY AND DIFFERENCE

§ 1. IDENTITY IN DIFFERENCE

1. The phrase " identity in difference " seems to the writer to admit a construction that sets together the two essential marks of reasonable implication as indicated above : the marks of sameness and limitation, or logically considered, identity and opposition. For when we return to our genetic point of view, we find that while it is the rôle of logical individuation to establish a meaning as identical, it is able to do so only by a process that recognizes differences also.

We note first that the stages in the development of meaning into its logical birthright, are those of generalization and Individuation singularization, the former establishing a meaning as Identical. that has certain illustrative particulars. These particulars were such only with reference to the marks used to characterize the general. But there always remains over a residue, the unused marks of the particular case whereby it remains in experience singular. For example, our much-cited friend the " horse " is not only a particular of the class horse, a meaning reached on the basis of the abstraction of certain marks of " horseness," but he is also this single horse, " Jim." This means that the whole meaning, in all its concreteness, is not exhausted by any treatment that construes it as in a class comprising numerical particulars. The reality, the existent thing, has the richer meaning that its full statement as singular warrants ; and this renders *its marks of difference.* The " horse " is individuated as having identical meaning with other horses ; but he is also judged in his singularity as different from others. In this case, therefore, it is true that identity implicates difference ; the identical class meaning implies particulars different from one another.

The only case in which this would seem not to be true is that in which the further abstraction is made that no concrete singular case is meant, but only those aspects of meaning are intended which are utilized in the constitution of the general. Thus I can talk about the "horse characters" of horses, maintaining an identity of connotation; but I do so with the presupposition that the sphere is now not that of actual existence, but that of abstract or logical meaning as such.

2. It may be said that this is to deal with one case only, that of different individual things in a class; and that it does not apply to the identification of one single object judged simply as self-identical. But from what we have seen above it is evident that it applies here also. For the very fact of rendering a meaning as common object of thought for different minds is to individuate it as general. Each individual's object, and each successive objective experience of the same individual, is a particular found different from all others.

In the control of reflection, which is common, the meaning even of the one single object becomes that of a particular experience among recurring and different experiences. Each particular

For different things and one thing.
experience that illustrates the recurrence of this one object is a different individuation for thought, just as each several object in a class of objects is a different individuation. All rendering of logical meaning establishes an identity which is subject to the further determination of differences.

3. This truth does not lend itself, however, to the view that thought as process proceeds by the establishing of identities in differences, except with the further explanation that its process is one of abstraction and generalization, through which the marks

Prelogical Identity in Difference.
of singularity or essential difference are left behind. For these marks are those of the concrete, the actual control; it is only the pale ghost of it that is reconstituted mediately in thought. The resort to "*identity in difference*" is, therefore, a resort to a prelogical mode of control, to an existence reference of one or another type according as the singularity is of one sort or another. It may be a mode of appreciation—one of imported singularity—in which case the difference is not one of external marks, but of experiences of feeling or direct appreciation. Or it may be one of the "essential" kind—the singularity that resists generalization—in which case it is a difference of perception, presentation, or some such simpler mode of control.

Looked at broadly, the meaning of sameness in difference

before the rise of judgment is one of "relationship," but not of acknowledged and asserted " relation "—a distinction developed on an earlier page. Where the sameness meaning passes into a relation of identity by an act of judgment, the relation of difference is given the same sort of rendering. So *identity in difference* found in the prelogical, becomes the *identity and difference* of the logical. Difference as a relation stands in the context of thought on the same footing as identity. It may be brought up into the context as subject-matter of judgment. We may say respecting *identity and difference*, that when judged as identical, a content has the presupposition of a larger whole of differences, and when judged as different, it has the presupposition of a larger identical whole.

4. The development of identity by successive acts of judgment, as experience is progressively rendered, issues no less in **Identity and** the establishing of differences. Of this we find certain **Difference.** forms recognized in logic, which we may treat under the names usually attaching to them. These we may set down as modes of identity *and* difference, as follows—Classification, Ordination, Definition. The development itself, as it proceeds in experience, is what is known as Induction, to which we will first turn. By the process of induction the " identity *in* difference " of prelogical meaning becomes the " identity *and* difference " of a body of related judgments of reflection.

§ 2. Induction

5. If what has now been said as to the nature of the judgment of identity is true, it follows that the formation of such judgments is just the positive side of the growth of knowledge or thought. Generalization, abstraction, singularization—all are cases of the development of identities by acts of judgment. So far we have considered the contents of identical judgment as issuing in appropriate meanings, ready formed or made up, and we have explored **The Growth** the motives found entering into them. We have now to **of Identical** develop more fully the proposal side of the process : **Meanings.** the aspect wherein it is instrumental and experimental, and especially that aspect as we find it in the more developed and conscious form in which it becomes explicit scientific method. It is by induction that such experimental treatment of experience proceeds ; and all my readers will agree, no doubt, that to reach an induction is to establish an identical judgment for a number

of cases. Indeed, induction may be defined as *the experimental establishment of judgments of identity.*

In order not to assume anything, however, we may ask the general question as to what induction is. We may be told that it is the passing from a particular or particulars to a general meaning ; or that it is the process of finding a common meaning among different and varied cases. On either of these views, the evident question before us is—" what shall I do with this, that and the other case ; are they to remain in isolation, or can I induce from them anything which they may all be taken to illustrate or exemplify ? "

6. Selecting out from the discussions of the subject the " canons " of inductive method as laid down by J. S. Mill, we may conduct the discussion with immediate reference to them. Let us ask the question of induction in this form, " When may I be sure Question of that among the varieties of natural happening, I have Induction. found a recurring, persistent, and invariable grouping of facts ? " ; or this, " given a certain set of marks now found together, how may I be sure that the present grouping is the invariable and necessary one, so that when I find one of the marks of the group I may confidently expect to find the others also ? " It is evident that wherever this is realized, I have established a judgment of identity, and my " induction " consists in my being able to read various cases of experience as now fulfilling this judgment.

For example, take the induction whereby we arrive at the judgment " all men are capable of speech." We may say that before the judgment of identity is reached—say by a child— the meaning " man " may not include the character of speech. A man is then heard to speak. The mark " speech " is hypothetically read into the complex "man"; and further experimental procedure is needed to establish a belief as to its universal correctness or truth. This makes it necessary to resort to some means of advancing knowledge, in order to determine the case. Thus the judgment is arrived at, that " speaking-man " is the true reading of the new identical meaning before read as " man." Sketch of This we have before discussed as the growth of a Induction. conceptual meaning. It is variously described in logic as " the search for causes," " the enumeration of cases," the " concomitance of phenomena," " the uniformity of nature," etc. But in all these designations, the same thought is more or less explicitly brought out, that a meaning already achieved is used experimentally to secure by further experience the definition and limitation of its comprehension. It is the normal and only method of discovery.

7. The stages of the inductive method as thus defined were substantially made out by Mill ; it is one of the great advances in the theory of scientific thought. Our genetic inquiry confirms the theory, but throws upon it a somewhat new light. We are able to see that there are three motives at work in the genesis of identity, each of which has its peculiar development.

First, there is the motive of actual and positive recognition, working itself out through the mazes of varied and conflicting experience. This is the motive of " recurrent sameness," hit off in Mill's canon of " agreement." [1] It requires the positive recurrence together, or concomitance in a positive sense, of the elements of the complex AB, B always appearing when A does. This **Agreement.** in so far justifies the acceptance of the whole meaning AB as recurring, persisting in its own type of existence and justifying *unless or until disturbed*, the treatment of all the things having this joint character as being of a class AB. Taken alone it affords the basis of what is called " analogy "— as in " this case of A is B, other cases of A are B also."

This is, however, clearly not yet either exhaustive or definitive ; there may still be cases in which A does not entail B, nor B entail A ; and there may be cases in which there is nothing about A to suggest whether it is or is not B. " All the men I know anything about are able to talk," is such a judgment of recurrent sameness or identity. It generalizes just these men, and leaves open both the question of speech in other men, and also the question of the identity of *man as man*, a universal —whether or not he is a speaking animal.

8. A second motive is found in Mill's canon of " difference." [2] It proceeds by invoking the principle of exclusion,

---

[1] Mill's canon of " agreement " runs : " If two or more instances of the phenomenon under investigation have only one circumstance in common, the circumstance in which alone all these instances agree is the cause (or effect) of the given phenomenon " (Mill, *Logic*, Book III, chap. viii. § 1).   In terms of our theory, this means that A, the first occurrence, becomes AB, the second occurrence. As a judgment of identity, A ((AB, it is restricted to just these particular cases. The phenomenon in question is, for these cases, identical with A.

[2] Mill's canon of " difference " runs : " If an instance in which the phenomenon under investigation occurs, and an instance in which it does not occur, have every circumstance in common save one, that one occurring

as in " whatever *A* is excluded from, *B* is excluded from also,"
or " *A* and *B* are always absent together." This reinforces the
expectation based on concomitance of the positive sort, since it
places both the parts of the entire meaning together in the
meaning " remote sameness," and so justifies, genetically, the
Difference. expectation of joint recurrence or recurrent sameness.

In fact, what more natural, as a resort of scientific
method, than that the experimenter, finding *A* and *B* together,
should then remove one and observe the removal of the other
with it. If we call the positive concomitance spoken of above
" concomitant presence," we may call this negative concomitance
" concomitant absence." The procedure amounts to *tracing
backward the genetic progression of the sameness meaning*, from that
of the "recurrent " to that of the " remote " type.

The investigator is then free to proceed to reinstate one, pre-
ferably the second, *B*, in a new combination with other elements,
and observe the re-occurrence again of the concomitant something, *A* ; thus illustrating the *forward progression in sameness*
or a new "agreement."

The method of difference goes farther than the recognition
of mere concomitance as agreement, and fulfils a farther
requirement of a full judgment of identity. Still it is not yet
what can be called a flawless or unimpeachable induction ; for
there still remains an ambiguity due to defect in limitation or
exhaustion. " Wherever I find a man I hear him speak," and
" I hear no speech when man is absent," these taken together
do not justify the universal " *man is a speaking animal* "
—an essential universal. It might be that only some men
speak, and also that no other animals speak. What then remains to constitute such a judgment.?

9. Evidently what is lacking is the factor which makes it
imperative that the concept man should include speech. This requires a movement that *divides the sphere of thought exhaustively*

only in the former, the circumstance in which alone the two instances
differ is the effect, or the cause, or an indispensable part of the cause,
of the phenomenon " (Mill, *Logic*, Book III, chap. viii. § 2). These
canons are discussed in most of the books of inductive logic. Adamson's
succinct account may be referred to in the writer's *Dict. of Philos.*, *sub
verbis* " Agreement (logical)," " Difference (method of)," " Concomitance (logical)," "Induction," etc. Under this canon we have *BA* (the
first case) becomes *B* (the second case), or *BA* ((*B*. The phenomenon in
question, absent from the second case, is identical with *A*, which is also
absent.

into two mutually exclusive classes, man and non-speaking things, and so reaches the predication " man is not non-speaking." That is, the motive of limitation must enter, due to the growth of knowledge of the sort that *allies non-speech with something incompatible with the meaning man.*[1] This is found in a discovery about the class of beings that do not speak, of such a sort that no **Exhaustion** case in that class can also be included as a particular **required.** in the class man. This supplies the element of necessity before lacking to the judgment ; without it the meaning is not a true or essential universal.

If, for example, a new species is found that does not speak, we cannot on the strength simply of our earlier experience of agreements and differences, at once say " therefore it is not man."

The matter may be put in propositions as follows :—

" Man is vocal, wherever I find him " (agreement) ;

" The not-vocal wherever I find it is not man " (difference) ;

I could not then say that men who are non-vocal might not still be come upon.

But if I now have an experience that correlates non-speech, as in the anthropoids, with certain anatomical characters which also exclude some of the essential marks of man, I can then say " the non-vocal are not-man," reaching the universal and exhaustive limitative judgment, " man is not non-vocal " or " man is vocal." Speech is added to the marks of man. Thus a judgment of class identity is reached to be carried as valid through future experience.

10. The essential thing thus secured, it is clear, is the establishment of a non-man, a non-B class. The inclusion in it of any case definitely excludes this case from the B class. We can now **This gives a** say " man must be articulate, for to take speech from **Contingent** him *places him in another anatomical class* than that **Meaning.** of man." That is, something already established and implicated in the meaning man would be incompatible with the proposed predicate. In this movement we come upon the essential motive to logical contradiction as will be brought out below, the " exhaustion " of the " B-non-B " sphere. The resulting meaning, " man is articulate," is a universal.

There is thus established a " contingent " meaning—" if *A* then *B* "—described already as one of dependence or conditioning.

---

[1] This it is evident, goes beyond Mill's third canon, that of " Concomitant Variation," which can be reduced, I think, to a combination of the two other canons.

11. There is a further movement to take place, however, before the judgment, now identical with respect to the whole meaning "man" thus recognized and made subject-matter, becomes identical also with reference to the mark through which its identity is predicated. In other words, the identity of the object may carry the specific mark, but the presence of the mark may not implicate the entire object. In the case given, "vocal man" is judged identical through its inclusion of the mark "articulation"— since the exclusion of "articulation" would destroy its identity—but there may be other things that could also be identified by this mark, taken with other characters. Man may belong with other beings in a larger group of "articulates," the differentiae of man, with respect to these others, being characters of some other sort.

"Plural cause" possible.

This is involved, though from a different point of view, in the doctrine of "plural causes." *B*, the effect, must always be present when *A*, its cause, is present; hence the advance that establishes a *non-B* class establishes also a *non-A* class. But it may be that *A'* is also present when *B* is, and that the establishment of *non-B* establishes also *non-A'*. In terms of cause and effect, any effect *B* may be due to the "plural" or several action of two or more causes, and further research is necessary to determine the further limitation under which the effect is identical with one or the other of them only.

Such further research involves, I think, a reversal of the terms; the predicate becomes subject and the subject is then subjected to the same analysis as before. By such procedure we reach a judgment of identity with reference to *B*. *B* is found to be *A* (and not *A'*). This then with the foregoing limitation of *A* to *B*, gives double identity or complete coincidence of meaning between *A* and *B*—what in the language of causation is the "universal relation of cause and effect."

For example, if we start out to investigate "articulateness," and by the process already described, limit it to man, then we can say both "man is articulate" and "the articulate is man." That is, man and speech are universally coincident meanings.

The outcome of this procedure is a second relation of dependence or contingence. Not only can it now be said, "if *A* then *B*," but also "if *B* then *A*." This is what is referred to earlier as "reciprocal" contingence.

Reciprocal contingence.

12. It now appears, also, in what sense limitation is at

work.   It makes possible the exhaustion of the sphere of control in two very essential respects.   In the first place, there is the presupposition of the limitation of the entire meaning to its sphere of reference or existence.   We mean or intend " real man " **Limitation** and " real speech."   But second, the intent of limita- **is essential.** tion works itself into the implication itself.   By the establishing of a *non-B* or *non-A* class within the sphere within which the *B* or *A* class is also controlled, the meaning becomes one of *exhaustion* in that sphere.   There is nothing in that sphere that is not one or the other, *B* or *non-B*, no matter what may be possible in some other sphere than that now presupposed.   The intent of incompatibility, or contradiction, or excluded middle is essentially an implication of exhaustion ; and exhaustion arises only from the motive of limitation.

13. It is not my purpose, at this point, to expound this as a theory of the meaning of cause, nor even to justify giving it that reference.   The object of stating it in these words is simply to indicate that it is the same problem, the derivation of the same meaning, that Mill treated of in his " search for causes."   Mill's analysis and resulting conception of method has its own validity, whether we call it a search for " concomitances," for " invariable   antecedents   and   consequents,"   for   " coincident **"Cause" not** dentities," or for " causes."   The question whether **discussed.** Mill did by this analysis further the theory of cause, or whether in the genetic research conducted here, which establishes the meaning called " coincident identity," we have come within sight of cause, remains a further problem.[1]

The result to be treasured here, however, is the discovery that induction is simply the method whereby the mind normally and   regularly   reaches   judgments   of   identity   in   experience. The maintenance and development of identities is but another name for the progressive individuation of logical meaning as **All discovery** such.   All discovery, invention, advance of meaning **Inductive.** by predication and proposition, is of the nature of inductive procedure.   It proceeds by the erection of a content as what it is, in relatively novel situations, in which it then proves to be what before it was not yet recognized as being.   The

---

[1] The reader should consult Mill's text for his distinction between "cause " as " sequence " and mere " co-existence " in time (*Logic*, Bk. III. chap. 22).

The distinction between material dependence or cause and logical dependence or ground (both considered as modes of   necessity ") is explained below in this chapter, sects. 20 ff.

advance is that a new judgment of identity is reached on another plane. The relative extension and intension of the context of recognitive meaning is thus constantly revised, by a process that is experimental and progressive. The identity is established on each plane by the recognition of sameness, the exclusion of otherness, and the limitation and exhaustion of range.[1]

14. After it has come, however, the judgment is no longer one of progression, discovery, adjustment, schematic proposal, but one of identification, retrospection, universality—a meaning of fixed logical relationships. The identity *in* difference of the concrete reading of experience—the "different" being the increment of content not yet determined within the whole identical meaning, the "other" or "not-same" of the limitative meaning— passes over into the identity *and* difference of logical negation and exclusion. Both the identity and the difference, as retrospective and logical categories are abstractions, both matters **But universal** of relational thought-content, having equally mediate **meaning is a** control and equally remote reference to the sphere **fixed Implica-** **tion.** in which the prelogical meaning was made up. The logical affirmative does carry difference with its assertion of identity ; but it is an abstract difference, one of logical opposition. The difference of immediate concrete experience, not yet made matter of logical judgment, is that of direct relationship within a content still under its own appropriate first-hand control.

15. It is not the implications for theory, however, that now concern us, but the further use and development of these meanings in the psychic movement. We find two processes proceeding from the establishment of these judgments of identity : one that called "simple enumeration" or "simple induction," and the other "deduction" or "deductive implication"—a process often contrasted in essential nature with induction. **Enumeration:** Indeed so urgently is the need felt of distinguishing **two cases** as widely as possible between induction and deduction that the former is often identified simply with "enumeration," and the latter in turn with what is known as "reasoning in universals." Both of these contrasted methods of operation, which are variants upon induction, must now be considered.

"Simple enumeration," so-called, takes place in two essentially different conditions. It may be the identification of like cases by the use of analogy—the pursuit of "recurrent sameness"

[1] It is shown below, chap. xii., in what sense "deduction," or argumentation through a "middle term," illustrates the same process.

as described above.   As such it is the first step in vital induction.
" So far, crows have always been black—here's a black bird—
it is a crow."   Restricted simply to this analogical use of
meanings, such an enumeration is not logical at all ; it is not
implication nor judgment.   We have found it already in the
child's schematic and habitual " construct," the vague inclusive
meaning within which, on superficial resemblance or from preferential interest, a new case may be interpreted along with old
ones.   The great maw of motor habit stands ready to devour
Simple   details that do not choke it, as the open bat's mouth
Enumeration takes in insects.   It is, however, an essential moment
in the inductive process as a whole, for it furnishes the larger
whole of agreements among which the necessary limitations and
exclusions are to be made.   Yet it is still true that without the
further factors in the whole movement, such enumeration is not
a process of implication at all.

The other sort of enumeration is a very different thing.   It
is the identification of instances by the use of a judgment of
identity whose universal character has already been established.
It involves no advance of meaning by including doubtful or unexplained cases ; but, on the contrary, it is a mere application
of the meaning already given.

For example, I am asked to assort the coins in a box ; I take
Application.   them one by one and distribute them in groups—
silver, gold, copper.   It is evident that I have here the
application merely to single instances, particulars, of meanings
already made up.   There is no essential induction as described
above, for no meaning is put in question, no problem is solved,
no thought advanced.   I am not defining identities, nor advancing
meanings, by such ticking-off of self-repeating cases.   This
movement of mere " application " has already been illustrated
above (chap. vii § 7) in the distinction between growth in
" extension " of a term, and growth in mere range in the use or
application of the term.

The difference between this and real induction, in the given
case, is seen when, for some reason, I find an ambiguous
coin, and look for some mark whereby to assign it to one only of
the classes.   *I am told to strike it*, and if it rings clearly it is
silver.   This enables me not only to place the coin, but it also
advances my knowledge of silver coins ; in this latter respect, it
is a remaking of my judgment of identity with reference
to this class of objects, and is a true induction.   The essential

advance resides in the fact, *not known to me before*, that silver coins " ring clear."

16. The judgment of identity and difference is, therefore, always a universal meaning. It is universal in respect to both its applications to the cases under it. In the first place, a content or meaning judged identical applies universally to the instances of its own recurrence ; it has in this function the force of a judgment

Identity always Universal.

of continuance or persistence. Secondly, it is universal with reference to the particulars that illustrate its general meaning. When I say " this book is from my library," I make a judgment of identity and difference that clearly intends both of these applications. It means that this book is a real persisting thing, always the same and identical, and always different from other books found in my library ; it means also that this is a particular one of the several books that make up my library. The general character of the meaning, from which its universality is an abstraction, extends both to the possible recurrences—the recurrent sameness—of the object, and also to its meaning as a particular in its class.

§ 3. THE INTENT OF VALIDITY : NECESSITY AND GROUND

17. We are now able to set together the shades of meaning that constitute, when taken together, the intent of logical validity.

Validity is

The two great aspects of meaning involved are those covered by the terms universality and dependent relation. In these great aspects of meaning certain more special elements of logical connotation are to be distinguished, in addition to those already treated of.

On the side of universality, we have the transition from the accidental to the essential ; from the empirical pursuit of identities

(1) Univer- sality and

to the recognition of identities as already established ; from the universal of fact to the universal of " necessity." The term necessity is used to introduce a shading of meaning which requires further discussion.

On the side of the relation of dependence, we have again an aspect of meaning that comes into evidence with the rise of necessity. It hits off that aspect of implication which attaches to each whole of a relation when considered as being made up of

(2) Depen- dence or Ground.

related or mutually dependent terms within the whole. It too presupposes the passage of the whole meaning from the stage of accidental and empirical discovery or fact, to that mode of universality which allows the isolation, in a self-contained whole, of the relations involved. In taking up these two modes of meanings, necessity and ground, we are following, therefore, the actual progress of determination from the schematic and problematical into that mode of relatively independent contingency that holds for thought as such. It is necessary to clear up this transition a little more fully before taking up these meanings for direct characterization.

18. If to start with, we simply assume a mode of implication that is universal in the sense of being " necessary," and " grounded " in the sense of showing the contingent relation between its terms, the question arises—how can such an implication come out of the accidental and empirical universals of experience ? Here, of course, we are sharpening for discussion one of the questions of historical theory of knowledge, and seeking to get light upon it from our genetic account of the development of logical meaning.

19. The actual factors in the transition from the mediate and joint control found in the ordinary judgment of experience to that of the exclusive control of reflection as such, are two. One of them is positive, the movement issuing in the common or synnomic force of the judgment ; and the other negative, the **Logical** movement establishing the exhaustion of the class **Necessity.** meaning by limitation. The former justifies the appropriate or common intent of universality—its necessity—the latter its relational character as logical " ground."

We may look at these two factors a little more closely. They constitute the genetic bridge from accidental to essential universals, and thus justify a theory that gives a natural history to the so-called intuitive or à priori principles of thought.

After a description of these meanings, we may go on to inquire into their origin and genetic rôle (below, § 5).

I. *Logical Necessity*. We have already developed [1] the aspect of meaning which issues in logical necessity. It appears in the relation of repetition which answers for all possible relevant cases. The identity of general and particular, in which all instances of recurrent sameness are rendered, is thus *necessary*. We found, it will be remembered, that even cases of singular identity issue, so soon as the point of view of community—the synnomic point of view—is taken up, in a relation of general and particular.

This then is the meaning of logical necessity. It is that aspect

[1] Vol. i. chap. x. sect. 27 f.

of the wholeness of the related meaning wherein it is *only and always what it is for common acceptance* ; whether this be the commonness of repeated experiences in one mind or that of different experiences in different minds. We may accordingly define necessity as that intent of the relation between particular and general in virtue of which but one universal judgment of identity can be used to render all the particulars. As there are no alternative renderings of the identity of the whole, each particular *must in the same sense mean the whole.*

It appears further that this meaning may be considered from two contrasted points of view. As pertaining to the sphere of meanings itself, it is a character of relational force ; it holds **Ground and** of the relations of context, between terms as such. **Cause.** On the other hand, the reference to the sphere of remote existence or control, wherein the whole meaning has its further fulfilment, is equally real ; and the relation considered as a meaning of fact or existence is also found to be necessary. This distinction appears in that currently made between logical dependence or " ground " and material dependence or " cause." The meaning of contingency or dependence has its logical rendering as a relation set up between separate items of meaning ; the relation of cause, on the other hand, is the rendering of the original material relationship that gave the meaning its contingent force in the prelogical stages of knowledge.

20. In brief, logical individuation, looked at in a broad way, is the achievement of an identical content by a process of induction. This process issues, when an exhaustive result is reached, in a meaning set up as a whole with certain general-particular relationships within it. Its isolation as identical releases the meaning from the need of further fulfilment, but it **Necessity** still has the control by which it holds for reflection. **within an** The relationships within the whole, therefore, just by **Inductive** **Whole.** being thus self-contained and " given " for reflection, are universal and necessary. They presuppose only the process of reflection itself by which they are set up for what they are. Alternative issues, or alternative fulfilments are, from the nature of the case, ruled out. It is then a mark of validity as such, that it be in this sense necessary.

21. II. *Ground or " Sufficient Reason."*—There is little more to be said under this heading. The logical ground of a given item of meaning is simply the whole of the relations that may with it make up the content of judgment. It is the logical

rendering of contingence and always has the force attaching to contingent meaning. As rendered in judgment such contingent meaning may now have some further description.

(1) It is always *analytic* from the point of view of the whole ; and from any other point of view it is not logical dependence or ground. If I say " you will catch cold if you walk in the wet grass," I assert a contingent meaning of material dependence or cause ; it becomes one of logical dependence or ground only

Contingent Meaning is Analytic when I make up the whole identical meaning " wet-cold," and find walking-in-wet-grass a case under this universal. The logical dependence consists not in the fact of a cold following upon the antecedent fact of walking when it is wet, but in the universal relation between the general and its illustrative case.

(2) For similar reasons, the meaning of logical dependence or ground is *unquantified* and *unexistential*. After the universal is made up in a judgment of identity, the whole is one of implicit relations valid for reflection ; as such they do not require reference to the sphere of fact. My statement is valid as one of logical ground, whether you walk in the wet grass or not, if it is

and Unquantified an essential universal, wherein both the sorts of intent, cause and ground, are found together. If you care to put the matter to the test of material truth, you may catch cold and so establish the relation of cause ; if not, the meaning still remains valid in the sphere of logical dependence or contingency, once it is established as a universal.[1]

So we might go through the marks of contingent meaning showing that they characterize the relation of logical ground. It is not necessary, however, to take space to do so.   But there is one further point to notice in furtherance of our general discussion. The question arises as to whether or how far the achievement of universal meanings of logical dependence banishes entirely the instrumental or experimental force of the meaning so rendered. It is not the general question of that intent of postulation which finally makes all implication experimental that is here referred to, but a special aspect of that question arising out of our account of induction. Its citation will show the contrast between formal or logical and material dependence.

22. We found that a partial induction may so far establish a

---

[1] *Pace* any exception that may be taken to this particular illustration.

concomitance of A and B as to give a "universal of experience."

Adequate Condition. This means that, so far as experience has gone, there is dependence between the parts of the entire meaning AB. But we then found that the transition from this to an essential universal required the establishing of reciprocal dependence, whereby a universal of identity was reached. It is interesting now to inquire whether this distinction in the material sphere between a *one-sided* contingent relation and a relation of *reciprocal* dependence or cause, holds also for the formal or logical relation of ground.

In the material sphere the two cases are carefully distinguished in current theory. The one is known as the case of " adequate " or " sufficient " conditioning, and the other as that of " necessary " conditioning. Either a flying stone or expanding ice is the sufficient condition of the breaking of the water bottle ; neither is then the essential nor necessary condition. In the **Necessary Condition.** case of logical dependence or ground, however, there is no such distinction. This appears from the fact that logical dependence arises only when the variations of alternative experience are once for all removed. The meaning is one of logical dependence only when a universal identity is set up in the whole meaning ; its illustrative cases are only those that show just the connection judged universal. It follows that the sorts of dependence recognized as logical and described in the following chapter on inference are all of the essential or necessary type. That is, logical relation and logical grounding have always the intent of necessity. It is only in other characters than that of relation, that propositions can express uncertainty. Both " conditional " and " disjunctive " contents are individuated as necessarily what they are.

23. This does not mean, however, that an alternative, disjunctive, or otherwise indefinite meaning may not be used in the judgment as one of its terms. Any meaning whatever may be so used. But in that case the relation of dependence holds as between it as a single term or proposition and its subject or **One Term may be indefinite.** predicate term. The B, that is, of the relation " B if A," may be itself any sort of a meaning, such as " x or y." For example, " either birds or beasts suit my appetite for game," " you will catch cold if you walk on the grass, unless you change your shoes." In each of these one term of the relation is in some respect alternative, but the relation itself is assertorial and necessary.

§ 4. CLASSIFICATION, ORDINATION, AND DEFINITION

24. The general mode of identity and difference issues in
" classification." The class is always, so far as it is logical, an
identical meaning, considered in its general aspect. Genetically
the class meaning is derived from the more practical sortings and
assignments of the prelogical treatment of contents, and has its
fundamental motive in the possibilities of effectively handling
The Class. such contents in groups or masses.[1] When the function
of generalization arises, the details or particulars are
rendered as cases within the general meaning or class. There are,
however, two ways of looking at the matter of classification
suggested by our present method of inquiry and also pertinent
to it.

A class may be any meaning individuated, as has just been
said, as content of a judgment of identity. The judgment is
An Identical not only inclusive of the cases within the class, but
Meaning. also exclusive or limitative with reference to other
and ineligible cases. It establishes distinctions within the body
of contents ; it is a matter of logical individuation. But there
is the further aspect of control, of reference to a sphere of existence.
The "identity *and* difference" of the logical succeeds the "identity
in difference " of the material ; and the question arises as
to the possible degree of coincidence of logical and material
classes.

25. It is evident that the general distinction between the
logical and the material holds here as in the matter of contingence. The reflective relation of contingence once established,
needing no reference nor control other than the identities of
reflective meaning, having no requirement of material truth,
Logical and there is no limit to the play of logical classification.
Material Any line of division or cross-division may be pursued
Classes. under the interest of its own pursuit alone, and classes
may be made for logical purposes which find no actual confirmation in nature. The demands of logical criteria as such
once fulfilled, the possibility of including cases in the identity of
a whole judgmental subject-matter once established—the processes of abstraction and classification move freely on.

On the other hand, material classification is a matter of
actual generality based on cases cited as particulars. The
classifications of natural history are made out by patient research

---

[1] See vol. i. chap. viii. on " Individuation."

into the actual concomitances and differences found in nature. So it is in all inductive research. These classes remain fixed as real identities and differences whatever sequences of logical validity and classifications of logical meaning may be formed upon them.

In view of this distinction we may say that all accidental or empirical universal judgments issue in material classes ; and **Empirical** these classes change and remake themselves in the **Judgments** progress of discovery. On the other hand, the essential **material** universals deal with established relations of dependence within the whole meaning ; and so long as the rules of the constitution of the whole are not infringed, rearrangements and reclassifications may take place according to the motive or interest at work. For this reason, the term " formal " is applied to the logical as such, as opposed to the " material."

26. The same thing may be said of " ordination "—the systematic arrangement of classes with respect to generality. From the point of view of existence the order is one of " quantity," **Ordination** the relative inclusion of class by class, or the taking in by one class of some or all of the individuals of another. The arrangement of genera, families, species, and varieties in natural history illustrates this growth of knowledge in ordination. The classes are said to show " sub-ordination," " super-ordination," etc., with reference to one another.

The ordination of logical meanings, however, is not so restricted. Given a universal judgment of identity, the relationships become a matter of manipulation as the special interest may dictate.

27. In definition, too, we have to make a corresponding distinction. A logical definition is one that arranges the content of an identical judgment so as to exhaust its relational meanings by ordination.

For example, the genus " man " gives the sphere of widest and most general control ; the species " mixed-blood," the lower class, subordinated under the former but super-ordinated with reference to the particular; and the **Definition and** particular, " American mulatto," is defined, with **Description** its differentiae from other particulars. If " Caucasian " blood be the differentia, then " a man of mixed negro and Caucasian blood " defines the term " American mulatto."

This may be interpreted as a definition that embodies an essential universal; it may be called the definition of a meaning, rather than the description of an object. " The mulatto is a man of negro-white blood " may be taken not to describe a class established on the basis of certain empirical marks usually found in men of mixed negro and white parentage ; but to apply strictly and only to cases in which such parentage is already known, no matter what the further associated marks may be. In this latter case, it is a definition of an essential and identical logical meaning. The " description," on the contrary, is merely a summary of empirical marks.

The logical definition is a judgment in *quality*, embodying identity and difference, affirmation and negation ; while the other case, the description, merely summarizes experience, and is a judgment in *quantity*. The latter generalizes cases on the basis of agreements and differences so far as experience has gone.

So also of the corresponding distinctions between material and logical classification and ordination : the former, the material, is in each case quantitative ; it is so far liable to revision in the growth of experience ; the latter is qualitative and not so liable.

In all these cases, also, the " material " is *synthetic*, so far as it contemplates or allows further accretion of meaning to the whole ; the " formal " is *analytic* of a whole meaning already made up.

§ 5.   REASONABLENESS AND REASON

28. We have now briefly indicated the nature of the transition whereby the material bond is loosened from a meaning, whereby its control as " true " yields to its control as simply " valid," whereby, in brief, it becomes *an implication for reflection*, and is no longer a *supposition awaiting confirmation*. It remains to explain and justify it.

We are now to approach a problem which in an important sense focusses our discussions of this mode of psychic life. This problem, isolated already in our preceding discussions, is a prominent one in epistemology. It is the problem of uni- The Question versality or necessity considered as being " absolute," of Validity " unconditional," " non-experiential," " à priori," etc. How can knowledge that is " reasonable " as material content turn itself into a judgment of " reason," whose mere statement is sufficient to carry universal and necessary force ?

However this problem may be put in the various theories of knowledge, it is, I contend, *one of control*. The distinguishing intent of validity in a relational content, is that of ground or implication within a whole meaning ; that of truth, experience, confirmation, is one of the acceptance or rejection of the whole meaning in some sphere in which it is put together and controlled. There is in all knowledge the germ of this contrast. The relational " what " is to be distinguished from the existential " where." So the question may be put broadly in this way : how can a system of implications, relations, elucidations— **one of** whatever term we apply to the relational content set **Control** up in a judgment or system of judgments—how can this become so detached from its sphere, from all spheres of empirical or material existence, as to float alone, so to speak, on the surface of reflection ? Or put a little differently—how can a body of relational meanings be set up in the control of reflection alone, as a necessary and self-maintaining system, requiring no appeal to a sphere of existence ? Or again—how can a given relation be valid for thought, whether or no there be any sphere of reference in which it is found to be true or false ?

We may reply by first showing in what sense it is thus cut off from the spheres of existence, and how it gets its validity, and then pointing out the sense in which it is not cut off from all such spheres.

29. The case seems to be plain, indeed, from the side of the actual process. The process of induction is one that secures the recognition of meanings as wholes, as identities, sustaining within their structure the relation of terms which their control in a given sphere acknowledges. There are, therefore, in every **Universals** case two chief elements of meaning recognized, the **under** related contents and the control sphere. When we **Empirical** **Control** say " this or that holds " in experience, we mean that it holds so far as the sort of experience presupposed confirms it. The empirical element then is resident not in the relationship as set up, *but in the confirmation or control of the relation* established by occurrences in this or that sphere. It would follow, then, that if this further reference *were no longer made*, if the experimental test were not invoked, there would be no further question of confirmation or of lack of confirmation, of acceptance or of rejection. The relation of terms would stand for just *what it is made up as being* in the body of reflective meaning. The critical question then would be—is there any experience that, by its own movement, cuts off the need of further reference to fact, and establishes a contingent meaning as universal *per se* ?

We have already pointed out that this requirement is suggested by the movement of reflection which asserts what has been called its own synnomic control over the contents of thought. The context of reflection is normally held under mediate control ; not only acknowledgment but also confirmation are there, and both assert themselves in and through the same related context. The further question is suggested—can reflection dispense, in any case whatever, with the factor of confirmation or empirical control ?

We have found in our analysis of induction above a distinction which will serve us here.   There is the case in which the relationships are not rounded into a limited and self-contained identical whole—the case in which the intent of disjunction still attaches **The Essential** to the contents set up.   This we have seen in the pre- **Universal.** ceding paragraph to be the case in the first two stages of induction, which give recurrent sameness or "agreement," and concomitant variation or empirical " difference." But there is the   third   and   further   stage in which the control required for the development of a disjunctive content is no longer invoked : when the limitation of the sphere of reference through exhaustion establishes a mode of control immanent in the judgment itself.   The meaning "A is not non-B " is the typical one.   It is simply a meaning of exhaustion.   This   requires   and   can have *no further confirmation from fact.*   The pendulum has swung over to the bare requirements of formal control, and a judgment of identity of the contingent and exhaustive type is constituted.

In short, what has happened is simply that resort is had merely to the inner sphere of reference whereby the movement of reflection itself becomes the presupposition under which the implication is set up.   This   is   a   sphere   of   self-subsisting relationships, apart from the material references by which their repeated application might be shown.

30. If we are right in depicting the growth of judgmental control as issuing in successive inductions from actual cases, the question then as to whether this process of integration or systematization does finally dispense with further experience, seems to be answered.   There is the case of repugnance arising from the **Universal** growth of two meanings which limit each other and **due to Con-** at the same time exhaust the sphere in which they **tradiction** are together controlled.   For example, the judgment " A is B," rendering the meaning *AB*, becomes a necessary universal so soon as the class *non-B* is developed in a way that

excludes A ; then the judgment " A is not *non-B* " arises. The meaning of disjunction as between the two classes B and *non-B* is resolved for the case of A so soon as experience is of such a character that A *is sometimes found in one class and is incompatible with the other.*

That this state of things may be realized there must be some experience of objects making up the B class, and some experience of objects making up the *non-B* class—both experimental
in   and empirical meanings—and then in addition, some-
Experience. thing about A that is incompatible with the *non-B* class. So we ask, how can this arise ? How can A be incompatible with *non-B* ? Does not this, we may be asked, assume that the *non-B* class is made up in a way to finally exclude A, a matter just as hard to account for as that B should be made up finally to include A ?

In answer to this last question, we have to say that the cases are different, that a meaning may be incompatible with another in the sense of being finally exclusive of it, when finality in the mode of inclusion would require indefinite extension of experience. This we may illustrate further, drawing upon our exposition of the development of prelogical meanings.

31. In the treatment of opposition,[1] we found that a privative meaning simply cuts off a content from everything else—giving the meaning " this and not other." This in turn may develop in either of two ways, usually both.

First, the inclusion of the positive construction may be widened, issuing in an indefinitely enlarged " this," while not changing the indefinite " other " ; whatever " this " may com-
Nature of prise there is always an indefinite " other " besides.
Privation. When such a meaning is taken up in the individuation of thought and rendered by a judgment, there can be no finality or essential universality about it. It suggests what the inductive process does when it proceeds by the methods of agreement and difference only. It simply establishes the meaning " this and not other " as a judgment ; but it is a meaning subject always to further extension with further experience.

But second, we saw also that the development of a privative meaning takes on a different mode when the " other " is itself
It passes into determined, giving the judgment " this and not
Limitation. that," in which both meanings are determined over against each other. Here the essential thing, from the point of

[1] Vol. i. chap. ix. § 4. See also chap. viii. § 9, of this volume.

view of the development of " this," is its limitation by the determinate marks of the " other." In this respect, therefore, the respect in which the limitation is present, the class " this " cannot be further extended, cannot grow by the further inclusion of or encroachment upon the " other " ; for the " other " is determined as a positive construction set over against the " this."

When this meaning in turn is taken up into the logical mode, its character is preserved. The opposition between " this " and " other " becomes not simply, as in the earlier case, that between *B* and " whatever-is-not-yet-determined " ; but between *B* and " what-is-definitely-determined-as-*not-B*." The marks, therefore, upon which the judgment of identity of *B* proceeds are those precisely by which the *not-B* class is also established.

In this case, too, the two classes *B* and *not-B* stand over against each other as exhausting the sphere in which the entire determination proceeds. For it is a further result of our earlier study that unless two determinations are in the same control, being, that is, meanings that may be rendered as a whole within **Exhaustion.** a given control, there can arise no opposition between them at all. It has been pointed out that judgments connecting such disparate spheres as the physical and the psychic, the semblant and the real, the humorous and the serious, do not have meaning, because the terms of each pair are irrelevant to each other. Only when a possible whole meaning can be made up with a unified control, to which the whole is referable by the act of judgment—only then is there an intelligible judgment.

The conclusion is now irresistible. If the *B* and *not-B* classes are in opposition in a final and necessary way, and if they exhaust between them the sphere in which *A* also falls, *then A, if not in one, is entirely, finally, and necessarily in the other.*

32. We find, therefore, in our storehouse of prelogical meanings, the stones for our present structure. The motives involved are two, both of which are familiar to us—both found to be requisite to the development of opposition. It is in the recognition of these that we laid the foundation for an adequate theory of negative meaning. They are—to put them more succinctly—first, the finality of a judgment of limitative opposition, rendered as logical contradiction,[1] and, second, the exhaustion of the sphere in which such a judgment of limitation

---

[1] In logical terms we may say that the intent of quantity (how many) passes over into that of quality (what and what *not*) and that material description passes over into logical definition.

is rendered. Given a meaning so constituted that both these motives are in force, then the intent of essential universality is present.

To take a case, suppose the opposition in meanings between " spoon and fork " to a child is established by the process of limitation. The early meaning " spoon " was something to lift milk with ; it was " this," and whatever did not lift milk was " other." The meaning " this and not other " was therefore privative, in the absence of any positive further determination of " fork." But with the practical necessities of the child, the meaning spoon grows in two ways ; first, it includes other suitable milk-lifting things, say " hand " and " knife "; and second, the dif-

Illustration. ferentiation of the " fork " as being of such a character that it is not available for the purpose (having tines instead of a bowl). The " fork " meaning is thus determined as once for all " not-spoon," by reason of the opposition of its marks—the tines—to what is essential in the determination of " spoon." There is then a judgment of limitation as between the " spoon " and the " not-spoon " class, the latter established by the positive determination of " fork."

Again " spoon " and " fork " are exhaustive meanings, so far as determination within the control established by the common use of the utensil for eating is concerned—one will serve when the other will not. That is, the class or control reference is exhausted between them. So both our requisites, limitation and exhaustion, are fulfilled.

Now the result. Given any new utensil of unusual shape, but in general eligible for processes of eating, the question arises as to the conditions of its use. The child determines it, in view of its shape, *as not a fork* ; but it serves the purpose of his eating ; there is then only one possible meaning for him to render in judgment, *it is a spoon*. This judgment is universal and necessary ; it is his intent and meaning that whatever eating utensil is not a fork *is and must* be a spoon.

33. We may put the whole truth then in the following sentence :—*Any meaning which is excluded from one of two mutually limitative and jointly exhaustive classes is judged to belong universally and necessarily to the other.*

We find, therefore, the foundation of the judgment of universal and essential identity in contradiction present within an exhausted whole of controlled meaning.

The case may be summed up in terms of what we have already

described as the "sameness" and "otherness" of the prelogical modes, when made matter of judgments of "identity" and "difference" in the logical. The type of sameness with otherness which gives the relationship of difference is that of two separately motived constructions each proceeding by limitation of the other, within the grasp of a common control process. The whole relationship is constituted in a sphere in which both are to be sought ; but each is in its own way set up with a restricted meaning within the whole. When the two limit each other we have what we had occasion to call "exclusive opposition" in the prelogical modes; it becomes "contradiction" when rendered in judgment. In contrast with it, we have the difference of two meanings, still controlled within the same whole, but not limiting or exclusive of each other. These are not contradictory but in some sense "consistent," with each other. We may, therefore, after certain concluding remarks, pass on to consider the two concepts of Contradiction and Consistency.

Exclusive Opposition becomes Contradiction.

34. The process of reaching a judgment of "reason," we now see, is not a new or strange feat. It is the legitimate outcome of empirical "reasonableness." Given an experience of exhaustion yielding a judgment of identity and difference, then the abstract rendering of this relation as a content of thought is only another simple act of logical recognition and individuation. The relation of necessity means the fact of exhaustion, but the fact also means only the relation. So the great mystery of the "essential universal" reduces itself to the act of judgment whereby *anything is not only what it is, but also not anything else or not what it is not.*

For example, the judgment *man is articulate* reached by induction, as explained above, is an "accidental universal" as long as it does not exhaust the natural universe by an established limitation. But as soon as such an exhaustion is established, or as soon as the term is *defined* as if there were such an exhaustion, it becomes an "essential universal." The judgment merely renders the relation of exhaustion, whereby man is of necessity and always not a non-articulate creature.

And it is not a mystery—this rise of the self-affirming universal of thought. It is just what occurs also in favour of external control processes when universal physical laws, such as cause, are set up. As a formulation for the world of fact, "cause and effect" is an abstraction from the actual control processes of the "external" world. This abstraction detaches these processes entirely from those of mind, and rubs out all suggestion of freedom, choice, acknowledgment, assertion, etc., by which the purity of the mechanical ideal of control would be impaired. So on the side of reflection when the whole body of meanings falls apart in this great dualism of spheres. Reflection, as inner control over contents related in judgment, becomes in its turn competent and self-legislating. It makes its own rule of identity its presupposition.

§ 6. Contradiction and Consistency

35. In logical contradiction we have the flowering of those original stems whose growth makes mental development a controlled and progressive process. In another place, I have intimated that there is no reason, in the nature of presentation—apart from motor reactions that organize them [1]—that contents should contradict each other or be inconsistent. Why should not two presented contents of any description be present together, as well as successively, if the conditions of organic stimulation allow? In certain modes of process in which the limitations set by this or that control are removed, there is no such thing as contradiction or inconsistency in contents that otherwise are so. There is the play of images, the license of semblance, the flow of *disjecta membra* of mental things, functions in which the requirements of consistency are not in force. Furthermore, there are the separations of different control spheres which we simply accept, not attempting to make connections between them. The contents are not relevant to each other; but there is no cry of inconsistency or contradiction. Virtue has no specific gravity, but I do not say that these meanings are inconsistent or contradictory. Two and two may quite acceptably make five in the realm of play.

In fact, there are three cases of relative detachment of contents, already given in the prelogical growth of meanings, which judgment conforms to and ratifies. First, there is the fugitive or uncontrolled, that which is so far a detached and unrelated item that it has no further development in connection with anything. This we may read off as not available for judg-

Presentations are not Contradictory

---

[1] *Mental Development*, chap. ix. § 1, in which the positive side of the process of motor assimilation or synergy underlying Identity and Sufficient Reason, is worked out; also *Development and Evolution*, chap. xvii., p. 260 and the context, where the organizing rôle of the attention is pointed out.

ments of relation except as just the detachment itself is acknowledged.[1]   Then, second, there is the relatively irrelevant, the relation of difference established between those worlds of fact or confirmation that do not intrude upon each other.   These are relatively independent spheres, in which different manifestations

Relevancy and Irrelevancy.   of the interplay of inner and outer factors of control are shown.   As between such spheres, the relationship of contents is unintelligible and meaningless, and " irrelevant " is the best term by which to render it.   This simply means that in the normal developments of these spheres, there are no larger control processes whereby relationships between the groups or classes themselves could be established. Third, we come to the contents set up within the same control, but individuated further as distinct classes, sub-classes, or individuals.   Here there is the possibility of alternative determination, of selective moulding of the material, of giving issue to what is indeterminate ; and this accounts for the rivalries and limitations that lead to exclusion and contradiction.   It is an affair of organization by disposition, interest, and activity as contrasted with mere presentation aggregates and complications of data.

36. As we have seen, the actual issue in every case is a determination of presented elements *under a control*, the control giving the resulting individuation or unit meaning.   This control always involves the organization or synergy of active dispositional processes embodying the interest or purpose of the moment. This we have already seen in sufficient detail in the theory of the early determination of objects.[2]   Be the relatively given datum, the objective content, what it may, still the demarcation and limitation of it in individual form and its setting in a system of units usable in the activities of the mental life—this is a matter

Contradiction is lack of Synergy.   of its being taken up for special treatment and use in the nets of more or less restricted adjustment processes. We have already illustrated the great types of such " synergy " in the analysis of the attention.   The grosser concentration processes select a whole meaning, the more refined designate its class, and the special co-ordinations in this or that case minister further to the individuation of the single thing. The one whole meaning thus becomes, by restriction and limita-

[1] The judgment by which such an item is classed as " inner " and so rendered as a logical meaning.   When so treated, it loses its detachment, however, by being referred to the specific sphere of the " inner."

[2] Vol. i. chap. iii. §§ 1f, and chap. vii. §§ 1f.

tion, a meaning in a larger sphere of control, occupying its special place in that control, and having its individual value for recognition and action.

This has its negative side in the fact that the adjustment processes are thus set upon contents that are specific, concrete, and mutually limitative. The control of an object as internal or psychic, is as definite and limited as is the control of the physical thing in its peculiar world. And the lines of development whereby these limitations and exclusions are established are rooted in the very mechanism of cognitive development itself.

37. If we look upon " contradiction," therefore, as the outcome of that restricted and limited individuation of objects which the development of positive meanings requires, then " consistency " may be looked upon as the obverse aspect of the same individuation processes. The only case of " inconsistency " is " contradiction." The various differences arising in the progressive determination of objects are not among themselves inconsistent, if they do not give rise to contradiction. Consistency may be looked upon, indeed, as relative unity and difference within the one control. It gives in all cases a meaning which is *not incapable of construction as a whole*, seeing that no element of contradiction is developed in it. At the same time, like the inconsistent, it does not take in the irrelevant, which is suggestive of a relation that has no motive nor meaning.

Consistency is unity and difference.

All the modes of identity and difference, considered above, therefore, save that of actual exclusion, are modes of consistency —subordination, super-ordination, classification, etc. They intend the relative differences of elucidation, grouping, restriction and range, that are possible within the whole identical meaning. Only that which cannot be rendered as a single whole with what is already given, is inconsistent with it and contradictory. The great line of demarcation, therefore, in the logical mode is—as has been urged already—that between wholes of identical meaning. Can two meanings, with all their inner relations, be taken up in the single compass of a new reconstructed whole ? That is the logical question *always*.

Its Modes.

§ 7. IS THE VALID ALWAYS TRUE ?

38. In view of the foregoing we may be asked, does not this dentify consistency or logical validity with truth ?—making it

ultimately dependent upon the reference beyond the inner
relations of the meaning itself ?   It does, in a sense—the sense
that looks to the actual make-up of meanings in a specific control
with the motive of limitation.   But there is an important further
question raised when we consider the body of reflective content
as in so far detached from the original material spheres.   It
will be remembered that we found limitation to be just the motive
that issued in contradiction and so justified the universal and
necessary character of thought.   So the question arises, if contradiction is an affair of material meaning, how can it also be a rule
of mere logical relation as such ?

The reply to this question introduces a consideration that is
of importance in our later discussions and is to receive further
treatment below.   The consideration is this, namely, that the
life of reflection, while thus cut off from certain control spheres,
is still reflection.   It is a process of personal belief, and it knows it.
The Valid is It is never cut off from the sphere of inner control,
believed. from the sphere of the actual movements of belief.
When we say that a matter is one of pure logical consistency or
contradiction, our last word in support of it rests on the *cogency*
of the reasonable and our *inability to believe* the contradictory ;
it must be true also, so far as ratification by judgment as reasonable establishes truth.   But another may say, " what
difference does that make ?—let us accept the contradictory statement, anyhow."   The reply is, " If you do so, you stop all
further acceptances, for this is repugnant to the act of acceptance ;
it fails of belief, which is the presupposition of reflection."
In other words, thought must have the presupposition of its
sphere of function and control.   Denying itself this, it must *postulate other rules of procedure ;* that is, *it must stop being thought,
and turn itself into some other sort of calculus,* from which personal belief is eliminated.

This is to say that reflection in fact cannot dispense with
one of its criteria, the dualism of self and the objects of thought.
There is the The act of belief is a determination of self with reference
knower. to its objects ; it raises the further problem—later
to concern us—of the " Knower and the Known."

39. This may be put in terms of the contents of judgment itself.
If we say that contradiction is material, and that on the basis of
such contradiction alone the isolation of universal and necessary
wholes of implication is made, then we may ask, what of the
further relation of such wholes *amongst themselves* ?   Of course,

the consistency of these wholes or units *inter se* may be estab-
Material lished as they themselves are, by a resort to some
references sphere, external, mental, or other.   But the question
of related
wholes. is, must it be ?   Is there no other way of establishing
it ?   The answer is, no, there is no other way ; for the acceptance
or control of the inner judgment function must be had, and
that is material.   The relation that seems to lack material reference, still has it in the resort to the control of personal belief ;
anything else falls short of that actual acceptance or rejection in
the mind by which the proposed whole of meaning is found
reasonable or the reverse.

This must be true, if we are to have clear notions of reflection, which gives a reconstituted content under mediate control,
within the mental sphere.   Material references of all kinds are
In mediated in it.   With nothing to mediate, it is without
acceptance. content ; with no mediation it is without form.   The
attempt to abstract its formal process from all content, gives only
another and more abstract meaning of the same sort, about
which the same question is again raised.   Personal belief is and
remains the final presupposition of implication as such.[1]   Implication is a system of *accepted relationships of consistency and
contradiction*.

Truth and It is here then that truth and validity meet and
Validity kiss each other.   The true is what finds control and
meet. confirmation in the sphere in which its meaning is made
up ;   the valid is the consistent whole of relations set up by
reflection in a sphere accepted as one of truth.   The valid may
not wait upon truth in a secondary sphere beyond the relations
which have been lifted from their first determination ; but it
must always return into the true through that belief reference
by which reflection itself is controlled.

40. Beyond this, indeed, there are two sorts of meaning ;
Otherwise the truthfulness or acceptableness of reflection
thought is may be discounted in either of two ways.   Either it
fugitive or may be discarded altogether, or it may be rendered

---

[1] It is evident, of course, that this is what writers in the theory of
knowledge have pointed out in various ways : the impossibility of universal
doubting, since doubt presupposes belief : the final reliance on consistency even though all logical content be called mere appearance (Bradley) ; the resort to " immediate acceptance," " primitive beliefs," etc.
Instead of Descartes *cogito ergo sum*, we might say *credens ergo cogito*.
" Beneath Descartes' ' cogito ' there is a deeper ' credo ' " (an annotation
made at this point by Professor Muirhead).

in various vicarious or substitutive ways through acts of *postulation*. In the former case, the course of reflection is uncontrolled, its materials simply float in a void, and if pressed to this conclusion all mental life is fugitive and unreal. For if it does not matter whether you and I accept the principle of consistency, then the direction both of our intercourse and of our personal thought is impossible. Dreams would do as well.

On the other hand, postulates may be resorted to. We may say, let us agree to treat the universal as not universal, the contradictory as consistent, and apply these postulates in lieu of the axioms of believed and satisfying thought. This is possible, the reactions of personal and common belief being alike treated as incidents in the rendering of some mode of " pure," " im-

rests on   personal," or " super-personal thought." But this is
Postulation. then a mode of postulation not of presupposition, and again we reach a calculus to which we cannot apply the term reflection.

While, therefore, the bond of connection between the material and the formal, the content and its control, seems to grow very attenuated, still it is never completely severed. A " thought " that is simply formal *about nothing and by nobody is not thought.* The abstract self-identical and impersonal " thought " of metaphysics is a myth—or at best a postulate ![1] What is taken for valid may not turn out to be true, but it must at least be *taken for true.*

[1] This is in general the defect of the type of theory called "logicism" (see vol. i. chap. i. § 3). It tends to treat logical categories, notably the "universal," as imported into, rather than as rising naturally out of, ordinary experiential process. It abstracts elements of form, reads them back into simpler modes, and so "constitutes" the whole development of knowledge in terms of abstract and essentially static "thought."

Chapter XII

INFERENCE

§ 1. Inference, Inductive and Deductive

WE are now in a position to suggest the general character of "inference" and to point out its principal forms. Since, however, inference is that aspect of implication that largely dispenses with the experimental reference of thought, it will not detain us long.

1. As soon as a whole of implication is isolated from the control **Grounded** conditions which would give it a material reference, **Implication.** it becomes a body of relations having the characters of mutual logical dependence within the whole. Then the processes called "inferential" or "discursive" in formal logic have their freest development. There are two aspects from which the modes of such development may be profitably viewed.

(1) A body of implication is constituted as *a single whole of conceptual meaning.* The processes are those whereby identical wholes are made up as subject-matter of judgment. It follows that the material control of these wholes is not the proper intent of inference ; that is already covered in the process of inductive procedure by which the whole arises as a judgment of identity. If, indeed, the term "inference" be used with reference to such material procedure, as in the phrase "inductive inference," **A single** it should be distinctly marked off from the further **Whole** use of the term "inference" for the elucidation of a body of implication within an identical whole.

We have seen that the inductive processes of discovery, having the motive of "proposal" and synthesis, are in sharp contrast to those motived by accomplished belief—those of implication and analysis ; and it is only with this understanding that we may adopt the current usage, and distinguish the two cases as those of "inductive" and "deductive" inference respectively. Inductive inference, therefore, is the process of the constitution of wholes of meaning in this or that control sphere ; while deductive inference or implication is a movement of thought, whether one of relatively simple inspection or one of relatively detailed elucidation, within the wholes already in some sense grounded or established.[1]

2. (2) The sort of inference just called deductive or discursive arises only when a meaning is set up as universal [2]; that is when **and Universal.** it is so far independent of material support that its implications show their own dependencies and grounds as necessary without further material reference. The " conclusion " is justified by the relations set up in the entire inclusive meaning that embraces the "grounds" or " premises." Given this meaning, then the conclusion must always and necessarily follow.

§ 2. DEDUCTIVE INFERENCE : IMMEDIATE AND MEDIATE

3. Immediate inference is the mode of grounded implication in its simplest form.   It is, in general, the case in which a whole meaning is rendered as explicitly intending certain logical **Immediate simplest form.** dependencies.   It simply states a whole of meaning in its universal intent, in any predicative or linguistic form.   The criterion of such an inference is the fact that no new additional meaning, nothing not already intended in the whole, is added to it in any changed form of statement that may be " inferred " from it.

This may be illustrated by the scheme of logical " opposition " as given in the text-books on formal logic.   The various modes of " opposition " given by immediate inference from the universal proposition A (" all A is B"), are as follows : the " contrary " E follows (" all A is not *non-B* "), also the " contradictory " O (" some A is not *non-B* "), and the " subalternate " I (" some A is B "), all of them variations of predication in quantity and quality. The same meaning, that is, may

---

[1] The use of the term " inference " for both of these has further justification below (sect. 10) where it is pointed out that the inferential factor in induction is really deductive ;   so that after all there is only one mode of inference.

[2] This is formulated in formal logic in the rule that no conclusion follows from two particular *premises*.   But that is true only when particulars are construed in quantity.   A particular judgment may well have universal intent, its quantitative reference being excluded, and so serve as premise to a valid conclusion.   By " universal " here is meant the intent to *apply to all its own cases*, as giving an identical meaning in judgment.

be rendered in such a way as to bring out explicitly any chosen phase of the entire intent.

We may then say of all such immediate inference, within a whole of implication, that it is always an identical and universal meaning, and that the movement is from one to another aspect of the relations of ordination, dependence, etc., present in such a meaning. From the point of view of the whole, the process is always one of elucidation.

4. In the further case, known as " mediate inference," and described variously by the terms " argumentation," " discursive process," " reasoning," etc., the process is substantially the same. It consists typically in the apparent connection or **Mediate** dependence of two or more relatively separate **Inference: the** meanings through their common dependence upon an **Middle Term.** element that enters into both of them. The common element is called the " middle term." The Aristotelian logic is in its entire structure only the systematization of the ways in which this middle term or common element of meaning may mediate wholes otherwise separately individuated. The result is that the assent of the thinker is held with reference to *the entire whole that comprehends both mediated terms*. The essential characters or criteria of such reasoning may be pointed out briefly as follows :

(1) The meaning deductively reached, the " conclusion," is in all cases an accepted implication, an identical judgment. *It intends the whole.*

(2) The validity, cogency, reasonableness of the conclusion, rests entirely upon the presence within the meaning of a body of implications or dependencies now organized as a whole. The movement is one of elucidation within *the given control or belief that gives standing to the whole.*

(3) It is " mediate " in the sense that the " middle term " is common to both premise-meanings ; *it mediates the premises* in which it occurs. Thus the relatively detached concepts of the premises, formerly held as more or less separate and irrelevant, fall together as one content in a new act of judgment.

Any " argument " will do to illustrate this. " The dog will bite for he is fierce " may serve. Put in Aristotelian form it **Argument.** consists of three separate judgments or propositions :

All fierce dogs will bite
This is a fierce dog
Therefore this dog will bite.

Applying our criteria we find (1) that the conclusion is a single identical or conceptual meaning, " this fierce-biting-dog " ; (2) that it is accepted entirely because of the earlier acceptance of the meanings " fierce-biting-dogs " and " this fierce dog " found together within a relevant control ; and (3) that this whole, the " conclusion," arises from the mediation of the " fierce-biting-dog " and " fierce-dog " meanings by the common element of meaning or middle-term " fierce."

Or again, taking a case having less evident material reference —" veracity being a virtue is praiseworthy " : we have—

> All virtue is praiseworthy
> Veracity is a virtue
> Hence veracity is praiseworthy.

The " praiseworthiness " that is universal to " virtue " goes over to the case " veracity " also characterized as " virtue," giving the new single meaning " veracity-virtue-praiseworthy."

§ 3. What is Deductive Inference ?

5. Having thus briefly pointed out the essential movement of deductive process,[1] whether immediate or mediate, as the elucidation of implication within a whole identical meaning, we may ask further questions as to its rôle and function. The first question is as to its relation to the inductive process. Seeing that we have found all discovery, all advance of meaning in a material sense, to be inductive, we may ask whether deduction ever issues in discovery or advances meaning, and if so, in what way.

Does Deduction give Discovery ?

There are two ways in which a body of logical meaning may grow by increments that extend it ; one is that aspect in which such a meaning is synthetic, and the other that in which it is " common," the aspect of " community." It may be well to inquire whether any light falls on the rôle of deductive process from our theories on these points.

As to synthesis, there is, in the first place, the case already pointed out in which two hitherto separate meanings, embodied in the premises, are brought into a new and fruitful connection.

---

[1] In another place, under the heading " conceptual interpretation of the syllogism," I have dwelt more fully upon the essential oneness of the meaning in which the whole process issues (*Handbook of Psychol.* I., *Senses and Intellect*, chap. xiv. § 6).

It would seem to be the function of the middle term to supply
or Synthesis? a link whereby the union of the two in a larger whole becomes possible. Here then there arises an apparent synthesis of the two meanings thus connected.

The case is really similar to that already discussed in the treatment of synthetic judgments.[1] We found, it will be remembered, that a synthesis is not really a logical synthesis, that is, not really a judgment, *until it is accomplished*; it is then that it is constituted a whole for belief, *whose terms are predicable by analysis.* The preliminary joining of meanings together for the
Synthesis may not be logical. purpose of experimentation, giving a "schematic meaning" or assumption, while instrumental to judgment and preliminary to it, is nevertheless not yet a logical meaning. The further testing of some kind whereby the whole, thus experimentally set up, is confirmed, so that it passes into an acceptance or judgment, takes place in a sphere of control *within which the synthetic whole can then be analysed.* This issues in material synthesis or real discovery. The judgment in which it is rendered, however, *is, for the mind that has reached it, now analytic.* This is one case.

6. Contrasted with this we found the case of further "application" in which there is the identification of new cases as illus-
New application of trating a meaning already made up; this meaning is thus given more extended application. In this case, it is evident there is no real growth in the meaning thus applied, no change in its connotation or intension; but only a widening of its application by the further inclusion of particulars. This is another case.

7. Now in what is called deductive process there are notable instances of both these typical cases. The latter result mentioned, that of widening of application, is the one most frequently
the Universal presented by arguments which introduce a middle term. They require a made-up meaning, a given universal premise, and the apparent growth or advance reached by the argument is merely a widening of the application of this meaning through the identification of cases not hitherto recognized as coming under it. There is really no growth in the definitive meaning of the so-called "major premise" or universal. The "minor premise" which introduces a new case and suggests the mark which assures the application of the major, brings with it other characters associated with the same mark or

[1] See chap. ix. § 1.

middle term.   So   the   application   of   the   major   term   is
widened.

For example—

> Machine politicians are all corrupt.
> Mayor X owes his election to the machine.
> Hence Mayor X is corrupt.

Here the universal major premise is the made-up meaning
" corrupt-machine-politicians," and simply by the identification
of " Mayor X " as having marks which bring him under the
class " machine-politicians," he becomes an illustrative case of the
full identical universal meaning ; that is, he is a " corrupt machine
politician." With reference to the meaning that the whole
conveys, there is no advance ; there is simply a new application
to an illustrative case.

8. But it is asked, does not the conclusion give a real advance
with reference to the minor premise ?—has not the meaning
" Mayor X " grown by the discovery of that gentleman's corruptness ? Certainly there is an advance in this respect, *but it is
not secured by the deduction*, which remains merely the recognition
of the eligibility of a new case. The actual material advance
comes in the establishing of the minor premise, " Mayor X is
Material
advance in
the Conclu-
sion. a machine politician " ; for it is only by this statement
which establishes the middle term that the inclusion
of the case among " corrupt " men is mediated. The
element of advance in knowledge, therefore, is not given in the
drawing of the conclusion, but is preliminary to it. And the
whole question of an advance in the content of knowledge by
deductive process leads back to that of the delimitation of what
we are to call deduction. Is deduction something additional
to the establishment of the middle term in the minor premise ?

If we rule out the advance that takes place in the establishment of the minor premise, we may say that deduction is the
recognition and statement of *the ordination of meanings*, with
reference to wider or narrower breadth of the major premise
meaning. It then becomes a process of elucidation of the implications now given in the whole identical meaning embodied in
the universal major.

9. But it may be asked—is the minor premise, which supplies
the middle term, always inductively established ? In answer to
this, three possibilities may be suggested.

First, the minor premise may be itself the result of a deduction.

In that case, this earlier deduction may be again analysed in the same manner, with view to discovering the element of real advance obtained in its minor premise. So it is clear that a chain of deductive arguments, each supplying a premise to the last, would finally lead back to some term that did not require for its acceptance further mediation through a universal; that is, one that was not deductively established.

The Minor Premise: Three cases.

Second, the minor premise may be itself a universal of the essential type—something already given for acceptance apart from processes of confirmation. In that case, the process of deduction seems to be simply the recognition of an overlapping or ordination of made-up meanings. So far as it constitutes an advance, it would be in the recognition of relevancies, coalitions, identities, groupings of meanings within larger wholes of thought. Of this we will speak more fully below.

There is left over, third, the case that serves to explain most argumentative procedure. It consists in the establishing by induction, in the large sense explained—the actual growth of experience through experimentation and identification—of meanings which have elements in common with larger wholes already made up. The result is the subsumption of the cases illustrating the newer and less extensive meaning, the minor term, under the older and more extensive, the major term.

Two Methods of Induction.

10. There is, however, in actual scientific method a reversal of this procedure that is often most profitable. Instead of awaiting the establishment of a minor premise, its truth is assumed or proposed, and a conclusion drawn with view to seeking confirmation of that assumption. The inductive establishing of this conclusion then goes to confirm the hypothesis of the minor premise.[1]

For example—

> Machine politicians are corrupt.
> If Mayor X is a machine politician, he is corrupt.
> He is corrupt, and this supports the surmise that he is a machine politician.

In both these cases, however, that of an inductive and that of a hypothetical minor premise, the real synthesis is, as was pointed out above, that of the making up of a meaning for a

---

[1] The argument called *reductio ad absurdum* illustrates this; the conclusion, found to be false, disproves the hypothetical minor.

Z

judgment, the judgmental conclusion being analytic of this meaning. These cases taken together exhaust the possibilities of advance of knowledge through argumentation.

11. Before leaving induction, however, we may note a point suggested by the use of a hypothetical minor premise as just described. The question comes up, how is this premise constituted ?—what gives it its relevancy and reasonableness ?—why is it fit, or supposed to be fit, to serve ? Only, we may reply, by a tentative and schematic inference, by which a new application of an old meaning is attempted. The very erection of an hypothesis in the logical mode is possible only by an extension of a meaning to a supposititious case ; it is the suggestion of a minor premise to a meaning already entertained, and treated as universal. All induction, then, is in this its first stage—its schematic or assumptive stage—essentially an act of deduction. Its validity is still to be made out by actual testing ; but its constitution as an advance for thought, a movement in meaning, an inference, is deductive.

We find indeed a certain unity now brought into our theory of inference. The one general movement is that of the application of a meaning *treated as universal* to new illustrative cases. In induction, this is done by assumption, schematizing, with appeal to fact for confirmation ; in deduction, it comes of itself through the recognition of the ordinations and subsumptions of meanings which are already largely made up.

This " coming of itself " is what gives deductive inference its peculiar character ; a new judgment simply " comes " from the juxtaposition of its terms. But it is just this that makes such a judgment a case of " application " of the universal, not of revision or extension of it. In induction there is the incubation period, during which the suggested proposition, the proposal, is held subject to confirmation, and the process is seen to be tentative. But in deduction the universal is so " ready for action," so to speak, the trap-door of belief is so poised, that when the unforeseen case, through its common element the middle term, comes forward for whatever reason, the recognition of the identity of the meaning in the new case *is* the fall of the door with a " bang." The tentative reading *as if universal* by which the preliminary proposal is set up for inductive research is equally self-acting ; but it does not seem peculiar, since in that case the actual belief does not occur. In deductive inference there is no reserve, no hesitation, since the very movement by which the view item is brought into the context is also its subordination under the universal.

12. If we say, then, that actual advance or discovery in the material sense is accomplished by induction, and that there is left over only the subsumptions and ordinations of meanings in resulting wholes, then our problem is reduced to the consideration of this process. This, it will be remembered, is the question we adverted to just above in speaking of the combinations of premises both universal.

Here we have what may be called, in a large sense, the *progressive adjustment of logical relevancies.* It would seem to proceed from just those motives that issue in consistencies and contradictions, in relative separations and relative unions of units of meaning, in adjustments made under the lead of dominant interests. If we say that the process called reflection, being a mode of control of contents, individuates its meanings by identification and ordination, by generalization, particularization, etc., then among such wholes all sorts of unforeseen combinations and relevancies must spring up. It may be illustrated at its extreme, in two actual cases, both cited from the domain of fact.

Adjustment of Logical Relevancies.

One case is that of the effect of new information or suggestion, coming through intercourse, reading, etc., on one's body of thoughts. The new information at once stirs up a relevant set of interests, and brings up to revival and resetting a wide ramification of meanings. All sorts of readjustments occur in the contexts of the mind, as selective attention unifies and synergizes its material. New and hitherto unforeseen relations spring up, simply because new juxtapositions appear about a new centre of relevancy. The new " point of view " is taken, a somewhat different and less habitual interest is excited, and contents before disjoined and seemingly irrelevant coalesce, while old unions are dissolved. All of this would seem to reflect simply the play of the inner synthetic process that makes the control of reflection what it is.

Case of getting information.

The other case to be remarked is also one of fact. When we " think hard," as we say, on a topic, we deliberately stir up all sorts and possibilities of relation among our wholes of meaning. We " try it on," we " schematize," we attend all around the topic, that its more recondite bearings may be brought out. All this again effects new juxtapositions, brings out possible middle

terms, puts ordinations to the test, and establishes the limits
Case of "hard of synergy and correlation.   In this, too, we simply
thinking." urge on the inner process of control by thinking hard,
and reap the advantage of seeing it overhaul its own arrange-
ments and dispositions of knowledge.

13. As   contrasted   with   inductive   testing,   the   processes
of argumentation as such would seem to be simply those of
ordination and re-ordination, subsumption and co-ordination,
juxtaposition and mediation, synergy and interference, among
the meanings consciousness has.   It does not introduce new data ;
it only mulls over and makes over the forms of relation.   It
shows the processes proper to the mode, working relatively free
from   intrusion   or   check   from   any further sphere of fact or
control.   It may be described as simply the process of the progressive adjustment of relevancies among logical meanings.

14. The growth of a content through the joint inductive and
deductive processes is that of a constantly enlarging conceptual
meaning.   I can do no better than cite the illustration and
exposition of my earlier discussion, conventional as it is.   The
instance is—

> John is (John) man
> (John) man is (John man) mortal
> hence John is (John man) mortal.

" This simply means that my experience of the reality ' John '
requires that I add to my idea John the marks of man, and the
Growth of   marks of man carry with them the mark mortality.
Conceptual So that my idea John must hereafter carry the marks
Meaning.   of man including the mark mortality.   The process
exhibits the striving of the mind to preserve the identity of conceptions through new experience (cf. Jevons, *Principle of Science,*
p. 66)." [1]

Put in terms of our formula for progression, in which the
sign ((means genetic change or becoming, we have :—

$$A \ ((\ AB$$
$$AB \ ((\ ABC$$
$$\text{that is } A \ ((\ ABC.$$

With this very brief account of the discursive operations we
must perforce be content, not only by reason of limitations of
space, but also of those of topic.   For our topic is " experimental

---

[1] Quoted from *Handbook of Psychol.* I., *Senses and Intellect,* 1st ed.,
1890, p. 302.

logic," and it is just in the relatively detached logical implication, having least apparent material reference, that logic is least experimental. The discursive operations never lose the experimental reference altogether, as we are to show more fully ; but in the theory of formal logic they are treated as if they did. Our treatment on the other hand, having indicated the aspect in which thinking has its purely formal side, must now go on to show that it is not purely formal after all.

It is in that connection also that the character of " community " referred to earlier in this chapter is to have further interpretation.

THE DUALISMS AND LIMITATIONS OF THOUGHT

Chapter XIII

TRUTH AND FALSITY [2]

§ 1. THE MEANING OF CORRECTNESS

1. Our discussion of truth may be considerably abbreviated in view of the preceding genetic discussions ; [3] for the lines of advance converge very plainly to a consistent point of view. It Rise of Con- has become evident that the progress of mind is marked trol Spheres. by the differentiation of control spheres into which the classified and dependable and typical modes of experience fall. All this has been traced in terms of the development of "dualisms." We find certain great psychic dualisms developing and undergoing constant transformation and restatement with the development of the mental life as a whole.

Further, it is simply a necessity of this development of dualism, as between the inner and outer control factors, that there should arise modes of what we have called "conversion." [4] This is necessary since the progress of consciousness is toward setting up its constructions under mediate control, that is as relatively remote from the original experiences with their direct coefficients. The entire development of inner control is, as we

---

[1] Being Part VII of the entire treatise on *Genetic Logic.*

[2] Much of this chapter has already been printed in the *Psychological Review*, July, 1907 (article " On Truth ").

[3] See chap. xi. of vol. i.

[4] Vol. i. chap. iv. §§ 3, 4.

have seen, to secure the more and more independent construction

Conver- of a content of presentation and thought; but it re-
sion. tains its reference back through some process of mediation to the sphere in which it is to find its direct confirmation
again. Images are read as memories and not fancies according as
they are convertible into experiences of the perceptual type. Private experiences make good only as they are convertible in turn
into the corresponding experiences of other persons besides.
Thoughts are true and valid when they find confirmation in
some more direct mode of experience to which they are "true."

We have, therefore, the rise of two modes of meaning: one
that of mediation, and the other that of lack or failure of mediation.

Mediation. The mediation of the mode of thought is that reference
to the further and more direct control which the given
construction requires. The lack or failure of mediation, while
not a negative thing in itself, yet arises from the same motive as
that whose positive requirement is mediation.

2. Now we have found it necessary to recognize at least two
great cases of outright mediation—cases in which the evident
value and rôle of a construction is to present an original control
and conserve its force, at the same time that it is made relatively
remote and mediate. These typical cases are those which we have

Two Cases. already found characterized by "mediate control":
namely, memory, taken in the broad sense of repro-
ductive imagery, and thought. Memory is a context that mediates
perceptual control by actual conversion into it; this we have
found in the three great cases of the physical, the social or
personal, and the merely temporal (the memory of events).[1]
Thought, too, is a context set up in a way that mediates the
control of the sphere from which its materials come, whatever
that may be.

Here we may add, that to deny this character to these two
modes of construction—whatever else we may deny of them—
is to destroy them, as the modes of psychic meaning that they
are. To make a memory inconvertible into direct experience

Memory and is to make it no longer a memory, but a fugitive or
Thought may fanciful image, an illusion, a dream; for such states
be Correct are differentiated from memories just in that they lack
this mediation of the coefficients of perceptual or other simpler
control. The character of memory, then, that makes it what
it is in the actual progression of cognition, is its *correctness*, its

[1] Vol. i. chap. iv.

accuracy, its way of "matching up" with the experiences whose control it mediates.

3. So it is with thoughts.   Their first and essential character, as a system of meanings set up in a mind, is this : they have a content that is not capricious, fugitive, disconnected, but one that mediates the sphere of control from which the contents were drawn.   Thoughts are correct or incorrect, according as they are referable or not to something or other in a world
or incorrect. in which there is a matching with the simpler contents whose control is thus mediated.   The correctness or incorrectness of memories we call their "accuracy" or inaccuracy ; that of thoughts we call their "truth" or falsity.[1]

I use the word "match" deliberately, only to discard it later on for the case of truth, since it is actually applicable to memory, and has suggestions that are valuable throughout.   In memory there is an actual image, a sort of visual or other picture, constructed on the lines of the original perceptual content, and we can often bring it up in mind so definitely that the real thing can be compared with it, and the details actually matched one upon the other.   I know when my memory leaves out a note, when my visual image leaves out a feature, so soon as I have the actual tune or shape reproduced for me, so that I can directly match the two.

In memory, the need of correctness is evident enough.   Action in the larger sense, on the part of the knower, depends upon the accuracy of the image that stands for the actual thing. The individual acts upon the thing ; then he acts similarly on the memory of the thing ; this he can do because the memory has this prime character of *mediating the thing*.

4. Admitting the analogy between the cases of memory and thought, we may then suggest for memory certain questions that are much discussed with reference to thought.   Are the memories, we may ask, correct *because we can act on them* instead
Correctness of on the things, or is the proper account the reverse—
and Action. that we can act on memories instead of the things *because they are correct* ?   In reply, I should say that the latter is the proper way to put the case ; since, while we cannot act successfully on what is not correct, we can establish correctness without implicating the motive to the specific sort of action.   That is to

---

[1] See the distinction of modes of correctness and incorrectness (with table) given in chap. x. sect. 10.

say, granted that action is implicated, and that it is necessarily carried out in actually securing the matching that confirms the correctness, still this is not genetically the motive to the acceptance of the memory item as correct. The same is true of truth, in my opinion, and so it may be well to examine the case of memory more fully here.

Suppose we take a case recently used by others [1] in discussing the question. A man is lost in the woods, and has a " thought " —in this case it would be largely a memory—of the way to get out. Of all the possible plans of direction, turnings, etc., he acts on the one that seems " right." He comes out at his home. Now what has constituted the correctness, or truth, of his plan ? —why is the thought of the situation on which he has acted to be labelled " correct " ? ·

The " action theory "—so to call it briefly—says the plan is true or correct because it has led to successful action : but for his success in getting out, his plan would have been false. The essence of the correctness or truth of the thought or memory is to be found, then, in its being a plan of successful action.

5. But certain difficulties with this are so evident that they " fly up and strike one in the face." Suppose we ask, how the case would have differed if the man had not got home ; would **The Action** he not still have used the thought as a plan of action ? **Theory un-** Yes, it is said, but not successfully. Then the critical **tenable: test** **is correctness** point is not merely the action, but the success of the action. Now what is *the mark of success* of the action ?—how does the man know his action is successful ? The only answer is, *by what he sees* or otherwise finds before him when he recognizes the familiar surroundings ; that is, by *the perceptual experiences* found to be what the thought or memory presented in image. Without this recognition or identification, *action is vain.* The test then is *a perceptual experience fulfilling* [2] *the details of the plan that guided his action.* Instead then of the action establishing or guaranteeing the correctness, it is the correctness alone that justifies the specific form of action. In other words, we are right in our first proposition made just above, namely, that action cannot get to its appropriate goal without the preliminary presumption that the thought that guides it is correct. Accuracy

---

[1] Russell and Dewey, *Journ. of Philos.* III. 599, and IV. 201.

[2] That is, establishing, confirming, realizing, in the sense of giving the same contents *with the perceptual coefficients attached to them.*

of imagery and truthfulness of thought are the conditions of the substitution of these constructions for the original things, which as guides to action they mediate. If the man fails to recognize his home when he sees it, the plan may still be true though to him his action has not been successful.

The "success" necessary, therefore, does not attach to acting thus or so, but to the mediation of the original physical control, for the individual's experience or for a larger social experience with which the individual's normally agrees.

6. Now let us take up the second statement, to wit, that correctness may be established without the motive to specific action. Suppose a schoolboy is put to drawing a map, and draws one that the teacher pronounces correct or truthful, using only the data of his history and geography books, together with verbal hints and instructions from others. Wherein consists the "correctness" of the map ? We are told by the action theory that it is correct or true because one might well act upon such a map, in going say from Baltimore to Washington. Very good, but is this the boy's motive for making this map just what it is in its details ; is this his reason for accepting the details as correct ? Suppose instead of doing what his teacher told him to, he had placed Washington north of Baltimore instead of south. Apart from any experience he has had, any promptings to action on his part, that would do just as well. What then has determined him, what has motived his actual construction in respect to correctness, what has guided and controlled the making of the map ? Evidently the fact that *he did what he was told to do, what all his copies required*, getting what, in other words, *could be converted into experience of a different cognitive order*—in this case into the reported experience of other persons. All this is what we have called " secondary conversion." It accepts the personal control of another person's thought as mediated by one's own present thought. This makes the thing accurate for oneself.

Success is due to Correctness.

Here the successful mediation of a socially common control has established the correctness of the personal thought, apart from any further mediation of the actual physical control in the country represented in the map.

7. Suppose again, instead of making a map, the boy is to give an account of a historical scene, or to narrate a series of past events. Here, as we have seen, the events, the transitive parts of the thought context, are *per se* subject to no further con-

firmation than that given by concurrent testimony.[1] It is the larger social control that mediates the by-gone events as true. The truth is tested by its social acceptability—its corroboration by testimony, written records, etc.—the process of verification

Correctness from Secondary Conversion. being that of secondary conversion into a recondite context of original testimony. In some vague sense, we might say that this could be tested by action; it does have, as all knowledge has, its following, its discharge of active impulses, always proper to the thought; but the motive to the acceptance of the result as correct is not that of doing something or going somewhere, but that of matching the details of one person's thought with those of another's.

We may put this a little differently in order to sharpen the essential issue. To act on a plan is to set up the plan as an end for

Action is means. realization. The action is merely a means to this end. Successful action is action that *reaches the end* set up— no longer as mere presentation, but as fact. Now how is one to know when he gets it ?—certainly this confidence is not given in the mere action, in the means. It comes only in the realization of the thing, the something of fact that the construction represented, the fulfilment that the end prophesied. The correctness, the truth, then, is the *end-realizing character of the presentation set up*.

These points seem to me very plain in the case of the control mediated by memory. I say to you that your memory of this or that is correct or incorrect. Of course, you can use it for practical purposes, to get the original things, if it is correct; and you can take the risk of its not being correct. Your justification in either case resides in your acceptance of its right to mediate a sort of experience called fact, reality, or existence.[2]

---

[1] Apart from the remote possibility of tracing out physical effects— substantive changes—following upon the event.

[2] It may be said in objection that by action is not meant alone the gross activity of going to or handling things, but also those functional processes of attention, etc., by which the presentation is constituted what it is. " What is true " is only another name, it may be said, for " what is," under these determining processes. The point recurs below ; we find the " truth " to be just the " what is " when the " is " is the control in which " the what " is acknowledged. But there our analysis is the same as here (as is anticipated in vol. i. chap. iii.), *i.e.*, we find that the control sphere is determined by coefficients of various sorts of existence and is not resolvable into the motor processes that operate with and upon them. As soon as there is a control meaning at all it is a dualistic or pluralistic control meaning.

8. We may observe, too, before going further with the discussion of truth, that correctness is independent of the mode of origin, and the degree of validity for theory, of the original control meanings thus mediated by conversion processes. However consciousness got the meaning " physical control," and however there arose the mediate controls by which physical and other objects are mediated, still the relative modes remain what they are in their respective progressions. Given a process involving memories, then the entire place and rôle of that mode would be destroyed if there were no conversion for it—no mediation into it of the coefficients already found in the earlier processes. There are in the progress of consciousness ways of returning to a relative immediacy ; this appears in the play and semblant modes ; but the character of such modes is shown just in this to be different from that of memory : their differentiae *do not consist in relative correctness and incorrectness.* They are not held to the original dualisms as memory is. Memory has its justification just in the relative correctness with which it mediates the coefficients belonging to the worlds of fact or existence.

Correctness assumes Controls.

In an important sense this is true also for thought ; it mediates but does not banish dualisms. Yet the processes whereby the mediating control of thought or reflection arises are so complex and their subsequent meanings so autonomous and seemingly independent, that the discussion becomes very much more complicated.

9. Before going on, however, I may point out a distinction that sums up the opposing interpretations suggested above, and shows itself sharply in the two current uses of the term " control." As used in my work, control is any coefficient or character of a content that classifies and delimits it, assigning it to a sphere in which *it is or might be present.* We may say of any presentation that it is or might be present in its proper class or sphere of presence or existence. Now on this view the development of knowledge is by the formation and development of these spheres of control ; and however far away from the original control coefficients a representative or ideal content may be, it still has

Two views of Control.

There is no valid sense in which these coefficients can be called " habits " or " motor complexes " ; for habit belongs at the pole of " inner " as over against external control ; and conflict of habits or of habitual selves is within the personal inner sphere that encompasses them (as in the larger synergetic process of attention).

the meaning that gives to it its assignment to that and no other control. From this point of view knowledge develops within the distinctions of control; there is development of knowledge in idea or thought only as the original controls are mediated by these modes—as we have just seen to be the case with memory.

10. Calling this the theory of *knowledge through control*, there is a variant upon it that may be called the theory of *control through knowledge*—the "control" of action, and through it of experience, by means of the mediating context of thought. This **Knowledge** is, as I understand it, the "control" of the *Studies in* **and Control.** *Logical Theory* and other works of the Chicago school so-called.[1] It is control of a personal sort—considered actively —management or effective handling of the details of experience, through knowledge, reflection, etc. This distinction is, in the sequel, important.[2] Both phenomena are real, "knowledge through control" and "control through knowledge"; but here it may be easily seen that the "control" to the latter theory is the "inner" or personal control of the former—one only of the sorts of control found actual by the present writer. The "control through knowledge" is a concept of the active functional relation between self and its world of experience; that of "knowledge through control" is one of logical or content relation between different modes of experience.

§ 2. WHAT TRUTH IS

11. We may introduce the discussion of the mode of truth as such by asking what would be necessary to constitute an active control process—a mode of action—as the sole criterion or mark of truth, and then ask whether thought or reflection realizes such a requirement. In this way, we throw into relief the differences between the two points of view already spoken of and secure the added interest that comes from having current theories in mind.

If then we ask what would be necessary to banish the requirement of correctness, considered as agreement or correspondence

---

[1] I hope here and below I may not be found to misrepresent these authors. The writers mentioned accept so much that I also hold to, that it seems desirable that we keep on "discussing." My use of the term "control" in the sense given it above goes back to my address on "Selective Thinking," December, 1897.

[2] It is developed in detail in the next chapter.

with some control read as external or foreign to the process, our answer is—it would be simply the banishing of the coefficients of externality. The question then would come back to one which we asked and answered in the first volume of this work—the question as to whether the active dispositional processes could be conceived as entirely making up, and hence as fully fulfilled in, the object as psychically set up, having no coefficients requiring reading as " external." This we found to be unrealizable for consciousness, such as it is ; for the existence both of things of the physical order, and of persons apart from oneself, requires the operation of the motives that mature in the mind-body dualism. In other words, the dualism of existences, as meanings of separate control, forbids a purely active determination of things ; the replica of the things—the image-objects—together with the variations in the correctness of these latter, are meanings that testify to the truth of this. Now, how is it with the higher mediation, that of truth, in which the terms of the dualism are those of reflection or thought ?

It must be admitted that we find here remarkable progress in the sort of mediation which would banish the external control factor, and so tend to reduce all controls finally to one, and that the control of active inner process. This aspect of the development may be spoken of first, before other motives are taken up.

Two great movements are to be noted : one that whereby the control of reflection as mode of inner experience is constituted, and the other that whereby the individual judgment becomes " synnomic " or competent without further control from other persons. Let us look at these two movements in turn.

12. The process whereby thought, functioning in acts of judgment, becomes a mode of mediate control, has already been described. It establishes a heightened and unified consciousness of self, as inner control function, standing in a dualism with all the objects of thought. These objects mediate the inner control which the self in judging exercises over the material it deals with. On the other hand, this inner control process arises by a unification of the more partial inner factors. There is, moreover, a redistribution of the objective meanings also, their resetting as outer pole of the dualism of subject-object. The question now urgent is as to whether the original controls by which the objects of thought were set up and recognized as

Marginal notes:
Action as Criterion of Truth.

Two Movements.

Reflection gives end of Action,

outer, etc., remain in any sense still operative, when the whole context is made one of ideas of thought.

There is, in fact, from the point of view of the personal life-process, no motive that arrests the original control-factors; we cannot say that they are banished. The objects of thought, like those of memory, seem to require fulfilment in fact. Yet we find certain complications now for the first time present. For whereas the objects of memory were in a sense " liftable " from the original things they reported, and were also on occasion actually lifted; yet this was merely incidental to the essential fact that whether thus separated or not, the two series dovetail together, submitting, on occasion, to all sorts of substitutions without confusion.

13. In the redistribution found in reflection there is no such continuity with fact. The mode of inner control through thoughts establishes itself in a much more radical way. The contents are not only " lifted " from things and reconstituted as meanings, but this is done by a mode in which the whole dualism is transferred to the inner world. The dualism is one of conscious reflection. In its mediation of the original existence spheres it sets up its own form of dualism, a new and characteristic **But does not** one. The question at issue now is whether, by becoming **fulfil the end.** a system both of whose terms are within the one inner control, thought loses the intent to refer to spheres of control other than itself. Put in terms of action this would read : granting that the control processes of the inner world are active—motived by purposes, ends, satisfactions, efforts, etc.—can this set of control processes find fulfilment in the mere contents it sets up, or must there still be a recognition of the external ? If the former, then any " truth " attaching to these contents would be derived from their relative worth as fulfilling personal purposes and interests. That is, there would be no necessity of going to a sphere of fact, to any sphere of simpler perceptual or memory process, to secure further fulfilment.

Only on such a supposition, I conceive, can an action theory of truth be put through—or any theory distinctively pragmatic. It would require the elimination of the external meaning of ideas, that is, the loss of any remote control reference. Only if ends were fully fulfilled in thoughts and thoughts had no further meaning than to serve as ends—only in such complete coincidence of thoughts and ends would further reference be unnecessary as corrective or control of either.

Now thought does not accomplish this—no more than does memory. Thoughts do not satisfy purpose ; purpose runs up against hard facts foreign to it. "If wishes were horses the beggars would ride." Interest does not stay with thoughts ; it seeks fulfilments in various external-seeming modes. The thought system mediates these remote controls ; it does not banish them.

14. The struggle of mind, however, to do what the pragmatists attribute to it, is interesting and pathetic. It develops a system of meanings that approximate and personate the completely "lifted" and self-contained.

Yet it cannot finally absorb all contents as only ends of action, completely dominated by processes of inner control, and rest with

Thought becomes Theoretical that. On the contrary, it marks its failure by going to *the diametrically opposite extreme.* It aims to banish dualism of self and things and instead effects the effacement of the self. It develops the neutrality of a purely *theoretical interest, and sets up a theoretically valid system of thoughts* —a system that is valid not because it can be acted upon, nor because it is true to anything else, but because, simply and only because, it is reasonable and self-consistent.

We have seen this motive in operation, and have described it as the prime and only progression proper to thought.[1] Thought is inductive, tentative, experimental, schematic, quantitative, existential, all the while recognizing the necessity of control from fact. But in the very bosom of this recognition of foreign control, it hits upon the contradictions and limitations in the body of its data that motive the validity peculiar to it. The whole,

as Implica- tion. set up as identical and self-consistent, then floats off in the ocean of logical form as such. Its validities take the place of former inductive confirmations ; its relevancies establish themselves within its own body ; its beliefs propagate themselves in the form of syllogistic conclusions ; and a body of implications is born that asserts its right to dispense with any further control than just its own constitution as a system of related meanings.

Now what has happened ? It is clear that something important enough has happened. It would seem that thought, the system of implications, has won a victory. The flow of valid relation would seem to take the place both of the concrete appeal to action, and of its dualistic mess-mate, the matching of thought

---

[1] In chapters x. ff.

by fact in a world of foreign control. Personal interest has become theoretical, and a body of logical validities has arisen to fulfil this personal interest.

15. This movement is analogous to the similar swing of the pendulum—just where we should expect it—in the mode of imagery, where the same two factors work out their respective places on a lower plane. Mere memory is everything, fancy is worthless ; memory is the thing to be interested in,

Analogous to correct Memory. it guarantees correctness and action ; it reports what actually is and must be. Therefore let us rule out preference, personal interest, the vagaries of desire ; let us recognize the " is," and banish the vain " might be." So here also ; thought sets up a system of relations that become valid for it *simply by being linked up together as they are.*

16. *But this is of course not final.* Personal desire, purpose, action, " find themselves " in the very process by which theoretical interest asserts its exclusiveness. A new dualism arises, between the self that thinks and the system of things it thinks about. The selections for action are not annulled even when the dictations of fact seem to be. Thought, even when most abstract, is after all a system of acceptances, beliefs, personal satisfactions ; and the demands of such intent are charged into the abstract forms of the syllogism. A whole world of valuation comes to find its embodiment in the system of thoughts. Thoughts are thus made ends again, just as before, and the external controls, the things of fact, are re-established for the " realization " of these ends.

We have to recognize, therefore, two general aspects of this progression of truth. First, there is the development of validity pure and simple taking the place of the inductive matching and conversion processes of external control. And second,

Two Aspects. there is the persistent return of the control of fact through the demands of action and appreciation in all the matters of concrete life. Both of these are so far irreducible. The satisfaction of active tendencies requires fact, at the same time that the demands of abstract validity tend to mediate truth in a system of static relations.

In short, *if things were different*, if the life of purpose and action did find complete fulfilment in thought, so that thought had no further reference than just this fulfilment, then such a meaning as " truth " would be impossible. The " valid " too

would have no meaning. The "good" then takes their place ;[1]
The True and thought fulfils desire and desire arouses and propagates
the Good. thought. There would be no further question as to the
existence of the desired in any realm other than or beyond thought.
For to suppose such a realm would open just the question of a
sphere other than that of purpose or action, giving something
beyond *for the true to be true to.*

I think we may safely conclude, therefore, in this matter of
the birth of personal judgment as a control mode, that while it
seems to show the possibility of bringing all the objects of thought
under a unifying principle of control by self, and so to subject
the whole content of reflection to the rule of personal action
and purpose, yet it works out differently when we consider the
actual result. Over against the self of control there is developed
a system of implication set up as universal, self-consistent,
and relatively independent of the processes of individual control
and desire. With the growing personalizing of the knowing
process comes the depersonalizing of the content of thought.
And thereupon there arises anew the mode of inner assertion
through purpose and appreciation.

17. From another point of view, also, we reach results of some
interest—the point of view of the "community," the common
meaning, of thoughts, suggested above (sect. 11) as a second
chief topic for our consideration. This introduces a somewhat
neglected but withal important set of considerations.

We found it necessary, it will be remembered, to recognize
as attaching to all judgment two modes of intent both of which
come under the general character of "community"; there is
community in the two senses covered by the statement that the
judgment is a content having both a "by whom" and a "for
Point of whom" force. Whatever is asserted is "synnomic"
view of in that *it intends to be true for everybody* ; and it is also
Community. "syndoxic" in that *it is actually held only by somebody.*
And these two aspects of community are not coincident. One
gives the force of the judgment as *fit for acceptance* ; the other
assigns the *degree of actual prevalence.* One indicates the universality and validity of the implication contained in the whole
meaning ; the other indicates the aggregate or catholic process
that acknowedges this validity.

---

[1] This is explicitly recognized and allowed by James, in his work
Pragmatism (" truth is a good, like health, wealth, etc.," says he). See
the discussion of " What Truth is good for " below, § 6 of this chapter.

Now the question of truth is necessarily a question of truth-to-whom as well as of truth-for-whom ; of acceptance in a social group, as well as of worth for acceptance by any single mind. And the interpretation of the nature of the truthfulness or falsity of a body of implications must not be one that mutilates the full two-fold intent of community.

18. First, then, looking at the synnomic force—the intent for-whom—of a logical content, we find that our description of the state of things requires certain further extensions. The solidifica-tion of the inner control, by which a self is determined over against the objects of thought, goes far to bring about the domi-nance of the selective and active control processes ; especially in cases of the more hypothetical and inductive research. For here the schematic meaning rendered as hypothesis is selected under the lead of personal interest. Allowing this—despite **Truth for whom.** the fact that in the result this tendency yields to that of setting up an independently valid relational content, as remarked just above—allowing, that is, that the pro-cesses of active control are thus greatly emphasized in the individual, still a further question arises as to the determination of the self in these active terms. Is the self that now judges, one of merely individual and private action and purpose ?—is the con-trol of the self-of-reflection in any sense a private control ?

No, it is not. All our work of analysis—and that of recent social psychology—goes to show that the self of judgment is the self of common function, of syndoxic control, of processes so interknit as among individuals that it is reached only by the **Not for the Individual alone.** elimination of personal and private factors. The self of judgment is not the private-self of appreciation and valuation ; that is expressly excluded in the terms whereby judgment is achieved. The factors of inner control are generalized inner data, read back and forth in the dialectic whereby the " socius " arises. All the way along, the child's self is not one that asserts his crude first preference or impression ; it is the disciplined and chastened self that has grown, by continuous processes of secondary conversion, into agreement with others. And the converse process shows the same result : the self that judges legislates its own result, so far as now and here accepted, back into the minds of others, *being obliged to intend it to hold for everybody.*[1]

[1] See chap. vi. §§ 7, 8 (with the diagram in sect. 26) for the discussion of the operation of the social " test."

The result for our theory of truth is clear. Truth is not a matter of merely personal interpretation, whether in terms of action or of cognition. Suppose we remove the factor of external control altogether and say that truth consists in availability of knowledge to minister to action ; still the question comes up, whose action ? Certainly not any individual's action ; this would reduce the " for-whom " to the realm of private preference and impulse, making the true that which ministers to personal gratification in a narrow and private sense. This directly contradicts the requirement of synnomic community. An interpretation in terms of action would require the sort of common function or action that would support and guarantee the intent of universal acceptance.

19. But this it is evident would again, in the larger social whole of meaning, destroy the distinction between true and good. If the truth becomes the socially available, in a pragmatic or utilitarian sense, it is then identified with the social end or good. **Social Action Theory.** What is good in the larger social sphere of welfare is the social end ; and this would then coincide with the true, determined as fulfilment of that end. The same result is thus reached on this construction, as on that stated above in individualistic terms, the determination of truth in terms of good, except that now *both terms are socially controlled.*

This result seems at first blush to be fairly just. The derivation of ethical good from social usage and habit and the reflection of social utility in individual conscience, do seem to result, in the processes of social history, in a correspondence between the accretions to truth and the accretions to good. But the difficulty with it would seem to be precisely that which we found with the similar correspondence between individual good and truth ; the difficulty of eliminating the factor of external control which appears in this case also in the realization of the ends. **Reduces True to Good.** Social or common thought could not of itself *fulfil* the social end : that could only come from "situations" that realized the thought. Social welfare is not—just as individual purpose is not—fulfilled *ipso facto* in the setting up of ends—in this case of common ends. There is still here also the need of converting the social ends set up into actual conditions of social life ; just as there is the corresponding need in the case of the individual's purpose. In other words, while the socially true is always that upon which *social action may go out* ; still there is the *recognition of actual social fact, which may not lend itself to what is desirable in action.*

20. The conclusion, then, is that the recognition of the synnomic character of the judgment function, while broadening out the reference "for-whom" to judgment process generally, does not remove the essential dualism between end and fact.[1] The demands of action are not fulfilled, but only mediated, by the thought context. So too with the coefficients of fact; they are **Fact is only mediated,** but not banished, in a socially available **mediated.** system of thoughts. The system, the entire accepted mass of social judgments, thus *mediates both controls*, the socially inner or synnomic and the external, physical and other,[2] in a new dualism, *that of fact and end*. Truth is still a relative conversion of the contents of social acceptance into the facts of a system of external controls. Socially considered, truth has an existential reference that is *not removed when thought is interpreted in terms of social desiderata*. As of the individualistic formulation, so of the "social": *the true can not be interpreted entirely in terms of the requirements of conduct*.

21. This result is further enforced from the point of view of the other aspect in which all judgment has an intent of "community"—the aspect "by whom," the aspect of relative catholicity.

Catholicity means relative actual *prevalence of acceptance*, or quantity of aggregate belief. It is that aspect in which meaning **Community** is always for a hearer no less than for a speaker, for **to Whom.** further propagation no less than for repeated statement. We have seen that in this aspect, as embodied in the linguistic forms of thought,[3] logical meaning never loses its hypothetical or schematic force; there are always in the social whole individuals still to instruct or convince, always a future of generations yet unborn to whom the linguistic is to be the mode of essential training in competent judgment. What shall we say as to the interpretation of judgmental matter as true, from this point of view?

We have to recognize at once that in this intent of renewed "proposal" to others the meaning lapses from the logical—**Proposal** the fully accepted or "synnomic"—to the prelogical, **Force.** the schematic and personal. That which is not yet accepted is, to the intelligence not yet convinced, problematical

---

[1] This is my line of answer to Professor Moore's attempt to restate the case in "social" terms (see the *Psychological Review*, July, 1907).

[2] The "other" including the other persons who are read as the centres of active and appreciative process.

[3] Above, chap. vi.

and personal. The question then becomes, how can such meanings, set up as suggestion or " proposal," become for that person truth. Evidently only by the processes of confirmation essential in all such cases of the growth of hypothetical proposal into judgments of acceptance. The processes are those of material confirmation, of experiment and induction. But this means a direct resort to those coefficients of control by which fact is established. It is a resort to the sphere in which the hypothesis set up finds its relevant control. The whole affair, then, the method of advance in the matter of diffusion, propagation, of gain in prevalence and catholicity—the process by which more individuals concur in a statement as true—is one that reasserts the external control. I see no escape from this conclusion.[1]

22. It means that the essential process by which relatively catholic acceptance, *by whom*, passes into " synnomic " acceptance *for whom*, a matter absolutely requisite to the availability of judgments for social use—that this process is one of *direct resort to the controls of fact*. It is, once for all, not a resort to the sphere of end or habit.[2] For the assertion at this stage of the individual's

Resort to   purpose or desire would only emphasize the divergence
fact.   that would keep the meaning forever in the selective
and a-synnomic stage of personal preference. Were I to decide every matter placed before me in the line of my personal interest, preference, or habit, the agreements by which common truth and value alike are reached would be impossible. There could be no truth, because there could be no judgment at all in the mode of " synnomic community "—no judgment of that universal import which implicates general agreement.[3]

---

[1] It has been brought against this that in my address on "Selective Thinking " (chap. xvii. of *Development and Evolution*), I made truth " not what is selected because it is true, but what is true because it has been selected." But this does not at all contradict what I now say ; for in that address I explicitly made the " *test of fact* "—the gauntlet of actual external control—part of the process of selection, just as I do here. *Truth is what is selected by the whole experimental judgmental process.*

[2] Except so far as racially or in individual habit, the two factors are concurrent (see the next note).

[3] This is, of course, not to deny that the habits of individuals are in large part common, and that action upon them is successful in mediating truth. But this is the case not because such habit is intrinsic to truth, but because the coefficients that are intrinsic have, all through the development of mind, controlled the formation of habit and moulded it to a common result. Habit becomes and is so far a measure of truth, because it reflects the adjustments of inner to external control.

The consideration of the community-intent of judgment, therefore, reinforces, on both counts, our theory of truth. As synnomic meaning thought is available for action *in so far as it is true*—it is not *true because available for action, either social or individual or both*. Of judgment in the forming, of meaning having a progressive intent " by whom," this is all the more true ; for the content not yet accepted could never be accepted, were the rule of determination anything else than confirmation in the sphere of control or fact in which the " truth " is finally to be acknowledged as open to common inspection.

23. There is, moreover, a further point to observe in the matter of community. It is a point that comes up in connection with catholicity considered as being a motive that recognizes the individuality of the single person. We saw that it is impossible to construe thought entirely from the point of view of the community of synnomic intent, that is, as a body of completely **Truth as** established and once for all given truths. The reason **involving** is that there is always also the intent of further propa-**other** **Individuals** gation and acceptance in a growing social whole. This latter aspect or intent of community must come into its own as well, and this recognizes further judgment process not included in the generalization of the personal attitudes, " for whom," whereby the synnomic meaning was constituted. This involves the singularity of individual judgment. The proposal made to single persons who do not believe is as real as the elucidation to the community of persons who do believe.

Of course, we are not concerned here with the implications of the acknowledgment of single individuals by others ; here we have to inquire only into the effect of such acknowledgment upon the theory of truth. This is shown in two ways that we may now point out.

In the first place, the process of conversion, whereby the proposed meaning passes over into judgment, is one of recognition of personalities. It consists in one's taking their thought as source of supply for one's own. The act of getting social confirmation proceeds always by such recognition of others as resourceful selves, whose knowledge is to be drawn upon. Thus the very **or other judg-** process by which thought is accepted as true implicates **ing Persons.** the recognition of a set of judging selves reaching a common result. The inference is that no theory of truth can stand that does not involve a mode of consciousness not only having the subject-object dualism—myself and what I think about—but also recognizing other individual subjects having a common body of acknowledged objects, or a common body of truths.   There is then a *common presupposition* in the implication of *truth*, but an *individual presupposition* in the implication of *belief*.   Truth is one ; knowers of the truth are many.   The commonness of any item of truth is achieved by the act of judgment ; but the progress of judgment, and with it the extension of truth, implicates *a group of persons individuated as singular selves*.

24.   The second point is that the individuals so implicated are, each for himself, a centre of inner control process ; and so are they all *in their meaning to each*—a set of objects having this character.   The social selves are, therefore, truths in the same **Individuals** sense that any body of contents is.   For me, it is true **are Truths.** that you are Mr. Brown, just as it is true that my hat is white.   The essential singularity of you, as Mr. Brown, resides in the meaning I must give you, of being a self which besides being a true meaning to me, *also has the common fund of true meanings with me*.   The true context of thought as a whole for each then, includes in it all the others who are also reaching the same true context of thought.

Here is a snag upon which instrumentalist theories often strike.[1] The readjustment of " conflicting habits " is depicted as a process of attention, a process of restoring equilibrium of action which, if more than a figure, must be *in the individual*.   And when it is pointed out that this is individualistic, resort is made to the social force of the content and of the social character of the self.[2]   But there is no *social attention*, no process of reconciliation of *socially conflicting wills*, except by a *return to the individual* as a centre of **There is no** action and thought.   This problem, whether set in **social judg-** terms of action (especially) or of thought (no less **ment process** **as such.** finally) must be solved in terms of the individual's experience, however fully it may also implicate common meaning. Either all controls, both other persons and external things *must*

---

[1] See for example A. W. Moore, in *Psychological Review*, July, 1907.

[2] Prof. Moore quotes here my *Social and Ethical Interpretations*.   That work shows the common character of the self-content, but does not for a moment deny the later logical individuation of singular selves.   In my present work I trace out this latter movement.   Moreover I am disposed to agree (and in fact I argued for it in the paper on " Selective Thinking ") that the mechanism of subjective control is, as Mr. Moore claims, that of attention.

be entirely and finally reflected in the common character of individual judgment, *or* thought in the individual *will reassert itself* as a mode of self-notself dualism, which is *also one of personal pluralism*. This latter is the outcome in the mode of thought as such, the mode of truth. The transcendence of personal pluralism by judgment is impossible, since judgment sets up its own dualism of reflection, and *the self of reflection implicates other subject-selves*. The position that objectivity arises only when conflict is not mediated by judgment, and that judgment brings a new immediacy, seems to me flagrantly untrue.[1] For when I judge, I set up and acknowledge a content *as object* over against myself. The dualism of fact and idea is mediated—in the establishing of truth—but just this it is that also erects the further dualism of self-acknowledging and things-acknowledged, together with that other most pregnant dualism of fact and end.

25. The true, then, is simply the body of knowledge *acknowledged as belonging where it does in a consistently controlled context*. The characters of truth are those attaching to the content of judgment as being under mediate control.

Conclusion. The meaning of truth is its intent to mediate the original sphere of existence meaning in which it arose. It is possible and actual, just as any other sort of relative correctness is, wherever there is an original experience having coefficients which the mediating later experience intends and invokes. It is strictly an experiential mode, since the controls which it mediates are those of developing psychic meaning whose growth comes by experiment and induction.

§ 3. FALSITY AND ERROR

26. A word about falsity by way of corollary. Our theory allows us to distinguish the different cases of the reference characteristic of a situation in which truth has its rise. Besides the case already described as that which issues in truth, it is evident that meanings that do not successfully mediate a control, that do not have grounding in a sphere of further fulfilment,

The False not the irrelevant may fail to do so for two distinct reasons. First, the process may be one to which such a reference simply does not attach, one in which the meaning is not relevant to the

---

[1] See the exposition of Miss Adams, *The Aesthetic Experience.* I suppose Miss Adams' is an accredited exposition—and I should say a very clear and able one—of the position of Professor Dewey and his colleagues.

sphere for which it may be artificially suggested. It is not true, for example, that the Matterhorn is praiseworthy. But it is not because the Matterhorn is not what it might be, but because the sphere suggested is one in which the content has no relevancy. This is the case of the absence of truth from mere irrelevancy.

The other case is that of the false. The false is that which is not irrelevant to the control invoked for it, but repellent to it. It involves one or more of those motives of opposition which we have pointed out as giving rise to inconsistency and contra-

but Relevant. diction. There is no question of falsity unless there be the suggested assignment of a content to a positive sphere to which it turns out to be repugnant. This embraces two different modes of the false, corresponding to the two modes, acceptance and affirmation respectively, already distinguished as the true and the valid. When I say, for instance, that man is not immortal, I mean both that I do not accept the concept " immortal man," its establishment in the control of cosmic fact not being made out, and also that I deny the predicate " immortality " to the subject " man," the connection not being logically valid. If we apply the term false to both these cases, we

The Invalid may then distinguish the "untrue " from the " invalid " or " fallacious." The untrue corresponds to the true, being a matter of belief reference to a sphere of existence, and the invalid corresponds to the valid, being a matter of inconsistency of implication or inference.

The concept of error covers both these cases of the false. Error is, however, a term of function rather than content. A false statement arises through a process of mistake or error. We

is also Error. may say that a man is "in error " either when he makes a mistaken judgment of fact, or when he falls into a fallacy of argument. His belief may be misplaced independently of the falsity of the content which he entertains ; for although he entertain what is objectively a true belief, he may reach it by a fallacious or invalid argument.

§ 4. How Truth is Made

27. With this general theory before us, we may gather up in certain concise statements the phases of the genetic process which justify it, and show the making of truth as a psychic meaning. We have in current discussion a variety of words, such as " agreement," " reference," " fulfilment," " grounding,"

"confirmation," "selection," etc., all seeking to express the essen-
The Truth tial way in which a content found true comes to have its
Progression. "true" intent. If our method of genetic exploration of
consciousness be sound, we ought to be able to point out exactly
the factors which are present in the experience involved in the
"truth progression." We have, in fact, in our discussions, all
the data for such an account of the making of truth.

In the first place we should have a care not to make the
relational affirmation of a statement something apart from and
added to its acceptance for belief. We have seen [1] that the
whole meaning is first of all the suggestion of a relationship, a
tentative context set up but not acknowledged. We cannot say
that this tentative proposal or suggestion is either true or false ;
it is a presentation, a hypothesis, a schematic or assumed whole
of meaning. Its establishment is an experimental process, a
trying-on of the suggestion in experience—in ways already
spoken of—and the result has the two separable aspects of
affirmation of the relation in the content, on the one hand, and
acceptance of the whole in a sphere of larger meaning or control,
on the other hand. The modal reference of belief, which is existential, is just what gives the relational implication its security. We
accept something, and by the one act of accepting it the relation
accepted, the "it" or "what," is also established. There are not
two different accounts to be given, therefore, one of the establishment of the relation and the other of its reference to a sphere of
Truth a control. The reference, agreement, correspondence, etc.
single Judg- —whatever one may call it—is not an obscure move-
ment of ment requiring a special explanation ; it is simply that
Acknowledg-
ment. aspect of a meaning experimentally secured and set
up by judgment, that denotes its linkage and assimilation in a
body of controlled contents. The so-called "reference" of truth
to what it represents or agrees with is merely the fact that it has
passed into a judgment of recognition in a larger established
context, and is now so intended, whereas before it was a
merely projected or suggested schema not so assimilated and
assigned to a setting.

The entire question of the making of truth, therefore, resolves
itself into that of the making up of judgments in experience. A
new truth is simply a new item of discovery, a new increment
to the entire body of content judged and acknowledged. To say

---

[1] Cf the diagrams given in chap. viii. § 2, figs. 10, 11.

that it refers to this sphere or that, is simply to say that all such knowledge is determined in this or that great class, controlled in somewhat relative detachment, in the progress of a specific interest. The item, just by its establishment, is in one of these classes and not in another. It is true for the one, untrue for another, irrelevant to a third—only because the actual progress of knowledge shows such divergences and convergences, correlations and irrelevancies in its flow and progress.

For example, I say, " The President is a reformer." Now how and why is this true ? Not because there is a valid relation between the " president " and " reform," which I then somehow by a secondary reference to a standard or sphere or something else find to hold, thus getting an agreement, a correspondence, or what not. Not at all. The truth is simply the establishing, by evidence of whatever kind, of the meaning " president " with the character " reformer "; the judgment of one identical " president," inductively established, is of a " reformer-president." That is the meaning established. The belief in the whole is simply the finding of the whole in the world of control to which such objects as presidents belong. The meaning has passed from the " schematic " or " proposal " stage, from the prelogical un-acknowledged stage, into the logical, judged, accepted stage.

A growing Determination.

28. That is the meaning of what is called " reference." Take any case one please : say the plan of action pursued in getting out of the woods. It is a suggestion, a schema, a proposal, not yet reduced, by proper linkage and relation in the whole of accepted and recognized meaning to which it would be relevant. We say it " refers " to such a sphere or whole. This means that it becomes true when it is assimilated to and integrated in the body of that class of experiences.

Truth as "Reference."

In all such use of the terms " agreement," " correspondence," etc., therefore, what we mean turns upon the fundamental difference between what is still only proposed, suggested, set-up hypothetically, on the one hand, and what is acknowledged as established and believed, in its place and class, on the other hand. And since any item of construction or knowledge may, in the pursuit of this or that interest, be treated in either way, these two grades or modes become generalized and compared. I distinguish between " sea-serpents " and " mermaids " possibly by saying that the sea-serpent is becoming well-attested ; the mermaid remains a pure myth. Now I do not set up standards with reference to which one of these proposed objects fails and

Reference is part of the Meaning.
the other succeeds. There is simply the increase of information, consistently built into the world of physical coefficients and control, which brings the sea-serpent within the range of a judgment of acceptance. The proposal is passing into belief. But the mermaid still rests in the limbo of imagined green seas and siren song. So far as the world of physical existence is concerned, only the sea-serpent is judged *in it* and so judged " true " ; as for the world of sea-mythology, there is an equally valid sense in which the mermaid is true : it is accepted as properly set in the context of that sort of mythological control and contextuation.

With these explanations before us, we find ourselves fully justified in using such phrases as " reference to a sphere," " agreement with " or " correspondence with " existence or reality, " conversion into a different mode," etc. These are comparative terms. The longitudinal " reference " is meant, as between different stages in the progression of meaning. The " truth progression " is simply the movement from proposal to belief, from question to acknowledgment, from assumption to presupposition.

29. The results are of so typical a character, and the intention so clear in all concrete cases, that it is quite natural and right to speak of a " correspondence " or " agreement " of the true with the corresponding reality or with the existing case. By the " reality " here is simply meant the established, the properly set and acknowledged objects, with their relevant connections, controlled as they are in a system. By the case

Truth as "Agreement" or "Correspondence."
whose " correspondence," " agreement," or " truth " is in question is meant the suggested item, the possible relevant and eligible construction, that is not yet reduced to its proper setting and control. While this is in question, there is an uncertainty of outcome that opens the way to all sorts of disagreement, lack of correspondence, irrelevancy, as well as to truth. The ordinary way of saying this is that the suggested thing lacks correspondence with reality, or has not yet made good its agreement with existence.

The question of the reaching of truth then is that of the securing of judgments, that is all ; and surely that is enough. It involves the entire theory of the progress of knowledge in the

All Truth Experimental
logical mode, to which our earlier chapters have been devoted. Our answer to the question then is given in the earlier pages, and none of them can be omitted. We may,

however, isolate the chief features of the process for concise statement, with a view to showing the essentially experimental and selective character of the rise and progress of truth.

30. First, we must say that whatever the true, it has not always been accepted as true, but has been once schematic and
at first, hypothetical. It has been established by a series of experimental processes of the " trial and error " type : by the process of induction, the one method of selective thinking. By this method all items of proposal are submitted to the tests of fact.

The tests of fact are numerous. They are simply the tests of actual assimilation to the mass of meanings already made up in a given control. Facts are simply the objects already established in this set of experiences or in that. Can the new proposal
and Selected join hands with these, be absorbed in the constitution,
as fact, the apperception, of the whole by new judgments of identity, new individuations of accepted meaning ? Such is the test of fact. It is the same in nature, whatever the system of control—physical, social, semblant, mediate, etc. It is always the same. For personal suggestions, the social is a test of fact ; for social suggestions the personal is ; for both, the physical is, and so on.

31. Second, the eligibles, the items brought up to the test, are the likely and seemly proposals. Just here is the racial, no less than the individual limit of eligibility. Mere image contents, *disjecta membra*—the rank " proposals " of the lunatic or the crank, whose judgment is not trained—these are not eligible, and of course they do not succeed. They have every right to try—but they are not selected. The fact is that the new proposal
from eligible is one that is likely ; that is, one that not only suggests
Proposals. an outright scheme of contents of its own, but has already that degree of setting and acceptance that gives its further development the more probability. In psychic terms, it is the earlier meanings, the contents already in their own way given in the modes and functions of life, that come forward for the crown of judgmental recognition. They are already so far relevant ; they have the fitness of their psychic parentage ; they have a " set " toward the place they are later on to occupy. This is the test of " habit " or " reasonableness." It is the candidates already in this sense " fit," that come forward to demonstrate their further fitness in the sphere of fact.

Putting it a little differently, we may say that there is a

platform of established truth ; a mass of personally and socially established meaning, all run through with the classifications and ordinations that earlier experience has justified. These are the worlds of existence and reality, making up the net stock-in-trade of the human seeker for new truth. Progress is by its gradual advance—a movement at the crest of the wave, so to speak. The new proposals are projected from such a platform, and being so far fit already, the new truth they achieve does not break with nor undermine the old.

The circulation, therefore, the progression, that shows the making of truth, is a movement as between these two great and necessary points of relative stability, habit and fact. Given what is established by the tests of habit, this and further readings are " proposed " for the extension of this set of meanings. Given on the other hand, the seeming fact, the raw, crude, brute outer or inner " that," it can become a " what," a thing of acknowledgment and belief, only as it shows its kinship with the established by being also reasonable. The judgment, whether personal or social, must be placated by the appeal to reasonableness, before it can be secured for conviction. Just as the proposal can be secured for confirmed belief only after it has been fitted into the control-context of fact.

§ 5. What the True is True to

32. Another aspect of the meaning of truth, confirmatory of those already mentioned, may be brought out by means of this further dualistic-sounding question—What is it that the true is true to ?—implying that the false is not, while the true is, true to something beyond itself.

Our former remarks indicate the correct answer to this question. The true is true to its own larger and more organized meaning.[1] When something is established as true, it is accepted in a whole meaning. As a single thing it is just and only the one intended ; when it is a particular, it is one of a general class ; when it is general or abstract it is such only in that there are the concrete and particular cases that illustrate the truth of its Truth a whole meaning. It is relevant to its context. What we Meaning. intend, therefore, when we say that there is some-

---

[1] I put to a sixteen-year-old school-girl the question : " What would you say it is that the true is true to ? " After some thought she said— " It is true to itself." " Why ? " " Because the truth is that which doesn't pretend to be anything else." There it is, in a nutshell !

thing to which a truth is true, is that there is a whole of apperceived or organized meaning in which the item, before detached, is now incorporated for our acceptance. The spheres of existence are themselves only certain sorts of experience generalized under their coefficients ; and to put an item into such a sphere can only mean to give it a fuller meaning by breaking down its relative isolation.

While this is correct for the theory of the functional process, it must not prejudice the character of these larger meanings for consciousness itself. We are right in saying that the " what " that truth implicates is a larger and typical whole of organized meaning ; but we must also treasure the results we have secured in our examination of the characters of that meaning. It is just the function of judgment to distinguish between the extent of mere psychic context as presented, and that further determination by which it is accepted or rejected with reference to a control. The coefficients of control are operative and upon them arises the dualism of the self and the external or not-self. The judgment of acceptance or rejection is the reading of a content as inner or outer, as being self or non-self, over and above its reading as being part of the judging person's system of thoughts. The act of reflection distinguishes explicitly between mere *presence to think about,* and *presence as being, besides being thought about.* This is the meaning to consciousness of existence or reality ; and while that too must be psychic and so a part of the whole meaning of the thing thought about ; still the intent of the true is to be something that is not interpreted psychically. To consciousness, to the judgment process itself, there is a " thing " beyond the organized meaning set up ; and the truth is true to this " thing." It is a fact that our subjective analysis will not and cannot expel from the logical mode—this intent of the process of reflection to reach a not-self. Just by the movement by which it becomes competent to judge anything at all, it judges things as apart from itself. [1]

True to its proper Control.

We may leave the matter here for the present ; but the fact should be signalized, that while we may find all so-called " reference " of truth a matter of inner organization of meanings, and in this sense merely an affair in intra-subjective organization,

[1] This matter will be taken up in the epistemological discussions of vol. iii. ; meanwhile the point is argued in my article " Mind and Body from the Genetic Point of View," *Psychological Review*, May, 1903.

still the psychic process itself makes and can make no such interpretation. It is essentially dualistic to the last; the very process
which sets up a self, a thing of inner control, sets up also a
not-self, a foreign control, in polar opposition to the self.

33. The difference between the two points of view, psychic
and logical, is undoubtedly due to the procedure of more
abstract theory whereby it sets out to examine the progression
of meaning in the individual. It finds all these readings of truth,
meaning, etc., subjective and individualistic. But this is not
what the process itself does; it proceeds by assuming and finding, supposing and using, social coefficients all the way through.
Only thus does it come to itself as an individual. Its meanings

It is dualis-
tic not sub-
jective.

are not those of "intra-" but of "inter-subjective"
function. The subjective outcome is therefore a
mutilation of the normal implication-system of judgment, an abstraction of part only—the individual inner control
process—of the whole set of meanings of the mode. It violates—
whatever justification it may have for doing so from other
considerations—that canon [1] of genetic logic which forbids the
isolation of a partial meaning from any mode in a way that
denies the other parts or members of the entire meaning of the
mode. In the sequel we will see that the need of epistemology,
as shown by our genetic results, is the radical purging of philosophy of this taint of subjective individualism.

§ 6. WHAT THE TRUE IS GOOD FOR.

34. Recent sketches that make truth "good for something"
seem to have more value from the further citation and criticism
of theories that make truth "good for nothing." But that
truth is "good for nothing" is hardly held by anybody,
and the strenuous reiteration that it is "good for something"
is about as commonplace and withal innocuous a statement as
psychology or logic can bring itself to take seriously.

The matter becomes worthy of attention only after a great
many distinctions have been made, and the questions that are
really of any vitality have been set in relief. Such distinctions

Truth good
for Some-
thing,

are those as to whether it be truth at large and in
general that is meant, or truth in each and every
detail of the true; whether it be truth to a possible
spectator, or to somebody who contemplates the *Weltall*, or to

---

[1] See vol. i. chap. i. sect. 26, "Canon V."

the individual to whom, for the present moment, the item of truth seems true ; whether again it be " good " in the sense of desirable to some one, or good in the sense of making a difference—a difference that may be undesirable or indifferent as well as desirable in some practical way.   I set forth all these possibilities, for the current writers who are " whooping it up " for " truth that is good for something " vary through this entire gamut of differences, and that with a rare confidence that at bottom they somehow mean the same thing.

35. It is evident that truth as a whole, the system of accredited thoughts, is from every point of view, a very valuable asset. **and for** Biologically judgment is a great adaptive or accommo-**Somebody,** dative function ; psychologically, truth is a great social instrument ; psychically, too, it is never quite free from the instrumental and practical reference, even when its pursuit seems to yield and to be motived only by the satisfaction of its own attainment.   So we may say without fear of contradiction that truth at large, the body of accumulated and accredited beliefs, is a thing of great human worth ; it is undoubtedly a " good."

So, too, of the obverse side of the shield.   It is clear that such worth is " for somebody " ; the biologist, the psychologist, the knower himself—according as the truth is determined from this standpoint or from that.   But here the more subtle distinctions begin to show themselves.

It is to be remembered that truth, being an intent of a body of established thoughts, is truth *to that process by which the thoughts are determined*.   The truth of a set of data to a biologist is not the truth of the same data to the psychologist, nor yet again to individuals of other classes than these.   It is a question of the determining interest, as well as of the given data.   The truth of " the wheels go round," is a different meaning to the observer of a passing bicycle and to the rider of that bicycle.   To the **in particular.** latter it is an intensely practical meaning, a judgment terminating on an immediate practical end ; to the former it is a fact of observation, a matter of no personal concern. To the mathematical theorist, again, the revolution of the wheels suggests a maelstrom of recondite curves, and his truth takes the form of a set of abstruse mathematical formulas whose connection with any further human interest is most remote.

36. We have, then, to consider the particular case, and to respect the type of interest engaged in the determination of this

or that as true. It becomes our part to ask, not as to truth at
Truth for the large or in general, nor as to truth as it might be to
Knower. some other than the perceiver of that truth ; but as to
the truth now set up, accepted, and believed—as to its value or
use to the one by whose process it is here and now truth. It is
vain to ask what it might or might not be to somebody that
hasn't got it ; or in a system in which it is not now found. For
then it might not be truth ; it might lose its force to the sceptic,
for example, or its character to the humorist.

This limits profitable discussion within narrower bounds. If
we admit that any truth is not what it is except as determined
by the mind that finds it true, and that truth may not be worth
what it is when set in a different context ; then what the present
meaning is to the knower himself is the really intelligible thing to
ask about. We can, of course, expand the circle of such determination to the nth power, provided we preserve its type.
That is, we can make the individual perceiver's truth as big as
we please—even to allowing him to have before him an infinite
system of valid implications. We can also consider him at any
stage of development, entertaining all the coincident meanings
that belong to that stage ; but it is essential that truth should
be considered only from that point of view from which it is truth,
and not from some other, from which it is an abstraction, eviscerated of its vitality, and supposed to be truth still, though not
in reality true to any living soul.

37. Now then—what we have is this. Here is a system of
accredited meanings, individuated as universal and identical,
controlled not only in a sphere having definite coefficients, but
also with " community " or common intent for other persons as
well, having its distinctive feature as knowledge in this and this
alone—that it is free from all question, that it is truth and not
hypothesis or assumption. Our question then takes the form :
How does what is true to him to whom it is true, serve, by being
true, as " good for something " to him ?

This is now a vital question. It resolves itself into this :
what motive, what active, volitional, appreciative, emotional,
interest, does truth satisfy or create ? The question of being
" good for something " can have no other meaning ; for " good "
Truth fulfils must mean in some way fulfilling, satisfying, serving
Interest. as end-state or terminus of a movement. When put
in this way the matter falls within our general problem
which deals both with the contents determined, and also with

the types of meaning that those contents embody. And we found the selective meanings, the fulfilments and appreciations to be always present with the recognitive.

This is the question then ; what motive, interest, disposition, does truth satisfy, what selective and appreciative meaning does it fulfil, in the economy of the process that discovers or contemplates it ? In reply we may point out two types of fulfilment—understood in this large sense, the fulfilment that truth is good for—and only two.

38. First, it serves the motive to its own establishment ; and second it serves the motive to its own further " pragmatelic " employment. In other words, it serves as terminus of *the motive to know the what*—the theoretical motive—and it serves the function of *means to any practical or other interest* that may be able so to use it. If we classify all those untheoretical interests, purposes, etc., these affective-conative dispositions as we have before as " uses," then we may say that truth is *good for knowledge, and also*, according to its availability, *good for use*. This is what the term " use " means when we ask, " what is the use of truth ? " ; we mean, *what does the knower do with it besides knowing it ?—what further use does he make of it ?*

It is both end.

We now have the question just where we want it, in order to point the advance in our thought. If we say that the mere knowing of a truth makes of it an end—the end, that is, of the interest of a theoretical sort—and contrast with this the use of truth for some further or remote end—the interest being untheoretical—then in this latter case, *the truth becomes means*. It is taken up in a movement *that goes beyond its mere constitution as truth*, and seeks a further end or fulfilment for which the true serves as means.

and Means,

Here we happen upon a familiar question, and a correlation is established that brings us, on a higher plain, back to considerations familiar to us.

39. The use of a cognitive content for a personal purpose over and above its mere constitution as object, is just what, all the way along, we have called " schematism," and described in various connections, as selective, semblant, appreciative, etc. It is just the movement whereby, all through mental development, a given " schema " of content, so far established under its own control, is selected to play a further rôle as fulfilling a personal interest or purpose not yet fully realized as

to further Ends

part of its meaning. The given meaning is "charged" with the intent to secure a further fulfilment or satisfaction. Now the case is the same, so far as method is concerned, whether the extension aimed at be theoretical or not. For the motive in one case no less than the other is now one of selective reading. The theoretical motive is also a personal one ; and, as we have seen, it is one of the many motives that may work itself out by the assumptive use of an established content of knowledge. Here is then our old and familiar friend the assumption,—the friend that laughs so often behind the schema of the given—and with him we have now again to deal.

The entire question is one of the continued operation of the selective and appreciative motive, now pursuing its development in the mode in which contents are definitely treated as ends, the object being to realize these ends, as personal purposes, by means of the contents already achieved.

In partial answer to this question much of our preceding discussion may be cited. For in the whole movement of development of knowledge by induction, the method has been just what we are now describing. There is the use of given contents experimentally, with trial and error, for the determination of new results. All this is motived by personal interest, but

Truth good for Satisfaction. interest of the theoretical type. So soon, however, as we classify this interest with all the others, with all the personal movements seeking fulfilment and satisfaction, calling the will-to-know one only of the various wills-to-be, then the others come in for treatment along the same lines. And any further distinctions whereby the cases are to be marked off from one another will be in order. Postponing, however, for the present, the consideration of the employment of truth *as means to further ends*,[1] we may now answer the question what truth is good for as follows : *truth is good for appreciation both as end and as means ; as end, it satisfies the motive to know, and as means it satisfies the motive to achieve further ends through knowledge.*

This conclusion may be put in a way that again " takes sides " in the dispute about the " goodness " of truth. If we ask why truth can in this way be a good, a good end or a good means, we have to say—*because it is true.* The fact that it is " good " does not supply its criterion as being true. It must

---

[1] See chap. xiv. §. 2

be true in its own way, in order to have the goodness that attaches to the way of truth. Anything that destroys the purity of the motives by which it is set up as a confirmed and accepted content of judgment, anything that vitiates the neutrality of its proper control in fact, any intrusion of will, appreciation, choice, in order to secure the good, destroys the truth and with it the goodness it subserves. Instead then of saying " truth is true because it is good," we must say " truth is good because it is true."

In other words, the distinction between the true and the good cannot be abolished. The " good" that truth is, is a specific good, attaching to what is in its own nature, the true. To call truth a " good," therefore, while in itself true, is only to conceal or ignore the proper question as to what the truth as a mode of meaning really is.

§ 7.   Truth Relative and Absolute

40. If truth be what we have described it to be, the question may be asked in what sense the antithesis of " relative " and " absolute " is applicable to it ?   What sort or degree of truth would be " relative," as over against another sort or degree called " absolute " ?

Any item of knowledge set up as truth is true, as we have seen, only as it is found in a system of truths. It is woven in a **Truth** context of ideas, and grounded in a control of fact of **relative to** some kind. It is then manifestly always " relative " in respect to the sort of relativity meant by implication in the whole of such a context.

The whole system of implication, moreover, is " relative " to other systems equally set up as identical contents, or held true under other controls. The playful constructions of the drama are relatively true as compared with serious life. The body of relations set up as " true " in fiction, is relative to the facts given in history or actual life. The general presuppositions **other Truths** of a sphere of control hold for the body of implications within that sphere, not as between that and other spheres. Each is then " relative " to the others.

All modes of truth, however, presuppose reflection ; have we not then in the presupposition of reflection a sphere that is not relative to any other ?

This would appear, were it not that the life of reflection is itself one of the spheres in which the control of the true is secured. So far as we deal with something as existing in the mental life so far we ground it in a control. The dualism of self as inner sphere and not-self as external asserts itself. To abolish this dualism, would be to abolish the concept of truth.[1]

41. This may be put in another way, also justified by our earlier discussions. We have shown that a set of implications is never entirely free from further postulation or hypothesis. Even in the deductive systems of meaning we found the reference to further extension, both of content as between different worlds of discourse, and also of " community " as between **and to Pos-** speaker and hearer. The proposal aspect of thought **tulations** is never completely banished; for varying postulates underlie even the most closed system of deductions. If, however, we should admit such a system of strictly given and closed meanings, say a system of *a priori* validity, the validity would then have to be merely that of implication, not that of the grounding that is essential to truth. So we have to say that all truth is in this sense " relative."

42. There is still another way of looking at the matter. We have just seen, and are to see again, that truth is itself not only truth but also fulfilment; that theoretical interest has motives of personal fulfilment, like any other sort of interest. True it stops with just the establishment of truth; but only on the presupposition that the meanings may be used as means to further **Truth a** purposes. The system of truth is then always one **relative** fulfilment among many, and its validities, however **Satisfaction.** final within their own system, are reset as means to further satisfaction no less than to further discovery. In short, there could be no valid truths set up quite apart from personal motives, and these personal motives, making up the personality as a whole, develop in connection with the same context, a mass of further meanings which subsume the truth system under the general requirements of appreciation. These requirements become intent of the system; it must mediate both facts and appreciations. The system as truth cannot be interpreted apart from the whole body of meanings of appreciation, except by mutilating the whole intent.

---

[1] As in supposing a context simply of reflection as such, without any further material reference, inner or outer.

I have raised this point merely for the sake of giving these negative considerations, avoiding, intentionally, the discussion of the term " absolute." In so far as absolute means not-relative, in the sense or senses indicated above, there is no absolute truth. If, taking another turn, we make the question one of " absolute objects "—objects cut off from the knowing process, and existing in some ontological sense—then it is the notion of reality and not that of truth that is in dispute.

§ 8.   THE COMMUNITY AND PERSISTENCE OF TRUTH

43. With the qualifications of the preceding paragraph duly made, we may recognize those elements in the meaning of truth that give it its quasi-finality—its finality for the consciousness in which it is accepted as true. These may be placed under the two characters of community and persistence.

As to its community, its commonness to and for persons, truth as implication is a judgment of finality. It is the character of judgment that it renders synnomic meaning, that is, meaning fit for all who may judge. This is differentiated from other meanings by its universality. Judgment gives a retrospective **As Synnomic** and general rendering of meaning as self-repeating **Truth is final:** and ordered. In its universal intent, every judgment sets up an identical meaning, good for personal judgment and acknowledgment everywhere. The meaning itself that is true then, apart from any question as to truth as an abstract relation, is final for the act of judgment itself.[1]

Its hypothetical intent, however, which reinstates the personal reading and questions the prevalence of the item of predication, is also a matter of " community," but of community as fact or external control. This takes away the finality in respect to universal acceptance or catholicity. We have then in these two **as Catholic** aspects of community the situation that a truth, set **it is not so.** up as true for all, is nevertheless admittedly not accepted by all.

This antinomy has an important bearing in the matter of the acceptance of the self-subsistence or absoluteness of truth ; for it motives *the discovery of the separateness of the given truth from the individual process of acknowledgment of it.* If my judgment delivers a truth as founded in an external system and

---

[1] See chap. iii. § 8, where this point is argued.

hence fit for everybody's acceptance, and nevertheless admits that other persons do not accept it, the further thought is allowed that it *would be the same, and would be still true, if nobody accepted it.*

A line of cleavage thus appears between the knower and the truth he knows, that is to meet us again further on. It is a meaning in the individual consciousness due to *the lack of coincidence of the two modes of community.* In recognizing the fact that truth may imply universal acceptance and still not be able to secure it, we allow that truth is the same whether anybody knows it or not. While the meaning of finality then, what is often called " the claim of truth to be final," is in one respect impaired, in that it is not universally accepted and may be mistaken—in another aspect the movement is the other way : truth hardens into the finality and independence of a closed system. If the true is fit for everybody, and there are those who do not admit its truth, then so much the worse for them. Truth is truth *coelum ruat,* and the sceptic may "go hang"! Mere knowledge of truth becomes a secondary matter ; truth stands in its majesty, with nobody, it may be, to see its perfection ; it is "Thought," with a big T, an absolute principle.

Of course, both interpretations are partial—abstractions from the full intent of truth considered in " community." This will be discussed later on and the actual dualism of the process by which this antinomy arises will be shown to be an unavoidable one. It is one of the movements that show the inability of thought finally to reach either a subjective relativism or an objective absolutism ; that is, in other words, its inability to reach any monism of control at all.

44. Persistence, however, is guaranteed in any case, both by the character of community[1] and also by the coefficients of the control that the particular truth system mediates. What is true persists as part of the content of the sphere in which it is true. The character of its persistence is then a function of the control.

Truth persists as its Control does. It is all covered in the result of our discussion of the rise of judgments of identity. The identical content is a " same " content, and the meaning "same " is either that of the recurrence of the external or that of the continuance of the inner. The truth that finds its control " outer " is recurring truth, to be found when wanted as fact, while any truth that finds control in the " inner " world is internally per-

---

[1] See chap. iii. sects. 56 ff.

sisting in the way of the continuance of the process in which it finds its rise.[1]

[1] An interesting correlation suggests itself when we take the point of view of community in a thorough-going way and consider the contexts established in others' minds as equivalent, for purposes of control, to those of our own organized experience (a point intimated already in several connections and explicitly stated in § 8 of chap. xiv.). If control by others' experience is in type control by fact, a matter of experiment and trial, then the resort to one's own organized knowledge may have the same interpretation. The tests of reasonableness, consistency, etc., then become tests of fact—a control as direct and compelling in the formation of truth as is the social control which is accepted as " external."

Chapter XIV

CONTROL THROUGH KNOWLEDGE

§ 1. The Two Mediations

1. The phrase "control through knowledge"[1] has been suggested in antithesis to "knowledge through control"—the latter being used to designate the processes of discovery as already depicted. We have been dealing with the progression, the advance, of knowledge; and have found that, all the way along, it is a matter of the recognition of a control which is in some sort of opposition, through tests of fact, to mere inner determination or presentation. However, the inner impulse **Knowledge and the two Controls.** to appreciate has been at work still. Knowledge inductively established has also had the intent that the content finally acknowledged should mediate also an inner control. Facts enter as control over ideas; but ideas also mediate relative control of the self over facts.

This is indeed only to say, in the terms of our present distinction, that the end in the case of discovery is just the knowledge, not the further use of that knowledge for remote ends. The knowledge process itself, rid of further purpose, is one of control by fact. But over against this, the mediation of knowledge through control, we find as well a control through knowledge. Not only does the context of reflection mediate a foreign control, whereby knowledge is set up as truth; it also mediates the inner control whereby knowledge becomes means to personal ends. The reference of the context to fact is for verification; its reference to self is for personal fulfilment.

Just what this latter reference means it is now our purpose to inquire. But in so doing it is evident that we go beyond the consideration of truth as such.

2. It is of the utmost importance, in my opinion, that this

---

[1] See chap. xiii. sect. 9. By "knowledge through control" is meant the determination of knowledge or the control of knowledge by resort to fact; while by "control through knowledge" is meant the use of knowledge for purposes of personal or inner control of experience, in varying situations.

distinction should be clearly understood. We may, therefore, seek to sharpen the line of cleavage between the two conceptions —" control of knowledge by facts," and " control over facts or experience through knowledge "—by showing the fundamental way in which certain present day distinctions are based upon its implicit recognition.[1]

Let us take a detached point of view for the consideration of the context of thought or ideas. Here is a context of presentations given to us for interpretation. We may consider it in the greatest detachment simply for itself, as having its own organiza-
Logical point tion and relationships ; so considered it is the content
of view of formal logic. Formal logic strips thought of its references, its implications, both of material truthfulness and also of worth for appreciation. For it, inference is purely a matter of relation, whether or not it be *about* anything true or anything good. There is neutrality as to further intent in both these aspects ; the ideal of such a discipline is pure validity. For it thoughts are subjects and predicates and nothing more.

3. Now it is evident that there are two ways of leaving formal logic behind. So soon as we ask what further meaning may attach to such a system of thoughts, we come upon the two conceptions just distinguished : either the thoughts represent
Instrumental and so mediate a control in which they are true, or
point of view they represent and mediate a mode of appreciation which they fulfil. In the one case, there is a recognition of a world of facts to be acknowledged or extended ; in the other, there is the intent to find worth or value in experience in and through the thoughts. By the mediation of control we have the development of the world of facts, for which the thought is instrumental. Here we have *experimental or instrumental logic*—

[1] I give this of course as my way of describing the difference of view between the theories, not " saddling " it upon any one. I cannot accept Dewey's account of our difference without modification—an account that makes my point of view " epistemological " and his own " logical " (*Journ. of Philos.*, May 9, 1907, p. 255). For while my own is epistemological, recognizing a dualism of self and not-self meanings, his view—although, as having the dualism of idea and fact in view, it can be called logical— as theory of control and reconciliation of the terms of the dualism, it is in its implications also epistemological ; for it implicates control largely of the inner or active sort. It postulates in other words a closed inner process, thus making the entire movement of experience " inner." To do this is, I think, to mutilate thought by banishing the " outer " control, while clinging to the " inner " ; but the position is still epistemological.

the science of the *control of thought by facts, or the extension of knowledge as truth.*

This science may be looked at in two ways according as facts or thoughts are made primary. We may consider the motive to be the *establishment of thought* by appeal to fact, giving "experimental logic," as a method of the proving of thoughts; **for Truth or** or we may consider the motive to be the *establishment of facts* in thought, when we have the science of the development of knowledge as controlled by facts : this is epistemology. We may with confidence write down both instrumental logic and epistemology as sciences of "truth"—the sciences of the *control of thought by facts.* Facts of any world is meant, of course ; and facts are experiences of an original order of control coefficient.

4. But now in contrast to this set of motives and the sciences that issue from them, there is the other great way in which the context of thought has meaning. The neutrality of purely formal logic may be departed from not alone in the way of establishing **for Worth.** truth by the control of thought by facts ; there is the other departure from neutrality found in the intent to fulfil personal purpose and interest. The system of thoughts is now set up not merely for discovery or confirmation ; it is made *means to the fulfilment of ends.* All the selective and purposive motives to individuation come up in the further reading of the context preferentially and so to speak "axiologically." [1] The mediation of thought is now not for control by fact and the embodiment of truth, but for the development of worth. Truth becomes means to satisfaction. All the interests besides the theoretical come into their own ; and the theoretical interest itself passes into a personal and selective motive subordinating its results as means to further ends.

This is what, I take it, such phrases in current discussion as "control of experience," "control of a situation," "dealing with things profitably," "readjusting conflicting habits"—phrases used by the various theorists of the "instrumental" school—really come to. Their emphasis is on the *management* of situations, the *manipulation* of experience, through the use of a context of knowledge. Knowledge enables us to cope with the worlds of things, facts, experiences, situations ; *to get something out of*

---

[1] "Axiology" is a term suggested, I think, by Professor W. M. Urban for the science of *worth-meanings* as predicates, as contrasted with "epistemology" which treats of predicates of fact.

them [1] *;* we use knowledge as means. The inner control factors—habit, attention, disposition, interest, constituting the self—by which the whole movement is motived, are left strangely unexplained by these writers. These are not logical terms ; they are affective-conative meanings of the nature of " intent."

5. This it is evident is the sort of mediation supplied to the factor of inner control by the context set up. The ideas are said to guide conduct, the knowledge to become practical insight, the concrete situation to yield to the interpretation and use that **Thought** thought suggests. All these expressions deal with the **mediates** relation of the reflective to the concrete, of the idea to **inner Control.** the fact ; but as soon as we use the word " control " with reference to it, we see that the " self " of judgment—the selective, purposive, set of factors—is the control that is mediated. By the knowledge, the insight, the facts are interpreted, the judgment guided, the self-factor, whatever its constitution, determined and advanced. There is then the control of facts through knowledge ; but it is in the interest of the inner synergetic process that counts as " self." [2] The motive is the personal one of reaching an end ; a meaning is set up as a desire, a remote worth, and the ideas are accepted as means.

Even the phrase " solving a problem," used so often by these writers, invites this criticism ; for the " solution " of the problem is in terms of " readjusted habit," " successful action," etc., all factors of just what I describe as advancement of " inner control " or " self." Such a " solution " gives, in fact, an expansion of self-feeling, and a sharpened objective plan of *what is true to fact* ; *it is dualistic to the core*.

6. If the disciplines that represent this departure from formal logic—this control of facts through ideas—be called in general " worth-theory," we find again two aspects or points of view from which such disciplines may be developed. The worth **Science of** meanings may be considered as predicates of the truths **Worth,** or facts, giving " Axiology " as recently suggested ; and the relation may be reversed, the thoughts being considered worthful as means to the establishment of gratifying truths.

---

[1] This is the suppressed premise of the whole theory. It substitutes " good " for " true," and fails to recognize the nature of the inner control, the " for whom " the good is " good." As soon as this is allowed, the correlative dualistic term, the " external " control, reappears, bringing in the epistemological problem of truth, or of " knowledge through control."

[2] That is, the organized self, over against impulse, partial habit, etc.

These two disciplines may be distinguished as, first, that of *worths as thoughts*, and second, that of *thoughts as worths*. The latter might well be called " Axionomy," inasmuch as it signalizes the control aspect, the thought being a factor that mediates the subjective control of truths.

The entire group of distinctions is founded on the fundamental one between the two possible controls mediated in the thought context. If the control of fact, then we have " instrumental logic " and " epistemology," the sciences of truth as established by this sort of control ; if control of the inner sort, then we **and those of** have the relative selection and utilization of facts **Truth.** through the mediation of the thought system as means. This gives the sciences of value or worth, " axiology " and " axionomy." These latter cover the whole range of disciplines often called " normative " or " ideal " ; those in which the contrast is made between the facts, the " is," and the ends set up as ideals, the " ought."

We are not to discuss the worth predicates as such ; for despite their interesting characters, they are still logical predicates and require, from our point of view, no special explanation.[1] What we are concerned with, however, is the development of the sort of meaning called above " axionomic," the meanings arising in the control of situations of fact through the worths attaching to the corresponding thoughts—the general theory, that is, of the development of selective meanings or ends, over against theoretical meanings or truths—the theory of " control through knowledge."

§ 2. Truth as Instrument of Inner Control

7. As to the meaning of the relation thus brought out between the two great worlds known as those respectively of " truth " and " worth," different views may be entertained. It may be held that the relation called truth, the relation of idea to fact, displaces the earlier dualisms of external and internal, since the external, now construed as truth, is brought within experience, and the

---

[1] The theory of their make-up and original content is now being worked out by certain authors (see especially W. M. Urban, *Psychological Review*, Jan., March, 1907 ; the same author's forthcoming work, *Valuation : its Processes and Laws*, is the only thorough treatment of the subject in English). Our discussion of these judgments as " assertorial " will be recalled (above, chap. ii. § 5).

problem of epistemology, as representing the "knower-known" **The External** dualism, now disappears. On this view, the whole **made Inner.** process becomes "psychic," in some sense, and the progressions are entirely those of the making over of fact into idea and the reverse, the turning of idea into fact. Thus the problem of logic becomes the fundamental and inclusive one, defined, however, as the problem of the development and meaning of truth.

This position, taken for itself, as representing a way of setting the problem of truth, has all the force of our own discussions behind it. It is true that the problem of truth is one of the conversion and rendering of objective and externally controlled facts as logical and reflective meanings. So far as content is concerned, we may say that all objectified content is capable **Theory true** of such a rendering. But the result would not be **of process.** exclusively in the sense often urged, the control of facts through knowledge ; but the reverse must also hold, the control of knowledge through facts. This latter is the problem we have discussed *in extenso* in our theories of the inductive development of the context of thought as truth. It is a mistake that is very prevalent—to ignore this latter movement, or to see in it merely a way of motiving the more effective use of experience. But to make effective use of experience there must be already a relatively stable body of truth which only the process of development of knowledge under control of fact could secure.

The whole position, indeed, is at best only a partial one, as appears from more profound considerations. We have anticipated our criticism of it on an earlier page, where we found that the pursuit of a neutrally valid system of implications, and of a fixed externally controlled system of truths, were equally impossible. For the establishing of truth is as much a matter of inner acknowledgment as of external fact, of inner reasonableness as of external confirmation, of theoretical interest as of common acceptance ; and the motive of full establishment requires fulfilment as appreciation as well as confirmation as fact.

8. The phrase "control of a situation" reflects, therefore, more adequately than its users seem to realize, the demand that there be a control not given in the mere logical relationships **Truth as** of truth considered as relation of fact and idea. In **Means.** recognition of this need of a genetic view that will not ignore the inner control motive, and the rôle of truth *as means to ends of fulfilment*, another point of view may be suggested.

It would seem reasonable to look upon the fact-idea relation not as one that abolishes the "knower-known" relation, but one that gives it further mediation and refinement. In other words, once start the progression of control on its dualistic career and we should expect to find new modes of adjustment being continually worked out whereby a *modus vivendi*, as between the inner and the outer, might be secured in experience and life. The function of revival, for example, seems to be a means of enabling consciousness to attach a control meaning to presentations in image, in anticipation of the actual objects, and so to **The Sense-** gain the benefit of such anticipation. The sense-**image dual-** image relation, then, is one of differentiation in the **ism as Means.** external control mode in the interest of the inner or adjustment factor. The self of the animal, however crude it may be as to its understanding of the matter, manages a situation better by having images in anticipation of the actual things. The image has then become in so far a "means" to the anticipation and effective handling of the thing. We would not say that the dualism of inner and outer had been abolished when the image comes to stand for the sense-percept ; but we can say that the image has been developed to play a vicarious rôle, *in the interests of the other control factor, the inner*, considered as embodying the motives to action.

9. So it is I think there. The meaning truth is one of substitution. The relation idea-fact is developed, not in the interest of the abolishment of the inner control factor, but of its advancement. The idea may be used vicariously for the fact, and as "means," subsumed under the more remote "end." Just as the animal profits by his memories to become a more competent self in action, so also does the man profit by his thoughts, to become a more competent self in both conduct and understanding.

So all the resources of logical implication become the instruments of the thinker—the self—who is in the midst of the situa-**So of Truth;** tions of life. The "problem" is a problem, a proposal, **it is Means.** to a self ; the adjustment is of a self to a situation ; and the whole set of objective meanings may be used schematically or hypothetically, turned into insight to guide experimentation, made means to the attainment of the ends of interest and fulfilment. The truth system becomes then *true within a selected world*—a theoretical, an ethical, an aesthetic world—which is the large end-universe in which satisfactions are being pursued.

That this is the case appears finally and, I think, conclusively

C C

from certain residual meanings which the other theories—the
theory of control simply within the logical, and that of control
only of the external sort—cannot interpret, but which our present
theory brings into their proper place. These are the meanings
" singular," " private," " privative," " ideal "—all meanings
whose characters have already been pointed out, but
whose final placing in the logical mode we have not
yet attempted. It will be seen, as we proceed, that
their omission has not been from choice, it has been because they
are *actually residual*, in the sense of being left over, after the
implications of the truth-system have been fully worked out.
As we develop their intent, it will be in order to show of each in
what sense it requires *a final dualism in the mode of thought.*

Certain Mean-
ings are
logical.

§ 3. The Logical and the A-logical

10. It should be borne clearly in mind that we have now found
the whole content of cognition submitting to the two great interpretations suggested by the terms means and ends. So far as
the object is set up as a body of implications, having meaning as
valid within the whole, so far it is motived by a theoretical
interest that terminates just upon this body of implications as
such. The reference to the appropriate control is part of its
theoretical intent ; its truth is its own meaning as confirmed and
established. Here knowledge is not means to a further
end ; it is itself end. It gratifies the curiosities, the
interests exploring and prying, the impulses to categorize, assimilate, and digest, to generalize and universalize ; all this is covered
by the term theoretical. The psychic movement itself finds its
fulfilment, its end, just in the discovery and acknowledgment of
a relational context of truth and validity.

Truth as End

But beyond this there is the attribution of further worth,
further instrumental or other worth read into the context of the
established. A further end is seen and aimed at in and through
the knowledge, which thus serves as means to its attainment.
Control through knowledge is purposive, end-serving.

Taking both cases into account, we may then say that all
thought process is motived by purpose—the *purpose either*
to know or to control through knowledge. In this sense all
logical meaning is selective ; it fulfils personal purpose and
interest, be that interest theoretical, on the one hand, or
practical, on the other hand. Having considered the
case of the operation of knowledge for itself, we now turn to the

in two cases.

case of the wider motivation that makes the theoretical only one of the interests and purposes of the mental life, and deals with the subject of end-meanings as such.

11. The more particular question, however, relevant to our own present line of thought is as to whether what we have already seen to be the method of reduction of meanings to a context of thought, making them theoretical ends, can so reduce all meanings —can make all the meanings of appreciation and fulfilment over into meanings of fact and truth, and so establish thought, and with it logic, as the final interpreter and arbiter of the meanings of the psychic life. If we find that the processes of logical rendering, of reduction, of the selective and interest motived meanings to those of relational content—to implication as such—without Can all Mean-residue, then such a system of thought would have ings be reduced to high claim to its traditional place in the rationalistic theoretical? systems of philosophy—claim to be allowed to perform this feat of supreme mediation. The theory of reality would quite properly give high credit to this rational mode, considered as one that could thus interpret all the varied meanings of more partial process, in a single whole both relational and satisfying.

The question then is: does any meaning persist in being a-logical?—not to be exhaustively rendered by acts of judgment?

§ 4. SINGULAR MEANING AS A-LOGICAL

12. Recalling our general descriptions of singular meaning,[1] the main characters of the mode stand out in relief. The singular is a meaning in which an object is individuated as one only, either because it is recognized as being " essentially " so—having marks that resist generalization—or because it alone fulfils the interest which finds it so—having " imported " meaning, beyond the actual marks that make it what it is in open and observable fact.

Now it will be remembered that while the singularity of actual marks seemed, at first, to make a case in which knowledge could not reduce the object to general or universal terms, seeing that The essential these processes have already exhausted themselves Singular upon it before the individuation as singular was a general in "Community" possible, still later on a mode was pointed out,[2] in which such a reduction of essential singularity does take place.

[1] Vol. i. chap. x. §§ 6, 7, also above in this volume.
[2] Above, chap. x. § 6.

We found the interesting character of community, which' is necessary to a judgment of identity, coming in to claim the singular object as a general of recurrence. For the generality of the meaning, its application to different particulars, is secured for the single object by its successive recurrences to one or to different persons. In other words, the reading of the singular object as persistently the same for its successive appearances, is from the point of view of community, exactly the same as that of a general meaning having different particular instances.

The singular meaning is then a general of recurrent experiences, just as the general of different cases is ; the difference is that the one is an occurrence of individuals in one mind, and the other a recurrence of like experiences in either the same or different minds. Experientially considered, there is in each of them alike a variety of particular cases generalized in a larger meaning.

This mode of singularity would seem then to be fairly reduced to logical terms. A logical rendering of the singular has been often simply assumed ; we have been able to discover its method only because we have found community to be an essential character of judgment.[1]

13. But the case is different with singularity of the second, the "imported" type. We have to ask of this, in turn, whether there is any way in which a judgment can render this mode of **But not** singularity in general and universal terms. In fact there is no way, and this sort of singularity remains over as a residual mode of meaning, after the most exhaustive operations of thought upon the object.

For when we ask how thought could render such a meaning, we find only two possible answers. It might render it as a fact, that is as being true of the object found singular, or as a proposal, a suggestion, a selective meaning. That is, when I say to you "none other such " I mean either to say something that you might confirm, reaching the same result with me, or **with import** to ask you to accept my experience of appreciation, in **ed singularity** an essentially private mode, which could not be directly confirmed. In the former case, I render a judgment of generality and universality, in community ; for I intend your acceptance of the meaning together with me as one of fact and confirmation,

---

[1] It is only in community that the reduction holds, since—as we will see more fully below, § 8—it is only by virtue of community that the successive recurrences to one mind yield a judgment of identity holding for all minds.

or, one which if inaccessible, is nevertheless still general in the sense given just above in which essential singularity becomes general. That is to say, the singular meaning is rendered as one of truth : it is capable of confirmation either by different persons, or by that equivalent process, the recurrence of experience in the mind of one.

But the alternative way mentioned of rendering a singular meaning is not that of finding it true. I say to you of my picture " none other such," meaning to express the appreciations It is Appreciative. that come from my more refined sense of values in the toning, shading, form, etc., which you do not share. Moreover, I myself do not attribute these elements of meaning strictly to the objective thing as its qualities. I say, " it suits my mood," " it sets my sentiments in a pleasant balance," " it calms my incipient activities." All this I may feel again and again and describe it in the same words, but this does not render it as an objective meaning. It is an "appreciative description," not a logical general that I express to you. The logical meaning is only an inadequate device for telling you that I find it good, in the way we both understand to apply to works of art ; but just how it is good, what the intimate thrill is that makes it good to me, that is not expressed.

14. The singularity of the object is in this sense imported or imputed. The predicates of worth are axiological. That is, they are worthful before being made logical. They take form in propositions, as the normal vehicle of intercourse ; but they Singularity as Worth Predication. are not exhausted in the generality of their logical form. They intend something about the attitude, disposition, gratification, interest, of the self, as well as something about the object that suggests the predication. In terms of recent worth-theory, these predicates are " projected " from the inner life, " sembled " into the object, and attributed to it by the sort of quasi-logical license called *Einfühlung*.

In terms of the distinction made above, the singularity of the one object may be either end or means or both. Its objective or essential oneness is rendered properly as the general of its own appearances, and thus the end of the theoretical interest Singular is both end and means. is fulfilled. In this aspect the truth of the singular is exhausted by the movement whose end is the establishing of fact. But its imported singularity is more. Its character as end to the theoretical becomes means to the appreciative interest that fills it with further personal worth. The object becomes a singular fulfilling worth to me alone, while it is perhaps besides a singular fact or truth to all of us alike.

15. It may be replied that this does not do, for although there be no reference to the external, there is to the inner control, **Are worths** and this is a sphere of existence for the establishment **inner Truths?** of truth no less than is the other. If the worth predicates are contents in the self-sphere, they can be confirmed there ; and the predicates are those of truth or fact after all.

This is not only plausible ; so far as applicable, it is true. There is such a sphere of controlled inner process which constitutes the world of experience, one practically of objective and factual reference. And in many cases, the singularity is evidently capable of just the reduction that this objection suggests. Suppose, for example, I say " I value this from my memories of it " ; this **As say events** would seem to be a case of personal appreciation. **of memory** But the worth here comes from organization in a body of contents, which though mental, are none the less subject to lawful recurrence, restatement, and common rendering. You reply to me, " yes, in that I join you, for I was there too when that remarkable incident occurred." Here is a case of the reduction of the meaning to strictly logical terms as truth in the sphere of the inner or psychic mode of memory.

16. Moreover in most cases of appreciation of singularity there is much that can be so rendered. So far as our lives move in similar grooves, our associations being much the same, and our ground-impulses similarly directed, we can in a large way compare, discuss, talk about them, with much common meaning. I say " I have a certain fear of that man "—the " certain " being **or common** the word that confesses the failure of my thought to **subjective** render the singularity of my impression—but you **happenings?** reply " I share your feeling ; I know just what you mean." Now there is really no further proof that we do mean the same thing, that we do share the same feeling ; but our lives and personalities being what they are, it is in many cases fair to say that there is here a real confirmation of the judgment that makes it common and true.[1]

All this it is plain, however, simply asserts for the inner sphere what we have already recognized for the external, the truth

---

[1] It is here that the importance of the question of emotional "constructs" or "generals" or of an "affected logic" as pointed out by M. Ribot, is seen. In what sense could we say that there is an affective or "faith" judgment? The matter is to be treated fully in connection with the aesthetic mode (vol. iii.).

of thoughts *within their proper control.* It goes as far as it can to resolve the singularity to that of the recognitive type. But it in no way militates against the position taken above that there is also a residue, in many cases—a mass of meaning that remains

No, they accompany inner or outer Truths. singular still because it is immediate in its nature. The selective personal readings, the ends set up over and above the truths taken as means, the proposals entertained only because they please, the preferences known to be private—all these meanings cluster on occasion about the fact, whether it be one of inner or of outer truth, and the assertion, or presumption, or assumption, of this meaning is axiological. Logical, indeed, so far as adequate, it is still never entirely exhaustive of the original experience of worth.

In this sort of meaning, therefore, the imported singular, the immediate worth experience as such, we have an intent that the drag-net of judgment cannot enmesh. It remains a-logical.[1]

§ 5. Private Meaning as A-logical

17. Similar things may be said about "private" meaning. In our earlier discussions we found that privacy could not be

Logical meaning not private. attributed to meaning in the logical mode, except in aspects which, indeed, were not logical. This appears as soon as we distinguish what is in any strict sense private from what is not. We found [2] that a judgment may render a meaning as actually held by only one person—private, that is, in the sense of lacking in aggregate community, or having least catholicity. But it also appeared that no judgment could render a meaning as not worthy or fit to be held by everybody, that is as not synnomic or "appropriate" in community. While, therefore, a judgment held by one person only is often called a "private" judgment, yet it is only by an indulgence of common usage that lends itself to confusion. For such a judgment still has universal intent, as invoking and legislating the agree-

[1] I have admitted above that it is rendered sufficiently well for practical purposes by the judgments of "appreciative description" that fairly differentiate and set forth its general framework and setting. Such judgments are developed in common, and constitute a great mass of *truth about appreciations*, as appears in the sciences of Aesthetics, Ethics, Economics, etc. But the variations of personal appreciation still show themselves in it all, and finally the remonstrance of feeling asserts itself in the cry "de gustibus non est disputandum." That is, the commonness of this may be "postulated," but it cannot be "presupposed." Cf. chap. vi. sect. 30. note.　　　[2] Above, chap. iii. § 10.

ment of all. It is, then, in the profounder sense a common and not a private meaning.

18. With these limitations set forth, we may go on to distinguish two modes of meaning to which the term "private" may properly be applied. They are the "imported singular," **Two further** the meaning of worth or appreciation just described, **cases: the** and the "fugitive" or detached mental content. **"Imported,"** These are both incapable of being rendered in judgment. The proof of this has already been given for the former in the paragraph immediately preceding this. Not to repeat that discussion, therefore, we may at once take up the second case mentioned—the private as detached or fugitive psychic content.

19. It is plain that "fugitive" contents may be taken up in acts of judgment. But in the degree in which we make them judgmental, in that degree we take away their mark of privacy, their detachment and fugitiveness. All determinateness **and the** of a content depends upon its relatedness in a larger **"fugitive":** "what," or whole of meaning ; to say anything about **the latter is** **judged as a** an image we must at least classify it. As a fact or **General.** truth, it has its presupposition of a sphere of control ; and a judgment of truth can be rendered about it only by making this presupposition. So of any other statements one may make of it—such as that it is fugitive in character, or detached— any such statement, by which it is described as in its place in the mental life as a whole, only succeeds in rendering those aspects in which the case is general,[1] not those in which it is singular. As of other singulars, this arises as a meaning of what is left over after the logical processes have done their work. There remains just the something that makes such a case singular, still unrendered in the judgments made about it.

This we have seen in our discussion of fancy-objects.[2] They are cases of the typically uncontrolled. Not only do they escape the rule of external reduction and control ; they are also unreduced **So of Fugi-** in that very sphere, the inner, in which their existence **tive Images.** is presupposed. In another connection it was remarked also that these fugitive creatures of the image world become the type of "unreality,"[3] seeing that they do not submit to the

---

[1] Including the "general of recurrence," by which such a content might be identified in the individual's experience. This further reduces the singularity of the meaning.

[2] Vol. i. chap. v. §§ 3, 4.

[3] Above, chap. ii. §§ 3, 4.

laws governing the play of controlled psychic process. They are not " funded " in the whole of lawful psychic happening, as " real " psychic objects are. They are in this very definite sense not only singular, but also private ; and in this they are in as definite a sense a-logical. They remain ungrasped, in their singular aspect, by the synnomic and generalizing function of thought.

These meanings then we may legitimately read off as being happenings, existential and pungent enough within their own sphere, the inner life, but yet not rendered by the logical mode of treating meanings. In this respect they are to be added to the appreciative singulars as being residual meanings in the sense stated above.

20. Writing this down, then, that the singular, in both those cases—the " appreciative " and the " private " singular—escapes the drag-net of logic, we still find a peculiar difference between the two. If we recall to mind the distinction between means and ends, as used in the treatment of truth, this difference will become evident. In the case of appreciation, the mere truth of an object is subordinated, as means, to the end of its pursuit, as gratifying or useful. The remote end of appreciation is superposed upon the meaning of truth. It is now this latter meaning, the intent of appreciation, that is singular and irreducible to judgment. In the case of the " fugitive " however, this is not the case. The Only the singular character here seems not that of appreciation, appreciative not that of imported singularity, but that of objective singular is end. character ; it is essential to an image, however fugitive, detached, and unmeaning it may be, that it have its own and no other set of characters. Its singularity as a-logical meaning resides then not in its end-fulfilling rôle, but just in the lack of it. It is meaningless both for truth and for worth just in that respect in which it is singular and private. There remains hanging about it only those effects of relief, release, freedom from law, irresponsibility, which sometimes do, indeed, become worthful after the burden and heat of the day ; but these cannot be pursued as ends through any process of truth, for they come often by the cessation of the pursuit itself, and in connection with an image that lacks the requisite relationships.

There is, therefore, within the range of psychic meanings, a sort of present object whose definition turns upon its lack of relation and control. Its presupposition is the general character of the mental life, that permits this sort of thing ; and its place in further theory enters into the conception we finally arrive at as to the meaning of mind itself. Here we may rest with the statement that it is not logical, although it is cognitive rather than appreciative.[1]

§ 6. PRIVATIVE MEANING AS A-LOGICAL

21. The conception of " privation " is again one familiar to us. It will be remembered that we found it important in two of its bearings, the recall of which will be sufficient for our further purposes. First, it was found [2] that in a case of opposition of the type of privation, there is an " indeterminate other," a penumbra of otherness lying about the object that is treated privatively.
Progressions " Let it be this and nothing else," is the appro-
of the "other" priate expression for meaning of this type.   Second we found [3] that such a meaning develops in either or both of two very different and contrasted ways.   The positive whole becomes enlarged with further information, so that the " other " of the privation is encroached upon. This is growth in affirmation or inclusion when it occurs in the logical mode.   In contrast with this, there is the positive determination of the content of the " other," as over against the original privative content.   The object meant or chosen is now definitely separated by a relation of exclusion from the now definite other.   This gives the meaning of exclusion, or exclusive negation, in the logical mode.

The point to be made here is that these two modes of progression of privation into the logical mode are the only ones, and that there is no room or place for " privation " as such when the
No logical   meaning has become logical. Logical meaning is
Privative.   definite affirmation or definite negation of a predicate. Even the disjunctive and alternative forms of meaning implicate belief in the determinate whole in which the disjunction occurs.

22. It may be said, however, that we do make judgments of the force of privation. This is true, as has been brought out in an earlier discussion.[4]   But such judgments render the *relation*

---

[1] If one doubts this, finding the singularity of privacy only in the affective setting, reverberation, active effects, etc., of the image—for which much may indeed be said—it does not really matter to my argument; for it reduces this sort of singularity to the other, the appreciative, which is still a-logical. Psychologically considered the point is one requiring close analysis.

[2] See vol. i. chap. ix. §§ 1, 2.

[3] Vol. i. chap. ix. sect. 10.   [4] Above, chap. viii. § 9.

of privation—a definite conception—not the fact or first-hand

Privative Re- meaning of privation. When I say "it is this and
lation may nothing else," I mean that the "this" is in opposition
be judged. to any positive "something else" that I might attempt
to predicate of it. The whole movement of negation rests upon
limitative opposition which is a movement of contradiction between
two positive terms. This does not suffice to render privation
as such, since there is always the infinite range of "othernesses"
meant in the privation, which are not yet brought to the test.
In fact privation is, as we have seen, one of exclusive interest,
not one of relational content. The "will to believe" has its
rôle here. I say "this and no other" not meaning to disparage
any "other," but to magnify "this"; not to reject "yours,"
but to value "mine." Not Caesar less, but Rome more !

If this be true, then we must admit a selective and appreciative
force in a privative meaning ; and this reduces it to the class
of singulars. In each such case, there is, besides the meaning
rendered in definite logical judgments, the intent to find the
object more than all these express. The privative object stands
as a fulfilment for the knower alone ; he does not expect anybody
else to find it what it is to him. It is therefore not logical.

23. In terms of our distinction of means and ends, the same
comes out. I may interpret my meaning of an object by a
succession of judgments of truth, thus giving a series of general
and synnomic meanings, either affirmative or negative in their
logical quality. But to reach a privative rendering of the same
object, all this truth becomes means. Suppose the object is in
a distant place. I cannot communicate to you the peculiar
tang of the fulfilment its presence would mean to me ; but I can

The Privative use the descriptions of truth to identify the object
is end not and request you to fetch it. When you do, or when
means in any other way by the use of truth or fact I secure
the thing, then only is the privative meaning fulfilled.[1] I then
come into the state of appreciation and end-fulfilment, for which
the description served as means. "Control through knowledge" serves its proper office, after "knowledge through
control" has defined and described the object as true.

Not stopping here to pursue further the positive characterization of privative meaning, or to signalize its further rôle in the

---

[1] In the forcible intensive of our negro phrase it is both the only one
and also the "*onliest* one"—the "onliest" of the only !

progressions of meanings—important in the extreme as this rôle

So it is a-logical. will appear in the sequel to be—we may simply note that this type of knowledge is not capable of logical rendering. It is a residual meaning, left over after judgment has done its work. It is then one of the modes we are here looking for. It is an a-logical meaning, essentially singular in its force, since it is the end-state of an exclusive and personal interest.

§ 7. IDEAL MEANING AS A-LOGICAL

24. One other type of meaning suggests itself as a candidate for standing in the present connection. It is the mode called "ideal" also given treatment [1] in an earlier place.

We may proceed by summarizing the characters of ideal meaning, giving only such detail as will suffice to render the present treatment intelligible.

A meaning is ideal, it will be remembered, according as it embodies an intent not yet reduced to the actual content taken to render it. It is a further projection of meaning in the lines suggested by the actual; but it is not yet realized in the actual. As thus understood ideal meaning is always of the selective and schematic type. Ideals of truth take the form of hypotheses, **Ideal mean-ing Selective** and suggest developments of meaning that may be found true. When the ideal intends embodiments not reducible to fact, it is selective and privative in the sense of ends. The two cases illustrate the truth already made out, that there is both the interest of a theoretical sort, that terminates on truth and makes completeness of fact its ideal; and also the pragmatelic interest that uses the fact as means to the attainment of ends. This latter establishes fulfilment or worth as ideal. In either case, the intent of the meaning, in respect to the ideal, is that of a further finding not yet rendered as true. The ideal is set up as end, even in the case in which truth is made end; for truth is then pursued by means of the preceding data of truth, and the ideal is a preferential and selective rendering beyond the present fact.

25. If this be true, then the ideal intent of meaning always escapes rendering as truth; for just by becoming truth it is made **Ideal is never Truth** means to a further end. The ideal forever entices, but never rewards us. So far as we get what we want, so far it is then truth; and the intent of the ideal is then

---

[1] Vol. i. chap. x. § 8.

either absent, or if present, it is prophetic again of further fulfilment.

Here then there is a further residual meaning, a meaning not
bagged by gunners armed with the weapon of judgment. And it
will have appeared already to the reader that the reason for it is
the one now familiar—that the ideal intent is singular. All ideal
and never reference, inasmuch as it is not reduced to truth, is
Logical. still a matter of personal end-meaning of the individual's selection. I may go beyond the judgments of truth
and find ideal values in this or that experience of fact ; but I do
not require that you agree with me, nor do I ask you to. The
object thus found relatively to fulfil the ideal is individuated by
my exclusive interest in finding it so ; and it is thus a singular
construction of imported meaning.

This meaning, then, like the others, may be classed as a
singular; it is a-logical.

26. In certain modes of meaning now mentioned, therefore,
to which different names may be given, we find "left-overs,"
residua from the logical processes ; they are a-logical. And in all
but one of them we find a common reason for this. They are
of the character of "singulars," all of them ; and in all but
one of them it is singularity of the selective and appreciative
type. The "imported singular," the "privative," the "private"
of exclusive interest, the "ideal," all get their distinction as escap-
All a-logical ing the net of judgment from the fact that they are
meanings worths, not mere facts, prospective fulfilments, not
appreciative
save the retrospective truths. The possible exception, the fugi-
"fugitive." tive singular, is a meaning of fact, but of fact detached
and private. It is a case by itself because it does not fall under
any control at all ; both the "control through knowledge" and
the "knowledge through control" find it unavailable. But for
its sphere of subsistence, the inner life, it would be an outcast
among things of the world.

27. We may now finally point the lesson to be learned for
our further work—a fundamental matter. Singularity, on one
hand, set up as end, is a meaning for which truth is means ;
generality, on the other hand, universality, truth, are matters of
fact, meanings of self-contained and logical implication. The
latter is a result, the former a prophecy ; one a category, the
other a hope ; one means what is true for the knower ; the
other means the fulfilments for the self that is the knower.

These contrasts introduce us to certain of the embarrassments of thought. Thought is unable to reduce end-meanings, appreciations, to the status of truths. This situation motives the progression out of the logical mode, as will be shown.

Resulting Dualism and Embarrass-ment. Here let us note that it is the movement of " control through knowledge "—the catchword of the school who find just this the shibboleth of the theory of truth —that lands the logical mode in this dualism and embarrassment. If all there is of psychic meaning could be read as they try to read it—as a movement of a logical sort within the body of presented contents—it would be different. But that omits just the motive to the whole movement—the habits, the dispositions, the urgencies of action, the interests, the attentions, in short the personal self in which the inner control process resides.

§ 8. Logical Community and the Difference of Discernibles.

In certain of our discussions we have reached positions which involved the recognition of the intent of judgment to hold for more than one individual. It will be remembered that in discussing the characters of judgment [1] we gave to this aspect of meaning the name of " community." We may now gather together the positions taken up in various connections, and show certain of their larger bearings.

28. (1) In the first place, it appeared that the process ordinarily known as generalization in logic is one in which a common meaning arises, that is, a meaning in community. The

The General in Extension. general meaning not only applies to each of the particulars under it ; but it also holds for different individuals.[2] The general-particular relationship remains the same whether the different cases that serve as particulars be observed by one individual or by many. This case is the one covered in logic by the theory of "extension." Certain variations upon it arise when we take explicitly the point of view of the community of the meaning.

29. (2) Second, we found certain peculiarities attaching to the meaning rendered as " singular." When only one object is meant, such an object is, as we have seen,[3] capable of the general rendering necessary to make it subject-matter of judgment, not

---

[1] Chap. ix. § 5.
[2] Chap. iii. §§ 8, 9, and chap. vii. § 3.
[3] Chap. vii. § 8, and chap. x. § 6.

from the point of view of the extension of the objective class—although this is the construction given it by formal logic—but **The Singular as General** only from the point of view of community. A single object can be generalized only from the point of view of the process that in some manner distinguishes in it different instances or particulars. This occurs in two ways, both of which show the absolute necessity of recognizing the character of community in logic.

The first of these is that in which the *one single object is actually experienced by different persons*, as, for instance, the observation in common of the " falling " of a star.

If we disregard those aspects of meaning wherein such a single object is one of a class of objects—then there is left over only that aspect wherein it is a single object to different persons. **when appearing to different Persons,** We have seen in detail how by processes of " secondary conversion " [1] between different minds this meaning arises. The point to consider here is this : such a meaning can become logical in the sense of having different cases to serve as basis of generalization, only if different experiences of one object can play the rôle of experiences of different objects : that is only if *community of experience takes the place of extensive quantity.* The experiences of different minds furnish the differences which become particulars under a general. The identity of a singular—say, for example, the identity of the shooting star seen by different observers—can be rendered in a judgment only through the generalization of the experiences of these observers, whereby the event is pronounced the same for all of them. This is a movement in community, or in a mode that preserves the force of community.

We may say, therefore, at this point that, but for the aspect of community attaching to judgment, *the logical rendering of a singular would be impossible.*

The other case of the rendering of a singular, seeing its great importance, may be placed under a separate heading.

30. (3) A third case is that of the meaning attaching to a single object when experienced *by a single person only* ; in what sense can such a meaning be rendered in terms of general and particular, and so become subject-matter of judgment ?

Here also it is evident that there is no implication of exten- **and to one Person.** sive quantity. The meaning is a singular because of the mark or group of marks which prevents its

[1] See vol. i. chap. iv. § 5, and above, chap. iii. §§ 6 ff.

generalization [1] with other objects in a class.   How then can we judge such an object the same, and expect others, if and when they experience it, to agree with us ?—or not experiencing it, still to accept our report of it ?

Here again we have an evident resort to community. If we consider the generalization in the instance just discussed above —that of one object seen by different observers—to proceed upon differences in experiences, the object being found identical through the *differences of its appearances* to the different observers, then the recognition of community gives us the same result here. Judgment in community renders meaning as holding *for different personal acts of judgment,* and the requirements of the case are met as well, and in precisely the same way, *when recurrent experiences of one person* are substituted for different experiences of more than one. There arise what we have called a " general of recurrence." [2] In both cases, the generalization proceeds upon the commonness of the various constructions of the meaning, whether these be experiences in one mind or in many. We have seen, indeed, in another place [3] that the process of conversion whereby the meaning of " sameness " attaches to an object is the same whether the recurrences of the meaning thus identified as the same be in one mind or One Meaning in more ; for there is either actual conversion, or the in Com- presupposition of it, from one experience to another munity in both cases alike. We reach, then, the striking result that a judgment of singular identity is one that may arise by the generalization of successive experiences in one mind ; and this generalization is read in community as equally valid for other minds. That is, we again come to the conclusion that a judgment of singular identity is possible on the basis of a single person's recurrent experience ; and that it is a judgment in community, having the force of commonness for all thinkers alike. But for the character of community, however, such a judgment would be impossible ; for there is no guarantee, apart from the intent of community, that the individual's identification of the object through recurrent experiences is socially available.

The cases now interpreted show clearly just what the intent of community really is. It is the intent that the rendering of

---

[1] See above, chap. vii. § 8.
[2] See chap. x. sects. 29 ff., and cf. chap. iii. sect 8 note, and sect 75, note 2.
[3] Chap. x. sect. 30.

an identical meaning by any one person implicates general judgment process, in whose ever mind it may be. It rests

Recurrence essential to General. upon the fact, which we have studied in detail, that such a judgment of identity is one of recurrent [1] appearances or experiences, whether the objects experienced are one or many, and whether the observers are one or many. The intent of community therefore is essential to judgment and is in certain respects independent of variations in the other characters, especially of variations in extension.

31. This result appears in an interesting light when we view the three cases mentioned in the reverse order. If we take a judgment of a single individual's recurrent experience of one object as given, we may ask what it involves besides his personal belief. The first additional element of the meaning is found to

Cases Reversed: General of Recurrence. be that this person expects his judgment to be confirmed by any one else who may experience the object. That is, the community intent is one that allows the substitution of another's personal experiences for one's own, or the intercalation of that person's experience in the series of one's own as in all respects equivalent to one's own. This carries over the meaning to the case mentioned second above—that of an object experienced by different observers.

Another implication then appears. Whenever occasions arise in which a judgment of identity in recurrence fails to establish itself, the experiences are read *as different objects* ; that is, a generalization in quantity takes place, whether or no there actually be more objects than one. The individual remarks, " I did not recognize you—I took you for a different man." This is precisely the same result *as if different individuals had disagreed in their several reports of the one object*. The judgment such individuals would reach after conference is that there are two objects of the same class ; and this is the result the one person reaches on the basis of recurrence. The step now taken is that whereby the single individual's treatment of recurrent experiences of one object is logically equivalent to the ordinary generaliza-

General in Extension. tion by one or more persons of different particular objects. But this holds entirely and only within the mode of community, since objectively there is but the one object.

32. We here come upon a principle which may be formulated alongside a celebrated historical dictum, the " identity, or same-

---

[1] " Recurrent," that is, in the general sense of duplicated or plural, not necessarily successive.

ness, of indiscernibles." While usually associated with the name of Leibnitz, on account of his use of it in his theory of " monads," it has been formulated in somewhat different senses by various thinkers.[1] We might describe it in Hegelian terms, as the principle of the " oneness of the many," and set over against it the principle of the " manyness of the one " which I prefer, however, to call that of the " difference of discernibles."

Identity of Indiscernibles. In the terms of our present analysis, the " identity of indiscernibles " means in principle that in the absence of discernible difference two or more objects are judged to be one and the same in recurrent experience. It is evident that we have here the process of individuating as one, objects which do not give experience of difference. This is, therefore, just the case we have pointed out as generalization in community and not in extension. The experiences may be anybody's or everybody's ; they are rendered in a judgment of singular identity. The experiences of different objects are equivalent to those resulting from the recurrence of one.

Difference of Discernibles. The same movement is capable, on our principles, of precisely the reverse reading—the reading formulated in the phrase " difference of discernibles." A single object is rendered, by reason of differences discerned in its several appearances, as more than one ; that is as having general force with reference to its own recurrent cases. The experience passes from that form in which a single object is found to recur to one mind, and also from that in which it appears as one to different minds, to that in which its several cases have marks of difference which forbid their individuation as one object.[2]

The principle of " identity of indiscernibles," when psychologically interpreted, expresses the movement in community

---

[1] Leibnitz, *Monadologie*, 9, and *Nouveaux essais*, II, chap. 27, § 1 ff. For citations from other authors, see Eisler, *Wörterbuch d. philos. Begriffe*, art. *Identitatis indiscernibilium*.

[2] The epistemological bearings of these principles are reserved for treatment in the later volume. Here it may be suggested, however, that all generalization illustrates the " identity of indiscernibles " and all singularization illustrates the " difference of discernibles." For generalization summarizes the aspects of meaning in which objects are indistinguishable or identical, and singularization fixes those aspects in which each object is discernibly different from all others. We now see that this latter process, the logical rendering of the singular, explicitly requires the intent of community, a result which shows the radical rôle played by the common or social factor in all the processes of thought.

whereby like experiences of more than one object may yield an object identified as one ; while that of the " difference of discernibles " expresses the movement whereby unlike experiences of one object may lead to its determination as more than one.[1]

33. Any judgment, by reason of its community, may be read in any one of three ways (cf. chap. x. sect. 29) : As meaning (1) more than one object appearing to one person or many, (2) one object only appearing to one person or many, or (3) one object only appearing to one person only. The process of generalization as such considered as a summarizing of likenesses in recurrent experience, can in nowise determine which of these three the actual meaning is to be. A paranoiac declares that everybody is persecuting him, because he generalizes recurrent experiences as all alike fit to excite his fear of others ; he is working under the principle of " identity of indiscernibles." At the other extreme we may cite the individual we call " subjective," who sees always in our conduct, however uniformly kind, new and varied signs of change. He in turn is magnifying the " difference of discernibles." The actual force in any case of normal judgment is determined by the control factor, the coefficients of fact which limit the meaning. The paranoiac's constructions do not allow the control that the actual differences in his attendants' action should secure ; the uniform tide of his fear obliterates these differences. Nor are those of the " subjective " man controlled as they should be in the larger meaning of kindliness that pervades the varieties of our acts. In his case the pebbles of variety choke the tide of sameness. Both are abnormal in that the facts do not get in their proper work.

Résumé and Examples.

34. It is interesting to note that there are forms of speech in which meanings based on the recurrent appearances of objects are rendered, whether such appearances occur to one person or to many. Propositions in which the predicate is modified by the words " sometimes," " always," " often," etc., may embody this meaning. " This woman is always vain " is a universal of appearance ; it is quantified in community : just as " women are always vain," equivalent to " all women are vain " has universal quantity in extension. Propositions in " sometimes," are particular in community (as " this

Quantification in Community.

[1] The most frequent cases of both these movements reflect types of interest and purpose. Exclusive interest requires the one object only, while large general interests allow differences without discernment (cf. vol. i. chap. iii. §§ 1, 2, and chap. vii. § 2).

woman is sometimes vain "), or in extension (as " women are
sometimes vain ") or both (as " some women are sometimes
vain "). This sort of proposition, rendering variety of appearances, which change with time and circumstance, has been said
by certain logicians to have " multiple quantification." [1] The
name is a good one, since the two aspects of meaning do both
render quantity ; but it is hard to see how the quantification
due to recurrent appearances of one object can be brought under
the ordinary logical doctrine of quantity in extension. If we
grant, however, that recognition of the recurrent appearances of
one object to one mind or more is psychologically equivalent for
the purposes of generalization, to the recognition of a plurality of
different objects, then in this movement which gives what I call
" community," the additional mode of quantity has its origin.

It will be remembered, also, that we had occasion to distinguish two modes within the notion of community. Community
" for whom "—the intent of a judgment to hold for many individuals as for one—is correlated with community " by whom "
—the further intent to suggest that the meaning may not be
universally prevalent or catholic as a fact, but may
be actually held by a certain number only. It is
evident that what has been said in this paragraph

Two Modes of Community.

about generalization in community, holds in the first instance,
of community " for whom," or community of " control " (as it
has also been called). The question may be asked whether the
other sort of community, that of catholicity, the relative commonness of the content as actually held in different minds, has
any logical rôle.

There are meanings, and of course forms of speech fitted to
express them, which not only recognize the recurrence of appearances as basis of the predication made, but also the limitation
of these appearances to a restricted number of persons. For
example, the propositions, " there are observations that indicate
that Mars is inhabited," and " Mr. Lowell holds that Mars is
inhabited," have both these shades of meaning. The reference
to a plurality of observers may be the emphatic element of
meaning, as in the proposition, " as to the truth of
evolution there is wide agreement among biologists."
Of course, every one would admit that such mean-
ings can be expressed ; it is a different thing to say that such

Quantity in Community "by Whom."

---

[1] See Johnson, " The Logical Calculus," *Mind*, 1902, and Keynes,
Formal Logic, § 70.

an intent is always present in the judgment. But if we are right in holding that a problematical shading of meaning attaches to all judgments, when they are actually current ; that all judgment intends personal belief, which is expressed in order to silence doubt or to extend conviction ; in short, that all judgment has an experimental and instrumental force, then here, in this mode of community, we should find its variations. Probably as a matter of fact the majority of cultivated people, if asked whether evolution is true, would say in effect, " Yes, most of the best biologists accept it." The ground of personal acceptance here seems to be relative prevalence, and the explicit recognition of this in such a judgment as that last cited brings out the presupposition of the mode of community " by whom " in the simple judgment of truth. Often the conditions of the appearance of the object or event to which the proposition refers require a meaning in catholicity. " Shooting stars are often red," " sea-serpents have no fins," " the moon is made of green cheese," are propositions that require this presupposition. They mean to report a certain degree of prevalence of the opinion or observation or belief, which the proposition renders, as well as the number of illustrative cases or appearances. These variations in prevalence or relative catholicity are a further sort of quantification. The implication made in respect to prevalence varies from the " singularity " of the opinion or judgment rendered as private, to the " universality " of the appeal, let us say, to the catholicity of " common sense." Between these lies the " particular " quantity of a proposition which renders the common judgment of a limited group.

The three modes of quantity, therefore, that may attach to judgments are (1) quantity in extension (as in " men are sometimes irritable "), (2) quantity in " community for whom " or " community of appearance " (as in " John is sometimes irritable "), and (3) that in community by whom or in catholicity (as in " we all find John irritable ").[1]

§ 9. How can the Singular be True ?

35. It will serve to sharpen our main result if we attempt to answer the question, how the singular can be true ; for we not only make singular judgments, but we do find them true.

The answer serves to illustrate the distinctions just made

[1] See the Appendix, III., for further illustrations.

The singular judgment is true in so far as it renders a singular meaning that is open to confirmation and inspection, having a control that can be reconstituted and a community that can be found to hold by some method of conversion. For example, when I say, " there is only one sharp leaf on the bough," I make a singular judgment that is true. But in finding it **Singular is** true, I appeal to fact, both as having external control **rendered as** and as being open to the inspection of others. Our **general.** different mental contexts agree. But when we now analyse the meaning, it appears that we have made the object general and universal in community although it renders a singular content. For the proving of the control involves the recurrence of experiences of the leaf, and generalizes them as cases for any observer, just as the finding of different leaves would do. The agreement with another person as to the one leaf gives the same result in community—i.e. different experiences, with the same general meaning—for both parties. So the singular as truth is a content rendered as general and universal in community.

On the other hand, when this is not possible, as in the case of a singular appreciation, as indicated above, no judgment of truth can be reached. Genuine appreciations do not thus repeat themselves, in a way to afford a general meaning of their cases ; nor are they open to inspection by others, in a way to yield community of truth. Such meanings remain outside the grasp of judgment.

While, therefore, the character of singularity betokens lack of quantity, this character differs for the two sorts of singulars. The recognitive singular lacks extensive quantity only ; it has quantity in community, and is thus made in a logical sense general. The selective or appreciative singular, on the contrary, lacks both modes of quantity ; it is, therefore, in the outcome, the only meaning that is finally and unalterably singular.

It may be remarked also that the privacy of a prelogical singular meaning—that of the schematic or assumptive as such— is entirely removed when such a meaning passes into a judgment fit for general acceptance in " community for whom." This, however, does not generalize the function in the same sense. The content of the singular becomes common ; but the individual's experience of personal function does not cease to be private to him. As pointed out above, only on occasion (see chap. x. sect. 30)—when the process is itself objectified by thought—does this process become subject-matter of a judgment of a truth.

Chapter XV

REFLECTION AS SELF-MODE

§ 1. The Dualism of Selves

1. Having thus found just where thought breaks down in one respect, it suggests itself to us that in the direction of the other aspects of the mode, there may be similar limitations. And in turning to the consideration of the " self " of the mode we may confine our remarks to this single question. Let us put it thus : is the mode of thought capable of rendering, in its peculiar way, all the meanings implicated in the function of " self," known variously as " subject," " subject-self," " knower," " rational self," etc., as over against " object-self," " objects of thought," " subject-matter " of judgment, etc. ? That is, is the meaning of *self as subject* capable of statement as object of thought, in a way that exhausts its subjective intent ?

We have here one of the classical problems of the theory of Subject- and knowledge. I shall discuss it now only so far as to Object-selves suggest an answer to the question we have propounded for our special purpose. The great attempts of philosophers have been, on the one hand, to show that the self as " subject " is nothing but the self as " object " ; and on the other hand to show that the self as " object " is only a sort of restatement of the self as subject ; or, yet again, to show that the self as object arises as a sort of cognitive screen or blind before the self as subject so that the latter is hopelessly obscured or hidden— the subject disappearing in the realm of the " unknowable," or the " thing-in-itself." [1]

---

[1] I may especially refer to two very subtle endeavours, one critical and the other analytic of the self : Herbart's in his *Metaphysik*, vol. i, and Bradley's in his *Appearance and Reality*. Bradley holds that the " self " is reached only as relational construction or object, and so loses " reality," since all logical construction gives only " appearance." His conclusion that it has disappeared as " reality " only means that in his view reality is not given in the constructions of thought.

2. Apart from theory, it may be said that thought renders all its meanings in relational terms, and that, as thus rendered, self becomes object, content, or subject-matter of judgment. As **Relational** to whether such a rendering of " self " deprives it of **construction** its " reality " is another matter. We now carry our discussion a step further by asking what are the implications of the relational meaning thus rendered? Does it exhaust the intent of the " subject-self " ?

The answer is, not at all. The self is made objective in the mode of reflection, in which the judgment of objectivity arises. That is, the construction of the objective self implicates a whole **does not** meaning or content that is what it is only *to a subject-* **exhaust the** *self over against this and other objective meanings.* **Subject-self.** There is the intent to be a subject, and this is part of the implication of the constitution of the object-self. This has been recognized so often, and has been given such emphasis in the literature of the topic, that it need not be further enforced here. Herbart's analysis cited above may be especially referred to.

3. Many changes of expression might be rung upon this result : such as that " a known implies a knower," that " an object implicates a subject," that " belief, acceptance, acknowledgment, etc., are unintelligible without a self that believes," etc. We may interpret the point variously from various points of view ; but from our more restricted one, that of the progression **Expressed** of psychic meanings, it is unambiguous. It means **in terms of** that the act of judgment, as a process of logical render- **Control** ing, cannot so mutilate the mode in which it itself arises, as to *destroy the union of content with control.* It cannot take its own control, the self-meaning,—in whatever element of content or function it may be·embodied—and make it object without again, *for that object, setting up a new phase of the same control.*

Put empirically, this admits of ready illustration. Whatever the actual elements of content may be that are made the vehicle of the sense or intent of self as subject, there is only one way of objectifying them in judgment, of observing and classifying them —namely, the regular and necessary way of controlling them as objective contents in a whole meaning of belief. Any such typical movement—say the observation of the strains and contractions identified with an act of attention—is itself a new act of the same sort, an act of attention ; it cannot be performed except as the very elements now made objective contents, or others vicariously for them, are set in action as control for the **And also of** effective use of the function. I must attend in **Content.** order to analyse attention. The analysis, therefore, that accounts objectively for the attention, does not exhaust the persisting control processes ; these escape the analysis. So with the self ; we do think about the self—and we can analyse the material so used—thus making it object of thought ; but the thought that does the analysing is going on just the same in a way that is not objective at all. The intent that motives the control is not itself rendered in the content that is controlled.

4. More positively, however, the subject-intent is a genuine and positive thing—the intent *to be*, the intent *of being*, the intent *that is*, the self. It takes on both the forms that the progressive determination of meaning shows, being both an **The Self Pro-** object of knowledge, the "empirical" or objective **gressions.** self when made content, and the "rational" or subjective self, when functioning as control. This duality makes it possible for us to trace its development in both the ways described as "knowledge through control" and "control through knowledge." These two movements are now to be considered.

§ 2. THE MEDIATED SELF AS "TRUE" OBJECT : SELF-KNOWLEDGE THROUGH CONTROL

5. The progression already worked out for objective contents generally, and called the progression of "knowledge through control," shows itself very evidently in the determination of the self-content. We have already concerned ourselves with the prelogical modes of this "progression," showing how the objective self is made up and individuated in persons.[1] We found that the self-content, the "me," in growing to be a body of contents individuated as the one personal self, is also read by a dialectical **Self-content** movement as the "alter" self of the social whole. **is "social."** There is a generalization of the contents in a "social" self, the "socius," which is read as you, me, or him, as the circumstances of the social situation require. The determination as "me and not you or him" is a movement of "singularization," wherein the marks of singular self-hood are read in the one case or the other. This process of singularization proceeds upon those essential marks of the inner life whereby each self

[1] Vol. i. chap. viii. § 9.

is a subject, namely, the marks of spontaneity, agency, continuous inner function, etc., which have been sufficiently dwelt upon.

It is this latter character, indeed, that distinguishes the contents that are selves from other objects. Each objective self is a case or particular of the general meaning " mind " ; but the very mark by which this generalization proceeds is that of *inner psychic process*, given only in the immediacy of the single person's mental life. It is then to be expected that this mark would become the basis of the further movement of individuation—as legitimately and regularly motived for the objective self as for **As func-** any other sort of object—by which each person is **tion self is** found to be more than a particular of the class mind ; **Singular.** he is also a *singular centre of inner process.* The inwardness of the self-object is part of its meaning as belonging to the class ; but its inwardness is also the mark that constitutes it an essential singular. John is " mind," together with you and me ; but John is, by the same right, also a singular mind, apart from you and me. He is one with us in the identity of the meaning of objective personality as such ; he is separate from us in that mark which resists generalization, the mark of inner control ; this makes him a subject-self only for himself.

6. There is, therefore, no essential departure from the process of " knowledge through control " in this case. The generality is found in what is taken up in judgment and rendered as common and social content of personality ; the singularity is found in the mark of separate inner control ; the latter is what makes the **A case of** single person singular, and this escapes the process of **Knowledge** judgment. The peculiarity in the case resides in the **through con-** **trol.** fact that the mark of singularity is here not like that which makes other objects singulars—marks merely objective— but it is the mark of inwardness or subjectivity. Persons are generalized as objects having in common the mark of subjectivity ; and the single person is singular in virtue of the same mark. Thus the self is, both for itself and also for others, a singular subjective inner process and also a generalized objective content.

Thus knowledge of self, as " me " or " you " or " him," is developed by the development of controls, the " inner " having its demarcation over against the " outer," as in the development of other objects. The self in both its senses is in contrast with " things," through the working out of the dualism of control modes. "Knowledge through control" is then the proper designation for the progression of objective-selves as of other objective contents.

The issue is a group of "selves" having a common meaning to each and also a singular meaning to each. The singularity to each is one of the marks read into the others as part of the common meaning. Each in short, thinks of all, including himself, as objects, and each of these objects having the singularity of its inner control process, is a subjective self as well.

7. To the objective self, the predicates "correct" and "true" apply, as to other objective contents. We have already discussed the question as to how persons can be remembered and identified.[1] About the same considerations apply when we ask how far a thought of a person can be "true." As objective construction, mediating an objective control, whether external as "another," or inner as "me," such a construction may be correct or incorrect, true or false, according as the new presented content is made up under the original control conditions, or not.[2] In this case the motive of conversion plays a great, if not the leading part, showing again the fact that one object may be individuated as The Self as a class. In the case of "others," of course, this is not "true." at all peculiar. I check off my thought of another by renewed experience of him ; by tests, that is, of fact. In thinking truthfully of myself, however, the case falls under the principal of the "difference of discernibles." Through the successive thoughts or experiences of my "me" as object, I generalize the cases, and thus establish a meaning that allows a real judgment of truth. The contents have the ground-tone of continuing and persistent sameness that belongs to the inner life, at the same time that—as in the case of my judgment of other persons—the successive experiences are, in their character of present singularity, different particulars under a general. Each case, however—to remark again the subtlety of the movement—while a particular of the class "me," is a member of that class as one person, by

---

[1] See the last reference.

[2] There are many sorts of "incorrect" and "untrue" self-constructions, as the pathology of self-consciousness shows. All the newer literature of divided and "obsessed" personalities recognizes this. The most remarkable cases are those in which the "subject," the I, as function or control, is so far detached from the "me" as to disclaim and disown it, saying "this is not the correct and true self ; it seems unreal" ; "I am not what I now seem." The literature of the subject is summarized by Hoch in the *Psychological Bulletin*, II., 1905, pp. 236 ff.

the singularity of its mode of control.   In other words, I judge myself truly in general terms, in virtue of the recurrence of the me in the intervals of my life history ; but I think each such appearance to have been that of a singular self of unique inner or subjective life.

§ 3.   The First Embarrassment of Thought

8. This inner singularity, then, though it is the mark upon which the generalization of the meaning of personality proceeds, is itself *never rendered in the judgment*.   What I think of when I say " I " may be the general self that includes " me " and " you " and " him " ; or it may be restricted to the " me " of the successive recurring selves of my own past history; but there is more : I mean also the subjective and immediate inner process which I am and which I also attribute to you as a singular sub-

The singular self escapes Thought.

ject self.   This intent is *not rendered in judgment* ; there is a dualism in the mode of truth, even when the " true " object is one's own personal self.   The subject-self is a singular meaning to the last.[1]   It thus illustrates in a remarkable way the a-logical character of singular meaning as already pointed out.   It is a case of the dualism of the " singular-general " which is characteristic of thought.   That which makes the singular a-logical, its immediateness, holds its own, even when its own child, the self, is identified and acknowledged in a judgment of truth.

We may place this mode of dualism, and its resulting embarrassment for thought, by recalling the aspects of the logical mode already worked out under the heading of criteria.   We found that all logical meanings present three criteria by which their differentiae, as belonging in the mode of reflection, are to be established ; they are *relational*, they are *believed*, and they are *objects to a self*.   In these results, the chief strands of

Failure of the Relational Criterion.

genetic progression converge upon the stage called reflection.   Now limitation upon the function, wherein its inability to render all meanings might be expected to become evident, should attach to one or more of these aspects of the meaning of judgment.   It clearly does attach, as we

---

[1] To illustrate this we may remark that the statement " I exist " is as a judgment a rendering of the " me " content common to all selves, with their character of singularity made mark of generality; but the statement also intends the inner personal process of control, which is immediate and incommunicable.

should expect, to one of these aspects, the relational. The failure of the meanings of the singular and appreciative types to get full rendering in judgment, marks the failure of relational construction in these cases. The imported singular and the appreciative, alike and together, refuse to submit to individuation as general and particular, as common and relational; they remain a-logical. We may put it down, therefore, that thought fails to carry over one of its criteria to these meanings, and so fails to become a universal vehicle of meaning. This is strikingly illustrated in the case of the singular self or subject.

§ 4. THE IMMEDIATE SELF AS " REAL " SUBJECT : CONTROL BY SELF THROUGH KNOWLEDGE

9. This remarkable phase of meaning, the subjective or control self, passes through a progression with the development of judgment, although it is not itself rendered as subject-matter. The functional control, which is just the factor of inner selfhood, is always present in the prospective tendency, the progressive organization, of the objective self. It is a segregated

Subject-self is affective-con-ative content mass of active and dispositional factors, which identifies itself with the purpose and interest of the special process going on at any time.[1] It is content of the affective-conative sort, not of the cognitive sort ; and, while not rendered in objective terms, it is still in no sense obscure or unempirical.

10. The presence of this factor in the entire progression gives what we call inner control ; and its development takes place through the context of ideas called the system of truth. The mediation of the forward-pressing, accommodative, active,

The Self is organized by adjustment. life is accomplished through the system of established ideas. In this system the realm of fact is set up vicariously, the fulfilments of the external are prophesied, the distant and remote are reflected in idea, as present and inciting, and the body of implication is interpreted not simply for what it is, a body of contents, but for what it might be, a body of fulfilments and satisfactions. The inner control becomes self-control—both control over self by the forming of habit, and

---

[1] This position, indicated in volume i. chap. vii. sect. 8, and chap. x. sect. 14, is developed by Mr. J. S. Engle, a member of my Seminary, in his Dissertation soon to be published, " The Ego in Relation to the Fundamental Functions of Consciousness " (*Philos. Monographs of the Psychological Review*, vol. i. He explicitly identifies " interest " with the subject-self or Ego. Cf. also his book *Analytic Interest*, etc.

control by self over things through the guidance of knowledge—
as the self-process is built up and organized.

This is the province of ends—simply this mediating of the
active life through ideas. The segregated and unified inner
control processes are what they are through the relative success
of the mediations of memory and thought. The self is simply
Self-con- this unified system. Its further advance is by the
trol succeeds same process now passed into the mode of reflection.
partial Im-
pulse and The context of ideas, of objects of judgment and
Purpose. discursive thought, is set up in the inner life as a
medium, a mediation, a means, to further accommodation and
adjustment. Thus the partial impulses, purposes, and interests
that represent the self of the moment, are systematized in the
whole self or personal character.

There is then a very real process of " control through knowledge," as recent writers have declared. But the essential thing
about it is not alone its relative detachment seen in the play
of ideas leading to facts or led to by them. Equally essential
is the advance of the inner control process, the self as subject, to
the organization of which the reflective context ministers, as a
system of means.

11. The ideas, therefore, from this point of view, are the
mediating factor merely in a new dualism, that between the self
and its whole objective and externalized world of not-selves
and other-selves. This is a compelling dualism, in the sense
that it is the essential form that the play of genetic motives
takes on in the logical mode. It is impossible to mutilate the
mode, by removing either term of the dualism, and dealing with
No Pure "ex- " experience " that is mere "validity," purged of a
perience" in self and of the ends of fulfilment that the self sets up ;
Thought. or "mere subjectivity," detached from the external
member of the dualism. Either procedure destroys the whole
process ; for it leaves no motive adequate to its continuance,
either as thought or as action.[1] The fact that the mode of
reflection *issues in a dualism of self and objects of thought* cannot
be blinked nor slurred over.

§ 5. THE SECOND EMBARRASSMENT OF THOUGHT

12. In this movement, indeed, we find another limitation
imposed upon thought. It cannot reduce the subject, the inner
control that its process implicates, to relational and cognitive

[1] See the Appendix, II. 3.

terms. The subject-self is a meaning that cannot be rendered by judgment. The rendering of "me" by judgment never exhausts the intent to be more than a thought of "me"—the intent to be a thinking "I."[1]

In this the second of those aspects of the mode of reflection found above to be criteria of thinking, another limitation and **The Self is** embarrassment is found. There is a residuum of **more than it** meaning in the intent of the act of judgment to **contains.** be more than it contains, to reserve from the drag-net of its own casting the hand that casts the net. Like the man who sees and knows himself in a mirror, the self sees and knows itself in the forms of thought ; but as the man, so the self may say, " what I see and know is not all that I am."

This residual meaning, to conclude, is the subject-self. It is not exhausted in the presentation of the object-self or me as knowledge. On the contrary it is immediate as subject, over against both sorts of objects, selves and things. In this sense then of being not remote nor mediate, but present and immediate, it may be called, as it often is, the " real " self ; as **It is immedi-** the objective may be called the " true " self, from its **ate and** status as a mediating content. The term " real " **"real"** should not, however, at this stage of our discussion be allowed to connote more than this ; it remains to discuss the proper meaning of reality both in this and in the other great psychic modes.[2]

§ 6. KNOWLEDGE AND ITS USE

13. In our discussion of what truth is " good for," we arrived at a conclusion that serves to bring up the third great

---

[1] We may note here the anomalous position of this inner or " subjective " intent of meaning in theories that get rid of the subject-self as actual self-consciousness. Those objective idealists who posit " thought " as such—objective. absolute and impersonal—find it " teleological," for instance, when the only possible teleological or end-subserving moment in thought is that which shows the control by and for a concrete self which uses the contents of thought as means to the progressive development of ends. It is a phase of the antinomy I have pointed out above (chap. xiii. § 9) as arising in community : the detachment of truth on the one hand, in an absolute system of " thought," and the requirement on the other hand, that truth should be good for something as ministering to " control through knowledge." Even when made most detached and absolute, the birth-marks of purpose, interest and fulfilment for a self, still attach to " thought."

[2] In vol. iii.

character of the mode of reflection, its third criterion, the attitude of acceptance or belief. We found, it will be remembered, that **Knowledge of** belief is an attitude, a mode of active endorsement and **the Known.** acknowledgment, which is always also an affirmation or denial of a suggested relational meaning. And in the discussion of the utility of truth, we found that all such logical contents are of use for the interests that at one time or another may seize upon them, either for immediate gratification, as merely theoretical, or as means to the gratification of more remote ends.

This means that the attitude of using knowledge is in some way different from the attitude of simply knowing. Of course, the gratification of theoretical interest, which is the attitude of merely knowing, is itself also a gratification of the attitude of using—the mode of use here being just progressive knowing ; here the two seem to flow together. But even here, there is a distinction, as has already been pointed out. The continuing interest **Knowledge** in knowing is not satisfied with the object already **as Used.** known. We do, indeed, take pleasure in simply running over our stores, as the miser tells over his coin, but that is not the real gratification of the theoretical impulse ; but rather a sort of personal emotion excited by possession. The full measure of our interest in knowledge is, on the contrary, to be found both in the pursuit of new knowledge, and in the fulfilment of a remote end of another sort secured by the use of the knowledge as means.

14. The reader will have no difficulty in seeing the bearing of this. All through our discussions, we have had to distinguish the attitude of genuine belief—of presupposition, acceptance, judgment—from that of question—of hypothesis, assumption, schematic rendering for the purposes of discovery. Indeed, **Judgment as** this has been minutely traced not only through the **Assumption.** prelogical, but also in the logical mode. The fundamental difference between what is merely suggested, projected, schematically and hypothetically rendered, on the one hand, and what is believed, on the other hand, has been abundantly made out. One is instrumental, prospective, questioning ; the other is recognitive, retrospective, deciding ; one assumes, the other accepts.

Coming now to the logical processes, with this distinction in **Knowledge** mind, we recall an important result. We found that **both Eluci-** no knowledge or thought process is free from a certain **dation and** **Proposal** shading of assumptive and problematical intent. When seemingly most isolated, as a body of implication or elucidation for one who accepts it, such a body of meaning always has the further intent to suggest, postulate, or propose something to one who does not. The proposal runs ahead of the elucidation, while the elucidation in turn motives the further proposal.

Not to dwell again upon the arguments in support of this, we may say that if this position—that all thought is in some sense, whether in its content or in its control, in its relations or in its community, *schematic and instrumental*—is true, a result follows that we must now record. It means, of course, that this intent is *ipso facto not rendered in the judgment that* **The proposal** *supports and suggests it.* Whatever is selectively set **Intent** up for testing is in so far beyond the scope of the **escapes** knowledge already accepted. The "prospective **Judgment.** reference" breaks over the limits of actual knowledge, and projects its hypothetical readings into the realm of the likely, the possible, the ideal. There hangs about all our knowledge, in fact, a future-ward reference, as actual in our meaning as is the past-ward; and the two but reflect our essential attitudes, the inner control factors, which are all the while assimilating the new data of experience and discovery, as well as elucidating the old.[1]

This has been already indicated indeed in two of our more partial positions. We found[2] a dualism between fact and end haunting us in our discussion of truth, and forbidding a strictly pragmatic theory. The instrumental end-serving character of thought is correlative with its correctness and its validity. Purpose may shape truth, but it cannot make it; it may use facts, but it cannot ignore them.

We found too,[3] it will be remembered, that the full intent of thought to be common, its intent of community, led to a certain embarrassment. Thought is fit for universal acceptance though nobody may actually accept it; yet it may be rendered in a form that reduces it to personal appreciation and purpose, to the schematic ideal of a single individual's end. Here the whole problem of the antithesis of truth and worth confronts us. The one intends what is static, complete, absolute; the other what is dynamic, teleological, relative.

---

[1] See the Appendix, II. 5.

In another place, I have dwelt in detail on this contrast of "prospective and retrospective reference" (see the *Psychological Review*, November, 1905, now chap. xvii. of the volume, *Development and Evolution*. See also the article by W. M. Urban, *Psychological Review*, January, 1906).

[2] Chap. xiii. § 2.
[3] Chap. xiii. § 9.

§ 7. THE THIRD EMBARRASSMENT OF THOUGHT

15. Here then, in this third character of the mode of reflection, we find yet another limitation. The ideal, prospective,
schematic meanings, although always present, are never reduced
A new Limi- to the relational content of thought. They are intent,
tation. not content, in the logical mode. They, too, *are not
caught in the drag-net of thought.* An embarrassment arises here,
also, to the theory that would say that all the vital meanings of
the psychic life can be rendered in the form of logical meaning.

§ 8. CONCLUSION

16. It would thus appear that thought has its very precise
The three limitations. One appears in connection with each of the
"S's." essential aspects of the mode, and in respect to each
of its three criteria. The *singular*, the *subject*, the *schematic*—all
these three—*play hide and seek with discursive thinking.* It cannot render them, any one of them. They are, indeed, the three
stumbling blocks—the three " S's " we may call them, the
Singular, the Self, the Schematic—in the path of any radically
rationalistic philosophical theory. They serve as the point of
departure for our discussions of the hyper-logical modes, and
of the further mediations of dualism, in the later volume on
" Real Logic." [1]

This may be for the present the end of our report upon this
topic ; but it is by no means at an end. It may suffice to point
the lesson of scepticism and reserve, in our future appraisal of the
claims of typical modes of meaning, to know that thought is by
no means entitled to its traditional monopoly of illuminating
material. Truly thought is a wise virgin, with oil in her lamp,
but there are others ! [2]

---

[1] We may note, too, that all these things escape Mr. Bradley's relational
screen—for what they may turn out to be worth !

[2] There are further embarrassments arising from the community
character of thought, which are in a sense complications of those mentioned. For example, the difficulty spoken of above (chap. xiii. sect. 43)
that while judgment essentially claims to reach its result by a competent
personal act, it nevertheless legislates its result for others and so denies,
in a sense, their right to do what it does. This appears in the allowance
of variations in prevalence of a judgment found by its author nevertheless
to be synnomic. One result admits the relative character of truth, its
subjectivity and dependence upon personal belief, while the other denies
just this. This and other more epistemological bearings of our results are
reserved for later treatment (in vol. iii.).

APPENDIX

I. TERMINOLOGICAL

THE terms suggested in chap. i. § 3 for attitudes of acceptance and assumption may be assigned their place in the larger scheme of terminology of the entire work, in the tables that follow (Tables K and L).

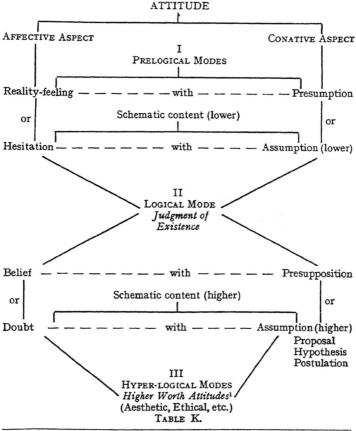

TABLE K.

---

[1] "Lower" worth attitude being recognized also in the prelogical modes.

Tables.

1. In Table K the entire affective-conative attitude involved in the apprehension of a content, as in its appropriate sphere or control, is given. It includes terms in use on the affective side as well (" Reality-feeling," " Belief," etc.), the contrast between the " presumption " and the " assumption," at the different levels, being indicated by the word " or." In this and the further Table L certain other terms are given which come up in the major discussions of this volume (" Implication," " Postulation," etc.), and have been fully defined. The latter table is constructed to show, in outline, the relation of the attitudes of acceptance or recognition to those of appreciation or worth.

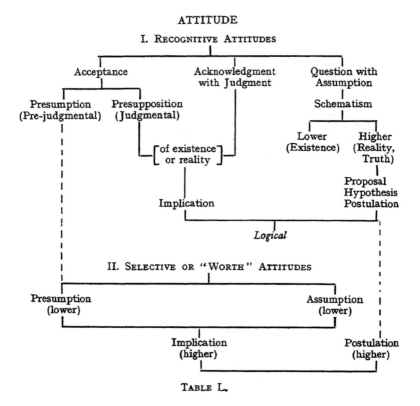

TABLE L.

II. Certain Explanations [1]

Professor Moore's remarks upon my book (vol. i.) in the *Psychological Bulletin*, March, 1907, lead me to make certain explanations. I shall refer also to criticisms made by others.

2. The treatment in my book is a compromise between two methods (as suggested by Professor Russell in the *Journ. of Philos.*). I find it impossible to treat each genetic " mode " in turn exhaustively, by a method that tries to make out longitudinal " progressions." For each topic, a certain before-and-after review is necessary, in order to get the movement of consciousness ; and this inevitably requires some repetition and restatement of the main characters of the mode in the interest of the particular problem under investigation. So it becomes a question, in order to reach the most effective exposition, of reducing this retracing to the minimum, without at the same time going over to a barren analytic and structural point of view.

To illustrate : in the second volume (chap. vi.) I find it impossible to discuss the linguistic embodiment of thought genetically without recurring to the general movement of development of thought, which has already been depicted in earlier chapters. There is, accordingly, a certain amount of repetition which is unavoidable. This appears also in the treatment of the " singular " in several connections.

As to the use of new terms—on that point, I simply take up any glove the critic may see fit to throw down. It all depends on whether the conceptions worked out are worth naming, and have not been named before (granting of course the relative appropriateness of the terms suggested). In this matter, it hardly behooves me to anticipate the verdict of the public ; but the opinion of the *Nation's* reviewer is this : " The vocabulary of well-considered new technical terms that this volume expounds is in itself a precious gift to psychological investigation. For with each of these new terms there goes a valuable new conception." This is by C. S. Peirce, whose opinion is of the highest. (See also what is said in the Preface.)

3. As to the " static absolute," which Professor Moore finds hovering over my work, I do not care for it—and who isn't tired

---

[1] Reprinted in revised form from the *Psychological Bulletin*, vol. iv., No. 4, April 15, 1907. Professor Moore's further remarks (referred to in turn in Chap viii. of this volume) are to be found in the *Psychol. Review*, July, 1907.

of it ?—because it is a purely logical resort, reached as a presupposition of an equally " static " truth. And as to a " dynamic relative "—to suggest a contrasted term—that sounds just now fresh and very modern ; certainly it is less hackneyed than the other. But when we look it in the face, what is its complexion ? It is a postulate of a *practical dualism*, as *crassly unintelligible* as the other is *logically over-theoretical*. I cannot rest content with a " dynamic " that has nothing outside to move it and no reason inside for moving ! If experience proceeds by readjusting to situations, whence comes the situation that " puts it up " to it to readjust ? Why does it grow discontent with its own habit-world ? Is a discreet unintelligible dynamic any better than a contentless formal static ? To kick where there are no pricks may satisfy a strenuous " relative," but beyond endangering our collections of precious antique china, its only result is to strain its own leg-tendons ! I am willing to stake the entire issue on Professor Moore's answer to the following two questions :

First, how can experience of the dynamic-relative type secure or utilize knowledge that is socially valid, without at the same time reinstating other things as valid along with the social fellows and the thinker himself ?

Second, how can an experience that has no environment save its own habit, and no reality save its present function, get up any " dynamic " at all ?

Or to put these two questions in one : In what sense is the will of the mother spanking the child part of the habit of the child, and why does the child's experience take on this particular phase of " relative dynamic " ?—this occasional and very disconcerting phase of habit ?

The " relative dynamic " is all right in its place ; but so is the relative " static." To be " relative," we must be *dualistic, realistic* and—" things are what they seem " becomes the motto of a " radical empirical " pluralism.

4. My own view, to be argued fully enough in my later volume, is that the aesthetic is a mode of experience that not only reconciles these dualisms and pluralisms, *content-wise—in a cross-section —* but also continues its mediation *progression-wise, longitudinally :* so that we can fairly say that in it experience has a way of finding its dynamics intelligible as a truthful and so far static meaning, and also of acting upon its established truths as immediate and so far dynamic satisfactions. In short, our relativisms are contrast-meanings, dualisms, instrumentalities one to another, and the

mediation and abolishing of these contrasts, dualisms, means to ends, removes the relativities and gives the only tenable " absolute." This is the " absolute " that experience is competent to reach. If you ask why this does not develop again into new relativities, I answer, *in fact* it does ; but *in meaning* it does not. For the meaning is the universal of all such cases of mediation. If the mediation effected in the aesthetic is one of *typical meaning everywhere in the progression of mental " dynamic,"* then it is just its value that it discounts in advance any new demands for mediation which new dualisms may make. The æsthetic is absolute then in the only sense that the term can mean anything : it is *universal progression-wise, as well as content or relation-wise.* It mediates the *genetic dynamogenies as well as the static dualisms.*

The following brief explanations are relevant to certain of Professor Moore's difficulties.

5. As to " meaning," I hold that after meaning arises as over against mere present content, then the content of necessity and by contrast also becomes meaning ; since consciousness may then intend or mean both, either, or the difference between the two. As I put it in vol. i.,[1] with the rise of meaning there arise *meanings* (in the plural). To hold a content to just its bare presence is to make it a meaning—after consciousness is once able to *mean* " *that only and not anything else.*" Consequently the use of " meaning " for what is had in mind (as in the phrase " *I mean* so and so ") supersedes the use of it for that merely which is attached to a content (as in " it means much "). When I say (in the former sense) " I mean chickens," I do not intend to restrict " meaning " to what the chicken suggests beyond the bare image. On the contrary, I intend the *whole bird.* Such, at any rate, is the usage adopted in this work.

As to the distinction between " general " and " schematic," between " belief " and " assumption "—that is one of the radical positions of my entire work, and I am glad to have it called attention to. It connects with and carries further the " assumption " theory of Meinong and the Austrian school. My second volume rests its interpretations directly upon this distinction. To say that " schematic " meaning or " assumption," is not " general," nor " universal," nor " particular," nor " singular "—all of which I do say—is to say that it is a mode of meaning *sui generis.* It is the *intent of question,* assumption, hypothesis, postulation, prospective reading—over against all the other meanings just mentioned

[1] Vol. i. chap. vii. §§ 1, 2, where the subject is fully discussed.

which are those of *belief*, acceptance, retrospective reading, proof. It means that the meaning of instrumental intent is *not the general, but goes before it*. A meaning can be instrumental *only to a general not yet reached*. And a " general " meaning, when made instrumental to further discovery, is then not general with reference to the outcome ; it has become in turn again " schematic," and instrumental to a new general.

So far from being antagonistic to an " instrumental " view, this furnishes the clue to it. On this distinction, *and this alone*—one destined I think to prove the most fruitful in the epistemology of modern times—the logical processes can be construed as essentially experimental from start to finish. This is the attempt of the present volume.

6. In respect to " effort " and the " subject," I do not resort to any hypothesis of " activity " in a philosophical sense. I find that, for the " knower " himself, the sense of effort—whatever its mechanism [1]—distributed variously as " efforts " here and there, is *segregated in a sense of control* which *is* the " self " of judgment.

As to the " inwardness " of thoughts—I hold that as thoughts they are in a context of reflection, recognized and intended as such ; but that there is always that belief-reference which acknowledges or assumes the original control-sphere. I reflect alike on " serpents " and " sea-serpents," but any intelligible use of them as meanings presupposes the reference to their respective existence spheres. This reference is for me the essence of " truth " as meaning. The serpent idea is " true " when referred to the proper sphere, and so is the sea-serpent idea.

7. One other point. While saying that the entire world of objects of experience or reflection is such to a self or subject, and is also referred to its original control, which " holds the entire system to its moorings," I mean two things besides. First, the original control, the " moorings," to which each idea or object of reflection is referred, is itself *the experienced* or made-up set of meanings of that original mode—as the reference of the idea " horse " to the perceptual horse-experience—the envelope of the developing psychic process *being nowhere ruptured*.[2] The controls, " foreign " as well as " inner," are all psychic meanings. And second, the dualism of controls does, as Mr. Moore suggests, live to the last within the sphere of logical meanings ; it will not down ; the

---

[1] The kinaesthetic theory is most likely, for me.

[2] It is however an envelope of inter-psychic or common, in no sense private meaning, as is argued in detail in this volume.

dualism of reflection itself is a redistribution, or *mediation, not a banishment*, of the control factors. But my conclusion from this is not a dualistic one, and not one of intellectualism ; but one of a-logicism. For the failure of the logical to transcend its own and the earlier dualisms is just the opportunity of a genuinely synthetic or unifying experience. The necessity of logic is the opportunity of aesthetic. It brings in a *new immediacy*. It is the cry of embarrassment of logical finality, on the one hand, and of pragmatic relativity, with its simpler dualisms, on the other hand, that has rung down the passages of history, and inspired the various solutions of immediacy, all the way from the logical postulates of pure identity, to the affectivist postulates of mystical contemplation. However ineffective these historical " immediacies " may have proved, the attempt recurs and will still recur. My own effort is to find out just what is universal and saving in this recurrent endeavour, seeing that genetic analysis shows the endeavour to be inevitable.[1]

III. ARGUMENTATION IN LOGICAL COMMUNITY

8. My intention in the treatment of logical community is accomplished in showing that there is a quantity in community based on recurrence.[2] It may, nevertheless, be useful to give examples of the sort of arguments involving community that play so large a rôle in our everyday life of thought. The first one I give is an argument clearly having force mainly for practical life and resting on a balancing of opinions. It issues in a judgment of comparison of expert with popular opinion. It assigns synnomic force or universal " quantity for whom " to the expert opinion, although the popular opinion has greater " quantity by whom " or prevalence (a relation anticipated above, chap. x. sects. 25 to 27). It is as follows (1) :

(1) " Most people agree that raw oysters are safe.
    Biologist's say they sometimes carry typhoid germs.
    It is the part of prudence to let them alone."

The next argument (2) is one of probability, having no immediate practical reference. It weighs one opinion against many,

---

[1] Dr. W. D. Furry's work, *The Aesthetic Experience, its Nature and Function in Epistemology*, Philosoph. Monograph of the *Psycholog. Review*, 1908, brings out admirably this resort to the aesthetic in the history of thought.

[2] See the first intimation of this given in the discussion of the " sameness of recurrence " in vol. i. chap. viii. sects. 16 f., especially sect. 17, footnote.

and the issue is made entirely on the basis of the relative number of individuals (quantity by whom).

 (2) " Astronomers generally agree that the earth is the only inhabited planet.

  Mr. Lowell say that Mars is inhabited.

  It is likely that Mr. Lowell is wrong and that Mars is not inhabited."

 The following (3) is an argument in community of recurrence, of the type that recognizes and utilizes the recurrent appearances of a single object, as experienced by a single individual, and deduces conclusions under a " general of recurrence."

 (3) " The man I met was not John—though any one else would have taken him for John—for he did not smell of tobacco."

 Thrown into syllogistic form this reads—

 " John always smells of tobacco, as I have personal reason to know.

 The man I met did not smell of tobacco.

 Hence the man I met was not John, though I alone know this."

 The last clause, " I alone know this," indicates that the conclusion has synnomic force although recognized as a belief based on private experiences. It illustrates the direct utilization of the recurrent experiences of one person only in a conclusion that is appropriate for the acceptance of all.

 The formal logician will call such arguments as this " loose," inadequate, and fallacious; but it is worth while pointing out that most of our conclusions, held with personal conviction and utilized for the guidance of life, while indeed loose and inadequate with reference to cogency in extensive quantity, are still cogent enough in the mode of quantity that they really intend. It all shows that the plain man cares more for the prevalence of belief and the drift of appearances than for the strictest arguments in Barbara and Celarent. And who would advise him to discard his rule of social conformity, and live by the syllogistics of the schoolmen ?

END OF VOLUME II.

INDEX TO VOLS. I AND II

When a term occurs in both volumes the page citations are placed in different paragraphs, those from vol. i. coming first.

When a term occurs in one vol. only the vol. is given before the first page-citation.

Butler & Tanner, The Selwood Printing Works, Frome, and London.